THE MICHEL HENRY READER

Northwestern University
Studies in Phenomenology
and
Existential Philosophy

General Editor Anthony J. Steinbock

THE MICHEL HENRY READER

Edited by Scott Davidson and
Frédéric Seyler

Northwestern University Press
Evanston, Illinois

Northwestern University Press
www.nupress.northwestern.edu

Copyright © 2019 by Northwestern University Press. Published 2019. Originally published in French under the titles "Quatre principes de la phénoménologie," "Phénoménologie de la naissance," "Incarnation," "Eux en moi: une phénoménologie," in Michel Henry, *Phénoménologie de la vie, Tome I: De la phénoménologie* copyright © PUF/Humensis, 2003; "La critique du sujet," "Philosophie et subjectivité," "Le *cogito* de Descartes et l'idée d'une phénoménologie idéale," "Ricoeur et Freud: entre psychanalyse et phénoménologie," in Michel Henry, *Phénoménologie de la vie, Tome II: De la subjectivité* copyright © PUF/Humensis, 2003; "Le concept de l'être comme production," "Difficile démocratie," "Kandinsky et la signification de l'oeuvre d'art," "Phénoménologie matérielle et langage," in Michel Henry, *Phénoménologie de la vie, Tome III: De l'art et du politique* copyright © PUF/Humensis, 2003; "Ethique et religion dans une phénoménologie de la vie," "Théodicée dans la perspective d'une phénoménologie radicale," "L'expérience d'autrui: phénoménologie et théologie," "Parole et religion: la parole de Dieu," in Michel Henry, *Phénoménologie de la vie, Tome IV: Sur l'éthique et la religion* copyright © PUF/Humensis, 2004. All rights reserved.

10 9 8 7 6 5 4 3 2 1

Library of Congress Cataloging-in-Publication Data

Names: Henry, Michel, 1922–2002, author. | Davidson, Scott, 1970– editor. | Seyler, Frederic, editor.
Title: The Michel Henry reader / edited by Scott Davidson and Frederic Seyler.
Other titles: Northwestern University studies in phenomenology & existential philosophy.
Description: Evanston : Northwestern University Press, 2019. | Series: Northwestern University studies in phenomenology and existential philosophy
Identifiers: LCCN 2019015761 | ISBN 9780810140677 (paper text : alk. paper) | ISBN 9780810140684 (cloth text : alk. paper) | ISBN 9780810140691 (e-book)
Subjects: LCSH: Henry, Michel, 1922–2002. | Phenomenology. | Life.
Classification: LCC B2430.H452 E5 2019 | DDC 194—dc23
LC record available at https://lccn.loc.gov/2019015761

Contents

Acknowledgments — vii

Editors' Introduction — ix

Part 1. Phenomenology

1. The Four Principles of Phenomenology — 5
2. The Phenomenology of Birth — 29
3. Incarnation — 46
4. Those within Me: A Phenomenology — 58

Part 2. Subjectivity

5. The Critique of the Subject — 71
6. Philosophy and Subjectivity — 83
7. Descartes's *Cogito* and the Idea of an Ideal Phenomenology — 108
8. Ricoeur and Freud: Between Psychoanalysis and Phenomenology — 124

Part 3. Politics, Art, and Language

9. The Concept of Being as Production — 143
10. Difficult Democracy — 168
11. Kandinsky and the Meaning of the Work of Art — 181
12. Material Phenomenology and Language (or, Pathos and Language) — 193

Part 4. Ethics and Religion

13	Ethics and Religion within a Phenomenology of Life	217
14	Theodicy from the Perspective of a Radical Phenomenology	227
15	The Experience of the Other: Phenomenology and Theology	238
16	Speech and Religion: The Word of God	246

Acknowledgments

Many hands have contributed to the completion of this project. First we would like to thank the translators who devoted their time, energy, and input to producing new English translations of chapters in this book: Justin Boyd, Christina Gschwandtner, Karl Hefty, and Michael Tweed. We would like to thank Presses Universitaires de France, Fordham University Press, the *Graduate Faculty Philosophy Journal*, and Springer for permission to use previously published materials included in this book. Importantly, we owe our gratitude to Northwestern University Press, especially Trevor Perri, for his encouragement and support of this project. The Department of Philosophy at Oklahoma City University contributed material support toward this project. Last but not least, we would like to thank DePaul University for its generous financial support. A University Research Grant was decisive in enabling us to accomplish this project in its present form.

Editors' Introduction

Michel Henry's philosophy is, from beginning to end, an original and profound reflection on life. In contrast with a naturalism that would define life in terms of living organisms or a set of physical processes, Henry approaches life in a phenomenological manner, which is to say that his philosophy is a reflection on the meaning of the lived experience of life. But our access to this phenomenon and its meaning, according to his view, has not only been blocked by the predominance of naturalism; it is also concealed by a set of philosophical assumptions that have guided the history of Western philosophy.

To overcome this forgetting of life and its proper meaning, Michel Henry pursues a reorientation of phenomenology that can rightfully be termed "radical." Henry's phenomenology of life is *radical* precisely because it situates life's original dimension beyond the realm of what is accessible to the natural sciences and even to objectivity as such, namely, by locating it in an affective immanence that escapes every attempt to objectify it. What this means can be shown, for instance, through Henry's concept of "knowing" [*savoir*], as well as through his critique of the reduction of knowledge operated by what he calls "scientism." For classical phenomenology, knowing is the result of both an act of apprehending an ideal meaning as well as the acts of intentional consciousness that make such comprehension possible. Therefore, knowledge ultimately depends on its constitution through intentionality, which is then seen as the most fundamental form of "knowing." The question is, however, whether this fundamental knowing requires, in turn, a foundation on an even deeper level. Pursuing this line of thought, one could ask how intentional "knowledge" becomes, for action in general and, more specifically, for conscious acts directed toward the acquisition of knowledge, the knowledge of a *subject*. In other words, how do we actually come to "know" that these actions are indeed *our own* actions? As Henry points out, such "knowledge" cannot be objective or even intentional. If it were, it would necessarily entail the distance that separates the subject from itself taken as object, which would make it ultimately impossible for the subject to recognize its acts as its own. The object of consciousness stands out in front of the intentional act of subjectivity and must therefore remain external to it. This configuration is, however, incompatible with the necessary and prior unity of the subjective action and subjective knowledge of that action. As Henry writes:

> In the outside the self, each "point" is still external to the self, in such a way that this "outside the self" is its way of appearing, an appearing that only has room for the outside and in this sense for what is other. In this place of radical externalization, then, no life is possible if to live is to experience [*s'éprouver*] oneself and not to experience [*éprouver*] something other. To live is to experience oneself in an immediacy so radical that nothing would ever be able to break the pathos of the flesh out of which this experience is made. Any placement outside of oneself of this pathos that is essentially non-ekstatic could only signify its destruction. The material phenomenological heterogeneity between the pathos of appearing in which life fulfills itself and the ek-static appearing which unfolds in the difference of the world and things, is radical, irreducible, and insurmountable. [See chapter 2, "The Phenomenology of Birth."]

In order to secure the self's relation to itself, intentional consciousness must therefore be grounded in a more fundamental form of knowing that is non-intentional. Such knowing is precisely what Henry captures through the concept of affectivity.

Affectivity differs from the object-oriented knowing that depends on the intuition of an object that would mark the fulfillment of the intentional aim. It is, on the contrary, the nonobjective and pre-intentional ground that makes such intentional processes possible. This ground is what Henry thematizes as *life*, and the type of knowledge that underlies every intentional activity is the "knowledge of life" [*savoir de la vie*], that is, the knowledge that life has of itself as a subjective activity. This also provides an initial clarification of the concept of *immanence* that Henry introduces in the earliest stage of his work, namely in *The Essence of Manifestation* (1963).[1] Immanence is that which "characterizes" affectivity, insofar as the latter appears "before" any object-relation. For this reason, affective appearing essentially differs from the intentional object given as transcendent; affectivity is irreducibly invisible. The notions of "affectivity," "immanence," and "radicality" do not refer primarily to philosophical abstractions; instead, they refer to life as a fundamental mode of *appearing*. The dead and lifeless, on the contrary, does not affect itself; it has no "relation" to itself and no ipseity. Thus, life is not simply one type of reality among others, but that *through which* everything appears to the living [*vivant*] as well as *that which* appears before anything else. This conception of life accounts for the radicality of Henry's phenomenology of life in comparison with Husserl's analysis of intentionality, for instance.

To be precise, Henry's phenomenology of life is based on two central theses. Its first thesis establishes the *duality of appearing*, insofar as there are, according to Henry, two essentially different modes of phenomenalization, namely affectivity and intentionality, pathos-filled immanence [*immanence pathétique*] and ek-static transcendence. The phenomenology of life, therefore, cannot be reduced to that which appears to consciousness as an object. Rather, its distinguishing characteristic is the fundamental role it ascribes to what *appears* at a purely affective level, which explains the meaning of the radical stance in Henry's phenomenology. Such a distinction within the domain of the phenomenologically given seems, however, to call for a complementary thesis. The duality of the two modes of appearing, as such, would not allow affectivity to be connected with intentionality. In this case, a purely affective givenness would simply be juxtaposed with an equally pure ek-static transcendence. The transcendent object, to recall, is *given as* transcendent; it is an object for consciousness and, thus, an object for a living subjectivity. But a "pure" transcendence would, however, not be connected to intentional consciousness in any way and would be totally inaccessible to it. In other words, it would be nothing for us, since it would be radically separated from subjectivity. Obviously, even the metaphysical claim of such transcendence would have to rely on something that is given, that is, accessible to subjectivity. This requirement is even more pressing for phenomenology, insofar as it strives to circumvent metaphysical theses through the *epoché* and through its focus on the "how" of appearing. This is why Henry's thesis of the duality of appearing must also be complemented by a second insight that accounts for the subjective givenness of transcendence.

This second thesis states that intentional givenness is founded in affectivity. It means that intentionality is always living activity and that it is inseparable from affectivity. Henry's phenomenology is thus a continuation of the tradition of transcendental philosophy, to the extent that affectivity provides the condition of possibility for intentional consciousness. Far from asserting a "pure" transcendence, the phenomenology of life anchors transcendence in immanence. That which appears in the horizon of the world as well as the world itself are not simply objective facts that would appear on their own ground. They are constituted by a living subjectivity on which they depend. As phenomenologically dependent and grounded in affectivity, the world is indeed nothing but a lifeworld [*Lebenswelt*]. As Henry points out in his critique of contemporary "barbarism," even the ideology of scientism, that is, the reduction of subjectivity to the objective and measurable, is a performance accomplished by transcendental subjectivity. "Barbarism" too is affectively determined, namely as a manifestation of life turning against itself. Husserl's analysis of the life-world is at the same time a critique of modernity and its paradigm shift in the empirical sciences. Expanding on Husserl's *Crisis*, Henry analyzes the occultation of the life-world through scientism as a tendency inherent to life, where life, unsuccessfully, aims to flee from itself and its pathos. Such an attempt is ultimately doomed to failure, because there "is" no world outside of life and because it is only through life that a world can appear. This remains true even when the world is reduced to an inert world of visible objects, since the visible world continues to be founded in affectivity's radical invisibility.

The duality of appearing, as well as the foundation of intentionality in affectivity, clarify the relation between immanence and transcendence: there is an eidetic difference between affectivity and intentionality as modes of appearing, but, at the same time, the latter is phenomenologically dependent on the former. This implies the primacy of affectivity, insofar as auto-affection is the condition of possibility of all appearing, or the fundamental mode of phenomenalization. The appearing of the world and of intra-mundane beings, on the contrary, is derived from affectivity. But the duality- and the foundation-thesis also seem to entail a third "theorem," namely that of affectivity's own phenomenological independence or self-sufficiency, that is, the concept of a pure immanence that stands in contrast to the dependent character of intentionality, as well as to the impossibility of a pure transcendence. Yet, is it possible to establish a pure immanence phenomenologically? In other words, how could we know anything about a pure affectivity if it is precisely something that escapes consciousness as intentional? So, just as the notion of a pure transcendence has been rejected, should we not likewise reject the claim of a pure immanence?

One possible response to these questions is to consider affectivity as a transcendental condition of consciousness. In order to be affected by something other, subjectivity first has to affect itself. A consciousness without auto-affectivity would not know itself; it would be without ipseity. Therefore, pure immanence could be deduced through a "transcendental argument" that regressively establishes its necessary presence as condition of the possibility for the consciousness of transcendent objects. But another possible response would be to pursue a direct phenomenological approach to pure affectivity. A transcendental deduction of pure affectivity, from this point of view, would not even be required—except for the purpose of *philosophical* clarification—since a direct access or "knowledge" of affectivity is already given in every act that it accompanies and makes possible, including objective knowledge. A transcendental argument is therefore only needed insofar as the concept of knowledge is restricted to discursive-objective knowledge, which is indeed the case for philosophy as well as for Henry's phenomenology of life itself. As a discourse, the phenomenology of life makes life the object of its reflection, thereby introducing a distance between life and the philosophizing subject. The phenomenology of life can therefore never access radical affective immanence, that is, seize or even describe affectivity as it is given in pure immanence. This conclusion is not surprising. It follows the traditional distinction made between philosophy and life, between the reflection on life and life as "enacted." Indeed, it seems almost trivial to distinguish the thought of life from life as it is lived through. Henry's phenomenology, however, allows for a conceptual clarification of this basic insight, which is accounted for through the thesis of the duality of appearing. But, as with all philosophy, it must content itself with an *image* of life.

It seems that the philosophical assertion concerning immanent affectivity is bound to be circular, insofar as it states that a direct access to affectivity (as a form of knowing) is impossible to philosophical discourse, precisely because affective knowledge is infra-intentional. Thus, what this form of knowledge is, and why it counts as knowledge, can only be known by this infra-intentional and affective knowledge *itself.* In other words, the knowledge of what life "is" can only occur as it unfolds in the experience of life itself. Here the word "experience" (*experience,* or in German, *Erfahrung*) can be misleading to the extent that it literally suggests an act of "peering out," that is, a directedness toward objects. This is why Henry conceptualizes life's self-appearing not as *expérience* but as *épreuve* (both terms being usually translated into English with the word "experience"). Life, in this sense, experiences itself through an experience of oneself [*épreuve de soi*] and it is only then that it can be said to "know" itself immediately. As a consequence, it is not sight anymore that provides the ultimate basis for knowledge, but experience in the sense of an immanent and invisible *épreuve.*

If life affects itself, then it must "know" itself in each living act, even if such "knowledge," being unable to appear as transcendent object, must remain invisible. There is therefore no other "proof" of immanent affectivity than the indirect one given through the transcendental argument. As we have seen, however, there are two forms of knowledge involved here: next to, and even embedded in the discursive level there is an affective one, identical to the movement of life, that is, a "knowledge" that life continuously has of itself. Life is thus a dynamic and uninterrupted self-appearing or appearing to itself, and this is exactly the meaning of auto-affection. The "knowledge" it involves is not indirect anymore but immediate. It accompanies the living as long as it is alive. Being both a specific and yet fundamental mode of appearing, it justifies an investigation in its own right, that is, a phenomenology of life. For the philosopher, however, the access to affectivity remains indirect, occurring under the form of the phenomenological reduction.

Henry's use of the term "reduction" is at least threefold: it refers to the concept of the reduction in Husserlian phenomenology, but also—and in a very different, even opposed sense—to the "reduction" operated by scientism, where reality is reduced to that which is objectively measurable. It is in opposition to this latter reduction—not to the phenomenological and eidetic reductions in Husserl—that Henry develops his own concept of the phenomenological reduction as a *counter-reduction*. Henry's counter-reduction radicalizes Husserl's critique of scientism developed in his *Crisis*. For Henry, it is not only the life-world, but life itself as an immanent affectivity, that is, "the word of life" without reference to the horizon of the world, that becomes the foundation of appearing and the condition of possibility for science, even for scientism itself. The task of the counter-reduction is therefore to lead back (*zurückführen* in Husserl) from the intentionally given life-world to the affectivity of immanent life. As far as radical phenomenology is concerned, such (counter-) reductive practice is fulfilled by the clarification of the concept of auto-affection, a clarification that is a central task of the phenomenology of life as a whole. As we have seen, this aspect becomes especially prominent when Henry thematizes auto-affection as knowledge or *savoir de la vie*.

But it is even more prominent in his recourse to Descartes, a paradoxical recourse if one considers that Descartes represents the rise of modernity and modern science. Paragraph 18 of *Incarnation* is thus significantly titled "The Cartesian Counter-Reduction."[2] It is certainly not Descartes's metaphysics of substance that is mobilized here, in which the mathematized approach of the *res extensa* is an ally of the Galilean revolution rather than of a phenomenology of life. As with Husserl previously, it is in the *cogito* of the "Second Meditation" that Henry finds a basis for a phenomenological reading of Descartes. Here the relation between the "I am" and the "I think" becomes, translated phenomenologically, the primacy of appearing over being, insofar as thought [*pensée*] equals, in such a reading, appearing itself. Hence, "this thing that I am" consists—as a "thinking thing"—precisely in its appearing, and its "matter" (or its "life," as Husserl suggests in §46 of *Ideas I*) is phenomenality itself. The decisive question is, however, that of the nature of such appearing or life. Henry's unique interpretation of the "Second Meditation" affirms that the self-appearing of the "I think," which includes every *cogitatio*, is nothing but an immanent auto-affection. The evidence of sight has been rejected by the "Meditation" and its radical doubt; the appearing in question must therefore be invisible. Alongside the ek-static appearing of the *videre* there is a pathos-filled appearing, the *videor*, that carries certitude: it is certain *that* I see (or, at least, that I have the impression that I see), despite the doubt attached to *what* I see. Hence, the affirmation of two radically different modes of appearing:

> The radical reduction is thus phenomenological in an ultimate sense . . . It shakes up appearing all the way to splitting it into two like a block of crystal broken by a hammer. And on the one side, it finds an appearing that it no longer holds in itself, in its appearing, as a self-justification and a self-attestation: it is seeing which in the light of its vision and in the undeniability of this light, is considered dubitable. On the other side, what is absolutely certain is the appearing in which seeing is given to itself without a *cogitatum* and without its light, without seeing itself and without being able to do so, in the Night of an absolute non-seeing. So, on the one side there is the appearing that the reduction reduces, and on the other side there is the appearing that can no longer be reduced. [See chapter 7, "Descartes's *Cogito* and the Idea of an Ideal Phenomenology."]

Since the intentional object's reality is doubtful, the certitude that I see cannot in turn be given through an act of intentional sight, but can only be internal (*intérieure*), that is, infra- or pre-intentional. Such is the process of the counter-reduction, insofar as it leads to the non-intentional appearing of an internal certitude proper to affectivity, which is nonetheless foundational to intentionality:

> Life must be understood as phenomenological through and through, as pure phenomenality and as the most originary mode in which phenomenality is phenomenalized. Life makes every other form of phenomenality possible. Yet, even though life founds phenomenality, its mode of phenomenalization differs fundamentally from that of the world. In order to avoid this equivocation, we will refer to it in terms of revelation.
>   The revelation of life can be contrasted point by point with the appearing of the world. Whereas the world is disclosed "outside of itself" such that everything disclosed there is external, the key feature of the revelation of life is that it does not have any separation within itself and never differs from itself. It only ever reveals itself. *Life reveals itself.* Life is an auto-revelation. On the one hand, it is life that carries out the work

of revelation; it is anything but a blind entity. On the other hand, what it reveals is itself. This is why the revelation of life and what it reveals are one and the same. [See chapter 3, "Incarnation."]

As an internal certitude, non-intentional appearing obviously escapes mathematical treatment and even objectification. It is synonymous with what Henry calls "affectivity" or "life." The Cartesian counter-reduction thus leads back to life as that which is radically invisible, and yet is the condition of possibility for everything visible. Performing the counter-reduction therefore results in an insight that bypasses sight and seeing. The certitude that is driven from the counter-reductive move finds both its origin and its foundation in the living activity of the subject. But since the living is in turn not its own foundation or origin, it is in Life, that is, in absolute life, that such an ultimate foundation has to be situated.

We have established that Henry's phenomenology of life grounds intentionality as well as the appearing of the world in a prior auto-affection, and that the analysis of auto-affection also establishes the concept of subjectivity as ipseity. But, one might ask, in what is auto-affection itself grounded? As far as the self-referential character of appearing is concerned, where the "self" of self-affection seems to be the last possible reference, this question appears to be devoid of meaning. Reduced to ipseity, individual subjectivity would be the final word for a phenomenological investigation of life. Such a reduction of life to the singular individual, however, will be questioned further by Henry, especially in his later works. At a minimum, it has to be asked if and to what extent auto-affection carries within itself a communal and supra-individual dimension, especially since it is shared by all of the living. This explains Henry's elaborations on the concept of affective community in *Material Phenomenology*,[3] before what has been called his Christian trilogy. On the one hand, auto-affection is the irreducible requisite for individuation, because it constitutes the living self as such. On the other hand, auto-affection is a prerequisite for intersubjectivity precisely because it is shared by all selves.

> For each impressional tonality whatsoever, it is the given to oneself in the self-givenness of life, it is this self-givenness of life itself that is Identical and that transforms even the most radical difference into an absolute equality, unequivocally designating the original place of it, its only possibility. [See chapter 10, "Difficult Democracy."]

It is from this being-in-common that the phenomenology of life is led to the idea of a community of the living. This does not only take place under the form of an affective foundation for intersubjectivity, but also under the form of a community marked by the solidarity of the living, at least as a possibility in principle.

In addition to indicating a mode of self-appearing, auto-affection also signifies, to follow Henry's terminology, the "suffering" of the self, as the terms "pathos" or "pathos-filled appearing" nominally suggest. What does it mean to characterize auto-affection as a form of suffering? For Henry, it is not the result of an "event" that would affect life from the outside, nor does it connote a negative picture of life as misery. Instead, it points to the facticity of the self in life itself. Affectivity is, for the living, not a matter open to choice, and the continuous process of auto-affection occurs independently from the will. In this sense, there is no escape from the affectivity of life. The more we try to flee from the self, the more desperate we become. But the attempt to reach the self is equally desperate. For we cannot reach what we already "are" in a sense that does not allow for any distancing. Henry's concept of life as adhering to itself explicitly refers to Kierkegaard, and his own concept of "barbarism" as a flight from life has to be read with the reference to Kierkegaardian despair in mind. Thus, the experience—*épreuve*—of one's own life always carries with it the experience of not being one's own origin. This is the new meaning that Henry attaches, at least in part, to the Husserlian idea of a "transcendence in immanence."

A further clarification is nonetheless needed. The transcendence that Henry refers to is never a region of being situated outside of life. Rather, it refers to Life itself as both the origin and foundation of individual life, which it therefore transcends. Given its ultimate and self-referential character, auto-affection cannot be seized through another form of appearing. This implies that the distinction between individual life and Life as supra-individual, that is, as absolute, can itself only be established within auto-affection. Following this line of thought, Henry distinguishes between a "weak" and a "strong" sense of auto-affection [*auto-affection faible/forte*]. The latter designates the absolute (divine) Life on which the individual life [*ipse*] depends. Life is therefore given, a givenness that, again, stresses its passive character as a prerequisite to any activity. Activity, in turn, is tied to Henry's concept of culture as the "culture of life." Absolute life as auto-affection—or God, as the Christian trilogy will clearly state—is the universal ground for all individual life. Therefore, for Henry, the community of the living is a community in the Life of God. This can be seen as Henry's decisive contribution to a philosophy of religion.

The essays collected here will help readers to glimpse the full scope of Henry's work. Together these essays show the underlying rationale behind Henry's original philosophical outlook and the broader implications that result from his original theoretical insights. Having gained this broad picture of Henry's thought, readers will then be well prepared to inquire into Henry's more extended reflections on the specific areas of interest to them. In what follows, we offer a brief survey of the major parts of this book and of the individual chapters included in it.

Overview of the Chapters

Part 1: Phenomenology

It is difficult, if not impossible, to understand Henry's thought without reference to the phenomenological movement. Phenomenology is a constant and important preoccupation throughout Henry's career, because he considers the phenomenological movement to be a necessary starting point for thinking today. Phenomenology clears away all of the metaphysical constructions of reality inherited from the philosophical tradition and allows for a fresh return "to the things themselves." Importantly, this return does not lead to the surfaces of things but to their depths, that is, to the origins of their appearing. In this way, Henry's thought clearly stands within the phenomenological tradition. Yet, in his attempt to reveal the origins of the appearing of phenomena, Henry is also highly critical of its actual development in the work of Husserl and Heidegger, and he demonstrates the limitations that they impose on the phenomena.

Henry's critique of phenomenology is articulated as early as *The Essence of Manifestation* and continues to be developed throughout his subsequent writings. His initial charge against phenomenology—in its Husserlian and Heideggerian variants—is that it succumbs to what he calls an "ontological monism." That is to say that it reduces all forms of appearing to one type of being. So, in spite of the supposed contrast between Husserlian and Heideggerian phenomenology, they ultimately share the same presuppositions about the nature of appearing. Influenced by the entire tradition of Western philosophy, they share in common a conception of appearing in terms of ek-stasis, or in other words, of an object that stands outside of the self.

In contrast with the ontological monism of the phenomenological tradition, Henry will reorient phenomenology toward another mode of appearing that is entirely opposed to the notion of ek-stasis and of appearing in the light. The appearing of life does not follow the pattern of an ek-stasis. Instead, it is a radical immanence in which life enters into relation with itself. This relation is not a representation or a form of illumination; instead, it takes place in the immediacy of one's relation to one's own living. The four essays presented in this part of the book provide examples of later developments in Henry's critique of phenomenology, published between 1990 and 2001. Each of these essays is developed with regard to a traditional phenomenological theme—the origin of appearing, the facticity of birth, incarnation, and intersubjectivity—and then unfolds the implications of a phenomenology of life for rethinking each of these themes.

The first essay in part 1, "The Four Principles of Phenomenology," was originally published in an issue of the *Revue de Metaphysique et de la Morale* that included a set of critical engagements to Jean-Luc Marion's book *Reduction and Givenness*. Henry outlines three principles that have guided the development of phenomenology leading up to Marion: (1) "so much appearance, so much being," (2) "the principle of principles" of Husserl's *Ideas I*, and (3) the motto "to the things themselves!" Henry then credits Marion with the discovery of a fourth phenomenological principle: "so much reduction, so much givenness." While Henry expresses admiration for Marion's breakthrough and acknowledges its importance for opening onto a pure appearing, he disagrees with how Marion applies this principle to the call and response structure. Such an approach, Henry contends, continues to identify appearing with exteriority; in contrast, he proposes a different concretization of the pure appearing of the call: the call of life. This call, instead of being rooted in exteriority, takes place in the radical interiority in which life calls one to life. Contrary to Marion's interpretation of the call structure, this pure appearing thus no longer has any traces of exteriority or of a relation to the world.

The next essay, "The Phenomenology of Birth," engages the question of the origins of appearing, or in other words, of how something comes to appear. Henry draws a sharp distinction between the appearing of a thing and the appearing of a living being. The appearing of a thing takes place in the light of the world; a thing appears when it stands outside as an object and is seen. But this mode of appearing proves unable to explain how a living being can come to appear, and this is why a phenomenology of birth is needed. The origin of the living being does not come from being perceived or from itself; instead, the living being comes into being through birth. But here Henry is not talking about birth in the ordinary, biological sense, in which a living being is born from its parents. Instead, his aim is to describe what he calls a "transcendental birth," which accounts for the birth of a self. In a transcendental sense, the phenomenology of birth entails that the self is not its own origin, but that it receives its existence from something else, namely, from life. Henry goes on to describe the process of a transcendental birth in terms of the pathos by which the self comes into itself through the initial embrace of life.

"Incarnation" engages the basic phenomenological question of the body. In Husserlian phenomenology, embodiment is understood as a dual condition in which the body operates both as an object and a subject. In its objective dimension, the body is an object among other things in the world. The subjective dimension of the body, by contrast, refers to one lived experience of the body and its powers, as something that is distinctly my own. Henry explores this subjective dimension of the body through a phenomenological analysis of pain and suffering. Pain is both localized objectively and also felt subjectively. But the original reality of pain is not a bodily intentionality that opens onto the world; there is a deeper and more intimate dimension of bodily experience. Henry contends that we can only gain access to our objective body and to the world, because we first have access to a transcendental body. The transcendental body is given in an original experience. This experience is revealed phenomenologically by the pure impression of pain as such, without any reference outside of the experience of pain itself. Likewise, the transcendental body is given as a pure impressional experience of the body; it points to what Henry calls a "Before-the-flesh"—a Before In-carnation—in which the stamp of life is originally placed on the body.

"Those within Me" addresses the phenomenological question of intersubjectivity. In other words, how is it possible for a radically individual life to be shared with others? This question was answered by Husserl in terms of an analogical apperception in which I perceive a likeness between my experiences and those of others. But this is an especially thorny question for Henry, due to his rejection of the primacy of intentional consciousness and his emphasis instead on the radical immanence of the subjective experience of life. Instead of proceeding through intentional analyses of perception, then, Henry's solution must chart a course through his phenomenology of life. Life, he contends, is not simply the transcendental condition of my self but of every conceivable self. Since all selves share this same transcendental condition, Life is what makes it possible for the self to enter into relation with others; it is the condition of the possibility of the experience of the other. This establishes an intersubjective community of the living who share Life in common.

Part 2: Subjectivity

This part of the book presents Henry's engagement with one of the central topics in twentieth-century philosophy: the question of the subject. The modern conception of the subject emerges with Descartes's *cogito*, which is a starting point for all certitude. This view is further developed by Kant's famous defense of the transcendental unity of apperception, or of the "I think," which can be added on to any representation. In the twentieth century, these traditional conceptions of subjectivity are called into question, whether by Heidegger's deconstruction of the history of the subject, or the structuralist pronouncement of the death of the subject, or various postmodern attempts to decenter the subject. The Henryan subject emerges after the critique of the modern subject. Instead of defining the subject through the activity of representation or the realm of light in which it occurs, this subject is rooted in affectivity, drives, and the bodily power to act. The subject's relation to these is described as an immediate identification and possession of them—they are not seen but felt. And this feeling of one's own affects, drives, and powers is the core of subjective life; it makes possible the other activities of representation and of cognition that traditionally define the self.

The first essay in part 2, "The Critique of the Subject," engages Heidegger's deconstruction of the conception of subjectivity that is developed within the philosophical description. There are two important landmarks of the subject that draw Henry's attention in particular: Descartes and Kant. Henry recognizes Kant's inability to account for the subject's experience of itself. Although the "I think" is a transcendental condition of the possibility of experience, the self can only experience itself as an object, but not as a self. Henry then returns to Descartes in search of an untapped resource for thinking about self-experience. Whereas Heidegger situates Descartes within a tradition of representationalism, Henry detects a different type of self-relation in Descartes. Prior to the "*cogito ergo sum*," there is a more direct and immediate self-experience in the "*videre videor*" ["it seems that I see"]. Because the philosophical tradition after Descartes has only understood the self as an object or as an activity of representing objects, the critique of the subject has missed the mark. Henry thus reroutes the critique of the subject so that it leads toward the discovery of an authentic form of subjectivity.

The next essay, "Philosophy and Subjectivity," offers a close reading of Husserl's account of subjectivity as intentionality. Henry criticizes Husserl for ultimately succumbing to the same problem as his philosophical predecessor, Kant. Just as Kant proved unable to account for an experience of the self, so too Husserl ends up being unable to provide a phenomenological experience of the transcendental subject as a condition of experience. Husserl's account of the transcendental subject as an intentional subject means that the subject itself ends up being treated as an intentional object; it thus appears only in and under the conditions of the appearing of objects. But this is to miss it in its constituting role and in its genuine reality. In order to discern this reality, here too Henry returns to the Cartesian doubt which reveals the self in its true reality in the "it seems to me that I see." This mode of givenness differs in kind from the givenness of objects. Its reality, as Henry interestingly suggests, is recovered by thinkers who considered themselves to be opposed to Cartesian subjectivity: Schopenhauer, Nietzsche, and Freud. Each of these thinkers, in carrying out a critique of the subject of representation, actually tapped into the more fundamental dimension of subjectivity rooted in the life of the will, the Dionysian, and of desire.

"Descartes's *Cogito* and the Idea of an Ideal Phenomenology" is a helpful elaboration of Henry's engagement with Cartesian philosophy, which is alluded to in the two preceding chapters. Here Henry provides a detailed analysis of the Cartesian *cogito*, beginning with the observation that it includes both a process of inquiry as well as something that is sought after. In pursuit of the essence or the being of the *cogito*, Henry draws a distinction between two types of *cogito*: a *cogito cogitatum* and a *cogito* without a *cogitatum*. Many of Descartes's most famous readers (Husserl and Heidegger, most notably) have interpreted the *cogito* in the former sense. But Henry contends that they have misunderstood Descartes's thought in a fundamental way. Cartesian doubt carries out a radical reduction that leads all the way back to a *cogito* without a *cogitatum*, or a thought without an object. The evidence for this claim comes from Descartes's statement that "it seems to me that I see"—this seeming is different from an observational statement; it points to a different type of appearing that does not depend on the relation to the external world. This new type of appearing, Henry contends, should serve as the prototype for the development of a new type of phenomenology—a phenomenology of life.

"Ricoeur and Freud" is a carefully developed critique of Paul Ricoeur's book *Freud and Philosophy*. The ambition of that book was to establish a confrontation between phenomenology and Freudian psychology. Ricoeur ultimately contends that, in spite of their differences, these two approaches share in common the search for meaning and that, in this sense, they can both be interpreted as hermeneutic disciplines. Both phenomenology and Freudian psychology begin with a challenge to straightforward or naive modes of consciousness and thus call for the passage from the surface of consciousness to the implicit horizons that remain unconscious. For Husserlian phenomenology, this leads to the discovery that every theme of conscious life is immersed in a set of potential horizons that remain unthematized and implicit. For Freud, of course, this leads to the discovery of the unconscious. While Ricoeur wants to argue that Husserl and Freud ultimately share the same goal of bringing what is unconscious into conscious life and becoming aware of its influence,

Henry distances himself from this hermeneutic reading by insisting that the realm of conscious representations and the realm of the unconscious are in fact two separate, and ultimately irreducible, domains. The mistake of Western thought, including Freud himself in his interpretation of the unconscious, is to presuppose that the unconscious can be assimilated into the structure of representation. But, as Henry contends, the realm of the unconscious is qualitatively different from representation. Instead of admitting light, it is a place of night; here the drives and affects have a direct and immediate hold over subjectivity.

Part 3: Politics, Art, and Language

Henry's philosophy of life is not merely an abstract engagement whose significance would only pertain to the history of philosophy: it generates a profound critique of contemporary society. The exclusion of life from theoretical and scientific consideration has practical implications for our everyday lives. Henry identifies contemporary "barbarism" with the paradoxical correlation between the increase of information and the corresponding collapse of culture. This spiritual malaise can be seen in many different guises, ranging from totalitarian forms of government to changes in higher education and all the way to certain approaches to art restoration. This part of the book, accordingly, displays the wide range of Henry's critical engagement with contemporary politics and culture.

The first essay in part 3, "The Concept of Being as Production," is one of Henry's early engagements with Marx and Marxism leading up to his two-volume study *Marx* (1975). The essay begins with a careful examination of the treatment of theory and praxis in Heidegger's "Essay Concerning Technology," through which Henry shows that Heidegger follows a long line of Western philosophy by reducing praxis to a form of theory. It is with Marx's conception of praxis, however, that the genuine meaning of production is discovered. This accounts for Marx's originality and importance as a philosopher. Praxis, as human action, can be understood according to the duality of appearing. There is a visible side of the action that can be intuited and objectified (the "what" of the action), but there is also a subjective aspect of action that cannot be seen (the "how" of the action). While the former aspect is governed by theoretical knowledge and the laws of the world, the latter aspect signifies the true reality of praxis and is rooted in the laws of life. Praxis thus reveals an original dimension of being and an original dimension of truth in subjective action.

The next essay, "Difficult Democracy," offers an interesting suggestion concerning how Henry might think about liberal democracy. This essay begins with a critique of liberal democracy for being overly formal.

Liberal democracies were founded on the rejection of traditional hierarchical forms of government. But Henry's critique of democracy observes, first of all, that representational democracy replicates this class division by establishing a division between representatives and those who elect them. But the deeper problem with democracy has to do with the threat of the rule of the majority, which means that a majority can overturn the freedom and equality that were the supposed foundation of democracy. Democracy, if understood on a purely formal level, thus enters into contradiction with itself. To resolve this contradiction, Henry proposes a material or substantive democracy which is able to provide an extra-democratic foundation for democratic values. The material anchor for the intrinsic value of the individual and the equality of individuals is to be found in life. It is through the transcendental birth of individuals that the members of a democratic community come to rank as separate but equal persons.

"Kandinsky and the Work of Art" offers a synopsis of Henry's extensive engagement with the art and theory of Wassily Kandinsky, who is the focus of Henry's book *Seeing the Invisible.* Kandinsky's discovery of abstraction parallels Henry's critique of Western philosophy, in the sense that it is a rejection of representationalism in art. Under the theory of abstraction, the meaning of painting is not to depict or represent the world; instead, its purpose is to shift attention to the elements that make such representation possible: color, point, line, plane, and so on. Each of these elements, Kandinsky contends, carries an inner, affective tonality, and the purpose of composition is precisely to arrange these elements in such a way as to produce a desired affective response. Kandinskian abstraction, according to Henry, thus provides a pathway into the phenomenology of life—for Kandinsky is painting the affective experience of life itself.

"Material Phenomenology and Language" is an important statement of Henry's view of language. Henry's account of a radical immanence that does not admit of representation raises the methodological question of how it is then possible for his philosophy to speak about this immanence. Does language about this radical self-relation not cast it into objectivity and exteriority? To address this issue, Henry distinguishes between the "language of the world" and the "language of life." The language of the world performs the task of disclosing the world. It has the same characteristics as the appearing of the world: the word is different from its referent; the word is thus arbitrary or indifferent to its referent; the word is unable to posit or produce its referent. By contrast, the language of life is described by Henry as a revelation of life. Its first feature is that it is a self-revelation. As a self-revelation, the language of life is identical with its referent. Instead of its referent standing outside of itself or being different from itself, life generates its own reality by experiencing itself through the word.

Part 4: Ethics and Religion

The focus of Henry's later writings turned primarily to matters of theological concern. His "Christian trilogy" consists of the works *I Am The Truth, Incarnation,* and *Words of Christ.* These developments apply his earlier philosophy of life in order to forge a philosophical approach to Christianity. But in so doing, they also raise new questions concerning the relation between the living individual and God as Life. Such questions run through the chapters included in this part of the book.

The first essay in part 4, "Ethics and Religion within a Phenomenology of Life," offers one of Henry's few statements on the topic of ethics in the context of his phenomenology of life, although the focus of this essay is clearly on the connection between ethics and religion. Religion is understood by Henry in literal terms as a bond that connects the living individual to Life. By contrast, ethics has to do with the way in which this bond is lived through by an individual. The relation between ethics and religion, then, comes to be treated as the relation between the way up and the way down. Religion, especially the notion of creation, refers to the way down; this is the way in which Life gives birth to ipseity. Through a transcendental birth, the self comes into its being as the offspring of Life. To forget this birth is to fall prey to the transcendental illusion of an autonomous, self-contained ego; it is to forget the self's prior bond with life. The way up, by contrast, is the way of salvation. Ethics includes the powers of the body and their ability to restore and repair this bond across the community of the living. The restoration of this community occurs through the commandment to love. Life commands love, Henry reasons, because life is love.

The next essay, "Theodicy from the Perspective of a Radical Phenomenology," offers an interesting interpretation of Leibniz's classic answer to the problem of the existence of evil. Henry surprisingly interprets Leibniz's essay as a thesis about the nature of the world. The world is characterized by its contingency, inasmuch as it is one world among other possible worlds. This means that if the world is to have necessity, it must be derived from outside of the world, and in fact, this is why Leibniz invokes God who confers a principle of necessity onto the world. The actual world, which includes evil and suffering within it, has been chosen by God because it is the best of all possible worlds. For Henry, however, the necessity of suffering does not come from God; instead, it is drawn from life itself. To live is to suffer because we do not create ourselves but receive our own life from life. From this perspective, Henry detects a new potential convergence with Leibniz, who speaks about the hidden connection between good and evil. Both belong to the pathos of life.

"The Experience of the Other" addresses the problem of intersubjectivity and of sociality, and in this way, it might be read as the converse of chapter 4 in this book, "Those within Me." Here Henry draws from the Christian doctrine of the mystical body of Christ to explain the community of the living. Just as his phenomenology of subjectivity has shown that I am not my own origin but am engendered by life, the same is true for other selves. Accordingly, this doctrine establishes that we are united together in life, specifically in the life of Christ, even before we come into life as a self. Living individuals are thus united in life in the same ways as members of Christianity are united in the body of Christ.

"Speech and Religion" is perhaps one of Henry's most widely read articles, because it was originally included in "Phenomenology and Theology," a famous set of responses to Dominique Janicaud's claim that a "theological turn" had taken place in French phenomenology and led it to deviate from its true direction. Situated within the context of this volume, this article gains even greater intelligibility. It draws from the phenomenology of birth to indicate that every self is a son, in the transcendental sense, who is begotten in life. It also utilizes the distinction between the language of the world and the language of life. Whereas the language of the world is rooted in distinctions and separation, the language of life is a self-revelation of life. Life is the word of God, as Henry understands it. This is why a theological turn does not violate phenomenology: they enter into relation when they speak the language of life.

Notes on the Translation

We would like to acknowledge the work of the many different translators whose work is included in this volume. While the translations that have been published previously have not been altered, when it comes to the chapters that are translated here for the first time, we have sought to be as faithful to the original and as internally consistent with one another as possible. For this reason, we have sought to retain Henry's use of italics throughout. He often italicizes sentences or parts of sentences in order to highlight a key point in his argument. Similarly, we have retained Henry's use of hyphenation; even though his usage is not consistent. He typically uses hyphenation in order to signal something important about the etymological roots of a term. For example, the hyphenation of the term "ob-ject" points to the two etymological roots: "ob-" is "in the way" and "-ject" is "thrown." So this highlights that an object appears in such a way that it is thrown out in front of consciousness and stands against it. Also, we have sought to remain faithful to Henry's occasional but inconsistent use of capitalization to highlight the use of a term as a substantive, for example, to contrast between the adjective use of "ek-static" and the substantive term "Ek-stasis." With regard to footnotes, we have provided references to the English versions of the texts to which Henry refers in his footnotes, when available. The endnotes that follow each chapter are Henry's, unless otherwise noted.

Some of Henry's terminology is technical and does not align easily with ordinary concepts in French. Several particular terms have been a point of discrepancy among the translators, and we want to explain the rationale for the editors' decisions on these points.

Among the terms that evoked different treatments, the first to mention are the verb *éprouver* and the noun *épreuve*. The term *éprouver* means "to experience" and broadly "to feel" or "go through an experience," and the term *épreuve* could mean a "trial," a "test," or an "ordeal." In this volume, we have chosen to translate both terms simply as "experience." The danger, with this choice, is tied to the fact that the word "experience" in its English etymology signifies a "looking out" and in this way runs counter to Henry's entire point about the experience of life: precisely that it is not a "looking out" but rather an affect. But the benefit of using the term "experience" is that it has a familiarity that does not make Henry's philosophy seem as if it were unfamiliar in an idiosyncratic or exotic way. In other words, it preserves the resonance of Henry's thought with the rest of the philosophical tradition and leaves it up to the arguments to establish his divergences from the tradition. To signal the presence of these terms in the original, we have put the corresponding French term in brackets when it seems relevant.

Another term is the French *pathétique*, which Henry uses quite often in his writings. *Pathétique* is not the same as the English word "pathetic," nor do we think it is necessary, as certain translators have done, to introduce an entirely new construction into the English language with the neologism "pathet-ik." Its equivalent instead is the term "pathos," both as a feeling and a passive undergoing. So we have used the term "pathos" when it stands as a noun, and the term "pathos-filled" when it occurs in adjective form. Also, Henry occasionally utilizes the opposing terms *naturant/naturé*. This terminology is derived from Spinoza, but it does not have a direct equivalent in English; accordingly, we have rendered it in terms of the Latin expressions by which this distinction is commonly known: *natura naturans/natura naturata*. Where a word or phrase is difficult to translate or simply deserves to be noted, translators refer to the French text in brackets.

Notes

For a more detailed account of some of the main ideas presented in the first part of this introduction, see Frédéric Seyler, "Radikal phänomenologisches Leben als Selbstaffektion: Die Lebendigen und das Leben," *Jahrbuch für Religionsphilosophie/Philosophy of Religion Annual*, Volume 16 (2017), 40–58.

1. Michel Henry, *The Essence of Manifestation*, trans. Girard Etzkorn (Dordrecht: Springer, 1973); originally published as *L'Essence de la manifestation* (Paris: Presses Universitaires de France, 1963).

2. Michel Henry, *Incarnation: A Philosophy of Flesh*, trans. Karl Hefty (Evanston, Ill.: Northwestern University Press, 2015); originally published as *Incarnation: Une philosophie de la chair* (Paris: Seuil, 2000).

3. Michel Henry, *Material Phenomenology*, trans. Scott Davidson (New York: Fordham University Press 2008); originally published as *Phénoménologie matérielle* (Paris: Presses Universitaires de France, 1990).

THE MICHEL HENRY READER

Part 1

Phenomenology

1

The Four Principles of Phenomenology

Phenomenology rests on four principles which it explicitly claims as its foundations.

The first—"so much appearance, so much being"—is borrowed from the Marburg School. Over against this ambiguous proposition, owing to the double signification of the term "appearance," we prefer this strict wording: "so much appearing, so much being."[1]

The second is the principle of principles. Formulated by Husserl himself in §24 of *Ideen I*, it sets forth intuition or, more precisely, "that every originary presentive intuition is a legitimizing source of cognition"[2] and thus for any particularly rational statement.

In the third principle, the claim is so vehement that it clothes itself in the allure of an exhortation, even a cry: *"zu den Sachen selbst!"*

The fourth principle was defined considerably later by Jean-Luc Marion in his work *Reduction and Givenness*, but its importance hits upon the entirety of phenomenological development as a hidden presupposition that is always already at work. It is formulated thus: "so much reduction, so much givenness."[3]

These four founding principles of phenomenology have two features that should be underlined from the outset. On the one hand, despite the claim of radicality implicit in their literal expression, *they remain in fact fundamentally undefined.* This indeterminacy is all the more serious and weighs all the more dangerously on the destiny of phenomenology precisely because it concerns a phenomenological indeterminacy in an essential sense. The first consequence of this phenomenological indeterminacy of the foundational principles of phenomenology is the purely formal character of the pronouncements to which they give rise, a character that removes a great deal of their rigor and, thereby, their fecundity.

On the other hand, in spite of their formal character, the four principles contain latent tensions that are hardly compatible with the coherence that one would expect from a system of presuppositions placed at the start of an investigation and charged with ensuring its unity. These tensions are such that, to speak candidly, they result in veritable contradictions.

Let us begin with indeterminacy. The first principle establishes a decisive correlation between appearance and being. This correlation impresses itself upon us with the strongest force because it is wholly immediate: when something appears, it happens to exist at the same time. This correlation is so powerful that it seems to be reduced [*ramener*] to an identity: to appear is thereby identically to be. When the principle says "so much appearing, so much being," it intends neither the extension, nor in any fashion the intensity of phenomenological and ontological determinations that it brings together, but rather the common identity of their essence. It is to the extent that appearing appears that being thereby "is." It is to the extent that appearing extends its reign that being also extends its own. And this is because they have one and the same reign, one and the same essence.

As soon as we consider further this essential identity between appearing and being, we are obliged to call it into question again. In spite of the supposed identity of their essence, appearing and being do not belong on the same plane. Their ontological dignity, so to speak, is not the same—far from it: appearing is everything, being is nothing. Or rather, being only exists because appearing appears and only to the extent that it does so. The identity between appearing and being is resolved in the establishment of the latter by means of the former. Here the essential identity means that only one and the same power is at work, that of appearing. Without appearance, as long as it does not appear, being is nothing—in the sense that it is nothing at all. Its essence, that which allows it to be, is found only in appearing, which has extended its own essence to it. Its essence consists in the fact of actually appearing.

By contrast, it is pure non-sense to inquire into the meaning of being as such or into that which would allow it to be in some fashion of itself and by itself, through its own power or will. Being itself has neither power nor will. It is nothing but a *flatus vocis*, unless we recognize in it the *sui generis* power that leads it to be and that leads all things to be. This is the power of appearing as it appears.

Phenomenology thus stands higher than ontology. Yet one must observe that this manner of expressing the precedence of phenomenology risks leading us into error. There are not two domains, of which one would prevail for some reason over the other, as if it would play the role of a precondition for the other one which would only be its product or effect. Phenomenology and ontology are not two different things; instead they designate the same thing, one solitary "thing" whose essence is appearing and which is constituted exclusively by it.

It suffices to cite here someone who, well before the development of modern phenomenology, seized the fundamental intuition of all pure phenomenology and was able to raise it to the level of its true concept—something which neither Husserlian nor Heideggerian phenomenology was able to do. At least twice, Descartes reduced being to appearing in such a radical manner that nothing remained of being or of any possible being that was not in substance appearing and, indeed, pure appearing. That is, an appearance in which what appears is the pure fact of appearing as such. In the *Regulae*, Descartes still understood the pure fact of appearing as such in a traditional manner and then designated it by a variety of improper titles, including *lumen naturale*. He then perceived it in its true essence in the piercing intuition of the *Meditations*, when he calls it the *cogitatio*. In the context of this problem, the relation between appearing and being is now laid bare: "thought alone belongs to [the mind] [*que nous sommes par cela seul que nous pensons*]."[4] This means: the being that we are and to which all being may be reduced (subsisting after doubt)—thus, being in its totality—takes the power of being from appearance and only from the power of appearance. This is formulated in the language of the problem of the *Meditations*: "I am, then, in the strict sense only a thing that thinks."[5] This means: being resides in appearing and is exhausted in it. Said otherwise, there is no being that would be different in itself from the appearing of appearance and that may not be reduced purely and simply to it.

We now arrive at the third principle: "straight to the things themselves!" Its announcement conjures up a duality of terms. This duality is not a fact of language but refers to what it claims to speak about: "*Zu*" on the one hand, and "*die Sachen*" on the other. "*Zu*" is the access to something, the possibility of reaching it, while *Sachen* designates something which is reached through this access, the content to which such access gives access.

At the very moment that we first proceed to make explicit phenomenology's rallying cry, to explain it in its simplest form, it is inescapable that we have both fallen back into the most traditional problem and that we have abandoned or rather rejected what the commentary on the first principle procured for us as an essential finding, namely, the identity of appearing and being through the reduction of the latter to the former.

Such is the contradiction. Being is no longer reducible to appearing. It no longer draws the power that makes it to be from the pure fact of appearing, if there are some *Sachen*, some things in themselves, which we should seek to attain and attain by following a certain path, by a means of access that is precisely nothing but the means to attaining these things. They are the end. Being is already there in itself before we recognize it.

The problem of appearing is certainly not resolved by that. In the imperative of phenomenology, the "*Zu*" that leads us to the things directly and without detour is precisely appearing itself. But this appearing, thought as a pure possibility of access, is presented henceforth as subordinate to that to which it permits us access. This subordination goes so far that it is not only the case that the possibility of access is involved in the attaining of the thing that is its true goal. Moreover, the access itself proves to be determined by this goal. It is the nature of the object to be known that determines the appropriate means of knowing it. This is to say that ultimately it determines the access itself, dictates what this access ought to be, which procedures and methodologies must be put in place in order to be able to grasp this object and to attain it in itself such as it is. Ontology's subordinate relationship to phenomenology is thus reversed now, since the thing constitutes the only goal by virtue of which the means of access were put in place and, moreover, since the nature of these means depends on the nature of the thing.

This reversal of the relationship between phenomenology and ontology brings us to an aporia. How can we know the nature of the thing and how it determines our access to it unless this thing and what we call its nature has already been revealed to us—in and through its appearing? To the claim that the nature of the thing decides the means of access, one has to respond as follows: it is the means of access to the thing that found and establish its nature; it is the act of seeing that determines the visual character of what is seen, hearing its auditory character, space its spatial character, time its temporal character, etc. Once we reject the naive idea that phenomenology is determined by ontology, once we reject that knowledge is determined by the thing known, a problem nonetheless remains: that of the duality presupposed by traditional thought and by contemporary phenomenology—although, to the contrary, this duality is abolished by a radical reduction of being to appearing.

The connection between being and appearing is established in the phenomenon. The concept of the phenomenon designates *something that shows itself* and thus unites the two significations of the thing, which are that of being, on the one hand, and the fact of showing itself, or appearing, on the other. The fact that something is only to the extent that it shows itself and that being inevitably refers to appearing, does not avoid the question of knowing whether "something" that shows itself by becoming a "phenomenon" is different in itself from appearing itself, even completely heterogeneous to it. What justifies this line of questioning is the fact that what is given in the phenomenon (at least, for example, in the mundane phenomenon) is given precisely as already there before the "discovery" of it that is offered by the phenomenon—before appearing establishes it in this condition of what appears and of what counts as a "phenomenon" for us.

A new contradiction now presents itself to us. The radical reduction of being to appearance finds itself supplanted by the inevitable dissociation of the two. Being is indeed independent of appearing, if it "is" in a certain manner, however obscure it may be to us, *before* being shown to us in and by the phenomenon.

The concept of phenomenon is itself affected by this contradiction and falls, at the very least, into ambiguity. In its positive signification, it expresses the primitive embrace between being and appearing, that unshakeable foundation recognized by the first principle ("so much appearing, so much being") on which phenomenology sought to establish itself. Why? As long as something appears, no critique can be made of its existence. One may well say, "This phenomenon is an illusion," but nothing has changed. Nothing has been done to this phenomenon itself insofar as its appearing has not ceased to occur and one limits oneself to it.

Shielded from criticism, the phenomenon is not protected from analysis. What analysis calls into question, in the first place, is not the connection of appearing and being but rather the reduction of being to appearing, that is, the idea that there cannot be any being other than appearing itself as such. To examine the issue more closely, in effect, the phenomenon does not at all imply the radicality of this reduction of the being of being to the appearing of appearing. Rather, quite to the contrary, it seems to presuppose their connection, however meager this may be, as well as their distinctness at least as an ideal possibility. If this distinction is inscribed in some way in what is phenomenologically the phenomenon, does it not make analysis necessary?

This distinction in the phenomenon separates what appears and the fact of appearing. The concept of phenomenon, in other words, is twofold: it is both ontic and phenomenological. From the ontic point of view, the phenomenon designates what appears, for example: this table, this proposition, this memory. But the ontic content of the phenomenon, or what common sense understands by that name, does not exhaust this concept. For it also implies, beyond this specific content, its phenomenality, that is, the fact of showing itself (or phenomenality) and that there can only be a phenomenon in this way.

Now it is necessary to think through how far this duplicity of the concept of the phenomenon goes, what results from the devastating rupture that it creates, and the primal unity of appearing and being. For it is no longer only about a simple notional distinction between the contents of the phenomenon and its pure appearing, if the former can vary indefinitely while the latter remains unchanged. This permanence of appearing, while that which appears constantly changes, implies a difference between the nature of the two. Traditional thought understands phenomenality as light—whether it is natural light, the light of reason, of the world, or of this world itself—the difference between appearing and what appears is a matter of absolute indifference, in this case the indifference of light to all that it illuminates, as Descartes says in the first "Regula."[6]

But, if in the phenomenon its contents and its appearing differ to the point of one standing with absolute indifference toward the other, if they revert each to its own side without anything in common with the other, how can their unity still be preserved in the phenomenon as that which establishes the phenomenon? The aporia of the phenomenon, however, only illustrates the aporia which now affects the relationship of appearing and being, upon which phenomenology thought it could establish itself. How would the content, the thing, and beings, be able to come into being by appearing and by its own act of appearing, if they are in principle indifferent to it? How, in other words, can being take its being from appearing if, in itself and in its nature, as the content of the phenomenon, it is irreducible to the phenomenality of appearing? It is the principle of phenomenology, the internal bond of appearing and being that is affected; and it is because phenomenology as a whole neglects or fails to clarify this principle that it has lost its bearings and finds itself adrift.

And how would it be otherwise as long as appearing and, at the same time, being itself reduced to its appearing are both presented as purely formal concepts? And as long as the fundamental principles of phenomenology remain in a state of complete phenomenological indeterminacy?

What indeed can the first principle ("so much appearing, so much being") mean if one does not know what appearing means and, as a result, what being means, a being whose being is appearing? How should one make sense of the proportional relation that unites them and which becomes a forever enigmatic proportion between two equally unknown terms?

Along similar lines, how can we understand the third principle ("to the things themselves") if the access to the things, which the *zu* expresses and which represent nothing other than appearing itself, still remains completely unelucidated? How can we understand this principle if we do not know *how things appear* or how to go to them in order to apprehend and know them? The very question of knowing if these things differ from the pure possibility that offers access to them and if, as a result, this possibility can and ought to be thought of apart; or if, on the contrary, things and access have only and are only the same essence; this question, which decides the ultimate claim of phenomenology to define being through phenomenality, even to reduce it to phenomenality, remains without an answer.

The same uncertainty, in turn, applies to the fourth principle: "so much reduction, so much givenness." This recent statement of a rigorous proportionality between reduction and givenness leads us back to the sources of phenomenology and to the first principle itself, at least as we have formulated it. For, as we shall demonstrate, the reduction understood in its phenomenological signification is nothing other than a reduction to appearing. That this reduction can be taken to a greater or lesser extent, according to a greater or lesser radicality—as the proposition "so much reduction, so much givenness" implies—does not only mean that it is important to define this concept of appearing in a rigorous manner by distinguishing it from that with which thought has always conflated it, namely, with what appears in it. If the radicality of the reduction ought to concern appearing itself, must not one think that appearing is not as simple as it seems in each of these statements that refers to it as a unique and monotone manner of a thing showing itself? To the contrary, it implies and puts into play fundamental differences and, beyond them, *an absolute difference between two heterogeneous modes of manifestation.* Everything that is ever able to manifest itself is manifested and revealed according to these modes. Thus irreducible to a formal univocal signification, appearing differs as such, according to the pure phenomenological material out of which it is made. Only an account of it—of the how of appearing—can lend a sense to the propositions that are based on it, notably the principles of phenomenology. Only this attention to the phenomenological substantiality of pure phenomenality can indicate whether or not pure phenomenality is homogenous with being and whether or not it is able to define and determine it.

Let us then adopt the perspective of a material phenomenology for the purpose of scrutinizing the founding principles of phenomenology more closely. What now stands before us is not only the ruinous phenomenological indeterminacy whereby phenomenology, as it is traditionally conceived, left vague the interior nature of its true object. The suspicion to the contrary is raised that thanks specifically to this indeterminacy and to the fact that effective and concrete phenomenological modalities of appearing are not fixed, a certain conception of phenomenality arises. This conception of phenomenality is presented immediately and usually to ordinary thought and at the same time constitutes the oldest and least critical presupposition of traditional philosophy. This conception of phenomenality is borrowed from the everyday perception of objects in the world and has become firmly established not as what it actually is, namely, a particular form of experience, but as the general structure of appearing and thus of all phenomena as such. This catastrophic confusion of the appearing of the world with the universal essence of appearing corrupts almost all philosophies in Western thought, to the point that critiques of them most often trace this confusion back to the beginning of their postulates and analyses. In Husserlian phenomenology, it is the second principle—"that every originary presentive intuition is a legitimizing source of cognition"—that exposes this confusion in its full magnitude.

This famous principle, the principle of principles, is given as the most fundamental, but beneath its apparent simplicity it conceals a double thesis that renders it contradictory. On the one hand, it explicitly aims at universality. That about which it pretends to speak, under the title of intuition, is that which makes possible every phenomenon and every experience in any domain whatsoever, and whatever might be the specificity of this phenomenon or this intuition. It thus concerns appearing in general. It is the universal condition of phenomena. It is phenomenality in its first and omnipresent structure, in its essence, which is designated under the title of "originary presentive intuition."

On the other hand, however, under the very same term "intuition," there is a particular mode of appearing that is intended and that is no longer a still undefined, simple concept. For Husserl, intuition signifies the structure of consciousness as "consciousness of something," as intentional. To be sure, it is fulfilled intentionality that, *stricto sensu*, the concept of intuition qualifies, but it is to intentionality as such that intuition owes its power of constituting phenomenality, of instituting the condition for the phenomenon. Intentionality gives rise to phenomenality. Intentionality thus proceeds by surpassing itself toward that which is cast in front of it as its intentional correlate, as a transcendent object. It is the transcendence of this object, its setting at a distance that constitutes phenomenality as such.

This unilateral definition of the pure concept of phenomenality, however given as universal, results in a limitation whose significance is not only gnoseological but vital. It is not only knowledge that, according to the most constant thesis of Western philosophy, sees itself confronted with an insurmountable finitude instead of being justified. It is our life itself that is put to the side, forgotten, and lost, if the essence of life is nothing other than that of original phenomenality, and if the phenomenality that draws its substance from the ek-static light of the world and from its transcendence excludes in principle this Archi-Revelation. But "intuition" is only a name for this transcendence; it implies in itself this unconscious but radical elimination of life.

The ultimate claim of phenomenology, of relating to phenomena in such a manner that it attains being itself within them, does not only run up against the difficulties and contradictions that have already been revealed but against an absolute impasse. By positing intuition as the basis for all experience and of all knowledge, of all that can exist for us, phenomenology displays the sort of appearing in which being never "exists" in its most original essence: it bursts forth in us as an infinite life that does not cease to give us to ourselves and to engender us to the extent that it engenders itself in its eternal self-affection. Far from being established in intuition, the connection between appearing and being is completely undone there to the point that, in the phenomenon issued from intuition and notably in evidence, being is neither presented nor given to us but rather is removed or, better said, abolished. To require being to offer itself in intuition and, if possible, under its completed form as evidence is to deny, in effect, that any other being than that which is intuited or intuitable is possible. It is to deny, finally, the mere "existence" of the original essence of appearing and being that are drawn from life. This second principle—which is in truth the first principle—is an act of murder.

This elimination by the principle of principles of that which, as the auto-affection of life, constitutes the Archi-Revelation of appearing itself, explains in first place the destiny of historical phenomenology. This tradition has never been able to break truly with the fundamental presupposition of Husserlian phenomenology. This is what renders Heidegger's criticisms of Husserlian phenomenology ineffectual. What makes being be is precisely not appearing understood in terms of the concept of intuition but what escapes irreducibly from intuition. As a result, one embarks, in effect, upon an unending quest, as they say, and becomes involved in a hermeneutic that is confined to the task of never finding what is in question. Besides, this is not the "meaning of being" but rather the force that makes being be. What is contrasted with intuition or intentionality under various titles—"Dasein," "transcendence," "ek-static truth"—does nothing other than to announce the condition of this intuition or of this intentionality. No other phenomenality in its pure phenomenological materiality is conceived or envisioned here than the phenomenality of the Ek-stasis wherein all intuition is deployed. Truly, the simple question of the possibility of an impressional phenomenological matter, such as that of an auto-affection in its pathos, never even comes to mind.

In the case of Husserl, the central lacuna of his phenomenology is the fact that it misses in principle, and notably in the principle of principles, the transcendental life that nonetheless constituted its primary preoccupation. This lacuna remains masked by the systematic character of the problem and the investigation that it arouses. Once intuition has been placed at the foundation of every form of possible being, a philosophy that seeks a universal phenomenological ontology can only be carried out through an exhaustive elucidation of the various possible forms of intuition to which different kinds of evidence correspond. In each case, evidence is the most perfect mode of intuition to which one could aspire for each form of intuition, and hence, for every domain of being. The meticulous and persistent pursuit of this grandiose project resulted, with the laying bare of new forms of intuition, in the discovery of new regions of being. And yet, this extraordinary broadening of human experience and of the domains of objects comes with a tragic limitation. All these means of access, skilfully recognized and described, are precisely forms of intuition from which life by its nature has withdrawn. Hence phenomenology produces in a purely negative sense a "reduction" of what it sought to expand and liberate: our relationship to being as a relationship founded in our own life.

It is the merit of the fourth principle, which designates without compromise the two key concepts of phenomenology and establishes a relationship of proportionality between them, to restore to the reduction a truly positive significance. Far from limiting, restricting, omitting, and thus "reducing," the reduction opens and gives. And what does it give? Givenness. The former leads to the latter in such a way that the expansion and deepening of the one is the expansion and deepening of the other: "so much reduction, so much givenness." This is what needs to be demonstrated.

The first discussion of the reduction in the *Lectures* of 1905 and 1907 remains weighed down with the ontico-phenomenological ambiguity that we have denounced. In his effort to reach the "pure phenomenon," the "phenomenon in the sense of phenomenology," Husserl does not distinguish clearly between what appears and appearing itself. This ambiguity corrupts the concept of "absolute givenness," of "self givenness" [*absolute Gegebenheit, Selbstgegebenheit*][7] which designates at the same time the thing given and the way in which it is given. The obtaining of things given in this way is now the goal of the inquiry. Hence, in the *Lectures* of 1905 the sense data constituted the absolute givens to which this first reduction led, whereas everything that surpasses these subjective and incontestable appearances, namely, the "transcendent" object constituted on the basis of them, is affected by a degree of uncertainty and thus is put out of play by the reduction. Auditory and visual impressions, for example, are certain, although the object intended through them but not actually given in them could indeed not exist. Or rather, what is directly grasped, the pure phenomena, are the conscious phenomena that intend the object, not what is intended by them.

However, one cannot forget that it is in the *Lectures* of 1905 that, with the explicit designation of the objects of phenomenology as "objects in their How,"[8] the decisive distinction is introduced between the given and the mode of its givenness, between the "object" and its how, which is nothing other than the How of its givenness, that is, givenness itself.

The distinction between the contents that are certain and those that are tentative is only the means for going back to the way in which they are given. This and only this renders them certain or not. From the reduction to givenness, even though phenomenology remains caught up in ontic ambiguity, is the path traveled since 1905 when the reduction was introduced.

As a consequence, the true sense of the reduction is never ontic. It does not have to do with establishing a division between the certain contents upon which, for example, knowledge might be established and other reputedly dubious contents. In principle, the reduction is phenomenological for the reason that it relates to the object itself of phenomenology, namely, to the How of givenness. How then are the contents given that can claim certitude and how are those that cannot? In and through the evidence for certain contents; and outside of and independent of evidence for uncertain contents. *It is never the certain contents, what is evident, which are able to offer a foundation for knowledge, but only that which renders them evident and hence certain, namely, evidence itself.* This is the sense of saying that evidence, and the evidence alone, is a principle; this is the sense of the principle of principles.

Under the purview of this principle, the analysis has already objected to the fact that all that matters, namely, the object of phenomenology—and with it every ontological determination receiving its substance from the original appearing and taking from this its ability to be—is lost. For the Archi-Revelation of Life never surrenders itself to the guise of evidence or merges with it. Our being, as generated in this Archi-Revelation and as living beings, is concealed as well. It is not a coincidence that, subordinating all ontology to the transcendental Ego, Husserlian phenomenology showed itself to be totally destitute when it was a matter of defining the "being" of this "Ego," or what could serve as it.

The disappearance of the original appearing and, hence, of the proper object of phenomenology under the purview of the principle of principles requires us to return to the reduction for the purpose of conferring on it a truly radical and new significance. What the principles of phenomenology presuppose is a pure reduction. By setting into operation the opposition between the ontic content and the appearing that makes it manifest, the reduction finally thematizes appearing in order to recognize it for what it is. For we have just discovered that this pure reduction directed toward pure phenomenality, instead of liberating it in its fullness, obscures in it its most primitive power. Extending the work of the pure reduction and pushing it to its fullest extent, *the radical reduction reduces appearing itself.* Within appearing, it sets aside this range of light that we call the world in order to reveal that without which this visible horizon would never become visible, namely, the auto-affection of its transcendental exteriority which actualizes itself in the pathos of Life that is never outside. Only a reduction that goes all the way to the end of its capacity of reducing, that suspends the ek-static Dimension of visibility in which every conceivable giving intuition and evidence itself flow, and that suspends all possible showing, can discover the original givenness, the givenness that by giving life to itself, gives to it to be life. And, at the same time, it gives everything in the world and every possible world, inasmuch as the givenness of such things never happens except in the self-givenness of life. Hence it is necessary to extend the reduction to its term, according to the "more" which radicalizes it so that givenness gives itself according to its own excess, an excess that belongs to it as its own possibility and without which nothing, not even the most trivial being, could ever be given. The trait that unites the method and the object of phenomenology, according to a yet unprecedented proportionality, is revealed to us now in the fourth principle: "so much reduction, so much givenness."

Three remarks are necessary here. The first is that the "more" which characterizes the original givenness is not limited to signifying the other domain of appearing that classical phenomenology had constantly lacked, this other face that is no longer the one which the world turns toward us. This other domain of appearing has no face at all, no conceivable visage, but is the non-visage of the invisible essence of life. Now that the duplicity of appearing has finally been recognized, it is not a matter of adding to the How of ek-static or intentional givenness from which the evidence benefits, this other unrecognized How by which life embraces itself according to the tonalities of its own pathos. The "more" of this new givenness signifies that in this wholly other way of giving, the finitude that strikes every ek-static horizon of visibility loses its power. In the horizon, all that is seen refers to the unseen, all that is real to the unreal, all that is given to the ungiven, such that all givenness is punctual, conditional, surrounded by unfilled horizons, by unaccomplished potentialities that are inevitably thus, submitted to the flow and disappearance as well as the vanity of hope. In Life, to the contrary, Life touches every point of its being and lacks nothing; everything is there in its entirety at every moment. But this is only possible because in this ultimate givenness of life there are neither adumbrations, nor aspects, nor horizons of fulfillment, nor contents coming to fulfill them: nothing that is beyond or below an irremissible experience, whose phenomenological material is a pathos and whose modalities belong to it in their plenitude each unsurpassable time.

With the reduction, Husserl wanted nothing to be lost but everything to be found again to a higher degree of consistency and legitimacy.

Hence he believed the *cogitatum* in the reduction to be that of the world itself. Within pure appearing itself, is the radical reduction which recognizes its duplicity for the sake of preserving the most original givenness of life, able to take advantage of a comparable result? By letting go of the reign of the visible and of every conceivable world, is it not affected by a lack of evidence? At the end of this unprecedented reduction which rejects all transcendence and all that is given by it, can one still say "so much reduction, so much givenness"?

Never, however, would affection by the world nor consequently by a being *happen* if this ek-static affection did not first affect itself in Life, which is nothing other than this primitive auto-affection. And because the world only has its being in life, because it "is" nothing other than a living cosmos, only the radical reduction which finds in appearing the ultimate dividing line between immanence and transcendence, only this reduction preserves what escapes transcendence in principle even while acting within transcendence as its condition.

All seeing, for example, carries within itself a non-seeing without which the eye would see nothing: the immanent experience that it constantly has of itself. This is, moreover, why there is a pathos in seeing, a seeing in desire, in boredom, in passion, and why it is submitted to such things. Concerning the radical reduction to pure immanence, it must be said that it neither forgets nor subtracts anything, but that it is by the reduction alone that what the reduction puts in parentheses receives its particular properties, while seeing, intuition, and evidence left to themselves do not explain what is in parentheses at all.

Not only the desirable, horrible, or odious character of what is seen but also seeing as such derives its own power from life. Our second remark is that only the radical reduction to pure immanence unperceived by Husserl and by contemporary phenomenology accomplishes the promise of losing nothing, whereas the reduction to evidence simply misses life and hence givenness itself in its original tenor.

The third remark concerns the relationship of a radical reduction to a pure reduction. A pure reduction was presented as coming at the outset onto a path that can lead to a radical reduction. It is necessary to put being out of play and to consider appearing in itself, if one wants to recognize its duplicity, the division in it between the two realms, and to understand their relationship, the foundation of finite givenness in the givenness which excludes every horizon and hence every limitation.

But here is what is important: although it comes first, a pure reduction cannot truly be accomplished if it is limited to itself. This is because, however pure it may be, the appearing that it isolates does not subsist by itself. Such is the primary and most powerful illusion of contemporary phenomenology: to believe that being phenomenologically defined as an ek-static dimension thus has a phenomenologically sufficient condition—ultimately, that transcendence is phenomenologically and ontologically an autonomous essence. Because the reduction has not led all the way to a reduction to pure immanence, the givenness that results does not remain only affected by an essential finitude: in fact, it gives nothing—and it gives itself less than any other thing. Because it has not accomplished vis-à-vis itself the original work of self-givenness, and because appearing was not produced as a self-appearing and hence does not appear, nothing else is able to appear in it. The other dimension of appearing, notably being, can only appear inasmuch as appearing appears in itself and as such.

But its self-appearing [*auto-apparaître*] is what the abstract appearing to which historical phenomenology was limited is unable to produce by itself. It is because the ownmost and innermost possibility of appearing remains unthought that it has always been understood as the appearing of something other than itself. But it is in itself foreign to the phenomenality of beings, as an appearing of what appears. *What appears in appearing is first and necessarily appearing itself.* This is what classical phenomenology never clearly perceived. It is limited to the theme of the phenomenon as it shows itself, and it only implies an abstract appearance which is unable to subsist by itself and which as such constantly refers to its opposite, to the opaque and dead element of ontic determination. But why did classical phenomenology limit itself to the appearing of beings, to the point of ignoring everything in appearing that would belong to a radically different order, if not because it took beings as its guide?

In the final assessment, and in spite of the illusory significations conferred upon an alleged subjectivity exhausted in its relation to things, the phenomenon of phenomenology was nothing other than Greek appearance. The critiques of subjectivity that have proliferated in our era are false critiques: they can at most find fault in the idea of subjectivity for faulty thinking—for example, ontic thinking—about the appearing to which they refer, which is the appearing of mundane things. Hence they remain unknowingly locked up in that which they critique.[9] It is here, by demanding the radicality of a reduction that suspends the phenomenality proper to being, that the fourth principle provides the path to a more original givenness.

The fourth principle emerges at the end of the problematic raised by Jean-Luc Marion, but he clarifies it retrospectively and gives to it a novel meaning. The subordination of ontology to phenomenology that has guided our entire analysis is explicit in the brief but decisive explanation of Husserl in the fifth chapter of Marion's *Reduction and Given-*

ness.¹⁰ The criticism too frequently and too quickly accepted by Heidegger against his master appears debatable. Fascinated by the new field of objects to which intentional analysis gave rise and set before the ego's gaze, it is true that Husserl too often restricted his attention to those objectivities rather than to the problem of being as perceived in the universality of its meaning. But one cannot forget that all of these fields of objects, and especially the field of the objects in formal ontology, is subordinated in the principle to a higher instance of another order. And this instance is phenomenological: the fact that it is designated under the improper title of the transcendental Ego does not truly impede us from signifying pure phenomenality as such. This is what appears clearly in the text of the *Ideen* of 1912¹¹ in which, freed from the ontic reference that did not cease from overwhelming Heidegger,¹² "the wonder of all wonders" is here "pure consciousness," "the phenomenon *par excellence*." It will no longer suffice to object that the "being" of this subject remains undefined, just as the difference between the "thing" and the "thing-for-consciousness" of the Husserlian reduction or even the objectivity of the objects of formal ontology remain undefined. For Jean-Luc Marion this means asking the question of knowing whether this Ego does not "except itself" from being, whether it does not situate itself "beyond being"¹³—a hypothesis that would suffice to disqualify the entire Heideggerian problematic of being, at least with respect to its claim to ultimate reality.

It is in Marion's direct confrontation with Heidegger throughout his work, which culminates in chapter 6 of *Reduction and Givenness*, that he completely disqualifies ontology in favor of a new mode of phenomenological thinking and perhaps a new phenomenology. The necessary overtaking of the existential analytic carried out in *Sein und Zeit* has for its principle motif the ontic preliminary of which the thought of being remains a constant prisoner. *Dasein* may be the only being [*étant*] in being itself [*être*] for whom its own being is an issue, but it remains nevertheless a being—from whence the critique that "indeed the meaning of Being (the second divergence of the *Seinsfrage*) cannot be read directly on any being whatsoever; a being, even *Dasein*, only ever allows one to read the Being of beings."¹⁴

By deliberately putting being out of play, insofar as it is in itself foreign to pure phenomenality, the phenomenological question of being passes through detailed phases of analysis and surmounts them all (the analytic of anxiety, the hermeneutics of the phenomenon of Nothingness) and arrives at the "irruption of Being itself, the 'voice' summons man directly,"¹⁵ which alone can define the ultimate enigma of the "phenomenon of being." Here, it seems to us, the subordination of ontology to phenomenology appears inescapable and, more importantly, this subordination implies the renewal of phenomenology itself in the depths of reduction with the unveiling of the givenness that exceeds all conceivable being.

Two decisive traits mark Marion's problematic insofar as it obeys the fourth principle. In the first place, it concerns the regression from Being to the claim or call of Being, a regression constantly required and completed in these closing analyses. Marion writes, "The *Anspruch* precedes and solely renders possible *Sein*."[16] "[. . .] the claim [*la revendication*]—more than being . . ."[17] "*Dasein* exposed itself to Being so as to become its site only inasmuch as it renders itself to the call that convokes it."[18] According to Marion, it is necessary "to think about Dasein in its totality starting from the instance that claims it and therefore it to itself as a there."[19] "The *there* . . . remains thoroughly determined by the call, since it serves only to respond thereto."[20] Hence the reduction, whose work follows the course and diverse formulations in historical phenomenology—the reduction of objects to the consciousness to an Ego, of "beings" to *Dasein*, of all beings to being—only leads to it in order to subordinate itself to something more essential and more originary, that is, to the claim and to the call.

Thus, what does the claim add to Being that is more fundamental and more primitive? What is the interpellation that it addresses to us apart from the fact that it comes, that *it appears to us* with neither mask nor detour, with neither intermediary nor delay, such that it is impossible for us to escape from its grasp or from what its immediacy contains? The call of being is simply its emergence in us; it is the embrace in which it gives itself to us at the same time that it gives being to us. Hence there would be nothing without this triumphal irruption of a revelation, which is that of the Absolute.

And it is here that we find the singular and surprising, if not stupefying, turn of this problematic of the call. After having established patiently that in accordance with the genuine sense of thematized being, it is the call, the way in which it embraces and takes hold of us, it is the *Er-eignis*, that matters. The problematic then reverses abruptly. According to its statement, what is introduced and essentialized in the end as in the beginning is not being, but it is not the call either: it is another call that has nothing to do with the call of being but rather one which renounces it in order to establish itself and reign in its place. Before we grasp the meaning of this rejection of the call of Being, let us see how it operates, how it is possible, and what instance higher than being and higher than its call may intervene here and dismiss being and its call.

This instance, which is the concept of boredom that Marion proposes in an entirely original problematic, is an instance of treating boredom as a "counter-existential": instead of providing our access to being, as a structure of *Dasein*, the power of boredom rather is to divert us from all that is. And this is so because it first diverts us from that which permits all beings to be: being itself. More radically still, the silent call that being ceaselessly addresses to the bored Ego is no longer of interest; the call "no longer says anything to it."[21] Boredom creates an extraordinary situation, one of the greatest danger and the greatest disgust, a situation in which the "Ego" is in some fashion no longer there for anything or for anyone.

From a Heideggerian perspective, one could take issue with this possibility of the Ego-*Dasein* detaching itself, in boredom, from being and its call. If, according to the existential analytic, *Dasein* is constituted essentially by its relation to being, if it is the being [*l'étant*] in being [*l'être*] whose own being itself is an issue, then how could one abolish the relation of *Dasein* to being without abolishing *Dasein* itself? Let us remember, it is through its most particular essence that *Dasein* "stands ek-statically in the truth of being"[22]—the truth of being which is nothing other than its fulguration, the illumination by which *Dasein* discovers itself from the beginning to be clarified in itself and in its innermost depths. But this illuminating fulguration is the call and the means by which *Dasein* is illuminated in its entirety, and from this moment, it is placed in the light of being, in the *there* of *Sein*. How could *Dasein* suddenly and miraculously cease to be? Would it not be necessary, in order for this to occur, that it cease to be what it is: *Da-Sein*? Now such a possibility is specifically discarded by Heidegger; as Marion writes, "doesn't that possibility simply contradict the very definition of *Dasein* as being-there, which it cannot not be?"[23]

The immense merit of Marion's work is that it seeks to establish in the analytic itself the possibility whereby *Dasein* may abandon the call which supposedly constitutes its essence. On the one hand, the surprise that provokes being and which carries out the same function of the call, "to grant *Dasein* to that which is destined to it and which, without amazement, could not manifest itself"[24]—this surprise implies at least the attention that *Dasein* lends to the call but that it can also no longer grant to it. The fact that the call is rooted in the eidetic necessity of the ek-static fulguration, in the truth of being, does not prevent but rather supposes the contingency of a response that can also not happen—in spite of the call, due to a boredom without limit whose radical refusal of every call can give rise to this idea. This can also be expressed, on the other hand, by saying that, if in its most intimate being, *Dasein* is the opening to the truth and thus to the call of Being, there at least remains for it—according to what counts without a doubt as another limit expression of boredom—

"the possibility of [*Dasein*] not being oneself," which in effect amounts to "revoking the call of Being itself."[25]

In addition to its originality, the interpretation proposed here also manifests an incontestable critical power. This power consists of turning Heidegger's major themes against his thought, or if one prefers, of proposing a new appraisal of them. This is the case with the sudden and singular vindication of inauthenticity; and it is true that *the possibility of* inauthenticity is nothing other than the possibility of revoking the call of being, denying in this way that "the reference to Being itself constitutes the final possibility of what I am."[26] Thus the famous analysis of everydayness is overturned. For, if in everyday existence *Dasein* conceals itself from its destiny as *Dasein*, as the Being which is destined for *Dasein* in its there, is it not the case that this destiny is not necessarily its own—is it not the case that another destiny offers itself to *Dasein*?

Now the simple possibility for the Ego-*Dasein* to have another destiny than that of hearing and responding to the call of being fundamentally disturbs its ontological definition in *Sein und Zeit*. For this possibility precludes *Dasein*'s ek-static relation to Being from being understood as the essence of every conceivable *Da*, as a possibility which is an essence, so that it is no longer seen as one simple possibility among others. The analytic of *Dasein* has ceased to construct the philosophy of the *humanitas* of the human; it is confined to indicating one of the virtualities of its nature.

As paradoxical as this final reduction may be—the putting out of play of being in its claim to define our being by its call—its meaning in every case is explicit and the last analyses attest to it: the disqualification of the call of being in boredom operates as a counter-existential; it has no goal other than opening us to another call, or rather to "[the wind of] every other possible call";[27] or better, not to any other call but to "the call as such."[28] It is here that the call of being is replaced by a kind of "model of the call,"[29] or again a "pure form of the call"[30]—the call as such. The motive for this substitution is this: every concrete call whatsoever, including the call that being addresses to *Dasein*, presupposes as its own possibility a pure structure of the call, its "model" or its "pure form." Marion writes, "Before Being has claimed, the call as pure call claims."[31] And again: "The claim of Being itself can call only in putting on this pure form."[32]

By subsuming the call of being under the pure form of the call, this problem of limits derives a double advantage: on the one hand, it does not contradict an immense heritage of thought from which it was nourished, but instead integrates it into a broader vision—and this especially concerns the existential analytic itself—that is opened to other modes of experience than those that are inscribed in the "phenomenon of being."

On the other hand, thanks precisely to this reference and also to every other possible reference, to every other call, this problem of limits keeps the refusal of the call of being, interpreted as the condition of opening of the call as such, from appearing too formal, to say nothing of appearing undefined and empty.

By contrast, consider the fourth principle. The fourth principle does not simply push the reduction to the limit, incrementally reduce the being [*l'étant*] to being itself [*être*] and then to the call of being only in order to lead us to some indeterminate X, to a model, to a pure form, to an Absolute, or to a Transcendent that would be defined in a purely formal way. Instead, it leads to givenness and its height, to the most original appearing. In the fourth principle everything is phenomenological. The reduction is phenomenological, first as pure reduction and then as radical reduction, because it explicitly takes phenomenality itself as its theme and in it the most original mode of its phenomenalization. And likewise, the givenness to which it leads cannot be thought as a form or as a model, but only on the basis of the how of this first phenomenalization.

Marion's thought proceeds down this path. For why would one substitute for being its call or its claim, except to identify what comes first within it, the fulguration of an appearing which submerges us and which, to the extent that it fulgurates, gives us being at the same time as itself? Now if this call of being itself should be rejected, so that the possibility of another call might open itself, so that a more essential call may emerge, what then does this ultimate substitution mean?

There is only one response to this question—to which we shall now turn. If the call of being is only its appearing, and if it is suitable for this call to prefer another phenomenality, such an opposition can only signify the opposition of two phenomenalities and thus of two phenomenologies. It implies the duality of appearing at the same time as indicating a hierarchy of appearing.

The call of being is the name for the phenomenality of ek-static truth. It is precisely because it finds its phenomenological foundation in ek-static truth that Heideggerian being can and must be subject to critique. There is a sense of "excepting" from being. The "à-Dieu," the "Otherwise than Being" of Emmanuel Levinas, and the "outside of Being" of Marion can only signify the dismissal of being for any other reason, because it has usurped even its name, and because it represents, notably in Heidegger, only a regional instance. This unthought but decisive limitation of the problematic, the thought that subordinates ontology to phenomenology, can be perceived as soon as this subordination is carried out. The essence of this Being whose call may be suspended, is the phenomenality of the world; the finitude of this Being is the finitude of every ek-static horizon.

The dismissal of being so understood—which "is" only in the comprehension of *Dasein* and relates to it as to what it "understands," as to a "sense"—is possible only on one condition, namely, that ek-static unfolding of appearing in the horizon of the world stands in strict contrast with its non-ek-static auto-appearing which is the essence of the pathos of Life. The dismissal of being is only possible phenomenologically. It is only possible if, in the absence of all ek-static phenomenality and in spite of this absence, something is still possible rather than nothing—that something is the Archi-Revelation of Life. "Otherwise than being" means "appearing otherwise." Only Life in its Archi-Revelation still "calls" and can "call" when being has become silent.

It is only because the "call" of Life is defined phenomenologically, because in its affective flesh and in the brutality of emotion or of love, that it never resembles anything other than itself [*à rien d'autre*]; and, in any case, it does not resemble the unveiling of a being [*étant*] in the world any more than it resembles the ek-stasis of being in the world—it is thus possible to speak of another call than that of being. And beyond the pathetic irruption of life in us, beyond its proclamation, whose words consist of our desire, our passion, our love, there is no pure form of the call, a structure of the call, that would be higher than or different from this pathos.

For the call is always defined. The definition of the call is phenomenological and is exhausted each time in its actual phenomenality. But phenomenality is never exhausted. Appearing rises again ever anew but in a way that is perennially its own. To recognize this "way" for what it is, in the How of its concrete phenomenological materiality, is not to limit oneself to a less elevated degree of generality than that of a pure form or structure of the call. On the contrary, to the extent that the structure of the call is usually described according to the bipolarity of the call and the response, the structure of the call borrows this disposition from an established mode of appearing, a mode in which opposition is constitutive of phenomenality—and this established mode is precisely that of the world. It does not matter that the pair Call/Response is substituted for the classic dichotomy of Subject/Object and, by virtue of this substitution, claims to renew our relation to being. How can one fail to see that it only reverses a relation conceived in both cases as constitutive of phenomenality, as preserving it. Far from escaping from the call of Being and from its implicit phenomenology, the structure of the call [in Marion] refers to Being and receives its own "structure" from it: the opposition of the Ek-stasis.

This opposition is understood as the basis of a kind of freedom. What characterizes the call, in effect, is that it waits for and solicits a response that may or may not be received. It is precisely with respect to this freedom of the response, its welcome or rejection, that Marion lays to rest the final possibility for the Ego-*Dasein* to "no longer assume the destiny of Being as that of its own being."[33]

But what characterizes the scope of life is that it precedes every response and does not wait for one. For in the irruption of life and in its flowing which passes through us and intoxicates us with it and ourselves, there is no gap, no recoil that would open the possibility of a response, of a yes or of a no. And this impossibility of every hidden recess and of every reply, this way of being riveted to oneself, oriented in every aspect toward all that one is, this impossibility is the eternal and irremissible, relentless and serene experience that Life has of itself at each instant; it is the wound that Life hollows out in us, that is our subjectivity itself, and that makes us into living beings.

And if there is no place here for a response that would give us the leisure of assuming or refusing the destiny of being, it is because, strictly speaking, we can no longer properly speak of the call. The other call, the call of life, stands beyond every call, for it does not put forth the proposition of whether to live or not live. The call of life has already thrown us into life itself, crushing us against it and against ourselves, in the suffering and joy of an invincible pathos. The call has already made us alive at the moment we hear it. Its sound is nothing other than the noise of life, its rustling in us, the embrace in which it gives itself to itself and gives us to ourselves in one and the same givenness.

And this means that in every living being there is only Life—a life that is not its own in the sense that one did not create, posit, or want it—but that which is one's own irreducibly and forever for the same reason: namely that there is nothing in oneself, not the slightest experience of the most basic impression, that is not the experience that life has of itself. There is not the least parcel of one's Self that is not the Self of Life. This is why we say that we are born of Life and that this birth never ceases. In the auto-affection that makes us feel ourselves at every instant, there is nothing other than the auto-affection of Life itself, its Archi-Revelation.

And this is also why the self engendered in life—this "me" according to Marion—is also an "I," an "ego." According to the admirable words of the mystics, life "cannot give only a little," because it can give nothing other than itself and thus the Ipseity that it engenders eternally in its self-givenness is equally in all that is living.[34]

Outside of being, otherwise than being, to be the being that relates to being and that only exists in this relation, which is only *There* for being, is only possible by way of a fundamental phenomenology and the radical reduction that it puts into play. What authority does the radical reduction exercise to set aside the call of being, along with that which is defined in its being by this call? Boredom, according to the sense that Marion confers upon it. But should we not also ask boredom the question that the author of *Reduction and Givenness* himself asked of the Husserlian Ego, which detached itself from all ontologies in the very act by which it constitutes them—the question about the place where this Ego can still reside, about the domain in which it dwells, and, finally, about its "being"?

Or still more precisely, does the reductive power of boredom reside in the fact that it is bored with everything and with being itself, or from the fact that, in being bored with everything and with being, it has not yet finished with itself? *For no boredom whatsoever could deliver boredom from itself.* Where then does this boredom now reside if not in Life, there where the connection between life and itself cannot become severed? It is the self-givenness of life that holds everything, which gives everything, which gives even boredom to itself when the call of being is silent, so that being is undone and so that being in relating to being is nothing.

"So much reduction": this final and radical dismissal, issued to being and all that is, to all that comes from it or goes with it, speaks and calls in its name—in the name of the world. "So much givenness": that which, in the absence of this being and its call, in the absence of ek-static appearing, gives nonetheless, gives everything—self-givenness, Life, and in it all those who live [*tous les vivants*], and the cosmos itself.

The fourth principle, as announced by Marion, does not merely provide phenomenology with a simple enrichment of developments already included in its historic presuppositions. By assigning to phenomenology previously unnoticed objectives, and greater ambitions, it leads phenomenology down new paths.

Translated by Joseph Rivera and George E. Faithful

Notes

This chapter was originally published in *Continental Philosophy Review* 48, no. 1 (2015): 1–21. It is republished here with permission from Springer Nature.

1. Translators' note: Henry fails to cite properly this originally German expression. Drawn from Heidegger and Husserl, in the German, *Soviel Schein— soviel Sein*, is a formula found in Jean-Luc Marion's *Reduction and Givenness*, trans. Thomas A. Carlson (Evanston, Ill.: Northwestern University Press, 1998), 59 and 203. The German is found in Heidegger's *A History of the Concept of Time: Prolegomena*, trans. Theodore Kisiel (Bloomington: Indiana University Press, 1985), 139. Heidegger writes exactly "Wieviel Schein jedoch, soviel 'Sein'" in *Being and Time*, trans. John Macquarrie and Edward Robinson (Oxford: Basil Blackwell, 1962),

60; Husserl writes "*Soviel Schein, soviel Sein*" in *Cartesian Meditations: An Introduction to Phenomenology*, trans. Dorion Cairns (Dordrecht: Kluwer, 1973), 103.

2. Translators' note: See Edmund Husserl, *Ideas Pertaining to a Pure Phenomenology and to a Phenomenological Philosophy: First Book*, trans. Fred Kersten (Dordrecht: Kluwer, 1983), §24, 44.

3. Jean-Luc Marion, *Reduction and Givenness: Investigations into Husserl, Heidegger and Phenomenology*, trans. Thomas A. Carlson (Evanston, Ill.: Northwestern University Press, 1998), 203.

4. René Descartes, *The Philosophical Writings of Descartes*, trans. John Cottingham et al. (Cambridge: Cambridge University Press, 1985), I, 195; René Descartes, *Oeuvres de Descartes*, 11 vols., ed. Charles Adam and Paul Tannery (Paris: J. Vrin, 1983): VIII, A 7 (henceforth cited as AT).

5. Descartes, *The Philosophical Writings of Descartes*, II, 19; AT, VII, 28. Henry's quote from Descartes, or its exact wording, cannot be located in the French citation he gives. (Translators' note).

6. See Descartes, *The Philosophical Writings of Descartes*, I, 9; AT, X, 360.

7. Edmund Husserl, *The Idea of Phenomenology*, trans. Lee Hardy (Dordrecht: Kluwer, 1999), 64.

8. Edmund Husserl, *On the Phenomenology of the Consciousness of Internal Time (1893–1917)*, trans. John Barnett Brough (Dordrecht: Kluwer, 1991), 121. The phrase may also be rendered in English as "objects in their ways of appearing" (*Gegenstände im Wie*). (Translators' note).

9. See Michel Henry, "The Critique of the Subject," *Topoi* 7 (1988): 147–53.

10. Marion, *Reduction and Givenness*, 141–66.

11. Cited by Marion, *Reduction and Givenness*, 163.

12. "The wonder of all wonders: *that* that being is," says the postscript of the 1943 *What Is Metaphysics?*; cited and commented on in Marion, *Reduction and Givenness*, 163. See Martin Heidegger, "Postscript to 'What Is Metaphysics?'" in *Existentialism from Dostoevsky to Sartre*, trans. Walter Kaufmann (New York: Penguin, 1975), 261.

13. Marion, *Reduction and Givenness*, 161.

14. Marion, *Reduction and Givenness*, 139. See also Henry's critique directed against the ontic preliminary of Heideggerian phenomenology in *The Essence of Manifestation*, trans. Girard Etzkorn (The Hague: Martinus Nijhoff, 1973), §§11–13.

15. Marion, *Reduction and Givenness*, 185.

16. Marion, *Reduction and Givenness*, 198.

17. Marion, *Reduction and Givenness*, 199.

18. Marion, Reduction and Givenness, 200.

19. Marion, *Reduction and Givenness*, 200.

20. Marion, *Reduction and Givenness*, 200.

21. Marion, *Reduction and Givenness*, 188.

22. Marion, *Reduction and Givenness*, 193. This is a quote drawn from Martin Heidegger, "Letter on Humanism," in *Basic Writings*, ed. David F. Krell (New York: Harper and Row, 1977), 205.

23. Marion, *Reduction and Givenness*, 194.

24. Marion, *Reduction and Givenness*, 194.
25. Marion, *Reduction and Givenness*, 195.
26. Marion, *Reduction and Givenness*, 195.
27. Marion, *Reduction and Givenness*, 196.
28. Marion, *Reduction and Givenness*, 197.
29. Marion, *Reduction and Givenness*, 197.
30. Marion, *Reduction and Givenness*, 197.
31. Marion, *Reduction and Givenness*, 197.
32. Marion, *Reduction and Givenness*, 198.
33. Marion, *Reduction and Givenness*, 195 (trans. modified).
34. Readers may want to note a divergence between the 1991 version of the article published here and the lightly reworked version published in 2003 in *Phénoménologie de la vie*. At this point, Henry inserts six paragraphs in place of the final four paragraphs of this version.

2

The Phenomenology of Birth

What does it mean to be born? Isn't being born coming into being, entering into existence, outside of which, before which, and after which there is nothing? From the outset, the question of birth thus seems to refer to the question of being which dominates the tradition of thought to which we belong. In this tradition, being is not truly thematized as such but is more or less confused with beings and is understood in terms of them. This fact, instead of contradicting the primacy of the question of being, requires the primacy of being to be fully established and the philosophical problem to be reformulated as a result.

To thematize being as such, however, does not lead philosophy to its ownmost task, nor does it truly correct the tradition. That is because being is never primary; it owes its own being to appearing as such. "So much appearing, so much being": this fundamental principle of phenomenology is disregarded when the traditional theme of ontology becomes a theme of philosophy once again. This is even more the case when one attempts to assign this traditional theme of ontology to phenomenology itself, as in the reactionary statement that "considered on the level of the thing itself [*sachhaltig*], phenomenology is the science of the being of beings."[1]

The attempt to lead phenomenology back to ontology by turning it into a mere instrument for a thinking of being is only a linguistic illusion which does not in any way affect the inevitable foundation of ontology in phenomenology. As for beings, there is only what appears, and as for being, there is only this appearing itself. The linguistic universality [*l'universalité langagière*] of the question of being only has a formal priority, if what it means to be is decided in these concrete modes of the actual phenomenalization of phenomenality, and in them alone, rather than in the empty concepts or preconceptions about it.

This priority of ontology, with the presumed universality of the meaning of being, is something that the question of birth comes along to shatter. For being born can precisely not mean coming into being as long as being lays claim to the realm of principles and thus to universality. Coming into being is a fact for every being: for rocks, for air, for water. Yet, none of these things results from a birth; they are neither born nor do they die, except metaphorically. Being born is a fact for the living and for the living alone. Being born thus does not result from being as a universal or from the "meaning of being in general"—such a meaning would be as suitable to rocks as to the living. This sudden impropriety of the meaning of being requires a reevaluation of the theme of ontology that is equivalent to a dismantling of it. For birth is not the work of ontology itself. Only a radical and pure phenomenology, which sets aside every foreign presupposition in order to thematize only appearing itself in its own phenomenality, can recognize and thereby distinguish between the appearing that belongs to the coming into being of the birth of the living, from that to which all the beings of the world and even this world itself owe their being. The term "being" in coming into being through birth and in coming into being through the world thus have nothing in common, except for the secret connection of the modes of appearing to which being always refers, a connection which is itself phenomenological.

The phenomenological transcription of the themes of ontology is possible because phenomenology has not been presented in a pure form in previous philosophy and traditional ontology has gone without a phenomenological foundation that determines it, unbeknownst to itself. The type of appearing that governs traditional ontology is the appearing of "the world," that is, an appearing whose phenomenality consists in the "outside" [*au-dehors*]. Coming into being—for this ontology that is transcribed from the phenomenology on which it is based—means coming into the world. But is not coming into the world, in anyone's eyes regardless of whether one is a philosopher or not, precisely the meaning of being born?

While it may be difficult to attribute the same being to a being like a rock that is shown in the world and to a living being who comes into the world through its birth, and to whom the world shows itself, this difficulty does not seem to be insurmountable. There is a phenomenological reason for this: the appearing in which the rock is shown is the same as the appearing to which living beings are open; it is the appearing of the world, the "outside." Because one and the same appearing confers being on the rock and on the living being, it is one and the same being that extends its reign over both of them, a universal being whose universality is based on the appearing to which it refers.

We should raise some fundamental phenomenological questions here, however. How does appearing confer being on the rock? By making it appear. How is it made to appear? By letting it be seen. How is it seen? The rock is seen inasmuch as it is placed outside of oneself. Being external to the self defines its appearing as well as its being—its being as such. If being can be conceived further as temporality, this is because "temporality is the primordial 'outside of itself' in and for itself."[2]

How does appearing confer being on the living? Is it also by letting it be seen, by putting it outside of oneself, in such a way that it is seen in the same way as the rock? In such a case, the phenomenological situation of the living would be the same as that of the rock; their difference would no longer be an essential phenomenological difference. Instead of generating an essential ontological difference, it would only be a difference on the ontic level. However, the living being sees the rock, while the rock does not see anything. This situation is completely paradoxical despite its apparent evidence. How could two beings—provisionally, we will continue to call the living a being—derived from the same phenomenological status present a phenomenological difference between them that is absolutely essential, in the sense that it affects their relation to phenomenality, namely, that one of them has such a relation while the other lacks it? How, in coming into being in one and the same appearing and in being illuminated by the same light, would the living receive the distinct favor [*l'insigne faveur*] of transforming itself internally into this light, in the illumination of appearing in such a way that it is no longer anything else but that, while the rock, illuminated by this same light, would remain foreign to this illumination, blind, forever opaque, and delivered over to a darkness that is so deep that we could only conceive it by the abstract negation of this clarity of the world in which everything that is able to exist for us is shown?

A crucial phenomenological difficulty arises here: one and the same appearing allows an x to appear outside of itself, but this x is deprived of the phenomenality of this appearing, and at the same time confers on this x, which has become y, the unheard of privilege of receiving it in itself in such a way that it identifies with it and is no longer anything but a sort of pure phenomenological matter. This dual condition can only be defined phenomenologically, yet it is independent from the nature of this appearing and its phenomenality. This appearing is presupposed to be the same in the two cases, because there is only one type of appearing. Whether something stands inside or outside of appearing owes nothing to the essence of appearing; it owes everything to what is originally and intrinsically heterogeneous to appearing and to its deployment: to beings!

In classical thought, the absurdity consists of the fact that this way of thinking is completely unable to justify the distinction on which it is based and which it considers to be essential, namely, the distinction between the subject and the object. The object is a being itself but is perceived in its appearing, which is outside of itself [*hors de soi*] as such, such that the ob-ject is being outside of itself and is seen and perceived as such. How, then, can the subject differentiate itself from this ob-ject, that is to say from the outside itself in which beings appear, if there is no other appearing besides this outside of itself, if "consciousness" of it is reduced to what is "outside of itself" as such (a condition that will be recognized in the "progress" of the philosophy of consciousness and notably by phenomenology for which, as is known, consciousness is essentially consciousness of something, intentionality, or in its ultimate definition, *In-der-Welt-Sein*)?

We are talking about birth interpreted as coming into being, which can only signify a coming into appearing and in which appearing is interpreted as a coming into the world. However, this designates two totally different conditions, and only one of them refers to birth and can serve to define it. Mundane beings are limited to entering and leaving this finite place of light that is the world; they are foreign to the phenomenon of birth as well as that of death. The phenomenality by which coming into the world through birth is defined thus does not allow for any distinction between what is able to be born and what is unable to be born.

This strange difficulty cannot be set aside as long as birth continues to be defined as coming into the world. When it is referred to being-in-the-world [*In-der-Welt-Sein*], the phenomenon of birth presents the singular trait that its connection to life, which seems essential, turns out to be erased. In order to clarify this new paradox, it is necessary to interrogate the relation of being-in-the-world [*In-der-Welt-Sein*] to life, a theme that is briefly examined in §10 of *Being and Time*. In this text, the major contemporary philosophies of life are set aside, and their theses are reduced to a few haphazard quotations. They are replaced by an analysis of life that reduces it to the claim that life is a particular kind of being [*eine eigene Seinsart*]. The poverty of this statement cannot, however, remove it from error, if it is the case that life is neither a type of being nor a being whose phenomenological presupposition is found in what is "outside of itself." That, however, is Heidegger's explicit thesis: "life has its own kind of being, but it is essentially accessible only in Dasein."[3]

What does it mean to be born when the access to life is derived from *Dasein* and from it alone? This access seems puzzling at first, since it is not specific—it is not merely a way of access to life but to every mundane being. To reach a living being inasmuch as this access consists of the living being's exteriority to itself, as is the case with the rock or the wall about which Fichte speaks, is at most to see this living being in the same way as one sees the rock or the wall. But one does not know why this being is attributed the characteristic of being alive—*it is in no way to become alive oneself*. Yet, that is precisely the meaning of being born: to reach life in such a way that one becomes alive oneself, taking part afterwards in the unbreakable experience [*épreuve*] of life, its suffering and its joy.

Can *Dasein* be the foundation for the access to nonliving beings, the access to living beings, and lastly the access to life in the sense that

Dasein itself would come to be alive? Concerning the access to nonliving beings, *Dasein* is nothing but that: it is the "outside of itself" in which every being is shown as "other" or as "facing" it. Concerning living beings, *Dasein* as "outside of itself" surely allows this being to be seen, just like any other being. But if this being discovers itself to be "living," *that* is something which no longer results from *Dasein* at all. Here, with respect to the living, we can recognize an essential law of appearing whose phenomenality consists in the "outside the self," namely, the disclosure accomplished in this appearing cannot explain in any way what is disclosed by it, in this case, the living character of beings. But if the character of being alive—the fact of being alive or the simple signification of being alive—is not derived from the appearing proper to *Dasein*, *then where does its phenomenological origin reside?*

Why is the appearing proper to *Dasein*, the outside the self that is constitutive of the appearing that it liberates, unable to provide access to life? This is something that can be understood right away. In the outside the self, each "point" of this "place" is not merely external to every other one, as in space. In the outside the self, each "point" is still external to the self, in such a way that this "outside the self" is its way of appearing, an appearing that only has room for the outside and in this sense for what is other. In this place of radical externalization, then, no life is possible if to live is to experience [*s'éprouver*] oneself and not to experience [*éprouver*] something other. To live is to experience oneself in an immediacy so radical that nothing would ever be able to break the pathos of the flesh out of which this experience is made. Any placement outside of oneself of this pathos that is essentially non-ekstatic could only signify its destruction. The material phenomenological heterogeneity between the pathos of appearing in which life fulfills itself and the ek-static appearing which unfolds in the difference of the world and things, is radical, irreducible, and insurmountable.

What does it mean to say that "life fulfills itself" [*la vie s'accomplit*]?[4] That life auto-affects itself, that the phenomenological matter of this original affection is a pathos, that the pathos of this auto-affection is a process, the eternal process through which life enters and continues to enter into itself—such that there is no other way to enter into life and to live it than in and through this process of auto-affection. That is why no access to the living of life is possible in the appearing of a world, and that is why in the latter life can only be represented as an irreal noematic meaning, whose character of being alive, a living being, as an objective character, is only stated. In the end, that is why the illusion that the access to life occurs in *Dasein*'s Being-in-the-World implies a disastrous confusion between the living of life and the external appearing of living beings. Their property of being alive refers to the living of life and presupposes it, instead of being able to found it and display it in external appearing.

Dasein's inability to give access to the living of life concerns it in the first place; it is *Dasein*'s inability to open itself to life by becoming alive itself. Because no life is possible in what is outside of itself, *Dasein* is in principle unable to come into life. One can find an unconscious avowal in Heideggerian philosophy of *Dasein*'s inability, which is understood existentially as being-in-the-world, to come into life. This occurs unexpectedly in a discussion seeking to establish the original character of the truth against all skepticism. Due to the fact that the truth is already presupposed with the opening of being-in-the-world as an opening of *Dasein*—and so is *Dasein* itself insofar as it is mine. Concerning the presupposition of the truth of *Dasein* understood as what always precedes and as such never has to be called into question, a question arises abruptly: "*Has Dasein, inasmuch as it is free, ever been able to decide and will it ever be able to decide whether it wants to come into Dasein or not?*"[5]

For *Dasein*, to come into *Dasein* is to be born. The question of knowing whether *Dasein* freely chose to come into *Dasein*, or to be born, immediately evokes a negative answer. Truly, this is a characteristic feature of being born and its mystery, namely, that birth is a sort of absolute beginning, and yet this absolute beginning presupposes something "before it." This antecedence of something "before" the absolute beginning of birth, that is, of something more absolute than it, is what makes the phenomenon of birth a limit experience, referring in the experience [*épreuve*] that it has of itself to something that seems impossible to live through [*éprouver*]. It is self-evident that there is no free decision concerning *Dasein*'s entrance into itself, which would presuppose that one would be placed in this before birth where one would be able to decide and adopt an attitude toward it. But it is a question of understanding precisely this impossibility of adopting an attitude toward it that is implied in every birth. Here one should avoid, on the one hand, the existentialist conclusion—for example, Sartre's thesis of a human being that is "condemned" to be free—which treats this impossibility as purely factual. On the other hand, one should also avoid the Heideggerian interpretation which, by reducing the "not" of not being able to the *Nichts* of Being and thus to ek-static phenomenality, only distorts the decisive phenomenon of *Dasein*'s impossibility of choosing whether or not to come into life.[6]

These two conclusions can only be set aside if the question acquires a radical phenomenological meaning, since here it is a matter neither of decision nor of freedom, neither of willing nor not willing. Transcribed phenomenologically, the question asks, how can one come into *Dasein*? How is the mode of revelation that gives access to *Dasein* revealed? The fact that *Dasein* does not itself choose to come into *Dasein* and that, according to another statement, it is not "brought to itself in its Da" [*nicht von ihm selbst in sein Da gebracht*], means phenomenologically that it is not in *Dasein*—in the outside the self of Being-in-the-world—that one reaches *Dasein*, in a way that takes place in it and identifies with it, and once placed in it in this matter and identified with it, to be able in and with it to relate to the world, "to have" a world, to-be-in-the-world. Thus our coming into the world presupposes our coming into *Dasein*, which, however, is not the doing of *Dasein* itself. How do we come into *Dasein* in such a way that this arrival owes nothing to it, owes nothing to the outside the self of being-in-the-world? The answer: in and through life. Instead of only having access to life in *Dasein*, it is only in and through life that we have access to *Dasein*.

If *Dasein* is itself only possible as a living *Dasein*, then the elaboration of the question of birth can be completed as follows. To come into the world presupposes coming into being-in-the-world itself, that is to say, into *Dasein*. But to come into *Dasein*, which does not bring itself into itself, owes nothing to it. Instead of resolving the question of coming into the world, the question of coming into *Dasein* is an entirely new phenomenological question, referring to a mode of revelation that is structurally different from that of *Dasein*. If we only enter into *Dasein* in life, the question of birth turns out to be displaced entirely. It lets go of the world and of being-in-the-world; none of these features—existential and categorical structures included—interests it. For if one only comes into *Dasein* in life, the question of birth is thus to know how one comes into life. Understood in its originality, the question of birth refers to an original birth, an *Ur*-birth which no longer has anything to do with what we understand initially and naively by birth. The *Ur*-birth about which we will now speak escapes from the sciences that relate to the world, as well as from traditional philosophy that has only thematized this type of relation.

To be born is thus to come into life. It is now a matter of understanding this proposition, because it includes at least two senses. But the most directly knowable sense is not the most essential one. "To come into life" means, of course, to come to life, to enter into it and to arrive at this extraordinary and mysterious condition of being alive. This mysterious character is attached to the phenomenological status of life, and the elucidation of this status is one of the essential tasks for a phenomenology of birth. This is only possible within a phenomenology of life and as a branch of it. But it is the second sense of the proposition "to come into life" that must be our focus now. Here to come into life means that it is in life and only on the basis of life that this arrival [*venue*] can occur. To come into life means to come from life, such that life is not the destination but the point of departure for birth, if one can speak in this way. This rootedness of every birth as an *Ur*-birth in the prior essence of life explains why the human as living—not the mundane human, the human being lacking this character of being alive, but the true human whose entire essence is to live—why this original human that we will designate as the living ego, is not at all originary. The living ego cannot be understood on the basis of itself, but only on the basis of this essence of life that eternally precedes it in the very process by which it continues to engender it as something that results necessarily from it, by which it continues to give birth to it.

How does life engender the ego in it, making it into a living ego? Inasmuch as it engenders itself and in the way it does so. Life engenders itself in the process of its eternal auto-affection, a process in which it comes into itself, crashes against itself, experiences itself, enjoys [*jouir*] itself, being nothing but the eternal bliss of this pure self-enjoyment [*jouissance*]. Living consists of this pure self-experience as a pure self-enjoyment; it is only possible in this manner and does not exist anywhere else. The fact that this auto-affection in which the essence of living is a process means that it fulfills itself as a movement, the auto-movement in which life continually comes into itself and is experienced. The auto-movement of life is a specific type of temporality, a radically immanent, non-ekstatic and pathos-filled auto-temporalization. This is the very temporalization of birth, and we will return to it. An ipseity is built in this auto-temporalization of the auto-affection of experiencing oneself in living life. This is because the experience of life is only possible as an experience that it constantly has of itself—and, consequently, because the structure of this experience is equally that of a Self. This is how life engenders itself as a Self. But no Self is possible except as a singular Self. And this is the case because the self-experience that fulfills itself in the process of the pathos-filled auto-affection of life is an actual one, a self-experience that is necessarily actual, this experience with its own content and as such singular, such that the self implied in this actual and singular self-experience is itself actual and singular as well. It is not really the particular content of self-experience that particularizes the Self that is implied in the auto-affection of this self-experience; it is the singularity of this Self that is engendered at the same time as it and in the same way as it, a singularity thus belonging to it as a matter of principle, which singularizes every "content" that is capable of being experienced by it. Myself, I am this singular Self engendered in the auto-engendering of absolute life and I am only that. Life is auto-engendered as myself. The generation of the singular Self, that I myself am, in the auto-engendering of absolute life is my transcendental birth.

But, inasmuch as this transcendental birth is accomplished starting from life or in it and inasmuch as my generation as a singular Self is thus possible only in the auto-generation of absolute life and as the actualization of it, the former is not separable from the latter. The singular Self that I am only arrives into itself in the coming into itself of absolute life and carries life within itself as its unabolishable presupposition, as its condition. Life thus crosses through all of those that it engenders in such a way that there is nothing within it that is not alive and nothing within it that does not contain this eternal essence of life. Life engenders me like itself. Generated as a singular Self in my transcendental *Ur*-birth, I am born. But, inasmuch as this *Ur*-generation is only a mode of the auto-generation of absolute life, which is not born, I am non-born [*non-né*].

Let's deepen each of these two points in succession. First of all, it is a matter of understanding why the singular Self that is generated in the auto-generation of absolute life is presented straightaway as a transcendental self or a transcendental ego. It is "transcendental" because here it is a question of its innermost possibility: its ipseity. Now the self [*moi*] and the ego [*ego*] are not the same thing, even though traditional thought slides from the one to the other in the most extreme confusion and without ever seeing that there is at least a problem in this twofold designation of the Self [*Soi*], no matter how constant it may be. The fact that the singular Self is expressed and must be expressed first in the accusative as a "me" [*moi*] conveys the fact that it is engendered. It does not bring itself into its own condition of experiencing itself as a Self, but it derives this condition from the eternal auto-affection of life. Because this engendering of myself [*moi*] in the auto-affection of life is phenomenological in a radical sense, as the original phenomenalization of this life as well as its immanent pathos-filled temporalization, what motivates the placement of me [*moi*] in the accusative can be detected in the following: it is its feeling of being entirely passive not only with regard to its own "states," including the most active ones, but also in relation to itself and its own "condition." Me, I am for myself, or better, I am myself but am not the cause of "being myself." I go through the experience of myself without being the source of this experience; I am given to myself without this givenness being derived from myself in any way. I affect myself and so I auto-affect myself. It is me who is affected, and I am affected by myself in the sense that the content that affects me is still me—and not something other: what is sensed, touched, willed, desired, thought, etc.—but this auto-affection that defines my essence is not my doing.

And thus I do not affect myself absolutely, but I am auto-affected and in this way engendered as a Self in the auto-affection of life. Myself [*moi*] ultimately refers to this character of being auto-affected of the singular Self [*Soi*] that I am.

Yet, even though the self [*soi*] is engendered in the auto-affection of absolute life and goes through the experience of itself passively and thus as a me [*moi*], this me [*moi*] is not only a me [*moi*]. By experiencing itself [*s'éprouvant*] in the immediacy of the suffering [*souffrir*] and joy [*jouir*] that are constitutive of this experience [*épreuve*], it enters into possession of itself at the same time as it is able to exercise each of the powers that traverse it. A new capacity is conferred on it, which is just as extraordinary as that of being a self [*moi*], even when it is merely the result of it. This is the self's [*moi*] ability to be in possession of itself, to be one with it and with everything that is contained within itself and that belongs to it as the many real components of its own being. Among these components, there are the powers of the body, for example, those of grasping, moving, touching, etc. It is through its pathos-filled experience of each of these powers that the self is able to implement them and thus to act—to use all the powers of its body and its mind. This experience is thus the ultimate power that gathers all of the powers within itself, the ultimate capacity by virtue of which it utilizes all of these capacities. Inasmuch as it advances armed with these powers and has them at its disposal, this self which has seized hold of itself and of everything that lives within it, is an I.

The I is written: "I can." The "I can" is not a synthetic proposition; none of the powers in it is added on to the essence of the I. Instead, the I as such is Power. It is the ultimate Power of being in possession of all its powers and capacities. It is this ultimate Power that is in substance the "me." "I, the ego . . ."⁷ This assertion by Husserl should not be taken as a mere haphazard way of writing, or as a tautology. It is because it is a me that the ego is an ego. "Me, ego . . ." marks the completion of the process of my transcendental birth.

Because it is rooted in a me, the ego has seized hold of all its powers and capacities in order to then exercise them freely and unlimitedly. This ego is lived through and experienced as a hyperpower that resides in all of its native capacities and all its functions. Thanks to this hyperpower, it puts them into play whenever it wants. Being in possession of them allows the ego to be free to seek their fulfillment. This free will is only the being-in-possession of these powers in the super-power of the pathos-filled experience of them, and the free will is based on it. We are never free with regard to anything external, but only within this super-power that has placed us within each of our powers in order to exercise them. The ego is thus only free on the basis of a me that necessarily precedes it, that is ultimately to say, this Self that is engendered in the auto-engendering of absolute life.

But this ego which carries all that in itself and results from it is actually lived as the fundamental "I can" (which has been described brilliantly by Maine de Biran) and at the same time, on the basis of this essence of its ego-ity [*égoïté*], as a free will. The metaphors in which the ego spontaneously expresses its own condition, or what it naively believes its condition to be, are thus significant. Within power and truly only being the proper interiority of this power to itself, it considers itself to be the source of this power, its origin, the place where this power takes shape and is gathered together in oneself. And once it is gathered in the self, it emerges from oneself—the self is thus the point of departure, the center from which it acts and soars, from which it radiates and exercises its function. In §25 of Husserl's *Ideas II*, one can find a constellation of these metaphors, all of which refer to the ego as this point of departure, this source point, this center of radiation, this *terminus a quo*, from which everything begins and is possible.

In these texts as well as in all those related to the ego, it is true that the Husserlian interpretation of the ego is overdetermined by an unquestioned and reductive conception of phenomenality, which likewise guides the development of European thought. The ego is tied to consciousness (this connection remains extremely confused), and consciousness is understood as intentionality such that this point of departure, this source point, this center of radiation, this center of operations, is precisely the point of departure, the source point, the center of radiation, the center of operations of intentionality. This overlaying of the concept of the ego as a source point with the concept of intentional phenomenality can be found everywhere. For example, note the following text: "All the multi-formed particularities of intentional relatedness to Objects, which are here called acts, have their necessary *terminus a quo*, the Ego-point, from which they irradiate."[8] This overdetermination of the concept of the *ego-punctum* through the presupposition of intentionality and more broadly of ek-static phenomenality—a presupposition which is also followed by the metaphysics of representation—results in the concept of the "subject" that guides modern philosophy. The numerous critiques of the subject in the latter half of the twentieth century result, in turn, from the very same illusory presuppositions.[9] Indeed, the ego has become the subject, the subject of representation, the I re-present myself before whom, to whom, and in front of whom everything is available [*dis-posé*], as something that is available before it, to it, and in the presence of it. And yet, the ego cannot be explained by this structure of representation, even if it does make this structure possible. The proof of this is that the phenomenological essence on which representation is based can be deployed without the intervention of any ego, understood as a pure "outside," as an ek-stasis, in the absence of any subject or ego. It is only when the ego is placed as a subject at the head of the deployment of the outside that the interpretation of it falls into a metaphysics of representation which relates the ego-subject to everything that is shown in this "outside" and in which it has become a mere condition of objects.

But then, where does the ego come from, if it is not from the "outside"? Where do we get the concept of the subject from, if it is not from a metaphysics of representation which instead presupposes something that its own phenomenality, the phenomenality of the outside, does not contain? For it is precisely a radical phenomenological reduction that delivers the ego to us (not the one practiced by Husserl, but one that puts intentionality out of play and even more radically the ecstatic phenomenology in which it is deployed, the outside as such)—the reduction which, outside of the world, limits itself to the sphere of life. The ego is not delivered to us in the sense that it would allow us to see that which, as a living ego, escapes from every possible vision and is never visible in a world. The Husserlian reduction only grasps the living ego in its irreal parts, in the form of idealities and potentialities, whereas its concrete living core is dissolved and reduced to the ideal limit of a purely conceptual "present." Truly speaking, no phenomenological reduction in the sense of a process of thought is able to deliver the ego to us. The radical phenomenological reduction about which we are speaking is only possible because, as a movement of thought, it indicates another place than its own, the one in which the ego comes into itself in accordance with its own mode of provenance. Where does the ego originate, if not from a phenomenological reduction?

The ego originates from its transcendental birth in life. This means: there is no other way of reaching the ego than the one by which it reaches itself within itself. But the way in which the ego reaches itself within itself is the same one by which absolute life originally reaches into itself. In the auto-temporalization of the pathos of its auto-affection, life is experienced in its essential Ipseity as this singular Self that is me [*moi*] and to whom the ego owes its being as an ego. This is how the birth of the transcendental ego occurs, and which, to emphasize once again, occurs in the absolute immanence of life. It occurs in such a way that this birth as an *Ur*-birth is not a question of the world or being-in-the-world. Here it should not only be said that one can conceive of purely spiritual beings,

THE PHENOMENOLOGY OF BIRTH

like angels or archangels, which would be entirely foreign to the world; it should also be said that this is the case for us.

To the extent that the ego is born in life in such a way that life remains within it as its condition, then a phenomenology of birth is brought before its second task. Its task is no longer to understand the generation of the ego in the pathos-filled process of the auto-affection of absolute life and to identify it with the fulfillment of this process; instead the task is to follow, if one might say, the opposite trajectory. We, living egos, are in the life of this ego which is always our own, in our life. How is something revealed in it, how is something given to it that has given it to itself and that, in order to do this, existed before itself? How does something that was born relate to something that was not born? In its transcendental birth as an *Ur*-birth, how do the living refer to this non-birth that is the self-engendering of absolute life?

Here we discover a paradoxical situation. On the one side, the auto-engendering of absolute life in which the singular Self is engendered precedes this Self as its presupposition; life is auto-engendered before it as an absolute before without which no singular self would ever come to life. On the other side, however, this presupposition of every conceivable transcendental ego is also its condition, namely, this auto-affection of absolute life that is constantly fulfilled and in whose actual auto-affection it is constantly engendered. If this self-fulfillment of absolute life were interrupted for a single instant, the ego would be destroyed. The arrival of the ego in the auto-engendering of absolute life is thus not an event that could be assimilated into what we ordinarily understand by birth. We are not born once in order to then lead our own lives. If that were the case, we would have to believe that living egos are in possession of each of their powers, freely using them afterwards and putting them to work; each ego would experience itself as a center of initiative and action. But the ego is only in possession of each of its powers and initially of itself to the extent that absolute life continues to auto-affect itself within it. This is because there is only one life, only one auto-affection, the very one in which the ego is auto-affected as the singular Self that it is. We are thus not born on just one day; instead we are constantly engendered in the absolute auto-engendering of life and in it alone. That is why birth is not an event but a condition. This condition of ours turns us into Sons—the transcendental Sons of absolute Life and not the Sons of human beings, of these empirical selves who are only the objectification of transcendental selves, who are Sons. Both presuppose the auto-engendering of the absolute life in which they are engendered at each moment.

The question is then as follows: how can we understand for each ego considered in its transcendental birth and thus interpreted transcendentally as a Son, the relation within itself between its presupposition and its condition? For, its presupposition consists of the auto-engendering of the absolute life that signifies for each ego an absolute before, whereas its condition—its condition as a Son—implies that this auto-engendering of life is within itself as what engenders it at each instant. How can what exists before in an antecedence that is hardly conceivable nonetheless remain at the same time within the ego as its condition, a condition which it cannot undo or cut itself away from? Are we not separated from that which precedes us? Is not the before necessarily past for someone who comes after it? Has it not been lost? And if this before is life, then has not the one who comes after this before of life already lost life? Is one not already dead?

It is here that the brief remarks made about the temporality of life appear to be decisive. We will set aside every misinterpretation concerning the before that precedes our birth—that is to say, the relation of our birth to what itself is not born—by recalling that the auto-temporalization of absolute life is essentially non-ekstatic. For it is precisely as an ek-stasis that contemporary phenomenology understands and defines the before in its very own possibility. In order for something to become phenomenalized as a "before," the one to whom this before is shown must relate to it retrospectively as something before itself, in such a way that one's relation to this "before" adopts the form of a specific ek-stasis. In the "outside" of this ek-stasis, the horizon of the before is discovered, and what is given within this horizon is discovered as what was "before." Through its ek-static nature, the horizon of the before is a horizon of irreality; it is irreal just like everything else that is shown within it and which, by showing itself in this way, no longer exists.

It is due to this twofold condition that the before of birth escapes, inasmuch as the process of the auto-temporalization of life is a radically immanent process in which no horizon is ever deployed. What is engendered never relates to what engenders it as an ek-static before. How can they relate to one another in such a way that what engenders it exists before and yet does not cease to exist? Every form of relation—of *logos*—which does not derive its possibility from ek-stasis draws it from *pathos*. Thus, a feeling does not relate to itself ek-statically but only in and through its transcendental affectivity. The original temporality in question here is precisely the temporality of its affectivity and its experience of itself which, although constantly changing, does not cease. So, whereas experience unfolds and what is experienced always occurs as newly experienced, what is experienced through this constant change is always the Self itself, just like the one who experiences it. The Self is an auto-movement experiencing itself [*s'auto-éprouver*] that does not cease to experience itself in its own movement, such that nothing slips outside and nothing can ever detach itself from this self-experiencing [*s'auto-épreuve*] movement, from this self-experience moving from the Self, nor from this Self itself. Such a remaining [*demeurer*] of the Self in its pathos-filled experience is its life [*son vivre*]. It is stronger than any change and makes every change possible. It is its co-substantial present with this life [*vivre*] from which it draws its essence—it is its living Present.

In its living, the living ego is something that is derived only from absolute life, just as it only derives its auto-temporalization from this life, from its eternal auto-engendering. In this auto-engendering (which does not cease to grow on its own in its experience of its own moving), life never leaves itself. In being carried by this life, the ego does not leave itself either; it finds itself to be possible at once as an ego and as a living being. The auto-temporalization of absolute life is a material phenomenological law of life. Two of its surprising properties are shown by analysis. First, in contrast with the constantly affirmed irreversibility of objective time and more essentially in contrast with the ek-static temporality whose temporality *is* the world, the temporality of absolute life is reversible inasmuch as this temporality is temporalized as suffering and joy. A passage between these fundamental phenomenological tonalities can be made in both directions, such that in this passage each of these two tonalities remains in the other as its phenomenological condition and thus as its own substance. Second, nothing irreal ever enters into this pathos-filled auto-temporalization of absolute life; instead, there is only the auto-movement of an endless self-experience in the reversibility of suffering and joy. That is the second material phenomenological law of life: everything is real in life, just as every reality is held in life.

These two laws of the pathos-filled auto-temporalization of absolute life allow us to define further the ego's relation to its absolute before, that is, to this life that engenders it at every moment. The ego only relates to itself in the self-relation of absolute life—and it is engendered in that self-relation. Put otherwise, the ego only deploys the constant self-experience of its living in the pathos of the auto-temporalization of life. Two points follow from this.

First, concerning the ego's relation to itself, it is non-ekstatic and a pathos. That is to say that life is all-pervasive [*omniréel*] within it; it is both intact and whole and, on that condition alone, is the ego possible as a life. Non-ekstatic means specifically that the living ego never relates to itself in a memory or in forgetting—but only in this absolute Forgetting that signifies the impossibility in principle of any memory: the Immemorial. Memory is not a category of ipseity. The living ego has neither past, nor future, nor present.

Second, concerning our ultimate question of the ego's relation to life, this relation is inscribed in the ego itself inasmuch as the ego only relates to itself, as this singular Self, in the self-relation of absolute life. It is this word "in" which is the problem, which is birth. This "in" is provided by the self-relation of absolute life, since it is this relation that, by joining life to itself, joins the ego to itself and at the same time joins it to life. Life can only be joined to the self to the extent that life is joined to itself. This self-relation, as a relation to life and as a relation of life to itself, draws its essence from life. It is thus at once non-ekstatic and a pathos. "In" life, the ego does not relate to any ek-static before; instead, it is in pathos and in this way alone that this ego relates to the Before of life. This pathos is thus determinate. It is the pathos of that which, in experiencing itself, experiences the experience that absolute life has of itself [*éprouve l'épreuve de soi de la vie absolue*], such that its radical passivity with regard to itself is its radical passivity with regard to life. The radical passivity of life with regard to the self has thus become, in its becoming-*ipse* [*ipséisation*] and in its singularity, the passivity of the ego with regard to itself. This mode of passivity is the most constant trait of every life resulting from a birth, of a life like ours. The condition of the ego is the pathos of its presupposition. The life of the transcendental ego is the phenomenology of its birth.

Translated by Scott Davidson

Notes

This essay was originally published in *Alter: Revue de Phénoménologie* 2 (1994): 295–312.

1. Martin Heidegger, *History of the Concept of Time: Prolegomena*, trans. Theodore Kisiel (Bloomington: Indiana University Press, 1985). Translator's note: Henry's page reference to [*GA* 20, 223] is inaccurate.

2. Heidegger, *Being and Time*, 302 [329].

3. Heidegger, *Being and Time*, 46 [50].

4. This question is formulated ironically by Heidegger with regard to the carrying out of acts that, according to Scheler, characterize the person. "But what is the ontological meaning of "carrying out" . . . ? ("*Aber welches ist der ontologische Sinn von 'vollziehen'?*") (*Being and Time*, 45 [48]).

5. Heidegger, *Being and Time*, 210 [228]. The English translation of *Being and Time* reads: "*Has Dasein as itself ever freely decided and will it ever be able to decide whether it wants to come into Dasein or not?*"

6. On this point, see Henry's critique of Heideggerian *Nichtigkeit* in *The Essence of Manifestation*, §42–43.

7. Husserl, *Cartesian Meditations*, §44.

8. Edmund Husserl, *Ideas Pertaining to a Pure Phenomenology and to a Phenomenological Philosophy: Second Book*, trans. Richard Rojcewicz and Andre Schuwer (Dordrecht: Kluwer, 1989), 112.

9. On this point, see Michel Henry, "The Critique of the Subject," *Topoi* 7 (1988): 147–53.

3

Incarnation

Incarnation, in the first place, refers to the condition of a being who possesses a body or, more precisely, a flesh. Are the body and the flesh thus the same thing? Like every fundamental question, the question of the body—or of the flesh—points back to a phenomenological foundation on the basis of which it can be elucidated. A phenomenological foundation should be understood as a pure appearing that is presupposed by everything else that appears to us. This pure appearing must appear first in order for anything else to appear and to be shown to us. Phenomenology is not the "science of phenomena" but of their essence, that is, of what allows a phenomenon to be a phenomenon. It is not the science of phenomena but of their pure phenomenality as such, in short, of their pure appearing. Other words can also express this theme that distinguishes phenomenology from all other sciences: demonstration [*monstration*], disclosure, pure manifestation, pure revelation, or even the truth, if taken in its absolutely original sense. It is interesting to note that these keywords of phenomenology are also for many the keywords of religion and theology.

There are two fundamental modes of appearing—two different and decisive modes through which phenomenality phenomenalizes itself: the appearing of the world and the appearing of life.

In the world, things are shown to us from the outside; they are shown as exterior, other, and different. These properties of things—of beings—do not belong to things themselves. It is only because a thing is shown in the world that it is presented to us in this way. Because the world understood in terms of its pure appearing consists of a primordial exteriority—an "outside of itself" as such—everything that is shown in the world is always already cast outside. It is given in front of us and outside of us, as an "object" or as "facing us." By appearing in the world, the body is something that can only appear to us as external and with all of the properties that result from this exteriority; our own body is like this as well. A body is only possible in a "world": each body is an "external body." If the world is no longer considered naively as the sum of things or beings—as a collection of "bodies"—but in terms of their mode of appearing, then the world is illuminated in the opening of this horizon of pure exteriority that Heidegger calls an "Ek-stasis." In this way, it is the arrival from the outside of this Outside that produces the space of light in which everything that we can see becomes visible for us, whether this is a sensible or an intellectual seeing.

In life, the difference between appearing and what it allows to appear—between pure phenomenality and the phenomenon—does not exist. The condition for establishing this unusual identification between phenomenality and the phenomenon is to understand life in its proper sense. Instead of taking it as a "thing" or, in terms of modern biology,[1] as a set of inert material processes, life must be understood as phenomenological through and through, as pure phenomenality and as the most originary mode in which phenomenality is phenomenalized. Life makes every other form of phenomenality possible. Yet, even though life founds phenomenality, its mode of phenomenalization differs fundamentally from that of the world. In order to avoid this equivocation, we will refer to it in terms of revelation.

The revelation of life can be contrasted point by point with the appearing of the world. Whereas the world is disclosed "outside of itself" such that everything disclosed there is external, the key feature of the revelation of life is that it does not have any separation within itself and never differs from itself. It only ever reveals itself. *Life reveals itself.* Life is an auto-revelation. On the one hand, it is life that carries out the work of revelation; it is anything but a blind entity. On the other hand, what it reveals is itself. This is why the revelation of life and what it reveals are one and the same.

This extraordinary situation is encountered everywhere life exists, even in its simplest modality: the impression. Consider an impression of pain. In the ordinary sense, a pain is initially taken as a "physical pain," which refers to some part of the objective body (a headache, a backache, a stomachache, etc.). For this reason, let's perform a reduction of pain that only keeps its pure impressional character, the "painful as such." This is the purely affective element of suffering pain. This pure suffering "reveals itself," which means that *suffering alone allows us to know what suffering is* and that what is revealed in the revelation of this fact is suffering itself. In this auto-revelation of suffering, there is no world "outside of itself." This can be recognized by the fact that there is no gap that separates suffering from itself. Riveted to itself and crushed under its own weight, suffering does not allow one to establish any distance from it. There is no route through which one could escape from oneself and what is oppressive about one's own being. Without any ability to put suffering at a distance, there is no possibility of directing one's gaze toward it. One never sees one's own suffering, pleasure, or joy. Pain is invisible, and this holds for every impression.

The invisible is not a negation. It should not be thought of based on the visibility of the world or in a purely privative way, since it is totally foreign to visibility and owes nothing to it. It refers to the primal and positive way in which the impression is experienced in an insurmountable passivity toward oneself, and thus as it is, in the reality of its impressional immediacy. Yet, it is never through itself or its own force that a particular impression is revealed in this way. It is only through the auto-revelation of life carried out in its absolutely originary immanence that every conceivable impression is placed within oneself. It is thus impressed on oneself as being what it is. For this reason, the auto-revelation in which each impression is experienced passively is not specific to any particular impression but concerns them all; all our impressions are, truly speaking, only the changing modalities of one and the same life.

This ever-changing impressional totality is our flesh. For our flesh is nothing other than *what suffers and undergoes, and supports itself and thus experiences itself and enjoys itself [jouissant] through continually renewed impressions.* Yet, like each of the impressions that comprise it, this flesh is only possible in life. Life's unity in its immanent auto-revelation is equally the auto-revelation of all these impressions; it is what makes them one and the same flesh.

Body and flesh are thus distinguished through the radicality of an originary phenomenological dualism. The body lacks the power to make manifest; it has to seek its manifestation in the world outside-of-itself and is thus constituted as a mundane body. The forms of the intuition of space and time along with the categories of representation under which the body is subsumed are nothing but the modes of the process of externalization through which it becomes a phenomenon. The flesh, by contrast, is an auto-impression in the process of the auto-revelation of life. Its revelation is derived from life and from it alone. Bodies are possible in the world, whereas a flesh never occurs elsewhere or otherwise than in life. Before inquiring further into the phenomenological properties that the flesh acquires through its arrival into life, it is first necessary to analyze briefly the relationship between the body and the flesh from a phenomenological point of view, that is to say, to ask *which of these two realities is the most essential in the sense of providing access to the other one.*

In the world, the body appears as an extended body, with forms and figures that allow it to be known geometrically. But a worldly body is not only an extended body owing its exteriority to the world outside-of-itself. It is also a sensible body. It has an impressional texture—it is red, dark, sonorous, painful, nauseating—which cannot be explained by exteriority alone. According to Galileo's analysis, which was repeated by Descartes in his famous analysis of the piece of wax in the "Second Meditation," the extended body has no color, sound, or odor on its own; it is neither agreeable nor disagreeable, neither beautiful nor ugly. Its sensible, axiological, affective layer comes from somewhere else than its ek-static structure.

This points out the following fact. Every sensible body that is seen, smelled, heard, touched, or moved presupposes another body that sees it, smells it, touches it, or moves it. The operations of this second body constitute the former and make it possible. In other words, it presupposes a transcendental and constituting body, a subject-body or a "subjective" body without which the former, the body-object-of-the-world, would not exist. This transcendental body is a principle but not the object of our experience, and thus the following question can be raised with respect to it: what mode of appearing ultimately gives rise to it?

In contemporary phenomenology, especially Husserl and Merleau-Ponty, the nature of the transcendental body still remains silhouetted against the horizon of the world and remains tacitly subordinated to it. This body, to be sure, cannot be reduced to an object of perception, since it is instead what produces such objects. This corporeal subject has taken the place of understanding in traditional thought. However, as long as the transcendental body is interpreted as an intentional body that casts us into the world and as an appearing whose phenomenality emerges along with the arrival from the outside of the Outside, then nothing has really changed from the traditional conception of phenomenality or from the conception of the body which results from it. Quite the contrary, our body is now "of the world" in the sense that it is no longer merely an object situated in this world but also opens onto the ek-static appearing of the world. It thus still belongs to the world and remains submitted to it in a radical way.[2]

Is this not actually how it is, one might ask? The acts of the transcendental body give colors, sounds, odors, etc.; these are the acts of our senses. The "distance senses" join us to things and can only do so to the extent that this "transcendence" of the ek-stasis of the world operates within them.

It is here that the aporia of every mundane theory of the body blocks the road. In the world "outside of itself," no impression or flesh is possible. The flesh can only be experienced in the immanent auto-revelation of life. Our body can indeed reach out toward the world, and this bundle of intentions can go out toward the sensible qualities of things. But the acts of the transcendental body—in this case the acts of our different senses—*can be carried out only because they are impressionally given to themselves in the self-givenness of life and only to the extent that they are given there.* How would we be able to see anything outside ourselves, if our vision were nothing in itself, if our hearing were not, as such, a "phenomenon," if touching and taking were not living operations experienced in themselves, capable of guiding themselves in their concrete performances?

The aporia of the mundane theory of the body is thus only another name for the aporia that confronts intentional phenomenology in general: if intentionality is what reveals everything, then how is it revealed to itself? Husserlian phenomenology was only able to avoid the spiral of an infinite regress by delivering transcendental life over to the anonymous.

But there is still more. Our transcendental body cannot be limited to our senses; they are not limited to that which intentionally reaches out toward things. The body is also the seat of originary, immanent movements. They are more than the movements that orient our senses and are indispensible to their effective functioning. *This body originally moves itself within itself.* This is how what appears to us from the outside in the external world—for instance, the objective movement of our hands—is in itself the self-movement of a power to grasp that remains in itself when it is accomplished. It is given to itself in the impressional self-givenness of life. If one considers this transcendental body more closely, it should be recognized that, instead of being reducible to an intentional body, its own intentionality presupposes—*a fortiori* in its self-movement that moves in oneself—this primal self-impressionality that excludes all exteriority. Moreover, this is the condition of the possibility of any power whatsoever—as impressionally given to itself in the same way as pain or suffering; it must be one with itself, never separated from itself, and in possession of itself. It is in this way and in it alone that it can deployed by oneself and act.

But if the powers of our body are only able to act in life, we need to carry out a complete reversal of the tradition. The original reality of our body is not our mundane body that is situated in the world and opens onto it; instead, it is our flesh in whose auto-impressionality all powers are placed in themselves and thereby able to be exercised. The flesh provides our access to the body—whether it is to sensible bodies in the world, our own objective, sensible body, or even the intentional body itself. Yet, *our flesh can only provide access to this body and through this body to the world, because it first provides us with access to itself—because it is impressionally given to itself where all self-givenness occurs, namely, in and through life.* Therefore, if it is no longer a question of examining the characteristics of the mundane body but rather of *the essential phenomenological properties that our flesh derives from life*, we must return to our initial question.

But, from what Life is it derived? Neither our impressions nor the flesh that they compose can bring themselves into themselves; they are only given to the self through the self-givenness of life. Likewise, this life itself—to the extent that it is ours—does not bring about the self-givenness that makes it a life. While our own life happens to lack this ability, only an Absolute Life contains this ability within itself, namely, the ability to bring itself into itself and to generate itself in and through the process of its self-revelation. It alone can make life exist somewhere. All other lives are only alive in it—in this unique and absolute life that alone has the power to live. Only the properties of this absolute Life—not as contingent properties, but as transcendental possibilities included in the process of self-generation—can account for the phenomenological properties of all conceivable life, including the essential phenomenological properties of our own flesh inasmuch as they come from life.

We thus need to inquire into this absolute process through which Life comes into itself, even if we can only do so briefly. To live means "to experience oneself" [*s'éprouver soi-même*]. No ipseity is possible without the experience of the self. But in principle this ipseity belongs to the absolute process in which Life comes into itself, engenders itself through the experience of itself, and reveals itself to itself. Life is not initially a concept; it is first of all a real life that is phenomenologically actualized. Ipseity, in which life experiences itself, is also real and phenomenologically actualized. It is a real Self, the First living Self in which Life reveals itself to itself, its Word [*Verbe*]. Because the Self is the most radical possibility of life and its Word, a Self is also connected to every conceivable life. And at the same time, a Self also belongs to everything whose condition of possibility is found in the auto-revelation of life—to every flesh and every impression. There is no flesh that does not have a Self within itself, such that this Self, which is implicated in the givenness of this flesh to itself, turns out to be the Self of this flesh just as much as it is the flesh of this Self. There is no flesh that would be an anonymous, impersonal flesh: the flesh of the world. There is no such impression either: there is no pain, suffering, or joy that would be the pain, suffering, or joy of no one!

We have used the words "flesh" and "impression." But why must the self-givenness of life within us, in our finite life, occur in the form of a flesh as well as in the multiple impressions that form its continuous thread? Haven't we said that all the characteristics of our flesh come from life, ultimately from the absolute Life that is the only Life that exists and from which no life, considered rigorously, can be separated? Without it, one would cease to experience oneself and also cease to be alive. How, then, does the absolute Life enter into itself in such a way that it can be the origin of our flesh and all its properties?

We answer: it does so in its own immanence. Since Life, in the immanence of its auto-revelation, remains in itself in a ceaseless auto-affection, this is also a property of our flesh. Nothing can ever separate us from it. It is an unbreakable thread without any fault line or rupture. Yet this immanence of our flesh should not be posited speculatively, like substance in Spinozism. It needs to be understood phenomenologically: how do we experience it in such a way that it is nothing but the revelation of absolute Life in us, as it is experienced in our flesh, and as our flesh, which in turn, is only ever experienced in this Life?

Affectivity, or as it could be said, a pure pathos, is an experience of oneself without any distance or gap, without the intermediary of a sense. Suffering is given to itself through affectivity. As we have seen, it is not given in its own affectivity, or in our own, but in the affectivity of absolute Life. Through Affectivity, absolute Life comes into itself, experiences and enjoys [*jouit*] itself. Affectivity is not a fact or a state; it is not one property among others. Instead, it is the ultimate possibility behind a process that continually occurs and is never undone—the eternal process in which Life experiences and loves itself eternally in its Word that is experienced and loved eternally within itself. *This Archi-possibility is an Archi-passibility whose phenomenological actualization is the pure phenomenological matter of absolute Life*—every auto-affection and every possible life exists in this originary Affectivity. And consequently, every flesh exists in it as well. It is only because our own life, in its finitude, does not itself have an *Archi-passibility, which is to say the ability to bring itself into itself through a phenomenologically actualized pathos*. It is because our own life is only given passively to itself through the Archi-passibility of absolute Life that we have a flesh like ours. *Every flesh is passible in the Archi-passibility of absolute Life, and every flesh is only possible through it.* Truly speaking, our flesh is nothing other than that: *the passibility of a finite life drawing its possibility from the Archi-passibility of infinite Life.*

We asked the question: what phenomenological properties does our flesh derive from life? We can see the answer better now: it does not entail any particular properties or any group of properties, however essential they may be. What the flesh derives from life is precisely its condition as flesh, that is, the auto-impression of suffering and joy that constitutes the pure phenomenological substance of every conceivable flesh. But this flesh—which derives its condition as flesh from life—cannot be limited to a multiplicity of impressions or specific sensations, or to a set of powers. The preceding analysis of these powers forced us to change direction. We had to abandon the phenomenological status of intentionality for that of self-givenness. To the extent that none of the powers of our flesh brought themselves into themselves, and were delivered to themselves without being willed and independently of the flesh's power, *each of these powers thus collides within itself with something that it has no power over or against; it collides with an absolute non-power*. For it is not through itself but only through the hyperpower [*hyperpuissance*] of absolute Life that each of these powers is given to itself, like the flesh for which it has become a power. Consider Christ's brutal response to Pilate who displayed his power to either release or crucify him: "You would have no power over me, if it were not given to you from above" (John 19:10–11).

Here again, we can see that this "givenness from above"—the Archi-givenness of life to every life—carries within itself the Archi-passibility to which every self-givenness of a life owes its ultimate possibility. What is given to every power through this Archi-givenness is not the semblance of a gift, or the semblance of a power; it is not a particular power, such as the power to take something or to move. Instead, this Archi-givenness is what places this power in itself, puts it in possession of itself, and makes it into a true power—*a power to be able* [*pouvoir pouvoir*]. It can then be used *freely*, as often as one wants. For freedom is not an idea but the actual exercise of a set of concrete powers. In the end, no power derives this power to be able from itself, and no human can claim it as his own.

If the self-givenness that makes every power a true and free power remains an Archi-givenness, how can we recognize that this Archi-givenness itself derives its phenomenological actualization from the Archi-passibility of absolute Life? Affectivity provides the phenomenological matter for this self-givenness that is constitutive of every power to be able. In modern philosophy, two admirable analyses provide evidence of this decisive situation. Maine de Biran interprets the *cogito* as an "I can" whose phenomenological possibility refers precisely to pathos, provided that *every actual action is an effort and that every effort is a "feeling of effort."* This is the ultimate phenomenological condition of all action, when it is considered not as the exercise of a power but explicitly as *the possibility of being able*. It is Kierkegaard who carried this intuition to its full radicality. In the crucial proposition from *The Concept of Anxiety*, he calls this—"the anguishing possibility of being able"—a proposition on which the Kierkegaardian theory of eroticism and of sin is based.[3]

The Archi-passibility of absolute Life is not a concept that one can freely introduce whenever it would be useful. It must be understood where it is located, that is, in the absolute process through which Life enters into itself and as the ultimate phenomenological possibility of this process. In the pathos of its auto-impressionality, our flesh becomes possible through this Archi-passibility of absolute Life. *This is what leads any phenomenology of the flesh back to a phenomenology of incarnation in a radical sense.* Incarnation thus can no longer signify merely the incarnate condition of the human being, with the constellation of problems tied to it: the problem of the body, of its relation to the flesh, of all the behaviors in which this flesh is involved, of action in general with its various affective "motivations" (which are its essence), eros, etc. In-carnation no longer refers to this actual flesh which is considered to be the paradigm of all facticity. *It refers to the arrival in a flesh*, to the process from which it came and in which it remains. In the extreme passivity and passibility of its finitude, it constantly experiences itself as being unable to give itself to itself and thus necessarily refers to the process of the Archi-givenness of absolute Life in its Archi-passibility.

There is thus a "Before-the-flesh"—a Before In-carnation—which resides in the Archi-passibility of Life. Through its reference to what is Before In-carnation, our flesh displays a strange affinity with other essential features of living beings. It ceases to seem like a mysterious and contingent addition to the condition of a living being, as if it were a sort of empirical appendix like our objective body. Instead, it becomes integrated into a network of properties that derive from an *a priori* that is older than the world. How can one fail to notice that the flesh's secondary situation in relation to the Archi-passibility of Life runs parallel to the secondary situation of the Self (thus of "me" and of the "ego") and of living beings in general? In any case, the intelligibility of what is in question—the living being in its ipseity and its flesh—implies that one must situate oneself prior to them in an original dimension. *This is precisely the same for each of the realities under consideration*, if it is the case that life can only exist in absolute Life, that the Self can only exist in the Ipseity though which this absolute Life comes into itself, and that the flesh can only exist in the Archi-passibility through which absolute Life's arrival in the self occurs. Life is thus a pathos, and in its originary enjoyment of itself, it is a Life of love.

"Before the Self" and "Before the flesh" are one and the same. They both refer to the Archi-passibility of Life because that is how Life is experienced in the ipseity of the Self, and thus in every conceivable Self, just as it is through this Archi-passibility that every flesh is joined to itself. This sheds a different light on the human condition. If the same experience of pathos makes the Self into a Self and the flesh into a flesh—*the ipseity of the Self and the auto-impressionality of the flesh*—then the Self and the flesh go together. The human is thus a *carnal living Self.* But this has nothing to do with the definitions that construct the human as a compound of spirit and matter, of soul and body, of "subject" and "object." Such constructions do not help us to understand anything whatsoever, today no less than in its first instances in Greece or elsewhere.

For the Archi-passibility of Life does not only illuminate our human condition, it also illuminates this Archi-passibility of Life itself. This is because our condition can never be explained on the basis of the world but only on the basis of Life. These premises of the human condition find their most striking expression in the Prologue of John. At the center of the Prologue, there is the Word. It is introduced in two ways, first in its relation to life and second in its relation to flesh. The unconditional affirmation of this dual relation overturns the horizon of Greek thought, which is also largely our own way of thinking today. The relation between *Logos* and life was only envisioned in the Greek world as an opposition. This was decisive due to the paradoxical fact that it provides a definition of the human being. Animals are distinguished from humans by their lack of a *Logos*. Here *Logos* signifies both Reason and the ability to speak, that is, to form ideal meanings. If one adds to this the fact that we, humans, can only speak about things and predicate various things about them to the extent that they are shown to us, then one can discover an original connection by which the Greek *Logos* is jooined to the appearing of the world (or of "Nature") and is identical to it. In spite of its apparent positivity, however, the history of Western thought will discover that this specific distinction between the *Logos* and living beings contains an insurmountable difficulty within itself.

Greek thought reveals this difficulty when it encounters—or better, enters into a titanic struggle with—Christianity. *Christianity does not know this aporia inasmuch as its Logos is no longer the Logos of the world but the Logos of Life, and its conception of the body is no longer the Greek conception of a mundane body, but precisely the conception of a flesh that only exists in life. Ultimately, it exists in this Logos of Life that is the Word of God.*

Two brief statements convey the initiatory revelation transmitted by John: "In the beginning was the Word," "And the Word was made flesh." We have already accounted for the former statement, if it is the case that the process of God's self-revelation (explicitly defined by John as Life) in His Word does not generate the Word at its end but in itself, as that in which this process consists: "In the beginning." As for the second proposition in verse 14, it too is illuminating if it is the case that a flesh can only have an auto-impression through the Archi-passibility of the Word of absolute Life. If the ultimate condition of possibility of the flesh is derived from the Word of Life, then the notion of the Incarnation of the Word is not absurd, as it would have seemed to the Greeks. Instead, it is rooted in the basis of things. Conversely, it founds the flesh's ability to receive the Word from which it is derived. In the insightful words of St. Irenaeus: "God can give life to the flesh," "The flesh can be given life by God," and "The flesh will be able to receive and to contain the power of God."[4]

Was the Incarnation of the Word necessary? Was it so admirable that it would have taken place without sin? All finitude presupposes the infinite, but the infinite owes nothing to finitude. The arrival of the Messiah can only be a gratuitous act by the power that governs everything. The Incarnation of the Word is not connected entirely to the historical arrival of Christ, however. For the Word that becomes flesh in Christ is the eternal Word of God. It is in Him that everything was created. This includes not only the world but also everything that is foreign to it: our flesh, the ipseity of our Self, and our life. When God breathed his life into dust from the ground, he turned it into the carnal living transcendental Self that makes up each human being. The body was only matter or dust, but the flesh was wholly alive. The arrival of each living being into its own carnal ipseity is part of the immanent generation of life. Incarnation, understood in terms of this generation, can help us to understand creation. It allows us to distinguish in creation between the process of externalization in the world and the embrace of the pathos of Life. It is through the dazzling light of John's Prologue that the book of Genesis is illuminated.

Christ's own words about himself, "the Incarnation is the Revelation of God," were repeated by his disciples. How this thesis came to be reiterated by the Church Fathers and thus by "Christianity" is the result of an unforeseen Archi-intelligibility, if the Incarnation is no longer understood naively as the arrival into an opaque body but into a phenomenological flesh. In the passibility of its unbearable finitude, the flesh is not merely experienced through the play of its ever-changing impressions (which are, in this respect, always the same). The flesh comes into itself, as an auto-impression, only in the Archi-passibility through which the Word of Life eternally embraces itself. In the flesh, then, at the bottom of its Night, the Eyes of God are watching us. Every flesh will be judged. That is the reason why with a unique lucidity—following after Paul and John, it is true—the Church Fathers understood the flesh as both the site of perdition and of salvation. The perdition of the flesh occurs when it becomes idolatrous of itself, takes itself as the source of its pleasure, and adores itself in terms of this principle as well as its effects. The salvation of the flesh occurs when, given to itself through its generation in the Word, it no longer loves anything within itself but the Word that connected it to itself in the beginning, and receives it as its essence in the Eucharist.

We called this an Archi-intelligibility, because the power of revelation at work here is foreign to any form of vision or "e-vidence," whether it would be sensible or intellectual. The latter allowed the Greeks (as well as the moderns) to adequately apprehend the content of the sensible. There are many degrees of this knowledge that can be divided into different "kinds" and evaluated in terms of their pertinence. That is the knowledge of the wise and learned. But here is what is new: the power of revelation is conferred on the flesh and this carnal power is the absolute. The pathos of life is vested in every living being as a privilege that no one can ever take away; it is the sign of one's election and the reality of life. This invincible revelation is inscribed in fiery letters in the invisibility of our flesh; it is given in each of the flesh's impressions, in each of its powers, in a "givenness from above."

Translated by Scott Davidson

Notes

The English translation of this essay was originally published in *Carnal Hermeneutics*, ed. Richard Kearney and Brian Treanor (New York: Fordham University Press, 2015), 128–44. This version has been corrected and modified so that it is more consistent with the other translations in this volume.

    1. In truth, following the Galilean reduction, modern biology eliminated sensibility, "subjectivity," and "consciousness" from its field of research. It no longer talks about life: "today we no longer study life in laboratories." Since its purpose has changed entirely, it is only the anachronistic use of the Greek name of this science that enables this confusion. François Jacob, *La Logique du vivant* (Paris: Gallimard, 1970), 320.

    2. It is this dual belonging of the body to the world as both seeing and visible—"touching" and "tangible"—that leads the later Merleau-Ponty to say about this body that is situated in the world at the same time as it opens us up to the world that "it is of the world." See Maurice Merleau-Ponty, *The Visible and The Invisible*, trans. Alphonso Lingis (Evanston, Ill.: Northwestern University Press, 1969), 178. For a radical critique of these theses, refer to Michel Henry, *Incarnation: A Philosophy of the Flesh*, chaps. 21 and 31.

    3. See Søren Kierkegaard, *The Concept of Dread*, trans. Walter Lowrie (Princeton, N.J.: Princeton University Press, 1944), 40. Translator's note: The Lowrie translation renders this as "the alarming possibility of being able." That said, I have remained closer to the French text, which reads "*pouvoir pouvoir.*" This connotes possibility, ability, and power, and so I have rendered it "the power to be able" throughout.

    4. Irenaeus, *Against the Heresies*, Book V.

4

Those within Me: A Phenomenology

What does it mean to approach the question of the experience of the other from a phenomenological perspective? Phenomenology's originality should be understood from the object that it has assigned to itself. Whereas other sciences study specific phenomena—physical, chemical, biological, historical, juridical, social, economic, etc.—phenomenology inquires into what allows a phenomenon to be a phenomenon, that is, pure phenomenality as such. Now, if one considers the historical development of phenomenology in the twentieth century in Germany and then for instance France, one will see that the central question of phenomenology, that of phenomenality or of appearing considered in itself, has received a unilateral response, yet one that we do not share. The conception of phenomenality that has served as the guiding thread in such analyses is the same one that first appears to ordinary thought, while simultaneously constituting the most ancient and least critical prejudice of traditional philosophy: a conception borrowed from the appearing of objects of the world and, when all is said and done, from the appearing of the world itself.

Thus, for Husserl, phenomenality is traditionally understood to start from consciousness, but consciousness is in essence intentional; it is nothing other than the movement by which it projects itself outside, so that phenomenality arises from this coming into the outside and is due to it. To reveal through such a coming into the outside, through putting at a distance, is to enable seeing [*faire voir*]. The possibility of vision resides in this putting at a distance of what is placed before sight and which is hence seen by it.

It is with Heidegger that the world's appearing finds its highest degree of elaboration. As early as §7 of *Sein und Zeit*, the phenomenon is explained according to the Greek—*phainomenon*—starting from the root *pha*, *phos*, meaning "light," such that appearing signifies coming into the light, clarity, or "that wherein something can become manifest, visible in itself" [*d.h. das, worin etwas offenbar, an ihm selbst sichtbar werden kann*].[1] The world is this ek-static horizon of visibilization in which all things can become visible, and with this "horizon," it is a question of exteriority, of the "outside of itself" as such, as the second part of *Sein und Zeit* explicitly states. There the world is identified with temporality, and temporality is nothing other than "the originary outside-of-itself in and for itself."[2]

The appearing of the world has three decisive traits. (1) Inasmuch as the appearing of the world consists in the "outside-of-itself," in the coming out of an Outside, thus everything which shows itself within it shows itself outside, as external, as other, as different. (2) The appearing that is disclosed in the Difference from the world not only makes different everything that is disclosed in such a manner; it is as a rule totally indifferent to it. Similar to the light spoken of in the Gospels which shines on both the just and the unjust alike, the appearing of the world illuminates all that it illuminates in a terrifying neutrality without any concern toward any thing or person whatsoever. There are [*Il y a*][3] victims and executioners, charitable acts and genocides, rules and exceptions, abuses, wind, water, earth, and all that stands before us in like manner, in this ultimate manner of being that we express by saying: "That is," "There is." (3) However, this indifference of the appearing of the world to what it discloses in Difference and which makes it anything but a Father for his Sons, a brother for his brothers, a friend for his friends—such an indifference, we say, hides a more radical indigence. *The appearing of the world is not only indifferent to all that it discloses; it is incapable of conferring existence upon it.* Doubtless, this inability of the appearing of the world to account for what it discloses explains its indifference toward it. Here, indifference and neutrality signify impotence and are derived from it. Heidegger, who was the first to think through the concept of the world in its originary phenomenological signification as pure appearing, failed to recognize this indifference (the anguish in which everything becomes indifferent), as well as this impotence. Disclosure discloses, uncovers, "opens" but does not create (*macht nicht, öffnet*). Thus is disclosed the ontological indigence of the appearing of the world, incapable on its own of establishing reality.

Now, according to us, *the appearing of the world is opposed trait for trait to the revelation specific to life.* Whereas the world discloses in the "outside-of-itself," such that everything that it discloses is external, other, and different, the first decisive trait of the revelation of life is that, not bearing any separation and never differing from itself, it only ever reveals itself. *Life reveals itself.* Life is a self-revelation. Thus, with regard to life, self-revelation means two things: on the one hand, it is life that accomplishes the work of revelation; it is anything but a blind, anonymous process. On the other hand, what life reveals is life itself. The revelation of life and what is revealed in it are one.

Everywhere where there is life one finds this extraordinary situation that can be recognized in each of life's modalities, even the humblest pain. Because, in ordinary apprehension, a pain is first taken for a "physical pain" and is referred to a part of the objective body, we apply to it the reduction that retains only its painful character, the "painful as such," the purely affective element of suffering. This "pure" suffering "reveals itself to itself," which means that only suffering allows us to know what suffering is. On the other hand, what is revealed in this revelation, which is the fact of suffering, is precisely suffering. Since, in this modality of our life, the "outside-of-itself" [*hors-de-soi*] of the world is absent, suffering is recognized due to there being no gap separating suffering from itself. Riveted to itself, burdened by its own weight, it is incapable of initiating in regard to itself any withdrawal, a dimension of flight by which it could escape both itself and what is oppressive about its being. In the absence of any internal distance, the possibility of casting a gaze upon it is excluded. No one has ever seen their suffering, their anguish, or their joy. Suffering, like every modality of life, is invisible. "Invisible" does not thereby designate a dimension of irreality or illusion, some fantasy world behind the scenes, but rather its opposite: reality.

So we have distinguished between two different and heterogeneous modes of appearing: that of the world and that of life. When philosophical reflection encounters an essential question, its first theme of research should be the fundamental phenomenological presupposition that serves as the support to and ultimate possibility of the reality that it is examining. For it goes without saying that the conception of any reality whatsoever is modified entirely depending upon whether one assigns the ekstatic appearing of the world or the self-revelation of life as its support. Consider for example a problem like that of the body. In the world, the body is an external body, the body-object of common sense as well as of the philosophical tradition and science. In life, to the contrary, the body is a subjective body consisting of the totality of our impressions and powers, themselves subjectively experienced and deployed. Furthermore, *the experience of the other is established on the level of the flesh and not only on that of objective bodies.* Such is the case of the relation to others in general, whose originary comprehension points back to the self-revelation of life and not to the appearing of the world.

A coherent and systematic problematic of the experience of the other which refers its possibility to the self-revelation of life should first show why the phenomenologies of the world have failed to account for such an experience, though they used it as their warhorse. There is no room, however, for such a critique in the context of this talk. Here I will limit myself to raising a major objection to those phenomenologies. Since the experience of the other is nothing other than a relationship between a plurality of selves [*moi*], the inner possibility of each of those selves [*ces moi*], namely the ipseity that comprises their essence, must be established first and foremost. And it is precisely this ipseity that cannot arise in the exteriority of the world.

The me [*moi*] is in fact a relation with itself [*soi*]. In exteriority every relation is a "relation to," in other words, a relation to something external, even a relation between two terms external to one another. In exteriority no relation to *oneself* is possible, as already shown by the analysis of the appearing of the world that projects [*jette*] everything outside-of-itself, disclosing thereby only the external, the different, the foreign. What can be shown, however, is how such a relation to oneself, constitutive of every Self, is only conceivable in life and occurs only in life. To live is "to experience oneself," as our own phenomenology has recognized in regard to the simplest modality of life, that of a pain, of a "pure suffering." In itself, suffering experiences itself without referring to anything else. But "to experience itself" in the manner of a suffering has nothing to do with the dead tautology "A = A" of the formal and empty subject of German idealism, nor with the "I am myself" of Husserl. For suffering, to experience itself means that it reaches itself, takes on the load of its own content, undergoes itself, suffers itself in a suffering stronger than any freedom.

This coming into itself of suffering is not brought about by the particular content of suffering. Such a coming into itself occurs equally in pleasure, satisfaction, joy, or desire. In each of its modalities and making each of them possible, it is life that comes into itself. Life is a process, the eternal process in which, by coming into itself it grabs hold of itself, expands itself, experiences itself and enjoys itself [*jouit de soi*]. This movement of life is a radically immanent movement, it is the movement moving in itself in which a life gives and reveals itself to itself without ever parting from itself, without ever getting rid of itself. In this immanent coming of life within its "experiencing itself" an Ipseity is constructed without which no self-experience is possible. Insofar as we are not speaking here of a concept of life but of a phenomenologically effective life, of a real life, the Ipseity in which this life experiences itself is also a phenomenologically effective Ipseity, a real Self, which, in principle, belongs to all effective life as its innermost possibility. There is no life without a living Self, in which this life experiences itself, but there is no Self except in the life that engenders it as that in which life becomes life.

Thus the first condition of every experience of the other is established if *such an experience arises whenever a me encounters another similar me*—an *alter ego*—and if, as a relation to itself, each me is possible only in the accomplishment of this radically immanent process of life, in its being engendered by this very process.

If one considers the phenomenologies of the twentieth century, one will surely see that they often raise the question of a plurality of me's [*une pluralité de moi*]. But this me is always taken for granted, in a kind of pre-philosophical naïveté that never questions its specific phenomenological possibility, namely, ipseity as such. Instead it is constantly presupposed or rather immediately forgotten. Thus, in Husserl, for whom the me functions as the source point of intentionality, its essence is reduced to that of this intentionality, in other words, to the "outside-of-itself" [*hors-de-soi*] as such. For Heidegger, in *Sein und Zeit*, *Dasein* is said to be "always mine." When the essence of this "mineness," of ipseity, is investigated, however, it is reduced to the process of self-externalization in which *Dasein* is discovered to be delivered over to the world in order to die there.

Behind these various interpretations, in our opinion, hides a ruinous confusion, which dominates the history of Western thought, between that of the ipseity of the Self and of the individuality of a thing. This latter actually acquires individual characteristics in the exteriority of the world, according to phenomenological categories of the world: space, time, the idea of this thing—categories which can be read on any identity card: born on ___, at such place ___, child of this man ___ and of this woman ___. Here, as in the positivist ideology that triumphs before our eyes, the human is basically only a thing, or better, a biological process.

Let's return to what is essential. If the Self relates to itself by experiencing itself in the absolute immanence of life and in it alone, phenomenology still asks: what does the phenomenological reality of this originary mode of phenomenalization consist of? What is the pure phenomenological matter of this originary self-revelation? This is a transcendental Affectivity that precedes every sentiment by making it possible—the originary phenomenological tonalities of this Affectivity are the suffering and joy in which the experiencing itself of life occurs, and thus every possible Self. Life is a pathos. *Every me is an immanent pathos-filled relation to itself.*[4]

If such is the case, every relation between me's [*des moi*] is ultimately an affective relation, whose laws do not have their principle in the course of the events of the world, but rather in the originary phenomenological tonalities of suffering and enjoyment in which the "experiencing itself" occurs. These relations unfold the affective potentialities inscribed in this originary "suffering" and "enjoyment" and for this reason, they have this character of an affective dichotomy, of a seemingly mysterious split between malaise and satisfaction, unpleasant and pleasant, pain and pleasure, suffering and joy, despair and bliss.

But if we can understand that the relations that are established between people necessarily imply living transcendental Selves stamped with the decisive traits of life—ipseity and affectivity, notably—we still face the most difficult question, that of the possibility of the relation itself: how is each Self able to step out of itself, one wonders, in order to encounter others, how is that Self with them or how are they in it? Does stepping out of oneself not mean to open up to the world so as to be able, in this world and due to it in some way, to be with them? That is how twentieth-century phenomenology has gone searching in the world for this possibility for each Self to escape its solitude—in the world and in its exteriority, in which, however, no Self is possible.

If each Self derives its possibility from life, if its effective reality resides there, its own like that of any other Self with which it must be able to enter into relation, then it is because the relation itself occurs in life, it is because *the life that is the condition of possibility of each Self also turns out to be the condition of the relation itself.* But what life are we referring to here? In what life is the Self given to itself if it must be able to encounter in this life all other Selves?

Let's examine anew this Self, this me that I am. "Me," wrote Husserl in a manuscript from the 1930s, "I am myself [*Ich bin Ich*]." We cannot confine ourselves to such a statement, as important as it may be. It is advisable to push the analysis further. Me, I am myself, but it isn't me who has given me to myself. My life experiences itself, but it is not the one that has brought it into this condition of experiencing itself; such a condition depends neither on its power nor its will. That is why my life, the ipseity of this singular me that I am, and all of my impressions are given to themselves in this radical passivity that confers on them this marvelous condition of experiencing themselves and of enjoying themselves, of living.

If it is not me, if it is not my own life, then we are led to ask what life does have the ability to give each life to itself, each Self to itself, making it a living being in the sense of a living transcendental Self. Only a Life that is able to give itself within itself, that bears the power of living, and is able to give life to all that lives is capable of such. It is in the self-givenness of this absolute Life that every finite life is given to itself, that each Self is united to itself in order to be this Self that it is forever.

But why would this absolute life confer this irreducibly singular Self on the living being that we are, if not because in its originary coming into itself, absolute Life generates within itself the First Self in which, experiencing itself, it becomes Life? Because the process of the self-generation of absolute Life, as the generation within itself of a First Self, is repeated in each living being; every living being also bears within it the Self without which no life, no living is possible.

It is in this way that, pushed to its limit, the phenomenological analysis of the Self leads us back to a "Before the Self" [*Avant le Soi*], to that which exists within it prior to it. That which exists in the Self prior to it is its coming into the condition that is its own, its immanent generation in the absolute Life whose process is repeated in it whenever it comes into itself. Thus *the transcendental condition of the possibility of every Self and of every conceivable me, or its immanent generation within absolute Life, is revealed to also be the transcendental condition of the possibility of the relation of each Self to all others, the condition of the experience of the other.* So if one wants to understand such a relation, one must never start from a Self or from an autonomous me. For considered in that way, the Self is never anything other than a monad, each enclosed within itself, experiencing its impressions and its emotions as that which is given to it alone, as "that which is given only to a single one" according to the language of psychology, and in fact incapable of encountering an other. It is only due to an analogical reasoning, of which the Husserlian "appresentation" is only a subtle disguise, that it could imagine what the other feels and which must be analogous to what it itself experiences in similar circumstances. But the experience of the other cannot be reduced to a "constitution" in the Husserlian sense, to a play of intentionalities whose correlate is only ever an irreal noematic meaning. If it forms the fabric of our life and belongs to it, then the experience of the other must be a real experience. The other must "be within us."

And here's how. It is in the self-givenness of Life that each Self is given to itself; it is in its self-revelation that the Self is revealed to itself; it is in life then, in this knowing of life, that the Self knows what it is. But the other—the other Self—is in the same situation; it is in the self-revelation of life that it is revealed to itself; it is also in life prior to being in itself. Thus they both are in life, and they are aware of life before being or aware of themselves. And just as it is life that leads each Self to itself, a Self that is itself only in life, likewise this same life leads it to the other, to the other me [*l'autre moi*], that is itself within life only through this one and the same Life. In this way they are originarily one with the other, inasmuch as they are first both in the same life and thus in it, the one in the other, in a kind of reciprocal phenomenological interiority whose place is this "Before" that precedes them both and that remains, however, in them as long as they are living Selves.

Thus it is that every conceivable community comes into being and is shaped in its originary phenomenological possibility. Consequently it presents certain essential traits. The first concerns what this community has in common or, if one prefers, its content: namely, transcendental life. Hence we see that such a content is not originarily (and consequently not necessarily) a "rational" content. Reason, as it is usually understood, is not what gathers originarily: it isolates as well. The old adage is quite correct: the madman is the one who has lost everything except reason. Besides, it is not only on the individual level that reason can prove to be destructive. It suffices to consider what is happening today before our very eyes in order to gauge to what degree reason left to itself, to a pure objectivism, to the calculating abstraction of modern technology, can strike at the heart of what is ownmost to the human, to threaten our "humanity" and at the same time lead all of humanity to the verge of ruin. *The content of all community is in reality everything that belongs to life* and finds its possibility within it. Suffering, joy, desire, or love, even resentment or hatred, bear within themselves a gathering power infinitely greater than the one that is ascribed to "Reason," which has, properly speaking, no power to gather as long as we cannot deduce from it the existence of a single individual, and thus lacks what must be gathered together in a "community."

Because what is common to every community is life, the community presents this other essential trait of being a community of transcendental living Selves, to the degree that it is only in life that such Selves are possible. Reciprocally, life is not possible without them, without the primordial Self in which Life comes into itself and that contains the potential and indefinite multiplicity of all possible me's [*tous les moi possibles*].

But it is the third trait of life that must be recalled here: before defining the content of what is in common, Life in its originary Ipseity constitutes the transcendental possibility of being-in-common as such, the relation as such, "being-with" in its precedence.

Being located in life, it follows that *every community is essentially invisible*. It has of course, just as our own life, as our Self, as our flesh, its "appearing in the world," but here again this appearing is only a simple appearance cut from reality. Therefore, even more than our visible life, our visible Self, or our visible flesh, the visible community bears within it the possibility of the ruse and of the lie. Isn't it the place where indifference and all other unadmittable feelings are constantly masked by social rituals?

Invisible, foreign to the world and to its phenomenological categories, to space and to time, the community's reality opens a domain of paradoxical relationships about which Kierkegaard had a brilliant intuition. Therefore, a real relationship can be established between transcendental Selves that are never seen and belong to different eras. A person can see their life turned upside down by reading a book by an unknown author from a previous century. An individual can become the contemporary of an event that occurred two thousand years ago.

The concept most lacking in Western philosophy is indeed that of *immanence*. In classical thought one finds it, under a thematic form, only in Spinoza, which makes him an exceptional thinker. However, for Spinoza the concept of immanence still has only a speculative function. It is only in a phenomenology of life that immanence gains its revolutionary significance at the same time as the entirety of its power of intelligibility. On the one hand, by excluding the "outside-of-itself" from the phenomenality belonging to life, immanence leads to a definition of life as pure pathos—this transcendental Affectivity of which we are speaking and which is nothing other than the phenomenological reality of immanence, its pure phenomenological matter. On the other hand, immanence allows the generation in the absolute life of all the living to be grasped as an immanent relation itself. Thus arises an entirely new concept of the relation, now exempt from the reign of exteriority. The ipseity of the Self occurs within Life; it is within Life just as Life is within it, in what we are calling a reciprocal phenomenological interiority. Because the immanent relation of Life to the Self that it generates within itself extends to every living Self, it is the relation between Selves that is overturned. No longer being entrusted to the exteriority of the world where every relation is an external relation between external terms, but to life instead, it is from life that it now takes its possibility as well as its reality; it is in life that I am originarily with others; it is in life that they are originarily within me.

In this philosophically novel conception of intersubjectivity as a reciprocal interiority of living Selves in life, is not the phenomenology of life found to be quite isolated? However, philosophy is not condemned to refer only to texts belonging to a canonical corpus reputed to be philosophical and delimited once and for all. Essential intuitions are also found elsewhere: in poetry, literature, in texts labeled spiritual, religious, or sacred. In the initiatory texts of John, for example. Does his famous Prologue express anything other than this process of the self-generation of life as the generation in life of a living First Self in which life experiences and reveals itself to itself? Is not such a process, placed entirely under the sign of a radical immanence, reproduced in the generation of these multiple transcendental Selves that we are—a generation that is their transcendental birth in life, in such a way that it remains in them just as they remain in it? In such a way as well that this immanence of Life in each Self is not only the transcendental possibility of every conceivable Self, but identically that of their reciprocal phenomenological interiority as an immanent relation within life.

These claims are as astonishing, as philosophically innovative, as those found in the theses of the Prologue to the Gospel of John, deciphering the immanence of the relation of Life to its Word in the immanence of this same Life to all of the living. To Philip, Christ declared: "Do you not believe that I am in the Father and the Father is in me?" (John 14:10). "If you know me, you will know my Father also . . . you will know that I am in my Father, and you in me, and I in you" (John 14:7, 20).

"The others in me . . . ," "Those within me . . .": no less astonishing is the title of this international conference organized in Porto in 2001. Is this title intelligible in any other way than in a phenomenology of the radical immanence of Life and of the relation that is established within it, between it and all the living, so as to make possible the relation of the living among themselves?

More remarkable still, however, is the fact that the topic of this international conference in Porto has been chosen by an eminent association of doctors. It is said that medicine is not a science. This means that it is not only a science, that it is more than a science. Since Galileo and Descartes, the new science is the geometric-mathematical knowledge of the material universe, a science which has made dazzling progress in the domain of biology and consequently in that of medicine. However, something else is at work there, *the intersubjective relation outside of which no medicine is conceivable.* The medical gaze is a transcendental gaze that is irreducible to a simple objective knowing. The examination of an X-ray or any other objective data passes through this gaze in order to bring into view a suffering that is to be eradicated or made bearable. Thus, the one who bears it cannot be separated from either the diagnosis or from the treatment. Those within me is also true of the doctor's connection to her patients. The phenomenological life of individuals comprises the final subject matter of research, of theory and of therapy. Here, "interdisciplinarity" is no longer an agreed-upon term or a pious vow; it is the work and daily bread of those doctors and philosophers, doctor philosophers would be a better way to put it, who share the same purpose: to return to a sick life its power and joy of living.

Translated by Michael Tweed

Notes

This text is based on a lecture given in Porto (Portugal) in September 2001, during an international conference of psychiatry.

1. Heidegger, *Being and Time*, 51 [28].

2. The original German reads: "*Zeitlichkeit ist das usprüngliche 'Außer-sich' an und für sich selbst*" (*Being and Time*, 377 [329]).

3. Translator's note: Here it is worth nothing that in the "Four Seminars" Heidegger himself remarks that "*Il y a*" ("there is" or "there are") is an inadequate and misleading translation of the German expression "*Es gibt*" (literally "it

gives"). In this context, however, for the sake of consistency we have used "there is." Nevertheless, as Henry is discussing the "terrifying neutrality" of appearing, the reader might find it productive to ponder the alternative: "it gives."

4. Translator's note: For an explanation of Henry's use of the terms *pathos* and *pathétique*, see the "Translator's Introduction" to Michel Henry, *I Am the Truth*, trans. Susan Emanuel (Stanford, Calif.: Stanford University Press), ix. The important point is to avoid any misreading that might occur due to the meaning of "pathetic" as commonly used in English.

Part II

Subjectivity

5

The Critique of the Subject

The critique of the subject is regarded as philosophy's principal teaching of the second half of this century—and already, to a large extent, of the first half. To each of the different forms it has assumed, a precise historical expression can be assigned. Indeed, so widespread is it that one would have to draw up a list of almost all contemporary movements of thought in order to take stock of its numerous but convergent formulations. We will restrict ourselves here to quoting, on the one hand, its philosophical rootedness in Heidegger, and on the other its extra or para-philosophical origin in the human sciences, notably in Marxism and Freudianism, which were to be crowned by structuralism—to say nothing of linguistics.

As diverse as these movements may be in their explicit aims and their qualities—meaning the level of reflection at which they are situated—they have a common outcome, namely the critique of the subject, which is to say, in the end, the critique of man conceived as a specific and autonomous reality.

But it is this specificity and this autonomy which must be understood according to the meaning bestowed upon them in the philosophy of the subject. Man identified as the subject (let us use for the moment this passive phrasing which occludes precisely what has to be illuminated) is not only a very particular and superior reality, but also one homogeneous with others. He is granted an exorbitant privilege in that there is in the end no Being or being except in relation to him, for him, and by him, and this insofar as he constitutes the *a priori* condition of possibility for all experience and thus for all that is and can be, at least for us.

It is in as much as he is identified as this subject that man appears as a super-being to whom everything that is has entrusted its Being, a Being which the subject henceforth has at his disposal and which he can make use of not as he sees fit (in which case he might just as well not make use of it at all, or respect it, fear it, etc.), but rather as that which is in its principle subjugated to him by way of its ineluctable and insurmountable ontological condition, as an ob-ject whose Being is the Subject.

The reader will be spared further repetition of these famous descriptions, except for the inclusion of one remark. These descriptions are those of our world—of the ravaging of Earth by Technology. Technology consists in the unconditional subjugation of the Whole of being, become the Ob-ject, to man, become the Subject—the Ob-ject of the Subject, then, disposed before him and by him, at his disposal [*disponible*] therefore, having no other end than this being at the disposal of, subjected to tallage and corvée as the serf of this new Lord.

We will not ask here how an illusion can have such power. How can the illusion by virtue of which man takes himself for the Subject and Master of things determine these things globally and in their effective reality, how can it confer its being on everything that is? Other, more urgent questions require our attention.

The common trait of all of the critiques of the subject just mentioned lies not in attributing to the illusion of the Subject the extravagant capacity to change the face of the Earth (this completely illusory conception of the illusion is peculiar to Heidegger; the other critiques of the subject see in it nothing but an illusion, unaccompanied by any effects, or having purely illusory effects, "ideological" effects, as they put it); more seriously than this, it lies in not knowing anything about this subject which is to be cut into pieces, and, in the best of cases, in being totally mistaken about it. Two questions must therefore be asked here:

(1) What is the Being of this subject which has to be eliminated, "evacuated" from the problematic?
(2) Who, contesting at once the right and the existence of such a subject, the right of man to identify with it, goes about its elimination?

At least twice in the history of modern thought, the subject has been the theme of an explicit problematic. The two philosophers to be named at this point, Descartes and Kant, are precisely the two greatest, the two whose influence has been decisive, who have given a rigorous meaning to the concept of subject in such a way that any critique leveled against the subject which does not proceed by the light of the foundational analyses of the *Meditations* and the *Critique of Pure Reason* would be meaningless. For various reasons, one of which will be mentioned in a moment, we will begin with the second.

How can one not be struck by this extraordinary conceptual situation: it is precisely with Kant, who relates the Being of all beings to the Subject, that the Subject becomes the object of a radical dispute which denies it all possible Being. Or to put it another way: it is at the very moment when philosophy sees itself clearly as a philosophy of the subject that the foundation on which it explicitly and thematically bases itself, and which it systematically endeavors to elaborate, escapes it and, slipping from its grasp, tips over into the void of inanity.

THE CRITIQUE OF THE SUBJECT

One cannot forget in effect how the rich developments of the Analytic end up, like a torrent which suddenly dries up, lost in the desert of the Dialectic. Now, this peculiar turning of the positive into the negative happens when the Being of the subject itself comes into question, when it is a matter of knowing if such a subject exists and, if so, what it might be. The "Critique of the Paralogism of Rational Psychology" in fact radically critiques the Being of this subject in such a way that anything one might advance about this Being includes a paralogism, so that if, in spite of everything, it must be spoken about, one can say only that it is an "intellectual representation."

Which means that "I think" (since we are dealing here with the *cogito*) is equal to "I represent to myself that I think." Which means that the Being of the subject is to be classed as the object of a representation, an object which on the one hand presupposes this subject, and on the other never contains by itself, insofar as it is represented, the reality—just as to represent to oneself a thaler does not imply that one has one in one's pocket. Thus, the foundation of any conceivable Being is stricken with an essential ontological poverty which prevents us from attributing to Being itself any kind of Being. Like it or not, it is the philosophy of the subject itself which has raised the most serious objection to the subject, to the point of rendering its very existence problematic. Kant may not eliminate the subject from the problematic, like the braggarts of today, but he reduces it to "a simple proposition," allowing us at the very most, and without furnishing the slightest reason to do so, the right to pronounce it.

We must now turn our attention more closely to our two questions: what subject finds itself thrown out of existence, and by whom? The subject thrown out of existence is the subject of representation. These two terms, "subject" and "representation," are tautologous. "Subject of representation" does not denote something which would have, in addition, that faculty of representing to itself (whatever it might be). That the subject is not something, according to the critique of the paralogisms, that it is not a being among others, as privileged as it may be, means: it is nothing but representation itself, the pure fact of setting forth as the opening onto an Outside, an Outside which is the world as such. The subject is not the opposite of the object; it is the opposite of the being. It is that which makes of the being an ob-ject, something which is set-forth, re-presented. The subject is the being re-presented as such, the fact of being represented—not as a being but as a being in its condition as object, objectivity as such, its unfolding. The subjectivity of the subject in the philosophy of the subject is the objectivity of the object. The proof is that Kant's analysis of the structure of this subject is nothing other than the analysis of the structures of objectivity (space, time, causality, etc.).

Why then does the subject unfold the Outside of Objectivity, of representation, why does it lead the being into the state of an ob-ject, a being-represented? So that it shows itself, and is something rather than nothing, to make it into a phenomenon. Representation is the essence of phenomenality. What Kant calls: consciousness, the I think, experience, which is to say pure experience, the condition of all possible experience. For Kant therefore, I think = pure manifestation = pure consciousness = pure experience = representation. If it is experience which gives Being to all things, representation is the essence of Being.

The subject thrown from existence, from Being, is the essence of Being itself understood as the structure of representation. By whom is this subject thrown out of Being? By itself. This is what the whole of the *Critique of Pure Reason* demonstrates. It is insofar as the subject grows its essence, its Being, from the structure of representation and is identified with it that it is impossible to confer on it any kind of Being. In fact, the structure of representation is on the one hand intuition, on the other the concept, and according to the explicit statements of Kant, we have no intuition of the I think and no concept of it either, so that we cannot know anything about it. This means that it is not a phenomenon for us and cannot be one. The deconstruction of the subject by the philosophy of the subject is a self-deconstruction, a self-destruction. By applying its own presuppositions to the essence of Being, the philosophy of the subject no longer finds any subject, any Being.

The historical self-destruction of the philosophy of the subject has been set forth here, however briefly, only because it implies this decisive consequence: that the essence of the subject, which is to say of Being itself, cannot consist in representation, because representation does not rest upon itself and cannot found itself, because to be does not mean to be represented if we are dealing with a being which actually exists in all its concreteness, which truly is. What then does "being" mean? Is there an essence of the subject which does not succumb to its own presuppositions, which is not given over in its very principle to nothingness? Or, to put it another way, this time from an epistemological point of view: is there a philosophy of the subject capable of thinking a subject other than representation, one whose being therefore would not destroy itself?

The founder of the philosophy of the subject and thereby, it is said, of modern thought, is Descartes. Descartes's problematic of the subject is characterized by two decisive traits, the full significance of which we are now in a position to see. The first is that it is a determined effort to contest the Being of the subject, to unsettle it and even to deny it—an attempt which is unparalleled, unprecedented, and unrepeated. With the first two "Meditations" it is therefore the Being of the subject and hence

Being itself which is most properly in question. All interpretation which aims to reduce the full ontological significance of the Cartesian problematic, to liken the Being of this subject to a being, indeed to a super-being, is nonsensical. For Descartes does not first of all ask himself what sort of Being he is dealing with as regards the subject, the *cogito*, but, purely and simply, *if* it is, and then how it is: he questions the how of any possible Being in general and consequently its pure essence.

The second trait of the Cartesian problematic of the subject is that the foundation of the Being of the subject, that is to say the recognition of *that through which this Being is*, presupposes as an incontrovertible condition that representation be ruled out [*mise hors jeu*], which means in the first place ruling out everything that is represented or capable of being represented, and secondly ruling out the structure of representation itself. For I can only doubt universally everything which is represented or representable, the sensible world and the intelligible world, to the extent that representation in general is itself dubious. It is the domain of representation as such, it is the light in which I represent to myself everything which I so represent, the things of this world as well as eternal truths, that is fallacious if what I see as quite evident in it—that $2 + 3 = 5$ or that "if I think, then I must be," etc.—can and must be deemed false, as Descartes deemed it.

The Cartesian problematic of the subject appears to us then to be a reduction. It is a question of knowing what can subsist, that is to say, what can still be when representation has been completely blocked, when "being" is neither the whole nor the part of the represented or the representable, nor representation itself—when being is not through representation. This block placed on representation, we might say in passing, brings us back to the situation encountered in the analysis of the paralogism of psychology, meaning now Kant's paralogism and not the one attributed to Descartes. For if when we begin to ask questions about it—about the Being of the subject—representation hovers in the void, is only a pure form without content, a simple expression, not even a concept, according to Kant's own terms, this is precisely because it *is* not through representation, through itself, but only is on the basis of its anti-essence—of the anti-essence of representation which is the essence of the subject. Let us see, then, how in Descartes the anti-essence of representation is posited as being precisely the essence of the "subject."

Such a position is reached, in abrupt but indisputable fashion, in article 26 of the *Passions of the Soul*. Once again Descartes suddenly practices the radical *epoche* of the world. He imagines the situation of a sleeper lost in his dream. If he is dreaming, everything he represents to himself in his dream is illusory, *is* not. But if in this dream he experiences sadness, anguish, any sort of feeling, this feeling definitely *is*, even though it is still a dream, *even though the representation is false*. This feeling, therefore, is not through representation but independent of it. Which means: without being projected [*posé devant*], without being represented and—if the representation is false—*on condition of not being so*.

How then is it projected? It is precisely that it is not projected, if to project is to project as a representation projects, by a kind of action which inscribes itself within the dehiscence of a first Outside which also renders it possible. It is because feeling is not projected that Descartes calls it a passion, determining its Being at the outset as a submission which is extraneous to any action, but above all to any Outside. What is this submission which is no longer that of some other reality, of an exteriority, which is the submission of the self—*feeling*? How does feeling submit to its own Being in such a way as to be definitively and indisputably possible? *In its affectivity and by it.*

But if affectivity, the self's submission to itself, the self's immediate and undistanced experience of itself, defines the Being of feeling, in this case the Being of all Being which subsists, which still is after the reduction, when illusory representation has been eliminated, then this affectivity, this pathos, let us say, through which all Being is primordially and unconditionally, is equally the essence of the subject, its subjectivity and the essence of all possible Being. It is only when, as happens at one moment in Descartes, the philosophy of the subject returns to this original essence of subjectivity and Being that the "subject" can become the theme of a philosophical discussion. Is it necessary to emphasize here what we briefly evoked at the beginning of this study; namely that, across the various historical forms it has assumed for a century, the critique of the subject has been elaborated in almost complete ignorance of that about which it speaks or thinks it speaks?

The most striking misunderstanding is Heidegger's, who explicitly and repeatedly identifies the "I think" as an "I represent to myself." One might argue that any great thought has the right to interpret in its own way those which precede it, that this is indeed its contribution and that, as inappropriate as this may be for the Cartesian *cogito*, the critique of representation nonetheless has considerable value as a critique of representation in itself, that is, of that which dominates Kantianism and through it the whole of modern idealism. But our point is that the Being of the subject, and the Heideggerian problematic which will subsequently lead to all contemporary critiques of the subject and serve as their foundation (acknowledged or not), has nonetheless lost, as far as the Being of the subject is concerned, all possible meaning.

As concerns representation itself, however, one could equally well

THE CRITIQUE OF THE SUBJECT

question the pertinence of such a critique. Is it really the structure of representation which is put into question, truly attacked in this critique? Yes, in the sense that it contests the right of a subject which sets itself up as the Subject to reduce, by that act, all of being to the state of an ob-ject for it, cast before it, by it, then cast back to itself, placed at its disposal and exploitable to the point of being nothing other than the object of this exploitation, as occurs in modern technology.

But this op-posing casting forth of the being as the object of the Subject does not come about *ex nihilo*, it must be possible, it must *be*. What Being, by which we mean what sort of Being, gives it leave to come about, to project, op-pose, and thus represent to itself everything which it re-presents to itself? What Being if not the Heideggerian Being itself, the transcendence of *Being and Time*, the ek-static Dimensional of *The Letter on Humanism*, the *Ereignis* of the late philosophy? A Being whose Being, in any case, whose coming into Being, whose being brought into Being consists in the original unfolding of exteriority and is identical with it. And this is because to be means to appear, and appearing appears in and through unfolding, as the exteriorization of exteriority, the Openness of the Open, which is the light of the world and the world itself. Only representation fulfills itself within this opening and does so precisely as one of its modes of fulfillment; its light is the light of the world, its ob-ject *is* the Greek phenomenon, that which shines in this light and presents itself to us as this shining and in it alone. The essence of representation is the essence of Being as Heidegger understands it; the critique of the philosophy of the subject is here nothing more than a repetition of it.

One might object here that the Greek being *is* not in the representation or through it. But the Greek being is through the same Being as the one through which representation will be (and hence everything represented in it). The Greek man does not represent to himself an object [*Gegenstand*], he does not cast it before him as a possession of this Subject which he is not. The Greek belongs to the Whole of being and lets it come to him as that which advenes, as that which is "counter" [*Gegenüber*] to him. But in the *Gegenüber* there prevails the same *gegen* as the one on the basis of which representation establishes itself—the *gegen* which makes possible the *Gegenstand*.

All of Heidegger's philosophy acknowledges this ultimate essence of Being, and not surely its representation but its essence; it is, indeed, an explicit affirmation of it. The philosophy of the subject is the metaphysics of representation, which is itself inscribed in the history of Western metaphysics. But the history of metaphysics is the history of Being itself. It is the Being which is destined for us, here as the *physis* of the Greeks, there as the idea of Plato, or again as the *perceptio* of Descartes, the representation of Leibniz or of Kant, the will to power of Nietzsche or of modern technology. It is not that the philosophy of the subject misunderstands itself, it is rather that Being induces it into this misunderstanding. The Heideggerian critique of the subject, reduced to the subject of representation and hence simply to representation, not only misses the true Being of the subject inasmuch as it can only be thought against representation, against all Difference; it is further doubly absurd because it has nothing to oppose to the Being of the subject it contests if not the very Being of this subject, because if there is after all a misunderstanding about the true nature of this Being and therefore about Being in general, this misunderstanding is precisely the doing of Being itself—one of its "tricks"—which it delights in playing on us or which it plays on itself.

With Freud, the critique of the subject remains naive, but turns out to be more useful, capable of opening up new paths. In a sense it also consists in a simple repetition. The subject that Freud critiques is the subject of representation—what he calls "consciousness," and rightly so if the structure of representation is that of phenomenality, its essence, and if consciousness designates nothing other than this pure essence, not what is conscious but the fact of being conscious, the quality of being conscious or, to use Freud's terms, *Bewusstheit*. It is remarkable that in order to justify what will become the first given of all his analyses—"the fact of being conscious . . . is the point of departure for all our analyses"—Freud calls explicitly on the philosophical tradition, and on what this tradition understands by "consciousness": "there is no need to explain here what we are calling consciousness, which is the same as the consciousness of philosophers and of everyday usage." Something which is stated with equal clarity is that what tradition, in other words, modern philosophy, as well as more distant philosophies, understands by consciousness is, precisely, representation: "let us call 'conscious' the representation which is present to our consciousness and of which we are aware, and let this be the only meaning of the term 'conscious.'"[1]

Even the most cursory reading of this text from 1915 reveals that:

(1) It contains the foundation upon which the philosophy of the unconscious grounds itself. That there is an unconscious is indisputable because there is such a thing as the non-represented: there are memories of which I am not thinking right now. The unconsciousness is posited in reference to consciousness understood as representation. It is in reference to phenomenality, understood as the opening of an Outside, that nonphenomenality claims to substitute itself for phenomenality thus understood, in such a way as to define the law of Being. It is the subject consisting of the "I represent to myself" which is edged out of the problematic; in other words, it can no longer claim to reduce its whole being

THE CRITIQUE OF THE SUBJECT

to its phenomenality, its "consciousness," its "I represent to myself," precisely because in its Being there is a host of things which it is not representing to itself, all its childhood memories, etc.

We said that this subject is excluded from the problematic: this is imprecise. It is rather maintained by it; it is to the extent that I understand my Being as the "I represent to myself," and thus "I represent to myself what I am," that I must confess that to the contrary I do not represent to myself everything that I am, that my consciousness is not coextensive with my being, that there is an unconscious part of me, that I am not master of my own house. The philosophy of the unconscious is here a sequel to the metaphysics of representation, it belongs to it. This will become clearer when we make our second point:

(2) Whatever is not conscious, in that it is not represented, is capable of becoming conscious, in that it is not represented, is capable of becoming conscious, in that it is representable—as for example with childhood memories. The unconscious still designates only the virtuality of what, in its actuality, could become conscious, that is, representation. The unconscious is not the opposite of representation; it rather names it as the law of everything that is, as its indefeasible phenomenality. It simply happens that under this law, in such a conception of the phenomenality of the subject, almost everything which has escaped the subject, which has escaped this particular phenomenality, is "unconscious."

The concept of psychoanalytic therapy is based on this metaphysics of representation; it is a question of *taking cognizance* [*prendre conscience*], of bringing to the actuality of representation something nonconscious which is secretly homogeneous with it and which can, for this reason, change into it—an unconscious constituted by "unconscious representations," in other words, which are not yet represented and which, ontologically if not existentially, are only asking to be. Classical thought calls out for the coming of psychoanalysis.

It is another subject which arises with the idea that unrepresented is also unrepresentable, that the original Being of this subject is no longer representation but its anti-essence. Freud in his turn runs up against such a subject, half perceived by Descartes, when he finds himself in the presence of an unconscious which is no longer provisional, no longer one phase in the history of representation, capable of completing itself in itself, in the actualization of its full essence. *The history of our representations refers back to a force which allows them precisely to actualize themselves or which forbids them from doing so. It is only this force itself which is irreducible to any representation.* It collapses in on itself in an immediation which is so radical and, in this immediation, it is submerged into itself in such a way that there is no room in it for any Difference, no distantiation thanks to which it would be possible for it to perceive itself, to represent itself—*to be conscious* in the mode of representation.

It is at this point, at this decisive difference with the metaphysics of representation, at the very moment when he is divulging the most original dimension of Being—the unrepresented and unrepresentable force which secretly directs all representation—that Freud succumbs once again to the presuppositions of this metaphysics. Because manifestation, pure experience, pure consciousness continue to be identified with representation and defined by it, hence that which escapes representation escapes all possible consciousness, is in itself unconscious.

Thus the subject is led back to its true Being, to the Being which signifies appearing and which exhausts itself in it—for, as Nietzsche states, "what can I say about any Being which does not come down to listing the attributes of its appearance"[2]—only to find itself forthwith removed from its own Being and from that which in general could confer a meaning on its concept. For the subject is nothing other than this: that which in making appearance appear, in the same gesture, makes be everything that is.

The intent of the critique of the critique of the subject is not to promote its return, like the return of a past reality which, tired of being neglected, would aspire to play once again a role on the philosophical stage. The critique has shown us that the Being of the subject has never been recognized; it is not its return that is announced in this critique, but its first coming.

One question cannot now be avoided: with Descartes, had not the Being of the subject been perceived, half perceived as we have said, in its peculiarity, as an antiessence of representation? How can all of philosophy after Descartes (or almost all) have been—as was Heidegger in the final analysis—so completely mistaken about the *cogito*? Or did this mistake arise in Descartes himself, by a kind of unlucky chance, or else for perhaps more essential reasons?

Philosophy is an approach to reality which habitually takes itself for reality itself, confusing the processes of thought with those of reality. In what we call "the *cogito*," we must distinguish the processes of thought which are realized in the first two "Meditations" in the form of a series of implications, of propositions, in the form of a text leading to the evident fact [*evidence*] that if I think then I must be. The *cogito* then passes for an evident fact, that is, for the completed form of representation. I think means I think that, I represent to myself that I think, that I represent to myself, etc.

As an evident fact the *cogito* designates the first truth and at the same time the prototype for all truth. When Descartes himself, before the end of the second "Meditation" and then explicitly in what follows it, enters into this kind of problematic which aims to found knowledge [*connaissance*] and, through it, all knowledge [*science*], without marking the rupture with what has gone before, he is not a little responsible for all the blunders which ensue. All the same, there is something vaguely uneasy in this transcendental theory of knowledge which will rule over modern thought; how can the *cogito*, which results from the radical critique of all evidentiality, be an evident fact itself, and moreover "certain," in such a way that everything rests upon it? It remains only to consider the *cogito* as a text, to submit it to a logical or historical analysis destined to uncover its faults or unconscious presuppositions, and to assess its difficulties.

Considered as designating reality itself and not its approach or knowledge, the *cogito* has nothing to do with thought processes or with thought itself, and even less with the text of the *Meditations. Cogito* means everything, except "I think." *Cogito* designates that which appears to itself immediately in everything that appears, or rather in pure appearing (pure appearing that Descartes calls thought). *Subjectivity* is the pathetic immediation of appearing as auto-appearing, such that, without this pathetic grasping of appearing in its original appearing to itself, no appearing—notably the aesthetic appearing of the world—would ever appear. Thus, for example, I can only see (whatever) in that I re-present it to myself on the basis of the ek-stasis of the World. But this ecstatic opening itself would not appear if it did not auto-affect in the very movement of its ecstasy. This auto-affection of ek-stasis is fundamentally different from its affection by the world: the latter consists in the Difference which the former excludes. "*Sentimus non videre*," says Descartes against hyperbolic doubt. But this can only be understood, sight being notoriously doubtful, if there is, in the originary feeling through which sight senses itself seeing and experiences itself, no seeing. Sight is—appears—only under the condition of a non-seeing.

It is in the face of the positive phenomenality of this non-seeing that Descartes draws back. Whereas everywhere, in passion, in sensation, in sight itself, affectivity is named as immediation, as the original essence of subjectivity, Descartes interprets it to the contrary as a disturbance brought into subjectivity by some foreign agent. Why? Because thought is light, the light of representation, the light of the world, the light in which things and their geometric shapes shine—Greek light. It is at its beginning, in its birth, that the aborted philosophy of the subject carries inscribed in it the defect that all critiques of the subject were to develop and lead to its extreme point: absolute objectivism, whether it be the naive objectivism of the science, notably the human sciences, or the ek-stasis of Being which, unbeknownst to them, serves as their foundation.

Such in any case is the teaching given to us in the critique of the subject, in the simple repetition of what it critiques. As soon as this repetition is perceived and understood, the philosophy of the subject becomes possible. The philosophy of the subject need not blush at its past, it need even less turn to it in nostalgia: it has no past. It draws its work and its tasks from itself; they remain before it.

Translated by Peter T. Connor

Notes

This article was originally published in *Topoi* 7, no. 2 (1988): 147–53. It is republished here with permission from Springer.

    1. Respectively, these are: Sigmund Freud, *The Unconscious*, in *The Standard Edition of the Complete Psychological Works of Sigmund Freud* (London: Hogarth, 1953–74), vol. 14, 172; *An Outline of Psychoanalysis*, in *The Standard Edition*, vol. 23, 159; "A Note on the Unconscious in Psycho-Analysis," in *The Standard Edition*, vol. 12, 260.

    2. Friedrich Nietzsche, *The Gay Science*, trans. Walter Kaufmann (New York: Vintage, 1974), 116 (trans. modified).

6

Philosophy and Subjectivity

By "subjectivity" we mean that which experiences itself. Not something that would have this property of experiencing itself, moreover, but the very fact of experiencing oneself considered in itself and as such. To experience oneself means to appear to oneself, in such a way that this appearing would have the meaning of an experience [*épreuve*], and would be one; and also in such a way that, since what appears is nothing other, qua subjectivity, than appearing itself; it is always and only as an appearing to itself of appearing that subjectivity is built up internally and unfolds its essence.

Constantly I experience the world, I experience the floor when my foot steps on it. But the floor does not experience itself; my foot is nothing for it, and thus is nothing. It is only in me and for me that the world appears and is given to me. Subjectivity is that which gives me the world at every moment, and if we understand by "world" the whole of what is, then subjectivity is the foundation of all things, the absolute to which they all refer, and without which they would not be.

Insofar as subjectivity experiences the world, or rather *is* this experience, it is not only the pure and simple experience of itself, the mute auto-affection, in which, for it, there is nothing other than itself; the world is also there for it. Without doubt we do not experience the world except on the basis in us of this first self-experience [*épreuve de soi*], which is absolute subjectivity. Nevertheless, the question arises of knowing how and why there is a twofold experience, the one which subjectivity has of the world, and on the other hand, the one it has of itself—two affections, so to speak—and of understanding the relation that unites them. Only radically elucidating the concept of affection can enlighten us. It is a question of knowing in each case what it means "to experience" and "to be affected by"; and to the extent that this experience or affection consists in the appearing itself, it is the nature of the latter that should be questioned.

Thus the task of phenomenology is proposed. Its object is not the collection of phenomena that concern the sciences, but what allows them in each case to be so: the mode of their givenness, subjectivity. With phenomenology, philosophy attains its proper object: it is the philosophy of subjectivity, and is distinguished in this way from all other sciences, notably from psychology—which also thinks it speaks of subjectivity, but misses it in principle, because it treats it as something which is (and which has, consequently, relations with the rest of being, with the organism, with the exterior world, the social milieu, etc.), rather than as the condition of all possible being.

The interpretation of the foundation of all things [τό ὑποχείμενον] as subjectivity happens for the first time in Descartes, whose *cogito* inaugurates modern philosophy. Already in antiquity, the Skeptics, by denouncing the illusion of a world in itself, and as such "objective" and "true," and by reducing it to its modes of subjective and moving givens, to sensations that are essentially relative, gestured in the direction of subjectivity as towards this final and obscure authority in which the being of things is resolved. In many ways, it is the effort to defeat skepticism that gave ancient thought its impetus to confer an apodictic foundation on knowledge and truth, even if this was still not understood in its final self-justification, qua subjectivity.

In Descartes himself, the extraordinary discovery of subjectivity in the first two "Meditations" does not reach its ultimate consequences. By making subjectivity the soul, that is to say, a reality distinct from the body's but finally juxtaposed to it, Descartes no longer regards it exclusively as givenness itself, as the source of all reality, so he can reduce subjectivity to a fragment of it. To the extent that he preserves its function as giving—qua *cogito* for all the *cogitata*—he nevertheless does not elaborate it systematically in his haste to get to the scientific knowledge of the world, which is all that really matters for him. This is how it has been possible to recognize subjectivity in its proper transcendental meaning without this giving rise to a fully developed thematic that is aware of itself and its stakes.

On the contrary, such a theme defines the phenomenological project in its historical point of departure in Husserl. It is carried out in the phenomenological reduction, which aims precisely to produce subjectivity as a theme that is open to be investigated exhaustively. This reduction, once introduced, takes on a twofold movement in Husserl's *Krisis*, which we can regard as his "final testament." First it is the *epoché* of the world of Galilean science, which Descartes had found in front of him, and whose development would overturn the mode of thought and the conceptions of European humanity, making it what it is. According to these conceptions, it is possible to display, despite the fact that its appearances and subjective apprehensions are relative and varied, a true being of the world, as it is in itself—thus beyond and independently of everything subjective. And this can happen to the extent that, in the knowledge of the world, one sets aside sensible qualities, and in a general way everything related to subjectivity, in order to attain as real being only the abstract forms of the spatiotemporal universe, the geometrical determination of which from then on constitutes a univocal knowledge. Thus from the disqualification of the sensible a "new nature" that is also "supra-subjective" arises, of which the intuitive given of the entire world is only a subjective presentation and which can be grasped thanks to mathematical idealities which count as limit forms of nature itself. "In his view of the world from the perspective of geometry, the perspective of what appears to the senses and is mathematizable, Galileo *abstracts* from subjects as persons leading a personal life; he abstracts from all that is in any way spiritual, from all cultural properties which are attached to things in human praxis."[1] The spiritual world, which is an object of the human sciences and obtained by abstraction from Galilean nature, is in no way symmetrical to it. Far from constituting a similarly closed, sufficient, autonomous universe, it is on the contrary, as human or animal spirituality, founded on nature, indeed in corporeality, and explicable and knowable through it. In all cases subjectivity is indeed only apparent and must be reduced, and science is this reduction.

Husserl's reversal of these theses, which support the scientistic and positivistic ideology of our epoch, is one of the landmark studies of philosophical thought. The scientific world of mathematical idealities cannot account for the subjective and relative world where the interests and objectives of everyday life develop, because that is what it is based upon. It is an idealization of this sensible and practical world and thus presupposes it as the ground on which it is constructed and to which it inevitably refers. On the one hand, it is only with respect to this life-world that scientific idealities have meaning. As idealities, on the other hand, they presuppose the subjective operation that produces them and in which idealization as such properly consists. Instead of reducing subjectivity to the status of a mere appearance, subjectivity is for the scientific world the principle that continually engenders it as the permanent condition of its own possibility. In the end, the nature on which every human or animal spirituality is built, *is precisely not the world of science and its abstract idealities*, but of life—the world that can constantly be intuited and experienced in the sensible modes of its subjective givenness. Galileo's illusion was precisely to have taken the mathematical world that was supposed to provide a univocal knowledge of the real world for this real world itself—for this world that can only be experienced and intuited within subjectivity.

Thus subjectivity does not only produce the idealities of the mathematical world of science, which inevitably refers to the life-world; *subjectivity first produces this life-world itself, since it is nothing other than the set of procedures and modalities whereby it offers itself to us, or even the fundamental methodology by virtue of which it exists.* Always and constantly we are thrown into a world that is given in advance and encloses within itself the totality of what is and can be for us, which is the *universum* of all beings, the terrain of all our actions and their ends. Every possible object, every preoccupation, is situated within the horizon of this world, which is in turn only this horizon. But all these ὄντα and this world itself are never there in a sort of immediacy and in some way by themselves, as the substrate of their qualities: they are so, precisely, only in the changing modes of their subjective appearance, in the "how" of these modes. The immediate is in truth the immediate of this givenness and actually overlaps with it.

The fact that we do not pay attention to these modes of givenness of things, and that we for the most part do not suspect them at all, changes nothing about their tireless operation in which this givenness is accomplished according to synthetically connected modalities. For an act of givenness is never isolated, and just as the perception of the face of a cube or of a house implies all the past or future perceptions of the other faces (of the internal and external horizons of objects, of memories and expectations, etc.), each actual operation that validates the world thus presupposes the infinite horizon of implicit validations that function together in the flux of absolute subjectivity—the totality of previous and background acquisitions of experience constituting, according to the play of these indefinite intentional references, the inseparable context of a living horizon. Positing, beyond the life-world that is always given in advance in its subjective fluctuations, a univocal scientific world, is only a subjective development of a higher degree, and it rests upon and presupposes all those that precede it.

We have suggested that the set of subjective performances, according to which the life-world is unceasingly produced for us as a unitary and universal value through its changing apparitions and subjective aims, remains most often hidden. And this is because, in conformity with its spontaneous attitude (whether it be theoretical or practical), natural life goes on in front of beings and the ends they constitute in its eyes, in such a way that it gets lost in them in a kind of ecstasy, of "bewilderment," Husserl says; and thus, lost and occupied with what alone has value in its eyes, it forgets itself. The naive conception of a world existing in itself, a conception that is reproduced in science, comes from the natural attitude in which life is constantly a life in the world and for the world, a life for which alone this world exists.

It is for life, however, that this world exists as its only preoccupation. For life: in all the subjective performances through which it never stops giving meaning and being to it. Except that in constituting all possible meaning and every type of being, subjectivity, which actually is this constitution, does not know it. The first *epoché* leads us from the scientific world back to the life-world that supports it inescapably. This life-world comes from a universality of interconnected subjective operations of which is it only the correlate. But this universal constituting life cannot be encountered or recognized in the natural attitude of life lost in the world. In order to discover it, a second *epoché* is needed, which, abstracting from our immediate living in the life-world, or if one prefers, our belief in this world, will take this "living-in" itself as a theme. In this way, a conversion of the gaze comes about, going from the life-world to its pre-given perceived for itself, that is to say, from the being to its givenness. This thematic displacement, which carries out a questioning backward from the real (and no longer scientific) world to the transcendental subjectivity that constitutes it, is the phenomenological and transcendental reduction, strictly speaking.

In the history of humanity, this signifies a total upheaval: it uncovers an entirely new dimension of being, a set of phenomena unnoticed until then and whose import is nevertheless decisive. These "purely subjective phenomena" are not juxtaposed to others, to those that make up the world of everyday or scientific experience; they found them, and are in these phenomena that are naively taken as such, precisely what makes them in every case phenomena, namely their very phenomenality. That this absolutely unique and original sphere could remain unknown for millennia is a surprising fact, as is the transcendental phenomenological reduction in turn—and phenomenology itself, putting a sudden end to this immemorial night in order to cast in full light, before our amazed eyes, the hidden depths of being.

On what condition? The *epoché* of the world must here be clearly grasped as that which allows the unveiling of subjectivity in its transcendental meaning as being the *Urregion* where all others have the foundation of their being and their meaning. The first *epoché* indeed takes place on the terrain of the world. In the natural attitude, I perceive the house and am inattentive to my perception of the house. I am always conscious of the world and never conscious of my consciousness of the world. But there is a reflection that is also natural, and to question consciousness itself in return, to take it in a thematic aim, is still to treat it as something that exists. So goes the habitual perception of humanity, even if it is understood in its spirituality: it is only the self-objectification of transcendental subjectivity and its decline to the status of a being. Only putting out of play of the world and everything that is, by snatching subjectivity from the condition of being and making its objectification impossible, preserves it properly as the ultimate constituting, the "absolute ego as the ultimately unique center of function in all constitution."[2]

The discovery of subjectivity thus occurs in a transcendental (and no longer natural) reflection, which frees my constituting and operative life as such, and it does so by installing me above this life that I dominate entirely. The category, "above which," intervenes in all of Husserl's descriptions and has a twofold role. It indicates on the one hand that the phenomenologist (transcendental reflection) has been able to put the belief in the world out of play, that he no longer lives in living immediately in the life-world. This ascending above lived experience, if it alters the latter, nevertheless shows it in its truth, namely in its functioning, as giving to the world the meaning of its being. Thus, the phenomenologist who no longer shares the belief in the world perceives it as such, as subjectivity that gives meaning. Not only does the phenomenologist perceive the subjectivity that functions in the final instance, but he also perceives in it the world that subjectivity constitutes, a world that he holds under the gaze at the same time as subjectivity, as the *cogitatum* of its *cogitatio*. By putting the world out of play the reduction does not lose it; it loses nothing, and even rather opens us to this world, no longer considered in its factical and naive existence, but according to its transcendental genesis, as a passive and active genesis.

These major themes of Husserlian phenomenology nevertheless put before us a paradox that is now important to assess: the subjectivity that constitutes original appearing inasmuch as it brings itself about in appearing—and thus as the source of all possible appearing—does not appear, and never itself reaches the condition of phenomenality. In order to do so, it needs something else, the intervention of another principle and its operation in a specific method, namely, the method of the phenomenological reduction. But what principle other than subjectivity comes into play here in a method that would be capable of uncovering it and making it manifest? Who performs the phenomenological reduction—we mean: Who looks into it and sees what it sees? Who, if not subjectivity itself? But if subjectivity, as living immediately in the life-world, is unaware of itself, if it does not experience itself, if it does not always already carry itself into phenomenality, then how can it do so later? In transcendental reflection, it will be said, to which the reduction precisely leads. But transcendental reflection is also a modality of the immediate life of absolute subjectivity, and as such it must bear in itself the same powerlessness that living immediately in the world does: thus if it is not always already carried into itself, namely into phenomenality, and by itself, by its own essence, how then could it carry out this task after the fact?

In fact, when reflection, which is subjective, intervenes, it does not simply repeat subjectivity's powerlessness in natural living, it redoubles it. It is not just in its immediate subjectivity and as every modality of subjectivity in general—as natural living in the life-world—that reflection remains blind, not brought of itself and by itself into phenomenality; what reflection is supposed to bring into phenomenality in front of it, in front of its gaze, is not subjectivity either and could not be, if it is true that in front of us, in the light of ek-stasis, there is only ever the world, and nothing but the world. Unaware of the subjectivity within itself, and as what it is, reflection manifests only this exteriority of a world. The pretension to entrust to the phenomenological reduction the discovery of subjectivity does not only posit, in an absurd way, that subjectivity is not, as such, its own discovery, namely its own immediate, internal promotion into the dimension of phenomenality that it defines. The supposed self-discovery of subjectivity in the phenomenological reduction is doubly impossible: first, if it repeats in reflection the inability of subjectivity to reveal itself in itself; and second, if it believes it finds this subjectivity in front of itself in a world, where it never is.

Let us begin with the second point. Subjectivity's powerlessness to attain itself in front of itself is not easy to recognize in Husserl's phenomenology. Its explicit presupposition, which founds it as a philosophy of subjectivity, is rather the inverse possibility, the possibility that subjectivity can grasp itself in its own being, in the perfect intuition of evidence. Let it suffice for us here to cite the following categorical claim: "The kind of being belonging to lived experiences is such that a seeing regard of perception can be directed quite immediately to any actual lived experience as an originary living present."[3]

We know that Husserl considered philosophy as the true science that reaches a perfect comprehension of itself in its final self-justification. This implies, as an ultimate explanatory principle, that it possesses a set of absolutely evident givens. Thus the necessity of a problematic of evidence, which defines, on the one hand, adequate evidence (that of a consciousness whose signifying intentions find their intuitive fulfillment), and on the other hand, apodictic evidence (whose content can be so only for what it gives itself, namely indubitability). So it is a question of knowing if any evidence of this latter sort exists anywhere. The questioning back from the world to subjectivity, is not only motivated by the fact that the latter constitutes the former and founds it; it results, at a deeper level, from what subjectivity provides for the requirement of apodicticity, the exclusive site where it is realized. While the experience of the world proves inadequate in principle—as it is only ever an induction, since each perception of the face of an object always refers to horizons of potential perceptions of it, and thus the possibility remains open that the subsequent course of experience might belie the present intuitions, that it might fall into dissonance, and the world into an always thinkable non-being—this is no longer the case for the immanent perception of the lived experience [*vécu*] itself. When my reflection is applied to my lived experience in order to grasp it, I have grasped an absolute in itself, whose existence cannot be denied in principle. "As soon as I look at the flowing life in its actual present and, while doing so, apprehend myself as the pure subject of this life . . . I say unqualifiedly and necessarily that I am, this life is, I am living: *cogito*. . . . in order for me to say necessarily and without restriction, I am, this life is, I live: *cogito*."[4]

With the gaze upon this life thus grasped in its indubitable existence, the reduction has delivered internal transcendental experience to us. Yet this experience, despite its apodictic character, is going to be the object of a critique so serious that it will call into question (1) the possibility for the reflective gaze, for any kind of gaze, to reach absolute subjectivity *in its very reality*; and (2) the dissociation Husserl makes between what he calls transcendent experience and immanent experience, namely of the world, on the one hand, and of subjectivity, on the other. So much so that the privilege of the latter, its ambition to constitute a sphere of absolute and indubitable existence, is seriously threatened.

The critique of transcendental experience unfolds in the *Cartesian Meditations* as a will to plumb "the range of apodictic evidence," and in §20 it arrives at the surprising declaration that "the possibility of a phenomenology of pure consciousness seems somewhat doubtful *a priori*."[5] The reason for this is that subjective phenomena present themselves to us as a "Heraclitean flux," where there are no "final elements," such that it would be vain to try to grasp them in fixed concepts, as the natural sciences do for their own objects. A possibility of overcoming the evanescence of the subjective modes according to which objects are given can nevertheless be found in the fact that "no matter how fluid these [modes] may be, and no matter how inapprehensible as having ultimate elements, still they are by no means variable without restriction. They are always restricted to a set of *structural types*, which is 'invariable,' inviolably the same: as long as it is an issue of a consciousness of a determined reality."[6] Thus, in phenomenological inquiry, one can see a significant sliding from the reality of concrete modes of subjectivity to the types that they obey, even at the core of their ungraspable becoming and of their disappearance into the depths of transcendental life. Eideticism comes to relay a mode of the given that claimed to exhibit the very thing in its effective reality and as an absolute, but proves incapable of doing so in principle.

Yet such a sliding is not occasional; we find it reproduced in a striking form in the *Krisis*. Speaking of "establishing *individual* transcendental correlations, as they factually occur and disappear," §52 affirms that

> not even the single philosopher by himself, within the *epoché*, can hold fast to anything in this elusively flowing life, repeat it with always the same content, and become so certain of its this-ness and its being-such that he could describe it, document it, so to speak (even for his own person alone), in definitive statements). But the full concrete facticity of universal transcendental subjectivity can nevertheless be scientifically grasped in another good sense, precisely because, truly through an eidetic method, the great task can and must be undertaken of investigating the essential form of the transcendental accomplishments in all their types of individual and intersubjective accomplishments, that is, the total essential form of transcendentally accomplishing subjectivity . . . The *factum* is determinable here only as *factum* of its own essence and only through its essence . . .[7]

This inflection of the problematic in the direction of the realm of pure and ideal possibilities is characteristic of Husserl's phenomenology, and it allows him to maintain and even to extend to the infinite the empire of apodicticity and *a priori* knowledge, even when reality can no longer be grasped in itself, but only starting from its essence and as a possible exemplification of it. But a possibility deciphered concerning an essence is not a reality, it is precisely only a possibility, by itself irreal, a possibility as ideal as the essence that governs it. So what is then questioned is nothing less than the claim that eidetic evidence delivers us "the full, concrete factuality of transcendental subjectivity," in person, which is also to say, in the unsurpassable singularity and individuality of each of its actualizations. However, to the extent that this singularity and this individuality are inherent in each of its modalities and belong to it in principle, it is indeed the full reality of this subjectivity that escapes from *a mode of givenness which is no longer the one it brings about in itself*—as a mode of original givenness identical to its own reality. Thus we see the phenomenological reduction carried out in Husserl as an eidetic reduction, given as different but inexorably connected to it. This eidetic reduction makes phenomenology the *a priori* science of the pure possibilities of absolute subjectivity, but it is the real essence of this that this eideticism misses.

That the thematic grasp of subjectivity allows precisely its reality to escape, and is only ever able to offer an irreal representation of it in the form of its ideal essence, is a situation that should make one think. It suggests that the mode according to which subjectivity is revealed originally to itself—namely, its very subjectivity—is precisely not the one in which the thematic grasp of it consists and that the reduction attempts—or any mode of grasping of this kind, in fact, whether founded in intuition or evidence, which ultimately means in intentionality. With evidence and eideticism called into question, the main presupposition of Husserl's phenomenology has gone adrift, and with it the claim to circumscribe subjectivity's original mode of givenness and to recognize it in its originality. We are thus led to our second point, to the paradoxical and ruinous reduction of transcendental experience, as an experience allegedly immanent and indubitable, to an intentional and essentially transcendent experience, subject to the vicissitudes of every experience of this kind. Such a reduction involves nothing less than the confusion of the experience of subjectivity with that of the world.

Before fleeing into eideticism and camouflaging its failure there, the critique of transcendental experience had for a moment aimed at the singular and concrete reality of subjectivity and did so in the following way. In the transcendental experience to which the reduction leads, "the ego attains itself in an original way," in such a way, however, that this achievement concerns only a "kernel" of life that is properly living, beyond which an indeterminate and obscure horizon extends to which my past belongs as well as the totality of my faculties and habits. At the outset a disquieting analogy is established between this transcendental experience and that of the world. Even if only the former lays claim to apodicticity, do they not both alike consist in a punctual evidence, in a standing-there-in-front-under-a-gaze, in such a way that evidence is precisely this "standing-there-in-front" as such, in its full phenomenological actuality, and in such a way that this ecstatic presence is gnawed away by the horizon of intentionalities that go unfulfilled—a horizon that confers on Husserlian experience its proper and absolutely general style under whose jurisdiction both transcendental and external experience falls? External perception (which, indeed, is not apodictic) is indeed an experience of the object itself—the object is indeed there in front of me—but in this "standing there in front, in person" [*in diesem Selbst da stehen*], the object possesses, for the thinking subject, an open and infinite set of indeterminate possibilities that are not themselves actually perceived. "*In an entirely analogous way*, the apodictic certainty characterizing transcendental experience of my transcendental 'I am' implies the indeterminate generality of the latter as having an open horizon."[8]

An open horizon of possibilities of experience not yet fulfilled means, in a general way, inadequation, which will be removed only with the intuitive fulfillment of these possibilities. Yet the fulfillment is only ever partial, which is to say that it never takes place—each fulfilled intentionality raises the horizon of all those that are not, each intuitive fragment surrounded by a wake of non-being in which everything is engulfed and with respect to which this morsel of presence, reduced to the actuality of a point-like evidence, and finally to the limit of an abstract present, cannot help but appear paltry. In such a situation, it becomes true to say, according to a too-seldom contemplated phrase of Husserl, "the *cogitatum* as *cogitatum* never presents itself as definitively given," unless "it is clarified to the extent that the horizon, and new horizons . . . which are unceasingly uncovered, become explicit"[9]—which also means that it enters into presence only in order to withdraw from it immediately, in favor of another content that is equally ephemeral—and this not only makes null and void the interpretation of Husserl's phenomenology as a "metaphysics of presence," where everything lapses into a plenary apparition without reserve or retreat. When such a situation characterizes not only the experience of the world but also transcendental experience, it risks bringing the same discredit upon the latter as upon the former, reducing it to a "Heraclitean flux" from which one hardly escapes except by demonstrating the structural types of its modes of flowing, that is, its ideal essence. Thus the law of fulfillment, as an always partial and provisional fulfillment, does not only strike a blow against the experience of the world. It is not just the world that is marked by an insurmountable contingency; transcendental experience obeys the same condition. The agreement that from a theoretical point of view is still problematic on the plane of inductive experience of the world is no less so, in the final account, in the sphere of transcendental life, and at the limit one can conceive, as Hume does, that it too sinks into incoherence and chaos.

The homogeneity between transcendental and worldly experience appears when the reduction is finished. Here the descriptions that transcendental phenomenology supplies are pursued in a twofold direction: first, they are noematic, insofar as their theme is the determinations that pertain to the intentional object; they are also noetic, insofar as they are considered as modalities of the *cogito* itself (perception, retention, memory, etc.), modalities that make the object what it is for us. But how can one not see that in this transcendental experience the noetic aim of the *cogitationes* and their grasp by the phenomenologist is homogenous to the relation through which these *cogitationes* refer to the *cogitatum*? That is why noetic experience is analogous to noematic experience and simply repeats its structure—because the noesis is itself the noema of this experience. Thus, in carrying out the phenomenological reduction in all its rigor, we preserve under the title "noetic" the free and unlimited field of the pure life of consciousness, and on the side of its noematic correlate, "the world-phenomenon, *qua* its intentional object."[10]

Transcendental experience is not only homogenous with the experience of the world; it is ultimately identical with it and properly founds it. We will perceive this more clearly if we probe this transcendental experience in its ultimate possibility. For reflection in Husserl is neither first nor self-sufficient; and it is not what succeeds in grasping transcendental life. Or rather, it is capable of doing so only because *this life is already there before the reflective gaze*, ready to offer itself to it. The being-already-there of transcendental life is the auto-temporalization by virtue of which each phase of this life slides into an immediate past that retains it, and this makes it possible for the attention to return to it, that is, life's possible reflection upon itself. Temporalization is the very running off, the sliding into the just now past, the first ecstatic dehiscence, the unfolding of the interval, and the opening of an Outside where something can become visible, offering itself to the gaze, which then turns itself toward what thus shows itself to it and takes this in view. The auto-temporalization of transcendental life is thus the emergence of the world, this world in its nascent state, and it exhausts itself therein.

How does such a world differ from the one the reduction has abandoned? By the fact that it is made up of the very modalities of absolute subjectivity, specifically the impressions and intentionalities that compose it. The transcendental reduction is what separates these two worlds, as its first formulation in Husserl's admirable lectures of 1905 shows. It consists, then, in putting out of play all of the transcendent apperceptions that posit, beyond subjective impressions—sonorous impressions that are actually heard, for example—a world of objects whose claim to existence always surpasses what really manifests itself (thus the existence of the object is posited as still lasting, even while the sensation that represents it is interrupted). The *epoché* of the world of transcendent objects allows only the immanent lived experiences of subjectivity to subsist, but, in their auto-temporalization, each of these lived experiences is already thrown into the ek-stasis of foreground of light: it appears as coming to us, present, just now past, and more and more past, in such a way that these modes of appearing—which together form "internal time-consciousness" and whose structure is also that of intentionality—only ever give us an object.

Here a singular situation is created that Husserl recognizes and assumes. The lived experiences of absolute subjectivity are the modes according to which the world's beings and the world itself are given. In the auto-temporalization of absolute subjectivity these given modes of objects give themselves in turn; the modes of their givenness are modes of internal time-consciousness, namely, the totality of protentional, retentional, and perceptive intentionalities that constitute the immanent duration in which all lived experiences take place—the lived experiences that constitute the world, the lived experiences that constitute time, and both self-constituted in this duration *as in a first dimension of transcendence, in this first world which is immanent duration itself.*

§18 of the *Cartesian Meditations* declares explicitly that the evident and punctual grasp of a lived experience in attention and reflection presupposes the opening of a horizon within which alone this lived experience can be perceived, and that this horizon is the horizon of immanent time objectified in the auto-temporalization of absolute subjectivity. If a world's first rising as a horizon of immanent time is not only homogenous to the experience of the transcendent objects that compose the objective life-world and scientific world, and even if it forms the first layer of that experience, and is thus identical to it in its foundations, this is because the immanent objects constituted in immanent duration are bearers of rays of intentionality which posit, beyond themselves, objects of the real world as ideal poles, identical to their subjective variations (which are these immanent objects themselves). Speaking of the great theories of physical nature, of humanity, of human society, of culture, etc., that phenomenology is bound to elaborate, Husserl declares that it is ultimately a question of explicating the synthetic unities of evidences in which these objects, which correspond to the main divisions of naive ontology, are constituted. These "synthetic unities of constituting evidences possess," he tells us, "an extremely complicated structure . . . ascending from the lowest objective basis, they involve echelons formed by purely subjective 'objects.' This last objective founding role is always filled by immanent life, which means by the life that flows by and constitutes itself in itself and for itself."[11]

The auto-temporalization of absolute subjectivity is this auto-constitution in which it constitutes itself in itself and for itself, which means that it itself is what gives itself to itself, in such a way that the revelation of subjectivity to itself is its doing, is a self-revelation, and also in such a way that the task of accomplishing this self-revelation and thus of realizing the full essence of subjectivity is entrusted to a temporalization, namely to the synthetically connected totality of protentional, perceptive, and retentional intentionalities that make up internal time-consciousness. In this threefold structure and in the unified totality that it composes, it is always intentionality that constitutes, and that makes visible—more exactly it is the first gap opened by the flow, and in which intentionality in turn unfolds. In any case, *the power that allows subjectivity to be seen is, in its origin as well as in the concrete modalities in which it is effected, strictly parallel to the one that allows the world to be seen, or rather is identical to it; in both cases it is a constitution, in the final sense of a making visible, and in the ek-stasis of time.* As we know, Husserl explicitly entrusted to a longitudinal intentionality, which runs along the flow of absolute subjectivity, the task of reflecting in that subjectivity its own reality bursting in temporal ek-stasis, and of reuniting all its moments in a synthesis which is constantly synthesized with itself in its own flow. These are the famous themes: "The flow of the consciousness that constitutes immanent time not only *exists* but is so remarkably and yet intelligibly fashioned that a self-appearance of the flow [*Selbsterscheinung*] necessarily exists in it, and therefore the flow itself must necessarily be apprehensible in the flowing. The self-appearance of the flow does not require a second flow; on the contrary, it constitutes itself as a phenomenon in itself."[12]

The reduction of the *essence* of subjectivity—namely, of its capacity to bring and to bring itself into phenomenality—to intentionality runs through all his work up to the *Krisis*, where it still has its categorical tone. From the first "Meditation" of Descartes, it is said that one must

> bring out again the most significant moment, even if it has not yet been developed, namely the intentionality that forms the essence of egological life. Another term for that is "*cogitatio*," to have consciousness of something, something that I experience, for example, or that I think, or that I sense, or that I see. For every *cogitatio* possesses its *cogitatum*. Each of them is in the widest sense a "belief," and consequently includes some mode of certainty—certainty itself, presumption, holding as credible, doubt, etc.[13]

The vast view that Husserl has of the history of philosophy, in all his works and particularly in *First Philosophy*, is always from the point of view and in the perspective of intentionality. That is what motivates, notably, the critique of British empiricism, one of the few forms of thought, admittedly, to have made subjectivity the foundation of knowledge of the world and as its explicit condition, but in such a way that, failing to recognize intentionality as the power that produces phenomenality, it reduces the subjective givenness of things to a dead inscription onto a blank slate [*table aveugle*].

We discover this reduction of the essence of subjectivity to intentionality when, in its auto-temporalization, subjectivity relates to itself *intentionally*, so as to reveal itself to itself—in intentionality, consequently, and through it. But when the flux appears in person to itself—*Selbsterscheinung*—and inasmuch as the flux constitutes itself, it must be said: "the constituting and the constituted coincide, and yet naturally they cannot coincide in every respect. The phases of the flow of consciousness, in which the phases of the same flow of consciousness are constituted phenomenally, cannot be identical to these constituted phases, nor are they."[14] When the flux appears to itself as it constitutes itself, as it relates intentionally to itself, and therefore in its phenomenally constituted phases, and when these constituting phases themselves give themselves only in this way, in and through intentionality—this means: they are never given as constituting, intentionality never gives itself as such, as operative in its functioning—which means that what makes visible is never seen.

What makes visible, however, is subjectivity. That it is never seen and that the principle of all phenomenality never becomes phenomenal in it and on the contrary remains foreign to it: that is the paradox of phenomenology. It is denoted euphemistically as the "anonymity" of transcendental life. Phenomenology is nevertheless assigned the task of lifting up this anonymity. It accomplishes this in the reduction, when the phenomenological gaze is torn from the world in order to turn itself toward the transcendental operations that constitute it. What then offers itself to phenomenology, however, is only ever a constituted; "the free and unlimited field of the pure life of consciousness," as we have seen, only retains it under the title "noematic": in its ultimate operation its own reflection escapes it.

In the auto-temporalization of absolute subjectivity, which serves as a foundation for this reflection, the same situation is repeated and brought to its paroxysm. The ultimate constituting power that is self-constituted in the auto-temporalization of absolute subjectivity, in truth, does not auto-temporalize itself; it never enters as such, as temporalizing, as constituting, into the constituted flux of immanent temporality. About this ultimate constituting power which is the I [*le Je*] "in its originality the most originary," the manuscripts of the 1930s will say that it "is not in time," that it is "without extension," "without duration," "non-temporal," "supra-temporal," etc.

But it is also nothing; phenomenology in any case proves incapable of giving it a status. And we see well why. Everything that is for the me [*le moi*], is given to it in and through the ek-stasis of intentionality. This is how the world "is." As for the me [*le moi*], it too is, only as it is for itself, as it relates to itself intentionally in the auto-temporalization of absolute subjectivity, and as we have demonstrated at length, in Husserl the experience of subjectivity is identical to that of the world. Both refer to an ultimate *natura naturans* [*naturant*], to the "I" functioning in the final instance, about which a 1933 manuscript declares in an essential way: "I am not only something for me, but I am me [*Ich bin nicht nur etwas für mich sondern ich bin Ich*]"—without being able to say anything more about this supreme authority which is nothing other than subjectivity itself. In a similar way, the critique of eideticism that, in some manuscripts, ends up calling into question the ambition to determine every factical lived experience in terms of essences—to the extent that the essences themselves are constituted and also refer to an ultimate constituting—in turn runs into the absolute of this supreme *Faktum* that escapes their grip.

This insurmountable difficulty rebounds upon the method and allows us to understand why this way of thematizing subjectivity never takes it in reality as a point of departure for its research. It is always the intentional object that plays this role, which serves as a "transcendental clue" for elucidating both the intentional syntheses that constitute it and the subjectivity reduced to them. Speaking of "the most general structure" that phenomenology proposes to elucidate, which is the intentional relation of consciousness to the world, Husserl says:

> In the particularization of that type, and of its description, the *intentional object* (on the side belonging to the *cogitatum*) plays, for easily understood reasons, the role of "transcendental clue" to the typical infinite multiplicities of possible *cogitations* that, in a possible synthesis, bear the intentional object within them (in the manner peculiar to consciousness) as the same meant object. Necessarily the point of departure is the object given "straightforwardly" at the particular time. From it reflection goes back to the mode of consciousness at that time and to the potential modes of consciousness included horizontally in that mode . . .[15]

This regressive analysis, which one cannot keep from qualifying as "reflexive," sometimes seems to start from subjectivity itself, and this is a possibility that Husserl himself recognizes explicitly (*CM*, §21). But the subjective modes that thus function as transcendental guides for the analysis of the most profound depths of life do not intervene under this heading except to the extent that they are also offered as intentional objectivities, as immanent lived experiences auto-constituted in the auto-temporalization of absolute subjectivity. The ascent to the constituting begins, in all cases, with what is constituted, and the constituting is given in turn only as its auto-constitution falls back into retention—otherwise, outside and independently of this process of ontification, it will only be a presupposition.

Husserl directed a profound critique against Kantian idealism, reproaching it for failing to recognize the phenomenological presuppositions that make possible the extraordinary "Copernican revolution" it carries out (which is nothing other than the reversal of objectivism into transcendental subjectivity). For if it is brought to its term, to make thematic something that remains "un-thematized" in the natural experience of the world—specifically, the *a priori* conditions of possibility of experience—implies that these performances of intuition and the understanding be torn from their transcendental obscurity and brought to intuition. But as for an intuition of subjectivity, Kant knew only the empirical intuition of it in the inner sense, which is still submitted to these transcendental conditions, instead of being able to display them. He is thus obliged either to abandon subjectivity for an empirical psychology, or to save the theory for a reflexive philosophy which lets go of phenomenology in order to turn into a metaphysics that can no longer claim to be a rigorous science (if the latter means to bring forth its own foundations with indubitable evidence). But Husserl's phenomenology is in the same situation to the extent that constituting subjectivity is incapable of revealing itself as such in evidence where it is only ever something constituted (however eidetic, categorial, and *a priori* this evidence may be). Problematizing its various types and the correlative types of evidence, Husserl wanted and realized an extraordinary enlargement of the concept of intuition, but it was of no use, at least insofar as it concerns the question of original subjectivity.

Thus an involuntary common destiny ties Husserl's phenomenology together with his prestigious antecedent Kant. Just as Husserl was constrained to take the allegedly "immanent" intentional object as a transcendental guide of his subjective, and notably noetic, descriptions, so we saw in the *Critique of Pure Reason* that the analysis of transcendental subjectivity is pursued as an analysis of the *a priori* conditions of every possible object, which in reality means, of objectivity as such. But when subjectivity is reduced to the structure of objectivity, it is nothing more than the essence of objectivity.

We thus discover a decisive phenomenological situation. As soon as thought truly proves capable of surpassing the naive and pre-critical opposition of "subject" and "object," an opposition in which they are each alike treated as beings, one that is conscious and the other that is not, the former that has the property of relating to the latter, which relates to nothing—as soon as subjectivity is no longer the subject but its essence, the essence of experience and of phenomenality, as soon as the object is no longer a being but its objective condition, which means objectivity, the advance into presence as the coming in front of us and thus, again, the essence of experience and of phenomenality as such—then it appears that this essence of phenomenality, thought here as the essence of subjectivity and there as the *a priori* condition of any object, is one and the same. Thus the Kantian subject exhausts itself in the relation to objects of experience, a relation which is objectivity itself grasped in its pure possibility—and Husserlian subjectivity, in intentionality, in consciousness of the object, which again means in the opening of an Outside that is the condition of all "constitution," which means of any object-presentation. It is precisely because subjectivity is nothing other than objectivity as such, as the horizon of transcendence where everything that is and can be manifests itself under the heading of a possible object, that the analysis of the latter, *qua* intentional object, passes for the analysis of subjectivity itself.

Yet the crucial situation denounced here proves to be absolutely general; Husserl and Kant figure in our analysis only as examples. Everywhere in modern thought the "subject" appears as the condition of the object; it is what brings a being into the condition of being-there in front of us, where the subject's being-a-subject is thus only the object's being-an-object, namely its objectivity. But subjectivity denotes phenomenality as such. It is in this way that the structure of phenomenality, the essence of manifestation in general, is interpreted as the condition of the object. When this condition is thought to its end, it can be described as the ek-stasis of a Transcendent, and finally as an "in-stance in the clearing of being"—*Inständigkeit in der Lichtung.* According to the teaching of Heidegger's *Zähringen Seminar,* because the philosophy of subjectivity had displaced, by situating it in the immanence of consciousness, this "in-stance in the clearing," it is necessary to put it back in its place, where it has always been. For the ek-static in-stance in the clearing of being remains in it and presupposes it. Thus the Greeks understood the object not as what a subject throws in front of and thus ob-jects to itself in its representation, but as what comes into presence starting from itself, and more precisely starting from a foundation that is this coming into presence starting from itself.

But this critique of the philosophy of subjectivity only repeats its own presuppositions and leads them to their ultimate consequences. Heidegger's work, the seminar's protocol claims, "consisted in the investigation of the radical implications of intentionality. Now, to think intentionality through to its ground means: to ground it in the ek-stasis of Da-sein. In a word, one needs to recognize that consciousness is grounded in Da-sein."[16] Thus subjectivity *qua* intentionality, *qua* "*ego cogito cogitatum*," leads to an improper formulation of the ek-stasis of being—*as long as it is and must be nothing other than the Condition of the Object, inasmuch as Being is this condition, and as long as there is nothing other to think*. With Husserl, the seminar says again, the object is saved, and is so *qua* intentional object, in and through intentionality. But this remains caught in the immanence of a consciousness, and with it, the object itself; it is in my subjectivity, in my consciousness, "as in a box." This immanence of subjectivity must be broken if one wants to deliver the object to the freedom of its own essence, to the primordial Outside where it remains.

What is the motive for the displacement that has come to pervert our primitive encounter with Being, what does the shadow that immanence casts upon the pure clearing of what is there in front of us mean—what does the irruption of Cartesian subjectivity in Western philosophy mean? Is it not necessary to pay attention to this nevertheless tirelessly repeated fact that the *cogito* is obtained in the radical *epoché* of the world—not only of the life-world where men and women live outside themselves in a sort of stupor, but of the subjective "world" itself, of the interior world of sensible givens that flow away in immanent temporality, and finally of the ideal world of essences that eidetic intuition delivers to us as stable elements that can be grasped in fixed concepts, of any possible world, whatever it may be? What metaphysical and hyperbolic doubt avoids, indeed, is not the whole of beings of the natural world, or the ideal realm of essences whose simple, mathematical natures furnish the prototype, it is their mode of givenness, it is subjectivity itself as evidence and as the foundation of this evidence. For the world—both of nature and of mathematical essences and ideal truths (the fact that two plus three equals five or that "as long as I doubt, it is necessary that I am," etc.)—is doubtful only because the milieu of visibility where it shows itself to us is itself doubtful. It is this milieu, the ek-stasis that runs through the gaze and the phenomenality constituted by it, it is the apodictic seeing of the supposedly indubitable evidence, it is the soil of Husserl's phenomenology and its final Heideggerian substructure—it is all this that doubt rejects.

But what then remains? *At certe videre videor,* says the "Second Meditation."[17] At least it seems to me that I see. What subsists at the end of doubt is the subjective experience of vision, the self-revelation of this vision to itself that, nevertheless, inasmuch as it is a vision of seeing, does not itself consist, *qua* revelation, in this sort of seeing—otherwise it would be doubtful and the foundation of any certainty immediately lost. Seeming, in other words, in which it seems to me that I see, and in which seeing feels itself—"*sentimus nos videre*"[18]—and reveals itself to itself, is not that in which this seeing attains its object, and is not the clearing of ek-stasis. The self-revelation of subjectivity is, however, nothing other than subjectivity itself, its original essence, *qua* ultimate foundation. Hypokeimenal subjectivity is the self-revelation of subjectivity to itself as such, exclusive of every transcendence and every ek-stasis, occurring before the world and never happening in it; it essentializes itself [*s'essencifie*] as a radical immanence. The interpretation of this immanence as the Depth on which everything that is rests—of the *sub-jectum* in its essence, and of subjectivity as subjectivity—does not mark an incomprehensible failure of the problematic, but rather the moment when it is equal to its task in returning to the true Beginning. For if it is a question of founding vision itself and assuring all evidence, this can only be by showing how this vision properly takes hold in itself such that, in this primitive immersion of subjectivity in itself, an immersion in which it touches every point of its being, there is neither vision nor ek-stasis, and in this way, neither doubt nor error.

This immediate possession of itself is the idea in its original Cartesian acceptation, it is the idea of the mind [*l'esprit*] insofar as it differs from every other idea,[19] insofar as, deprived of objective reality and reduced to its material or formal reality alone, to the pure *cogitatio*, it is the power by which this is revealed to itself as *cogitatio* and as it is in itself, and is thus its self-revelation, the revelation of thought to itself, and not of something else, of an alterity, or of any kind of objectivity—the revelation of a *cogitatum*, or the representation of an objective reality. This is why the formal reality of the idea does not designate something formal, the simple form of a content situated outside it, but, in the absence of all exteriority, the proper reality of thought, precisely its material reality, and specifically the phenomenological materiality of pure phenomenality insofar as this no longer consists in an ek-stasis, but in immanence—in the idea. By the term "idea," "I understand this term to mean the form of any given thought, immediate perception of which makes me aware of the thought."[20] Thus the ideas are in Descartes first the radically immanent modalities of subjectivity—not the givens of internal time-consciousness but what, before any constitution or self-constitution, belongs to the very materiality of absolute subjectivity: sensations, feelings, passions, fears, volitions, and everything that must be considered as "ideas that are only in our soul."[21]

Thus the Cartesian reduction, if one wishes to denote doubt in this way, has nothing to do with the Husserlian reduction, which is neither its enlargement nor its deepening, but a ruinous misinterpretation. The Husserlian reduction disqualifies the world only in order to take into account its givenness, the consciousness of the world as such, intentionality, so that for Husserl consciousness is identified with consciousness of the world and is properly reducible to it, the *cogitatio* to the relation to the *cogitatum*, and phenomenality to ek-stasis. What is passed over in silence, or rather, totally overshadowed and lost in such an explication is nothing less than the original essence of subjectivity, namely, its original arrival in itself in the idea of the mind, which means in a sphere of radical immanence where there is neither *cogitatum*, nor intentionality, nor world. The aporia that shatters Husserl's phenomenology, its inability to assign a phenomenological status to the ultimate constituting, to the I "which functions in the final instance," is a result of his misunderstanding of the most original dimension of phenomenality, a dimension perceived by Descartes as the *cogitatio*, as "knowledge of the soul," about which the

"Second Meditation" establishes that it precedes and founds the "knowledge of the body," which is to say, consciousness of the world. For vision (the *inspectio* of the *intellectus*, for example) is precisely not possible unless it is has already arrived in itself, in its vision, so as to be this, and to be able to do what it does.

Husserl's phenomenological reduction, on the other hand, is accomplished as a thematic displacement whereby thought turns from the world to itself, in such a way that this perception of oneself is still intentional and what it perceives as its noema (this is still intentionality) is a consciousness of the world. This constitutes at once the how and the content of transcendental experience, an experience in which phenomenology has not the least idea of what the essence of original subjectivity is. This deficiency appears from the moment of Husserl's first efforts to grasp the nature of lived experiences. "If the peculiar character of intentional experiences is contested, if one refuses to admit . . . that being-an-object consists phenomenologically in certain acts in which something appears, or is that of as our object, it will not be intelligible how being-an-object can itself be objective to us."[22] Because the being of the subject—the "specificity of the lived experience"—is for it only the being-an-object of the object, because the subjectivity of this subject is thus only the objectivity of the object, phenomenology repeats the presuppositions implicit in classical thought, presuppositions that post-Husserlian phenomenology will make absolute.

The Cartesian reduction is not content to shift the theme from things to the mode of their givenness; it traces in this givenness a line separating the phenomenality of being-an-object, allegedly doubtful, and distinguished and circumscribed in this manner from, on the other hand, a more ancient revelation. Since what appears (the being) is put out of play, it is a question of a decomposition of appearance itself, where original subjectivity denotes the way phenomenality comes to it independently of all ek-static mediation. That is the way the first two "Meditations" mark a decisive turn in the history of human thought; the subjectivity they introduce is no longer the Greek appearance of the object, a Nature sprouting up, the principle of knowledge and science, but what by making these ultimately possible, always remains unperceived in them.

How does phenomenality bring itself about as such? This is a question that cannot, however, remain in darkness or become a mere speculative affirmation if the "how" is phenomenality itself in the eruption of its Parousia. Undoubtedly a method that looks everywhere to see and grasp in the evidence of intuition (that is, in the horizon of a world) what it makes its theme, in this case the original phenomenalization of phenomenality, seems inadequate if it is true that this phenomenalization occurs neither in the world nor as its appearance. *The ultimate anonymity that Husserl's phenomenology stumbles upon is the acknowledgment of the non-ecstatic condition of absolute subjectivity and its simple consequence.*

If subjectivity never arises in front of our regard, it nevertheless accomplishes its work in us; it is this regard, or rather its first arrival in itself, the first semblance in which it seems to me that I see and *by whose effect I do see and am capable of seeing*. But what is now in question is this ultimate possibility of seeing (and also of hearing, touching, sensing, imagining, conceiving, remembering, and desiring), subjectivity's original arrival in itself—and more exactly the phenomenological mode in which it is realized. The arrival of subjectivity in itself is its auto-affection, which is thus neither a concept nor a presupposition, whatever its nature that may be, but the primitive Fact as a feeling of oneself where phenomenality flows in itself, its first phenomenological effectuation. In what does this consist? What feels itself without this being in the ek-stasis of a sense or a thought is, in its essence, Affectivity. Affectivity is not some thing. As the primitive form of Affection, it belongs to and properly constitutes the givenness of everything that is. It is not a psychological determination juxtaposed against others—to sensation, imagination, conception, volition, doubt, certainty—but the fundamental How in conformity with which these modalities first arrive in, are felt, and are experienced in oneself; it is the pure, phenomenological materiality of this experiencing of oneself [*s'éprouver soi-même*] and, in this way, the principal, concrete possibility and essence of absolute subjectivity.

Thus there are two affections united in subjectivity and together defining its being, two fundamental modalities according to which the givenness of all that is given to us is essentialized. According to the first of these modalities, affection is an affection by the world; its structure is intentionality, and the phenomenality in which it consists is transcendental exteriority whose unfolding it secures. The following remarks of Husserl, for example, pertain to this ecstatic affection: "The world is effectively experienced . . . it is experienced in a 'living there' as being simply 'perceptually there.'"[23] According to the second of these modalities, affection is an affection of subjectivity no longer by the world, but by itself, an auto-affection; the phenomenality in which it consists is transcendental affectivity, the power of feeling feeling itself, which is identical to the original essence of subjectivity and makes it Life. Inasmuch as it reveals itself to itself in the auto-affection of its affectivity, subjectivity is not only life; it is in principle individual and singular, since it is ipseity as such. The phenomenological method's abandonment of these essential determinations of subjective life, namely individuality and singularity, is indicative of its failure.

The philosophy of subjectivity begins with the distinction of the two fundamental modalities by which phenomenality becomes phenomenal, a distinction unperceived by early phenomenology, whose goal was nevertheless to elucidate subjectivity systematically. Failing to recognize in this what makes it subjectivity, it could not help but abandon the concept of it and lose its bearings in post-Husserlian developments, in thought of the world. Thus the will to defeat objectivism, which is the eternal task of philosophy and alone can preserve for it an object properly its own—despite the pretension of the positive sciences to reduce everything to their type of knowledge, to an object proper, whatever may be the precautions taken to mask it, culminates in failure.

With several exceptions that it is not possible to examine here (for example, that of Maine de Biran, who is the only one to think the question of subjectivity in a thematic way: *is there a mode of internal apperception?*), the history of human thought hardly propounds subjectivity except in figures. These take on a particular form when they are introduced in doctrines claiming to be scientifically objective. Thus we see in Freud's 1895 *Project for a Scientific Psychology*, the "nervous system" is determined by the capacity of its neurons to receive two sorts of excitations, those which come from the universe, and those whose source is in the organism itself, in such a way that, the "excitation" being the representation of the affection, these two modes of accomplishment as exogenous or endogenous excitation only inscribe a twofold ontological receptivity in the organism—the transcendental receptivity with respect to the world in the unfolding of ek-stasis, on the one hand, and the transcendental receptivity with respect to oneself, the self-receptivity of absolute subjectivity as living subjectivity, on the other.

Yet the laws that regulate the two modes of affection are fundamentally different. In the finite site of ecstatic light the being appears only insofar as everything else that is, shirks away from this condition of presence, and thus everything that shows itself to us in intuition, in evidence, does so only in a series of indefinite references (according to the play of pre-traced horizons Husserl studied) to what does not show itself, before disappearing in turn. On the contrary and in principle, it belongs to the original auto-affection of absolute subjectivity in its affectivity never to lose what is given to it, namely itself, in such a way that, driven back to itself, driven back to being and submitting to it in a submission stronger than any freedom, it is what it is forever. In this pathos of being with respect to itself and in its powerlessness to overcome the connection of primordial Suffering that attaches it to itself as "suffering undergoing itself," the essence of being as the essence of subjectivity resides. Subjectivity is being itself, the subjacent and what persists identical to itself. Thus we see in the 1895 *Project* the neuronal system, which figures absolute subjectivity unconsciously, cannot free itself of these endogenous excitations and offers itself as an ego [*un moi*] "perpetually invested," since the possibility of putting them at a distance no longer exists, because affection *qua* auto-affection never ceases, because life has no power to undo itself from itself. The shift from the principle of inertia, which tends to abolish the quantity of energy invested in the organism, to the principle of constancy, which is content to lower the level of it, camouflages and expresses, in the language of the science of 1895, the structure of absolute subjectivity.

Still more interesting is the Nietzschean figure. Nietzsche, representing Schopenhauer's ingenious distinction between the Will, which signifies immanence, and Representation, which is founded in ek-stasis, and pushing it to its limit, refuses from the outset the classical reduction of subjectivity to a consciousness of an object, in order to conceive it on the contrary as Life. Not only does he understand this as the original affection of being in its pathos (Dionysus) and thus as Affectivity, as determining, further, every Imago of the world (Apollo), but also, deliberately installing himself in life in order to experience its real possibilities in himself, he uncovers the history of Suffering and joy, where these are the fundamental phenomenological categories in which our experience of being properly consists. Even more, in this play of the Absolute with itself he glimpses their internal connection, the incessant passage of ontological tonalities one into another, before and interdependently of any production of an image.

It is paradoxically the philosophies of the Unconscious that offer the last figure of subjectivity to us. For in their contradictory and confused manner, they say at least that the Ground [*Fond*] of Being is not the Dimension of ecstatic visibility, and that neither is there intentionality in it. And this is the case as long as the life that we are, as the auto-affection of absolute subjectivity, has no face and never allows itself to be met or perceived in a world.

Added to the properties that in each case determine what conforms to the modes of its phenomenological givenness (which means the affection that constitutes the essence of subjectivity) is the fact that everything that appears to us in an Outside arises from an unreality in principle, and is never the very substance of our life, which knows nothing of the Difference of ek-stasis and is not produced in it. Thus Husserl, in his own way of elucidating, had to abandon this reality in favor of the intuition of ideal essences alone. Thus Schopenhauer and then Nietzsche and even Freud, believing themselves opposed to Descartes on this point, denied thought any ontological claim. But it is the final reasons for this decisive situation that must be founded apodictically, just like the possibility for a thought to grasp, still in the apodictic mode, what escapes it in principle. The philosophy of subjectivity remains to be done, and phenomenology has to begin again.

Translated by Karl Hefty

Notes

1. Edmund Husserl, *The Crisis of European Science and Transcendental Phenomenology*, trans. David Carr (Evanston, Ill.: Northwestern University Press, 1970), §10, 60 (henceforth denoted as *Crisis*).
2. Hussserl, *Crisis*, §55, 186.
3. Edmund Husserl, *Ideas Pertaining to a Pure Phenomenology, First Book*, trans. F. Kersten (Dordrecht: Kluwer, 1983), §45, 146 (trans. modified).
4. Husserl, *Ideas*, §46, 100.
5. Edmund Husserl, *Cartesian Meditations*, trans. Dorion Cairns (The Hague: Martinus Nijhoff, 1950), §20, 49.
6. Husserl, *Cartesian Meditations*, §21, 51 (trans. modified).
7. Husserl, *Crisis*, §52, 178; *Husserliana* VI, 181–82.
8. Husserl, *Cartesian Meditations*, §9, 23 (trans. modified).
9. Husserl, *Cartesian Meditations*, §9.
10. Husserl, *Cartesian Meditations*, §15.
11. Husserl, *Cartesian Meditations*, §29, 64 (trans. modified).
12. Edmund Husserl, *Lectures on the Phenomenology of the Consciousness of Internal Time*, trans. John Barnett Brough (Dordrecht: Kluwer, 1991), §39, 88.
13. Husserl, *Crisis*, §20.
14. Husserl, *Lectures on the Phenomenology of the Consciousness of Internal Time*, §39, 88.
15. Husserl, *Cartesian Meditations*, §21, 50.
16. Martin Heidegger, *Four Seminars*, trans. Andrew Mitchell and François Raffoul (Bloomington: Indiana University Press, 2003), 71 (trans. modified).
17. Descartes, *The Philosophical Writings of Descartes*, II, 19; AT, VII, 29.
18. Descartes, *The Philosophical Writings of Descartes*, II, 27; AT, VII, 40.
19. Descartes, *The Philosophical Writings of Descartes*, II, 298; AT, VII, 443.
20. Descartes, *The Philosophical Writings of Descartes*, II, 113; AT, VII, 160.
21. Descartes, *The Philosophical Writings of Descartes*, I, 212; AT, IX, 27.
22. Edmund Husserl, *Logical Investigations*, vol. II, trans. J. N. Findlay (London: Routledge, 2001), V, I, §8, 93.
23. Husserl, *Crisis* §63, 219 (trans. modified).

7

Descartes's *Cogito* and the Idea of an Ideal Phenomenology

I would like to offer a phenomenological reading of Descartes's *cogito*. A project like this gives rise immediately to great reservations. These are connected to the very intention of trying to understand one thought on the basis of another one that came later. This later thought, which is perhaps more elaborated, has undergone countless influences. It has procedures and conceptual systems that did not exist at the time when the doctrines that we are seeking to clarify were formed. So instead of clarifying, doesn't this retroactive projection threaten to falsify what was contained in the intuitions that we would like to reactivate? Can a phenomenological reading of the *cogito* be anything more than an "interpretation"?

It could be the case on one and only one condition: on the condition that Descartes's *cogito* constitutes the act of the birth of phenomenology itself. In this case, a phenomenological reading of the *cogito* is not only possible: it is the only one possible. My first thesis is that phenomenology defines the only way of access to what is thought and must be thought in the *cogito*.

But this thesis is true only with the addition of this essential precision: the phenomenology that must serve as our guide in order to arrive at the buried intuition of the *cogito* is not the same one that we understand today by this name, namely, the movement of thought inaugurated brilliantly by Husserl, then followed by Heidegger and the other philosophers who were inspired by them. This Husserlian or Heideggerian phenomenology is what I call historical phenomenology. Regardless of whether it claims Descartes and especially the *cogito*, or whether it explicitly criticizes it, in either case this phenomenology has missed what is at stake in the *cogito*. Only an ideal phenomenology, which would be what it ought to be, is able to grasp the *cogito* in its radicality.

But if it is not the phenomenology of Husserl, Heidegger, or someone else that is able to introduce us to the hidden truth of the *cogito*, then one will ask: who do we address? Which phenomenology will carry out this task? A phenomenology that is born in the *cogito* and is identified with it—that is, an ideal phenomenology that is able to define its object as well as the means of attaining it. But is it not circular to understand the *cogito* in light of the phenomenology that is born in the *cogito*? The *cogito*, it could be added, is quite difficult to understand if it can only be understood on the basis of itself in a type of self-understanding whose nature is poorly understood now.

Let us first try to show why the *cogito* is so difficult to understand. This difficulty is due to the fact that two totally different things are meant by the term "*cogito*." First, it is a problem, that is to say, a movement of thought proceeding along a series of implications and evidences and aiming to define a certain reality. This process of thought has a specific structure to which I just alluded in speaking about implications, evidence, etc. But its most general structure is the structure of thought itself, because this process is precisely a process of thought, its unfolding according to its own modalities.[1]

The "*cogito*" can also mean that which is sought in the problematic that is expressed through different Cartesian texts, this "reality" whose true nature the process of thought attempts to understand. What then is this reality which is the theme of the *Meditations*, especially the "Second Meditation"? It is the nature of the human mind. For this nature of the mind is thought, the essence of thought. The *cogito*, according to the dual meanings that we just recognized in it, is thus the process of thought that aims to grasp the essence of thought. Whence the idea of reflexivity that is often linked to the *cogito* by commentators.

Here is my second thesis: it is that the essence of thought which the problematic of the *cogito* aims to grasp does not have any relation with the nature or the essence of thought that unfolds in this problematic, that is, in this process of thought. Even though in both cases we say "thought"— *cogito, cogitatio*—the realities designated by one and the same word are separated by an unbridgeable, inconceivable abyss. As a result, it is this reference to two "things," which are completely heterogeneous and irreducible to one another, by the same term and, it seems, by the same concept, that is the major obstacle to understanding the *cogito*. It thus follows that every attempt to base this understanding on the study of texts and words, or on language, is non-sense. Only the prior understanding of the *cogito* can actually give a meaning to the words and the problematics in which we are trying to express it.

It is thus necessary here to sketch for the first time the structure of these two "realities" that have been confused disastrously in the utterance "*cogito*": on the one hand, the structure of the thought whose implications unfold in the first two "Meditations," for example, and on the other hand, the essence of thought that this problematic attempts to define. We will understand the structure of the thought that unfolds in this problematic under the title "*cogitatio-cogitatum*." The essence of thought to which this problematic refers will be understood under the heading of a "*cogito* without a *cogitatum.*" This presupposes that something exists as a *cogito* without a *cogitatum*, as a *cogitatio* without any objective reality, and moreover, that it is this *cogito*, this *cogitatio* without a *cogitatum*, that is exclusively and essentially what Descartes initially has in mind.

If we compare these two utterances: "*cogito cogitatum*"/"*cogito* without a *cogitatum*," a doubt emerges for us: can they truly refer to two completely different "realities" excluding one another? Do they not, instead, include a common element that is indicated by the *cogito*—such that the first utterance appears richer by including, in addition to the *cogito*, the *cogitatum* which is absent from the second utterance? Unless—it is already time to reaffirm our thesis—the *cogito* in the "*cogito* without a *cogitatum*" signified something entirely different from the "*cogito*" in "*cogito cogitatum*" and thus that the first *cogito* had no relation with the second one.

What, then does it mean to say *cogito* in "*cogito cogitatum*"? This utterance seems so simple, but we are prevented from understanding it as long as we consider it as the formal prototype of a two-term structure, which is present in many possible iterations. For example, I think that the tree is losing its leaves, or even I think about the tree without its leaves, I imagine it this way, etc. The *cogitatum* here is the tree with or without leaves, perceived or imagined or conceived. And just as the *cogitatum* is a being—the tree—likewise the *cogito* refers to me who stands in front of the tree, or who imagines it or who remembers it.

If we follow Descartes, however, we have to immediately bracket the last statement that was put forward. The tree, the *cogitatum*, is a being, but surely not the *cogito* of this *cogitatum*.[2] What then is the *cogito* of the tree, which is not at all similar to it, which is not a being but rather the appearing of this tree, or put otherwise, the "consciousness" of it? That is really our question, and it suffices to show that the only access to the *cogito* can be phenomenological. The question is: what does this appearing,—the appearing of the tree, the *cogito* of the *cogitatum*—consist of?

Let's reflect further on this latter term: the *cogitatum*. We have said that the *cogitatum* is, in the present case, the tree with or without leaves. But it could be a path or a human being on a path or its image or its memory or its idea or some artwork or beauty, etc. However, if each of these cited terms, in spite of its differences with the other terms, is called a *cogitatum*, this is because in reality the *cogitatum* is neither the tree, nor the human being, nor someone's memory, nor some mathematical proposition. More precisely, each of these terms is a *cogitatum* only insofar as it is thought—*qua cogitatum*. But the *cogitatum qua cogitatum* is the *cogito* purely and simply, the *cogito* of the *cogitatum*.

It is thus necessary for us to correct what is pre-philosophical in an initial approach to the *cogito/cogitatum* structure. By following the text word for word, we thought that it implied two terms: the *cogito* and the *cogitatum*. On the one side, there is I who represent myself, and on the other side there is what I represent to myself. And we now understand that this is not the case: the *cogito* is in no way opposed to the *cogitatum*. It does not differ at all from it, if we conceive the *cogitatum* as such, the tree "as it is thought." *Cogito*, in the *cogito cogitatum*, is a *cogito* when I think the tree. It is the being-thought of the tree; it is the fact that it is thought; it is thought as such and nothing else. The *cogito* is thus identical to the *cogitatum* understood in itself—*qua cogitatum*.

In what will very quickly become the language of traditional philosophy, the above distinction between the *cogito* and *cogitatum* is the distinction between the subject and object. Here again is something very simple and evident: there is the subject who thinks on the one side and the object—the tree—that it thinks on the other. Is it not strange, however, that thought might stand on the side of the tree, around it, in the fact that it is thought and only "exists" as thought, as well as "in" the subject? This enigma disappears once we understand that the subject is nothing other than the fact that the tree is thought, its being-thought. But the being-thought of the tree is the fact that it is an ob-ject, that it stands out there, in this first outside of the objectivity in which alone a being can become an object. The subject is not opposed to the object but to beings; it is that which, opposed to a being, turns a being into something that stands there in front [*se tient devant*], the ob-ject. The subject is the object as such, or as we said previously, the *cogitatum qua cogitatum*. But the standing in front of the ob-ject and thus of every being that becomes an object is equally what allows it to be shown, its appearing—the appearing of the tree, its *cogito*.

Let's turn for a moment to the historical destiny of the *cogito* and especially to Kant, who will have a heavy influence on historical phenomenology—on Heidegger even more than on Husserl. The *cogito*, the I think, for Kant, is the subject, and it is quite remarkable that this subject is considered here on its own independently from the question of its being, from any passage from the *cogito* to the *sum* which is reputed to be a paralogism. This pure subject, discharged from the question of its own being, is reduced to a pure "I think," but it is not closed onto itself. Quite the contrary, it has the structures of objectivity, of "standing in front," which are deployed according to the pure intuitions of space and time as well as the categories of the understanding. As a result, the forms and the categories are only the conditions of every phenomenon to the extent that they let it be seen. And they do this inasmuch as "standing in front" resides equally in all of them. In each of them, it is this "standing in front," this being placed in front, that makes things visible.

To be placed in front is to be represented. In order to say that "I think," the subject is the subject of representation, that is to say that representation shows [*fait voir*]. That is what the *cogito-cogitatio* is. Inasmuch as it shows, representation is also foundational for being. To be is to be represented; it is to be as represented. Heidegger helps us to understand that this all comes from Aristotle in speaking about the state of rest that characterizes Aristotle's *Physics*. He writes: "The house standing there *is exposed* in unconcealment in that it is established in its outward appearance and stands in this appearance. Standing, it rests, rests in the 'ex' of its exposure [*in diesem Aus des Aus-sehen*]."[3]

It suffices to project this Heideggerian reading of Aristotle retroactively onto Kant in order to understand what is essentially Descartes's *cogito*. According to Heidegger's explicit and repeated statements, the *cogito* means "I represent myself" and means nothing but that. The most important trait of Descartes's *cogito* is that it is tied to the idea of certainty. The *cogito* emerges out of doubt, but this doubt happens in view of the indubitable, in and for the relation to it. What is certain? What is indubitable? Truly speaking, there are two things. What is certain is the tree, not in itself but only as it is represented, that is to say, placed in front, disposed, exposed in this Before, in the clearing [*apérité*] of a fundamental Outside. What is certain is this ecstatic Dimension, such that everything that is gathered into it and is shown in it, turns out to be certain as well. "What is presented-to no longer permits any doubt about what it is and how it is" [*das Zugestellte in dem, was es ist und wie es ist, keinen Zweifel mehr zulasst*].[4] This foundation of certainty through the act of placing in front that is representing, is something that Heidegger expresses unequivocally: "Re-presenting is a presenting in complete certainty" [*das Vor-stellen ist ein Sicher-stellen*].[5]

What Descartes would claim to establish with complete certainty, however, is not only or even primarily the *cogitatum*—it is the *cogito* and its *ego*, the person who wants to be self-assured and at the same time to establish its mastery over everything that it represents, preparing the way for the reign of the Will to power and the unleashing of technology. Heidegger's extraordinary preoccupation with founding the *ego* of the *cogito*, an ego over which Descartes passed so quickly—a preoccupation that logically should have led him more profoundly than any other commentator into Descartes's thought—can, however, lead us astray. In fact, the Heideggerian account of the *ego* adds nothing to the structure of representation; instead, it leads back to this structure as that with which the *ego cogito* is identified.

This is how, according to Heidegger, the *ego* is necessarily implied in the *cogito* reduced to an "I represent myself." For "every 'I represent something' simultaneously represents a 'myself,' me the one representing (for myself, in my representing). Every human representing is—in a manner of speaking, and one that is easily misunderstood—a 'self-'representing."[6] Of course, this should not be understood to say that in every representation the ego would be proposed as the correlate of this representation, as if in representing the tree, for example, I represented myself along with the tree, next to it, in a vague and marginal consciousness, at the very least. It is in a much more essential way that the ego is implied in its representation: inasmuch as in representation everything represented happens to be represented for the ego, in front of it, to it, and before it. The ego is thus presupposed in every representation not in an *a posteriori* manner as an object that it will discover. but in an *a priori* manner as the one in front of whom, to whom, and before whom everything will necessarily be represented. This reference of every possible represented object back to the ego implies that the ego is dis-posed before itself in every representation. It is because this disposition of the self before itself constitutes the structure of every conceivable representation, that, as Heidegger adds masterfully, one does not have to pass from the *cogito* to the *sum*. The "I am" does not have to be deduced from the *cogito* in any manner. It is implied in the *cogito* as "I represent myself" and is identical with it.

I have said that Heidegger did not understand a single word of Descartes's *cogito*. Does this, like any excessive statement, need to be corrected, even reversed? Might he not, instead, be the only one to have understood it? Yes, if it were a question of the *cogito/cogitatum*. And here we understand perhaps something more: the reason why Heidegger always exposed what he critiqued with such depth and why philosophical repetition always takes on such a magnitude in his work is that he thinks the same thing as what he critiques. This is how it is in the case of the *cogito*. The critique of representation—one of the major Heideggerian themes—only has a limited meaning: it denies to the human the right to establish itself as the "I" of the "I represent myself," as a master of nature and of everything that only exists in being re-presented, posited, and dis-posed in front of oneself—unlike the Greeks who are listening for what arrives. But if through this contrast between the *Gegenstand* of representation in the moderns and the *Gegenüber* of listening to Nature in the ancients we raise the fundamental phenomenological question of pure phenomenality, of appearing as such, then we can see how this contrast dissolves. For it is the very same appearing that founds the Greek *phainomenon* and the phenomenon of the moderns, namely, the one that is illuminated in ek-stasis and from which the "I represent myself," in turn, draws its power to make something manifest by placing it in front, in and through ek-stasis.

The proof of this abolition of every fundamental phenomenological difference between Greek phenomenology and that of modernity is provided by the Heideggerian history of Western metaphysics. By establishing the continuity of this history, the *cogito*—as a *cogito/cogitatum*, as an "I represent myself"—marks one of the avatars in the transformations of this one and the same appearing.

Let's return to our analysis. *Cogito/cogitatum* is the structure of thought unfolding in the process of thought that aims to grasp the essence of thought. Is it not also the structure of thought in general, its essence? This is how it has been understood: every *cogito* is a *cogito cogitatum*, a consciousness of something. The whole of modern phenomenology, as well as the whole of philosophy of today or yesterday, has in one way or another adopted this self-evident interpretation. Let us limit ourselves here to remarking that both Heidegger who critiques it and Husserl who advocates it, say exactly the same thing about the *cogito*. Heidegger says: "All willing and asserting, all 'affects,' 'feelings' and 'sensations' are related to something willed, felt and sensed."[7] For his part, in §20 of the *Crisis*, Husserl writes concerning intentionality in Descartes: "Another word for it is *cogitatio*, having something consciously, something, e.g. in experiencing, thinking, feeling, willing, etc."[8] In these interpretations and in many other ones, we see the structure of the process of thought—the *cogito/cogitatum*—extended endlessly in order to define the structure of thought in general and thus the essence of everything that exists. And this is based on a phenomenological presupposition that guides the entire history of Western thought. What then does the statement that we contrasted with it mean: a *cogito* without a *cogitatum*?

This statement evidently expresses a reduction. It puts the *cogitatum* into parenthesis in order to consider only the *cogito*. Is this not the very same reduction that Husserl placed at the beginning of his phenomenology? Whatever modifications he may have placed under the reduction, whether it is restricted to the certain givens of consciousness that are called immediate givens and through which objects are constituted, or whether it is concerned increasingly and soon exclusively with the transcendental modalities of this constitution of objects, in either case the reduction has established a division between those conscious phenomena that are considered certain and those that are constituted in it and are not certain. These "conscious phenomena" in relation to constituted objects are the *cogito* in contrast with the *cogitatum*. And one can understand that since the former constitute the latter, the *cogito* allows the *cogitatum* to be recovered, this time founded and justified, and thus that the reduction does not lose anything.

To put the *cogitatum* into parenthesis, even provisionally, in order to consider only the *cogito* is, however, something that has become completely impossible, according to our preceding analyses. As long as one considers the *cogitatum* naively as some thing and the *cogito* that faces it as something else, then one can bracket the *cogitatum* and keep the *cogito*. But as soon as one understands that the *cogitatum* in itself, *qua cogitatum*, is nothing other than the *cogito* and nothing other than appearing as such—the appearing of the tree, for example—then to bracket the *cogitatum* is to suppress appearing itself. It is to plunge into an inconceivable Abyss, an absolute nothingness. For we are placed in front of such an abyss for the flash of an instant with Descartes's *cogito*, that is to say by doubt, by the radical reduction that comes before our regard for the first time and which is what we have to think. Expressed in the statement "*a cogito without a cogitatum*," this reduction not only brackets the *cogitatum* but also the *cogito* itself, which is to say the statement "*cogito cogitatum*" in its entirety. But what remains and can remain then? One can recognize Descartes's question.

The radical reduction, in this case Cartesian doubt, develops through three essential moments that do not mark three steps of a problematic, but refer tacitly to what is intended in it. In the first place, this reduction puts beings out of play: every conceivable being, including material bodies in nature as well as mine or myself as a being. It is no longer a question of saying with Heidegger that in Descartes "the human . . . becomes certain about itself as the being which, in this way, posits itself on the basis of itself," and that "the *Meditations* . . . keep within the sphere of the question about the *ens qua ens*," that in the history opened by the *cogito* "the truth of beings has become certainty" and that "the ego is the truest being," etc.[9] Relative to the *cogito* without a *cogitatum* that I will call the original *cogito* from now on, such propositions have lost any sort of possible meaning.

But, if the Cartesian reduction acts initially as an ontic reduction that strikes all beings in general without taking pains to consider them one by one, this can only be because it already puts out of play what is their condition, namely, the appearing in which each of them is shown as a phenomenon and only "exists" in this manner. It is this way of appearing that is considered dubious, and it is only for this reason that everything that is shown within it is disqualified in an *a priori* manner. The ontic reduction is thus in reality a phenomenological reduction. This is the second moment of the *cogito*, this extraordinary moment where what is set aside is appearing itself as such.

Two remarks are needed here. First, it is the phenomenological character and no longer the ontic character of the reduction that explains its sudden extension. While it is initially limited to that which there are some reasons to doubt (for example, the sensible), it is suddenly released and takes hold of everything that exists and even of the indubitable, the rational truths. If there is nothing extravagant about this, if it is not the work of a madman but a simple eidetic necessity, this is because the problematic of doubt afterwards does not consider what appears in appearances or, for example, that two plus two equals four, but the appearing of this appearance. Once this appearing becomes dubious, once the seeing that lets me see that two plus two equals four becomes fallacious as seeing, once its showing [*faire voir*] in itself becomes denaturation, occultation, and trickery, then what is seen by it is certainly not like the way one sees it and perhaps does not even exist at all. And this holds for the seeing that lets me see the world, as well as for the seeing that lets me see my dreams. Truly, it is because there is only one and the same seeing at work here and because it is fallacious in itself, that everything seen by it—the world, dreams, and rational truths—are only crazy fantasies to which nothing corresponds anywhere. The hypothesis of the evil genius does not imply any rupture, an abrupt appeal to an infinite will about which one does not know here what it can be. The hypothesis of the evil genius is phenomenological; it is the reduction itself, the hypothesis of the falsity of appearing that is enough to destroy everything.

My second remark follows from this. The presupposition of the falsity of appearing, even though it would not be the presupposition of absolute Nothingness, entails in any case the collapse of all possible knowledge and notably of phenomenology. For phenomenology always sought to base itself on appearance, and more precisely, on appearing. For if one scrupulously respects this aim, it is hard to see how it could be denied—how appearing, if one restricts oneself rigorously to it, would be able to be false. Here, to restrict oneself rigorously to appearing no longer means to restrict oneself to what appears in appearing as it appears, but to restrict oneself to pure appearing as such, as it appears as appearing—for example, to restrict oneself to the light as it shines. Who could doubt here and contest appearing in the actuality of its appearing, the flash of light in the actuality of its act of shining? This is, however, what Descartes does, and we can only understand the third moment of his reduction by going to an extreme point of a radicality that seems to make it impossible.

Here one must ask: what appearing does Descartes challenge, in defiance of the force that belongs to all appearing as such in the way it actually appears? We have said this many times: it is seeing. "Therefore I suppose that everything I see is false" means that sensible seeing is the first example of that which, like the senses in general, imagination, memory, concepts, etc., functions everywhere like seeing, on the basis of a transcendental seeing whose *intuiri* of the *intellectus* presents the settled form. And what is in question is the essence of seeing, its appearing, the *cogito cogitatum*, placing in front—"in complete certainty," as Heidegger said—the Outside where this position happens, ecstatic truth, the "outside myself" where there "may perhaps be nothing at all," as Descartes said.[10] This is what is announced at the end of the radical reduction by a brisk return to sensible seeing, to something that everyone understands and that nobody challenges insofar as everyone sees and is sunk into their own seeing, or to say it with Husserl, because seeing is an absolute that "cannot be demonstrated or deduced."[11] But with the brackets placed around this "outside myself" where there is "perhaps nothing at all," are we not placed before the Abyss of this Nothingness? And once more: What remains?

It is fortunate that Descartes answered precisely this question: *At certe videre videor.*[12] At the end of the reduction in which brackets are placed around seeing, what remains indubitable is this seeing itself. More precisely, seeing as such is dubious (and consequently everything that it sees), but "it seems to me that I see" is absolutely true. And that is only possible if the appearing in which seeing consists, in which seeing sees what it sees—*cogito cogitatum*—differs essentially from the appearing in which seeing is given to itself, in which "it seems to me that I see." It is on this condition alone that the former can be false and the latter true.

What does it mean, for the appearing in which seeing sees what it is seen, to distinguish it essentially from that in which seeing senses itself? It means that it is distinguished in its very appearing, in the pure phenomenological matter out of which this appearing is made. Here appearing is ek-static phenomenality, ek-static truth, and it is false—there it is sensing, sensing oneself—a *cogito* without *cogitatum*, to appearing crushed against itself, immersed in itself, submerged by itself. Its power of revelation was accomplished in the pure suffering and enjoyment of itself before the emergence of a world, before any Outside, before this space of light where the *cogitatum* unfolds inasmuch as it is one.

The radical reduction is thus phenomenological in an ultimate sense. With an unrivaled violence that seems to be close to madness, it clashes with appearing itself and challenges it in its own appearing. It shakes up appearing all the way to splitting it into two like a block of crystal broken by a hammer. And on the one side, it finds an appearing that it no longer holds in itself, in its appearing, as a self-justification and a self-attestation: it is seeing which in the light of its vision and in the undeniability of this light, is considered dubitable. On the other side, what is absolutely certain is the appearing in which seeing is given to itself without a *cogitatum* and without its light, without seeing itself and without being able to do so, in the Night of an absolute non-seeing. So, on the one side there is the appearing that the reduction reduces, and on the other side there is the appearing that can no longer be reduced. This prompts the question: how can the reduction reduce the first type of appearing but not the second one? This situation is all the more strange since the first type of appearing is the light that everyone sees, where Being is there in an immediate demonstration [*monstration*], that everyone has within themselves as that which one is, as one's "consciousness" or one's *Dasein*, whereas no one has ever seen the second and never will.

Let's note that here we are touching on the very core of Descartes's meditation:

> But it still seems (and I cannot resist believing) that corporeal things—whose images are formed by thought and which the senses themselves examine—are much more distinctly known than this mysterious "I" which does not fall under the imagination. And yet it would be strange indeed were I to grasp the very things I consider to be doubtful, unknown and foreign to me more distinctly than what is true, what is known—than, in short, myself.[13]

But yet if what stands there in front of me with an undeniable clarity is struck down by the radical reduction of pure appearing, of this pure light, whereas what is hidden from this light in my night is all that remains "certain," this can only be the case for three reasons: (1) there is actually a duality of appearing, and it each time differs in what accounts for its appearing, in the matter of its pure phenomenality; (2) the former is dubitable and the other is not; the second founds the former and establishes its being as well as its indubitability; and (3) only the second is autonomous and absolute, whereas the former is only founded. Together these three theses compose the fundamental Cartesianism delineated by the reduction and that we are thinking under the heading of the *cogito*.

Only one text contains these three theses and affirms the duality of appearing according to whether its pure phenomenological matter consists in the ek-static light of seeing, in this case in perceiving, or instead in pathos. The dubious character of seeing is established by the fact that it cannot determine whether what it allows to be seen exists or does not exist, whether it derives from the domain of dreams or of the truth. For what is in question here is not a being that is perceived, imaginary, or oneiric. Different from a being as well as its being, it is an "I know not what" that conceals itself from ek-stasis, an Arch-revelation situated in the impressional flesh of pathos and in everything that is affective. This Arch-revelation can occur even if the "world" would not exist; it remains absolutely certain even if every ecstatic truth would be fallacious. "So, often when we are sleeping and sometimes even when we are awake, we imagine certain things so forcefully that we think we see them before ourselves or feel them within our body, although they are not there at all. But even though we be asleep, we cannot feel sad, or moved by any other passion, unless it be quite true that the soul has that passion within itself."[14]

There remains the third and final thesis, namely, that pathos alone places seeing in seeing and grants it certainty—seeing thus never derives this certainty from seeing itself, but from its pathos. This pathos does not only define seeing—as desire, anxiety, love—in relation to what it sees; it first makes it possible as a seeing affective itself and experiencing itself as a living seeing and in this way alone: as a non-seeing [*non-voir*].

It is only this non-seeing, which is immanent to every possible seeing as an auto-affective pathos, that reveals it originally to itself, establishes it in certainty, apart from any evidence and any possible seeing. It is only because this ultimate foundation escapes from all evidence that the doubting of evidence, instead of reaching it, uncovers it for what it is, as the unique foundation. The massive and decisive theses that close the "Second Meditation" result from the auto-affective pathos of every possible ek-stasis, namely, the givenness of every conceivable object presupposes the self-givenness of this givenness. This self-givenness differs structurally from ek-static givenness due to the fact that it is without any horizon, any profiles, or any temporal development. It is absolute, whereas ek-static givenness is finite like the place of light that it handles. Descartes expresses the absoluteness of this Arch-givenness by one of the most powerful litotes of our language in saying that the nature of the human mind, or the soul, "is more easily known than the body."

What is the soul? Is it possible any longer to evade the problem of the *sum* that we have passed over in silence throughout this exposition? Does not Descartes explicitly say *cogito ergo sum*, or better, *cogito, sum*? Is it not here that Heidegger's ultimate objection is justified, namely, that the *cogito* is not original because it is based on an unclarified presupposition, that of being? For I would never be able to say "I am," if it were not on the basis of at least an implicit pre-understanding of what it means to be, of "the meaning of being in general."

The meaning of being in general is always thought on the basis of beings. It is to think being as a being—*ens qua ens*, as Heidegger said about all of the "Meditations"—and thus to think of beings as what exists and thus to think at least confusedly about being as such. From its first step, however, Descartes's radical reduction put beings out of play as well as being. This is attested by his scathing reply to Gassendi, who had objected that I could not say "I am"—literally "I am a thing that thinks"—if

I did not already know what an animal or a plant is and thus "what one calls a thing or indeed what a thing is in general."[15]

Where then does Descartes get and where can he get the *sum*, if it is not from what exists, or from being itself? The answer: from the *cogito*. *Sum* thus does not signify a being that is analogous to the being of a tree or animals, or even that would be "being itself" as such. Everything that is ontic and ontological has been put out of play by the reduction. What, then, is this being of the tree which would also be mine? The being of the tree, or of the wall, is, in Fichte's words, something which contains within themselves the fate of Western thought, "its being outside of its being."[16] It is the tree in its own exteriority in relation to itself, outside of itself—the *cogitatum*, the object. The being of the tree is its appearing as the exteriority of this Outside. To be is always to appear, but here appearing has cast outside of itself what appears and only discovers it as other, foreign, external, irreal, an inert being whose living interiority forever escapes.

The *cogito* from which Descartes draws the *sum* proceeds from the radical reduction that has put out of play beings, the being of this being, and being itself. Phenomenologically speaking, the radical reduction has put out of play the appearing that is thrust outside of itself: the *cogito* whose *cogitatio* is the *cogitatum qua cogitatum*. The original *cogito* proceeds from this reduction. It is not the simple appearing of the tree or the wall in naive perception and in the worldhood of a world, but the Arch-revelation, the Arch-affection in which every possible affection is auto-affected, including every ek-static affection by a being. For this Arch-affection is autonomous. It is neither a being nor being, but is identified with an Arch-facticity that is engendered in the Arch-revelation of this Arch-affection. The term "*sum*" designates this Arch-facticity.

What facticity does this involve, more precisely? What fact is announced here? The pure fact of appearing considered in itself and as such, the appearing of appearing inasmuch as it constitutes the being of being and allows it to be—to the extent that one can still speak of being, since it is no longer a question of what exists or of its being.

In the radicalized reduction, taken to its culmination, the pure fact of appearing has been reduced and brackets were placed around the appearing that appears as the ek-static Truth of Being. Why? Because such an appearing does not bring itself into appearing and does not itself produce its own appearing. If it were left to itself and delivered over to itself, it would not appear; it would not be the pure and simple fact of appearing—the Arch-fact that must carry all the others.[17] Only the pathos of its auto-affection can bring the ek-static appearing of Being into itself. Only this Arch-affection as an Arch-revelation does and can make appearing a "fact." Descartes calls this Arch-facticity "*sum*": the *sum* of the *cogito*, from this Arch-revelation then, whose phenomenological matter is a pure affectivity, revealing in and through its own affective flesh, outside and independently of ek-static Being.

How could we not notice here that when he tried to express the connection as he did—at the culmination of the reduction, in the paragraph on the evil genius—or, as I would say, the Arch-connection between the Arch-revelation and the Arch-facticity, Descartes expressed himself in these terms:"Here I make my discovery: thought exists; it alone cannot be separated from me"—*haec sola (cogitatio) a me divelli nequit.*[18] It is as if it were in a radical immanence rejecting all Ek-stasis that the most original revelation happens and as a result of this most original auto-affection, of the work of life in us, what we call the "self."[19]

In a recent book, Jean-Luc Marion stated what I have called the fourth principle of phenomenology: "the more reduction, the more givenness."[20] Unlike the ontology or the metaphysics of which it is an avatar, the fourth principle of phenomenology can lead us back to the abyss of Descartes's intuition and allow us to rediscover it. For it is at the culmination of the reduction that beings have been bracketed, as well as the givenness that gives them and which the Arch-givenness is given "outside of being," outside of horizons, outside finitude, independently from every side and from every perspective. In this self-givenness, life gives itself immediately to itself in totality—it is an omni-givenness that gives everything inasmuch as everything is given in life, including not only life itself but every ek-static affection as well.

Naturally, what occurs in the auto-affection of life as engendered in this auto-affection—which we call our soul—has nothing to do with what we see and perceive as a being. Life has other ways. The reduction taken to its full radicality opens on to them, and the task of a radical phenomenology is to elucidate them. The fact that Descartes went on to follow other paths does not matter to us here. As the point of departure for this radical phenomenology, the *cogito* can be the recommencement of it today.

Translated by Scott Davidson

Notes

The first version of this text was presented under the title "Descartes's *Cogito*" at a seminar directed by Jean-Luc Marion at the École Normale Supérieure on January 9, 1991. The text published here has been revised and renamed in 1996, for a presentation made the same year at the École Normale Supérieure.

1. The *cogito*, as a process of thought, is expressed though a number of texts; it is thus also a linguistic process, which cannot be totally independent from language or its own morphology. Whence the importance of knowing whether the texts are written in French or in Latin, in the absence of their being in Greek. As both a process of thought and a linguistic process, these texts recount a certain history that is analogous with those that are recounted by other texts, philosophical ones but also literary or dramatic ones. According to some, the *cogito* belongs precisely to a literary genre; it is, for example, a sort of drama putting into place a true plot that keeps the reader in suspense. Or it is a spiritual exercise like those that were practiced at the time. As a philosophical text, a drama with a plot, or a spiritual exercise, it is in any case a cultural object that is answerable to all the types of analysis that are valid for objects of this genre: historical, social, and psychoanalytic analyses, but also grammatical, logico-grammatical, and logico-mathematical, since in any case it is a text.

2. "I am not that concatenation of members that we call the human body. Neither am I some subtle air infused into these members, nor a wind, nor a vapor, nor a fire, nor a breath, nor anything else I devise for myself." Descartes, *Philosophical Writings of Descartes*, II, 18; AT, VII, 27.

3. Martin Heidegger, "Metaphysics as History of Being," in *The End of Philosophy*, trans. Joan Stambaugh (New York: Harper and Row, 1973), 5.

4. Heidegger, *Nietzsche*, vol. 4, trans. Frank A. Capuzzi (New York: Harper and Row, 1982), 105.

5. Heidegger, *Nietzsche*, vol. 4, 106.

6. Heidegger, *Nietzsche*, vol. 4, 106.

7. Heidegger, *Nietzsche*, vol. 4, 108.

8. Edmund Husserl, *The Crisis of European Sciences and Transcendental Philosophy*, trans. David Carr (Evanston, Ill.: Northwestern University Press, 1970), 82. And also: "The life of the soul, which is through and through a life of consciousness, the intentional life of the ego, which has objects of which it is conscious, deals with them through knowing, valuing, etc." (85).

9. Heidegger, "Metaphysics as History of Being," 30, 23, 47, respectively.

10. Descartes, *The Philosophical Writings of Descartes*, II, 16; AT, VII, 24.

11. Edmund Husserl, *The Idea of Phenomenology*, trans. Lee Hardy (Springer, 1999), 30.

12. "Yet I certainly *seem* to see," (Descartes, *The Philosophical Writings of Descartes*, II, 19; AT, VII, 29).

13. Descartes, *The Philosophical Writings of Descartes*, II, 20; AT, VII, 29.

14. René Descartes, *The Passions of the Soul*, trans. Stephen H. Voss (Indianapolis, Ind.: Hackett, 1989), §26, 33.

15. Descartes, *The Philosophical Writings of Descartes*, II, 250; AT, VII, 362.

16. Johann Gottlieb Fichte, *The Way towards the Blessed Life*, trans. William Smith (London: John Chapman, 1849), 50.

17. Here again, this is something that neither Husserl nor Heidegger perceive, and this is the reason why we have put them in parallel in spite of their seemingly divergent readings of Descartes's *cogito*. The fact that the appearing of the *cogito* is reduced in reality to that of the *cogitatum qua cogitatum* can only ap-

pear on its own through a sort of doubling back that only underscores its initial inability to do so instead of removing it. This can be seen in both of their readings. Husserl states: "Descartes asked, as you will recall, after he had established the evidence of the *cogito*: What is it that assures me of this basic givenness? Answer: clear and distinct perception [*la clara et distincta perceptio*]" (Husserl, *The Idea of Phenomenology*, 37). Heidegger writes "ego cogito . . . sum" (Heidegger, *Nietzsche*, vol. IV, 112). Concerning the illusion of conferring a power of self-revelation on a *cogitatio 2* that it lacks, see Michel Henry, "The Phenomenological Method," in *Material Phenomenology* (New York: Fordham University Press, 2008).

18. Descartes, *The Philosophical Writings of Descartes*, II, 18; AT, VII, 27. And later: "Which of these things is distinct from my thought? Which of them can be said to be separate from my thought?" (*Meditations*, II, 19; AT, VII, 29).

19. The immanence of this auto-affection is indicated in all the fundamental texts where Descartes considers the *cogitatio* or the idea in itself; on this point, see Michel Henry, *The Genealogy of Psychoanalysis*, trans. Douglas Brick (Stanford, Calif.: Stanford University Press, 1993), chaps. 1–3.

20. Jean-Luc Marion, *Reduction and Givenness*, 203 (trans. modified).

8

Ricoeur and Freud: Between Psychoanalysis and Phenomenology

Ricoeur's book *Freud and Philosophy: An Essay on Interpretation*, first of all, presents one of the best expositions of psychoanalysis available today.[1] The power of Ricoeur's conceptual structure is deployed there in the form of a very clear and extremely rigorous analysis. But, because Ricoeur is a philosopher, this exposition is wholly different from a restatement, however articulate it may be. It is a critique in the Kantian sense of the term, an "epistemological critique" that aims to "deduce" the realist concepts of psychoanalysis—notably, the concepts of topography and energetics. That is to say that it justifies them and does so by showing "their power of regulating a new domain of objectivity and intelligibility."[2] For this critique will put phenomenology into play and into question, to the point that the whole book can be read as a debate between psychoanalysis and phenomenology. It is not the case that phenomenology is introduced as an arbitrarily chosen prerequisite, in light of which one would try to offer a philosophical interpretation of psychoanalysis. Instead, *one and the same problem is judged to be decisive, that of meaning*, and calls for these two major theories of modern culture. This problem assigns them both to the same theme and the same work: to decode the deep meaning, the "true" meaning of human behavior, by starting from their apparent meaning and passing through it. Which of these two disciplines utilizing its own system of categories and its own methods is best able to handle this task and goes furthest in the ultimate understanding of the human psyche? The stakes of Ricoeur's problematic are to put phenomenology to the test by psychoanalysis, and likewise to put psychoanalysis to the test by phenomenology inasmuch as they both constitute a hermeneutics.

The appeal to phenomenology, as we said, is not gratuitous; it is motivated by the failure of the trial launched against psychoanalysis by the epistemological critique and especially the American epistemology that is more or less tainted, it should be said, by positivism and scientism. This trial, Ricoeur declares, is unanswerable "as long as one tries to place psychoanalysis among the observational sciences."[3] But this enterprise itself reveals itself to be completely inadequate, if it is the case that the analytic situation is initially a "situation of language." Henceforth, "the concepts of analysis are to be judged according to their status as conditions of the possibility of analytic experience, insofar as the latter operates in the field of speech."[4] These concepts, for Ricoeur, are then essentially the ones that take into account the relation of the signifier to the signified. As such, they belong essentially to the hermeneutic sciences (for example, to psychoanalysis) and define their task and their method in terms of interpretation. The analytic relation to the object is thus irreducible to a description of observable objects that epistemology takes as its univocal criterion. Instead, it is only intelligible in reality with the help of procedures that are closer to historical understanding (such as Max Weber's "types") than to the positive explanation used in the natural sciences. Even if the foundation of the psyche refers to facts of nature as Freudian energetics leads us to believe, our access to them—and this will be Ricoeur's crucial thesis—can only occur through the mediation of the mental representatives of energy, which are all signifying processes and as such are justifiable by an interpretation. With undeniable evidence, it is here that the need for a return to phenomenology arises, which is understood as the hermeneutic discipline par excellence or rather as hermeneutics itself.

The striking parallel that Ricoeur introduces between phenomenology and psychoanalysis has its point of departure in a reading of the reduction as the dispossession of immediate self-consciousness, a dispossession at the end of which the initially intended sense that was taken to be true comes to appear dubious or suspect. Clearly, Ricoeur interprets the Husserlian reduction in a Hegelian manner: it has become a critique of immediate knowledge. And it is true that Husserl's philosophy of evidence, posited as the "principle of principles," is inevitably accompanied by a critique of evidence to the extent that one can place evidence at the foundation of being and knowledge only on the condition of unequivocally identifying what evidence is, what merits this name, and what is not evidence. For this critique of evidence perhaps extends much further than Husserl would have wanted, and Ricoeur instinctively plays on the extension of this critique in order to bring phenomenology and psychoanalysis together as much as possible.

The Husserlian critique of evidence is twofold. After showing that the intended object is only a subjective appearance that is limited to the instant and fleeting like it is really given, the entire context of objective reality is reduced to a presumptive series of potential evidences and as such non-evident. The same critique can be brought to bear, in a menacing way, on the *cogito* itself for which a living and concrete core, which is also limited to an evanescent present, escapes into the always open horizon of potential givenness, the co-intended, the implicit, and finally the unconscious.[5]

But there is more. If one considers the *cogito* no longer from a quasi-psychological point of view as a privileged given (however fragile and fleeting it may be), but in its true transcendental meaning, as a power of constitution, *as the power to constitute the meaning of everything that exists for us*, in and through this meaning, then it is another difficulty, or the same one in a more formidable form, which emerges for us. As an operation of constituting meaning, as the ego "functioning in the last instance," transcendental subjectivity remains in an "anonymity" that contradicts its claim to define appearing as such, that is to say, in its actuality.[6] Let's say it right away: this is the ultimate failure of Husserlian phenomenology, which is unable to resolve its ownmost problem, that of phenomenality—more precisely, the problem of the how of the original phenomenalization of phenomenality—that provides hermeneutics with its main argument. For if the ultimate power of constituting meaning thus itself escapes from phenomenality, if, as Ricoeur says, "intentionality is broader than thematic intentionality,"[7] then one is faced with a situation whose full implications must be unfolded. For they will also define the task, or better, the very nature of this hermeneutics for which the phenomenology of meaning and the psychoanalysis of the unconscious will appear as two modes of its fulfillment—unless, on the basis of their shared presuppositions, they are in fact only one and the same investigation.

Phenomenality thus only reigns on the level of thematic intentionality, which, as Ricoeur clarifies, "knows its object and knows itself in knowing that object."[8] This is immediate consciousness. To say that it knows its object means that its object is shown to it. To say that it knows itself in knowing the object is to say the same thing. It means that, in constituting this object and letting it be seen, it itself is nothing other than the appearing of this object, the pure appearing in which it is given to us. However, to affirm that operative intentionality, in exercise [*die fungierende Intentionalität*], overflows thematic intentionality or rather remains in the anonymous, and that it does not show itself as operative, is only to limit the scope of thematic intentionality itself and to affect it with a major limitation, from the phenomenological point of view. It is to affirm that, at the very heart of the act of showing, there is something that is not seen, such that the product of this act is not only that of a showing but also that of a not showing. What is thus pro-duced in the light is never completely or entirely there; the totality of its meaning is not exhibited there, inasmuch as it is also the result of a power that in itself is not shown. "The invisible unknowing of intentionality in act," to repeat Ricoeur's own terminology, entails the result that its correlate has or can always have another meaning than the one that is disclosed to the regard of the thematic intentionality that is immediately self-conscious about the object, namely, everything in this object that results from the intentionality in exercise and its hidden operation.

This distinction between thematic intentionality and anonymous intentionality, which is an entire post-Husserlian current to which Ricoeur refers explicitly,[9] is expressed in the form of a historical distinction between a meaning that is already constituted by the operation of an intentionality unbeknownst to itself and the apperception of this meaning by the thematic consciousness that *finds* it in front of itself without being able to understand it truly, that is to say, precisely without itself consciously constituting it. This disjunction is also the one that is introduced between non-reflective consciousness and a reflection on it that is always delayed but attempts to recover the factual meaning and make it fully intelligible by reactivating its genesis. This is precisely what is impossible, if it is true that the ultimate operative intentionality, that of reflection itself, always remains, as operative, in the anonymous. The project of an absolute knowing in the Hegelian sense, that is to say of a total recovery of operative intentionality, is broken up by its essence, that is, the inescapable primacy of the unreflected in relation to the reflexive, which is at the heart of reflection.

What results from such a situation is the emergence of a meaning that is not comprehended. More precisely, it is *the possible separation of meaning and consciousness* inasmuch as consciousness is placed before a meaning that it has not constituted on its own and consequently whose true tenor escapes it. It is unconscious. "It is possible to define the mind directly without appealing to self-consciousness by the aim of something or some meaning."[10]

A meaning is there without being understood, an unconscious meaning. That is to say a meaning that does not know about its truth, a text to be decoded and offered to the possibility of decoding, because it proceeds from a prior constitution. It is meaningful in itself, a meaning belonging to the region of meaning, to a hermeneutic domain whose components are all the elements of this genre, meanings that are not yet understood and thus remain to be understood. That is all that is needed for a hermeneutic, whether it is phenomenological or Freudian. It is the ideal material that is predestined for its treatment.

One can thus find in Husserl the explicit description of a situation that provides hermeneutics with its proper terrain [*terrain d'election*]. It involves the essential distinction between the active and the passive genesis of meaning. In the former, the ego actively and consciously intervenes in the constitution of a meaning that it creates through the help of specific acts, whose appearing it somehow oversees and which it is then able to reproduce as often as it wants. In passive genesis, to the contrary, the same ego is placed in a very different condition, which is no longer one of mastery but of submission to the object-meaning that it encounters but does not create. The passivity in question here is not like the simple reverse or reciprocal side of the productive activity of the categorical objects of reason, its modalization in a *habitus* and the correlative passage from meaning to an acquired state. Passive genesis functions instead as the indispensable prerequisite of active genesis in the sense that it brings a pre-discovered field of objects that are presupposed by categorical syntheses. For this genesis does not only produce the objects that will be found by the ego. Inasmuch as it is an operation that is originally constituting, it is carried out in the ego but without the ego, independently from its will and its consciousness. This is precisely the reason why all of its products are given as an opaque and already existing world. One knows the place that these passive syntheses of association and of temporality occupy in Husserlian phenomenology, on which they confer the character of an archeology of meaning. Since endless syntheses have constituted true layers of overlapping meaning, from archaic meanings that are passively pre-constituted up to thematically intended meanings—which includes, however, their fall back outside of phenomenological actuality and thus engenders, on the level of active genesis itself, increasingly thicker layers of passive sedimentation—then the investigation must inevitably be pursued as a continual effort to exhume these escaped meanings, the deepest and most fundamental of which have never been conscious. An act of noematic consciousness refers back to and implies an act of noetic consciousness; this is the explicit program of phenomenology and what makes it, in an exemplary fashion, a hermeneutics.

We have now become aware of the fact that the active intentionalities that constitute the archaic and fundamental meanings cannot be reduced merely to the processes of association and of temporality as they are in Husserl. They are also processes of desire, of the activity of drives and affects—which have the dual characteristics of being an essential passivity and unconscious. Thus the theory of passive genesis and, more broadly, phenomenology as a whole will sketch out a philosophical structure that offers a special welcome to psychoanalysis. Shouldn't this be understood as a hermeneutics of desire? "Is it not sufficient," asks Ricoeur, "to extend to desire and its objects this explication of layers of meaning, this investigation of an 'original foundation'? Is not the history of the libidinal object, through the various stages of the libido, just such an explication by means of successive retroreferences?"[11]

No sooner than desire has provided the model for an unconscious production of meaning and thus has demonstrated the possibility that a meaning exists without being conscious, does bodily ownness [*corps propre*]—Merleau-Ponty's flesh—come along to provide a concrete example of this model. Is it not precisely the seat of desire, of a set of "signifying behaviors" in which meaning is not offered as the ideal correlate of a theoretical or a representative intentionality but as this behavior itself, as a meaning found in a body, whose principle is indeed an intentionality but an "intentionality made flesh" in some sense, thus this body itself as an intentional body?

Perhaps under the influence of the thesis of the "Paris School" or simply in agreement with them, Ricoeur defined the analytic situation as a situation of language. But it is to language itself that one must first apply the model of unconscious meaning. To do so, it suffices to recognize that before every "explicit apophasis," that is to say, before being formulated thematically in an ideal statement in the form of a proffered discourse, all meaning is already at work and precisely as a "meaning at work" and actualized by a behavior. The proffered or explicit meaning is usually only an expression after the fact of this operative meaning that it presupposes.

This analysis of language, if it is connected to the analysis of perception, allows us to enter more deeply into its essence and find the same dialectic of absence and presence without which language would be unintelligible. For, to speak is to mourn the object, to renounce an actual presence (the presence of the mother, for example) in order to recover it as a form of absence in the sign. But the most primal experience, perception, already figures into this play of absence and presence, if it is the case that nothing is ever intended without appearing against the background of the co-intended and that each fragment of intuitive givenness, each side of the object, presupposes and refers to the indefinite horizon of potential appearances. This is why perception is surrounded by a horizon of absence, that is to say of unconsciousness, such that every actual presentation appears sadly limited with regard to the background from which it arises. While this finite presence is the presence of a meaning that is thematically intended by consciousness, the apparent meaning would be unintelligible without the totality of underlying meanings which are archaic and fundamental but remain sunk in the Night. Ricoeur can thus write: "Phenomenology turns out to be just as radical as psychoanalysis in contesting the illusion of immediate self-knowledge."[12]

This is because the ruler of phenomenality, which brings about the thesis of this radical finitude that opens onto an overwhelming primacy of the unconscious, is perception, that is, the world. As this decisive text admits: "The ambiguity of 'things' becomes the model of all ambiguity of subjectivity in general and of all the forms of intentionality."[13]

It is a characteristic of Ricoeur's thought, of its lucidity at the same time as its integrity, that he marks the difference between psychoanalysis and phenomenology, at the very moment when a unique agreement is established between them. This difference consists in the fact that, in Husserlian phenomenology, the becoming conscious that brings to light sedimented and lost meanings takes shape as a continual progress that nothing opposes in principle. Like the progress of perception, the process of the elucidation of awareness, although endless, is nonetheless accomplished no less spontaneously as the immanent teleology of intentional consciousness and as its own movement. It continually gives rise to new horizons of meaning and explicates them as well.

In psychoanalysis, by contrast, conscious and unconscious systems are separated by a bar that will be extremely difficult to cross. It implies, in any case, the introduction of totally different procedures from those of reflection and of traditional phenomenological elucidation. What gets reawakened by bringing them to light is no longer the intentional references which are established naturally and in some sense necessarily between the apparent sides of a cube or a house, for example, and those that do not appear but will certainly appear if "we move around" these objects. The associations that analysis will confront do not have the docility of the associations of the world of representation—which constitute the objectivity of the world of representation and are homogenous with it, visible or readable in it, and at the limit, are identical to its visibility. The associations of analysis obey, to express it simply, another principle than that of intentional thought, namely, forces. As a result, it is impossible to disclose their true meaning, that is to say, to go back to the desires and drives that determine it, without first mastering these very same desires and drives, and without using a method that makes this mastery possible and thus the modification by which the mastery over nurtured, or apparent meanings, will be effective.

It can then be understood why the phenomenological method and psychoanalytic therapy differ completely. For psychoanalysis can only be the therapy that it claims to be by changing levels. It must abandon the *telos* of an elucidation that, in the unfolding of intentional references, remains trapped in thematic and apparent meanings, in order to plunge into a reality of another order, into a play of forces which nourishes meaning. "To plunge" is understood in its proper sense: the psychoanalyst enters into this world of forces, becomes one of them, in the confrontation with the forces of the sick patient. By modifying them through this confrontation and in this way alone, the psychoanalyst modifies at the same time in the patient the power that produced the meanings at work: neurotic symptoms, hallucinations, phobias, stuttering, forgetting, etc.

Here it would be necessary to be able to reproduce the subtle analyses through which Ricoeur shows how the analytic treatment is always divided up. The method of investigation that must result in the correct interpretation is only an "intellectual part" whose effectiveness is subordinate to its insertion in the intersubjective relation of the analyst and the analysand, a relation that is established between forces and between resistances. It is a resistance that was really at the origin of the neurosis; consequently that is what must be defeated first in order for awareness to become possible, so that the work of interpretation can, and only then, become fruitful. For the victory over resistance can only happen in the course of analysis, by means of the transfer that reproduces the traumatic situation and tries to provide another outlet for it. The remembrance that Breuer's catharsis sought to accomplish, as if it were a properly intellectual and autonomous phenomenon, is replaced here by a repetition and by the reawakening of the forces and drives at the origin of neurotic symptoms. These symptoms are only substitute forms of satisfaction that can only result in failure. To what extent the transference appears as a repetition of the traumatic situation, that is to say as an instinctual conflict, can be seen in that the sick person seeks the same substitute satisfaction in relation to the analyst and in that the work of the analyst, who plunges into this lived relation with the patient, is to ensure that the patient avoids the trap of the past.

"Knowledge" [*savoir*] is only introduced into psychoanalysis within a dynamic and conflictual relation whose denouement alone will make possible the emergence of this knowledge as the power of healing, which will be the power of this knowledge. In the end, this justifies Freud's thesis that "the pathological factor is not his ignorance in itself, but the root of this ignorance is in his inner resistances; it was they that first called this ignorance into being, and they still maintain it now."[14] A treatment is thus only worthy of the name of psychoanalysis "if the intensity of the transference has been utilized for the overcoming of resistances."[15] For these reasons, Ricoeur is able to conclude that there is "an economic problem that completely distinguishes psychoanalysis from phenomenology" and that "the philosopher schooled in phenomenological reflection realizes his exclusion from an experiential understanding of what occurs in the analytic relationship."[16]

What Ricoeur's thought discovers here, under the heading of the "economic problem," is truly something that his reading of Freud confronts from the very outset, namely, the enigmatic world of energies and forces that are at work everywhere as the *true natura naturans* [*naturant*] of the mind and of every Freudian construction. This confrontation is developed in two steps. The first, whose main twists and turns have already been sketched out here, follows the trajectory that leads from the description of the immediate consciousness which is stuck in the aim of fallacious meanings *to the power that produces them, without consciousness or itself knowing this*: to the unconscious drives whose *topoi* and energetics tend to define the game [*cerner le jeu*]. But it is perhaps only by letting go of the consciousness that lacks the ability to exhibit the truth in its *Sinngebung*, in its donation of meaning, by performing this major decentering of the foyer of meanings at the end of which this foyer is placed in the unconscious.

This step of displacement is painful; it is the step of the "anti-phenomenology" that forces the human being to recognize that the meanings in the midst of which one lives and debates do not come from oneself but from powers that surpass oneself and for which one is a mere plaything, notably, the powers of language and desire. In the course of this "reduction not to consciousness but of consciousness," it is necessary to lose everything that involves the object of representation, its subject, the ego itself, and to undergo a triple humiliation that consists of no longer being the master of the universe, of others, or even of oneself.

The second step is very different. It manifests Ricoeur's extraordinary effort to reintroduce in the field of hermeneutics what seems to escape into the confines of the mind and the organism: brute force, the quasi-physical, blind energy, which knows nothing about the light where meaning shines and which, inherited from the Schopenhauerian Will, does not want to know anything. So, how can drives enter into relation with the world of meanings deployed by intentional consciousness that seems to define the humanity of the human being and thus the ultimate aim of every investigation seeking to return the human being to itself, to tear it away from dark powers? This is possible, *inasmuch as a drive enters into the mind*, not as itself or in its own reality, but through the intermediary of "representatives" that are precisely its representatives in the Psyche and constitute its basis. The representatives of the drives, with a physical, bio-energetic, material force, differ from the drives just like representation differs generally from what it represents, for example, from natural beings. As representations, the mental representatives of the drives are similar to the representations of consciousness; they are homogenous with it. The fact that they initially remain plunged in the unconscious does not prevent them, since their being is determined by the structure of representation, from being representable and thus suited to representation. They aspire to it as their true condition. The general essence of the mind is to be a reality that is still unconscious but is directed toward consciousness, as a representation—and that is how "conscious" is understood in both Freudian psychoanalysis and Ricoeur's hermeneutic phenomenology.

For, it is not only the representations whose proto-constitution is the work of desire that are first delivered over to the night. The representations of perception are also submitted to the law of this radical finitude about which we have spoken, which holds that only one of them is offered to the brightness [éclat] of intuitive presence while the others remain captive to the shadows, or this state that the metaphysics of representation has always called "virtuality." Precisely because mental phenomena contain within themselves the same essence as phenomenality, that of consciousness as representation and as intentional consciousness, they are submitted to the same law of transformation of virtual consciousness into actual consciousness—of the becoming-aware of consciousness understood as this becoming itself. This is how the interpretation of mental reality as representing drives and as representation can be led back to phenomenological actuality and can place back into the light of meaning that which hides from it in its original and ownmost being. The hermeneutic reading of psychoanalysis is illuminated in a single stroke, there where it draws its motivation as well as its mode of fulfillment: "There is a point where the question of force and the question of meaning coincide: it is the point where instincts are designated in the mind by representations and the affects that 'present' them."[17]

The theory of the representative [Repräsentanz], masterfully explained in two passages of this great work on Freud,[18] forms the key to unlocking the hermeneutic interpretation of Freudianism. After the critique of immediate consciousness and its reduction by topical and economic explanations, it allows for the beginning of the opposite movement, that of the recovery of meaning and thus of the recapturing of human autonomy and freedom, by the human being who has been displaced from itself. What founds this vast movement of becoming conscious that places psychoanalysis back within the orbit of Western thought is the ontological and structural homogeneity established between the unconscious and conscious systems. On both sides of the bar that separates them, and in spite of this bar, the same definition of mental reality reinscribes all of it, whether conscious or not, within the realm of meaning. Ricoeur's claims about this are quite explicit:

> For it is in relation to the possibility of becoming conscious in relation to the task of achieving conscious insight, that the concept of a psychical representative of an instinct becomes meaningful. Its meaning is this: however remote the primary instinctual representatives, however

distorted their derivatives, they still appertain to the delineation of meaning; they can in principle be translated in terms of the conscious mind. In short, psychoanalysis is possible as a return to consciousness because in a certain way the unconscious is homogeneous with consciousness; it is its relative other, and not the absolute other.[19]

The return of meaning—the becoming conscious of the mental representatives of the drives, and through their mediation but only through it, of the original drive of desire—is not a simple return to the point of departure. What is regained does not coincide with what has been lost. If the intentional consciousness that defines the humanity of the human being is saved, this consciousness and likewise this humanity appear profoundly changed at the end of the journey. It is a solitary consciousness that was displaced from what it believed itself to possess, namely, the meaning of its own existence. The decentering of the foyer of meanings leads to "another place of meaning" that Ricoeur calls the "transcendence of speech or the position of desire."[20] But the discovery of this second place derives again from a consciousness. The disjunction that is performed by the realism of Freudian topography, "this disjunction with respect to my consciousness is not a disjunction with respect to all consciousness."[21] The great work of interpretation in which private subjectivity—that of the analyst as well as the analysand—surpasses itself results in a consciousness of truth, or rather, it is the fact of this consciousness that coincides with the hermeneutic field inasmuch as it constitutes itself, in and through this work, as the new foyer of intelligibility where the rules that guide interpretation are elaborated, and where its true meaning can be perceived.

It is in and through this hermeneutic field that the system of mental processes is constructed that lay bare interpretation. The Freudian reality of topography thus remains subordinate to a consciousness that gives meaning, to the scientific consciousness of the truth; it is relative to this universal hermeneutic consciousness: "this reality only exists as a 'diagnosed' reality."[22] That is how the whole Freudian enterprise that accomplishes an archeology of the human subject can appear as an "extraordinary discipline of reflection." It is internal to it and ultimately blends with its own movement, such that consciousness—the immediate consciousness of the apparent meaning—is only lost so that reflection—the apodictic knowledge of scientific truth—can be saved.

To this rigorous thought that is able to pull together psychoanalysis and phenomenology in order to turn them into corresponding and complementary moments of a single grandiose process of reflection, we will pose a double question: *Which phenomenology accords with which psychoanalysis?* And we already have the answer: it is a phenomenology of intentional consciousness, of the consciousness that gives meaning, that is suited to a psychoanalysis that is itself understood as a decoding of meanings. Or, to say it more categorically, *it is within the same philosophical horizon, constituted by shared ontological presuppositions, that phenomenology and psychoanalysis can be seen as the Same: as a hermeneutic.* This horizon belongs to classical thought which, through its seemingly most different formulations—those of Husserlian phenomenology and Freudian psychoanalysis, for example—is dominated by an identical concept of consciousness, that is to say, of phenomenality. It is all the more essential to recognize clearly what this concept consists of, insofar as it is clearly in relationship to this concept that the antithetical concept of the unconscious, in turn, can be defined and understood.

The fact that the concept of consciousness around which all of psychoanalysis is organized is borrowed from classical thought is something that Freud states explicitly: "there is no need to characterize what we call 'conscious'; it is the same as the consciousness of philosophers and of everyday opinion."[23]

What is this self-evident concept of consciousness, that everyone understands, and that there is no need to explain? Another text states this explicitly: "Now let us call 'conscious' the conception which is present to our consciousness and of which we are aware, and let this be the only meaning of the term 'consciousness.'"[24]

Consciousness is representation. This proposition means: representing, which is to say the act of placing something in front is, as such, in accomplishing this placement in front, what pro-duces consciousness, that is to say, the phenomenality which consists of the fact of being placed in front considered in itself—such that nothing can become conscious unless it is placed in front, re-presented, and enters into the condition of representation.

But this phenomenological presupposition of the metaphysics of representation is absolutely universal; it directs all of Western thought and especially Husserlian phenomenology. To say that consciousness is intentional, and in a proposition that is aimed expressly toward its essence, that all consciousness is consciousness of something, is to confide the manifestation of everything that exists, including the manifestation of meaning, to the original emergence of exteriority, to a primordial transcendence. It matters little whether one conceives this emergence as the objectification of a Subject who is exhausted in it or as the clearing of a Nature that illuminates it. In either case, phenomenality consists in the opening of an Outside where every possible object becomes visible, in the ek-stasis of Being. The thoughts that relentlessly denounce Western metaphysics, understood as this metaphysics of representation, thus remain submitted to its rule as long as they confuse the phenomenality of Being with this ek-stasis that we are talking about.

The connection of consciousness and the unconscious on the basis of this ecstatic conception of phenomenality is easy to understand. It comes down to the observation of the finitude of the place where a being stands as an ob-ject, to the finitude of ek-stasis and of Being, which is understood starting from it. It is this finitude that presides over the exchange of themes between Husserlian phenomenology and Freudian psychoanalysis, an exchange that is demonstrated by Ricoeur's reading and results in their identification, or at least in the parallelism that is established between them as hermeneutic disciplines. This is what Ricoeur is referring to when he writes: "Every mode of being conscious is for subjectivity a mode of being unconscious, just as every mode of appearing is correlative to a nonappearing, or even a disappearing, both signified together, co-signified in the presumption of the thing itself,"[25] when he speaks profoundly about the "full significance of the perceptual model" for phenomenology—and, let us add, for psychoanalysis itself inasmuch as it remains under this perceptual model, that is to say, the unthought presuppositions of a metaphysics of representation.

But does the concept of the unconscious have any other function than to mark this finitude of representation and the ek-stasis in which it is rooted, to the extent that all intuitive presence is inevitably surrounded by an obscure horizon of empty potentialities? Would it not rather signify for Freud—even if unconsciously—*a radical calling into question of the metaphysics of representation and thus of the mode of phenomenality that is modeled on perception*? Although psychoanalysis largely remained derivative from classical thought, should that lead us to forget that its true historical origin, as Freud states, is found in "the great philosopher, Schopenhauer, whose unconscious 'Will' is equivalent to the mental instincts of psychoanalysis"?[26] The will constitutes the foundation of our being and is defined precisely by the exclusion from itself of every possible representation. It is thus not representation, even in the form of a "representative" of the drives, that constitutes the Foundation of the Psyche, but the being-outside-representation to which all these fundamental forms of our experience that are called Will, drive or desire. Although they never arise before our regard, in a world, aren't they nonetheless experienced by us, in the abyssal Night of our primal subjectivity, as what we are? Is it not remarkable that this archaic dimension of existence, this Foundation which is the basis of Being and of our own being, is designated by Freud as the unconscious and at the same time, as Energy and as Force?

If one refers to the 1912 "Note on the Unconscious," it can be seen that a singular turn of the problematic occurs there. The "justification" of the unconscious by the latency of most mental contents (that is to say of virtual representations such as memories that we are no longer thinking about) gives way to a consideration of the force and efficaciousness of unconscious thought, a force and efficaciousness that they owe, it seems, to their very unconsciousness. It is as if action were only conceivable in the Night of this subjectivity before the world, where every power and every force enters immediately into self-possession, without the least separation opening up between it and itself, without a Difference through which it would then be able to represent itself, to contemplate and to see itself—but it would no longer be able to act, inasmuch as, separated from itself by the distance of this first objectivity, it would be prevented thereafter from rejoining itself, from taking hold of its own power and deploying it.

Thus the emergence of an "active unconscious,"[27] that is to say, of an action that finds its site and its possibility in the radical immanence of an archaic subjectivity, carries Freud's thought outside of the field opened up and traveled by a metaphysics of meaning. Here it is the competence of a hermeneutics submitted to the presuppositions of Western thought that is in question. If force and the Energy that is the Foundation of the Psyche find the possibility of their being, that is to say their possibility of acting outside of representation, is the problem truly to return this type of a being, in spite of everything, to the being of this representation, to inscribe it against all opposition in the hermeneutic field? Has not the psychoanalytic cure shown that interpretation, that is to say the declension of meaning, is subordinate in a decisive way to the work of forces and thus to what they are in themselves, prior to interpretation? Is it not then precisely the being of force that needs to be thought in terms of its own essence? Does not its status outside-representation signify the negation of all phenomenality—or rather only the negation of the phenomenality that shines in the Greek phenomenon and that modern philosophy gathers together in representation?

In the depths of the psychic unconscious, there do not only exist unconscious representations (which really do not exist but only exist as the illusion of a metaphysics that does not conceive of being otherwise than as being-represented, and that actualizes it in this form even when the phenomenality whose task it is to promote has disappeared); there are also affects. However, according to a decisive statement by Freud, an affect is never unconscious: "it is surely of the essence of an emotion that we should be aware of it, i.e., that it should become known to consciousness."[28] The foundation of the psychic unconscious is never unconscious and is only called so inasmuch as it insurmountably rejects the visibility of the world from itself: this fact places phenomenology and psychoanalysis before a single essential task. The task is no longer to explain this foundation of our being through a light that excludes it in principle; instead, it is to think on its own terms the archaic dimension where phenomenality originally becomes phenomenal as affectivity. When psychoanalysis is put to the test by phenomenology, it is called to understand the status of these deepest layers of the psyche which determine our entire life, otherwise than in a purely negative way, as the simple rejection of consciousness [*Bewusstheit*]. When phenomenology is put to the test by psychoanalysis, it imposes the same program and requires phenomenology to provide a rigorous definition of the archaic dimension of the Psyche, of its essence as irreducible to that of natural beings and thus to an "unconscious" that would be identical to the unconsciousness of things, for example, to the biochemical processes of neurons.

The problem is thus not to propose a purely hypothetical interpretation of how material processes come to be represented in the Psyche[29] but, within the psyche and the interior of phenomenality itself, to draw the line of demarcation that divides between, instead of the conscious and unconscious systems naively realized by the topography, two heterogeneous and originally connected modes through which phenomenality is originally phenomenalized: in the ek-stasis of a world and in the impressional flesh of affects. They are heterogeneous to the extent that the latter excludes the ek-static Dimension in which the former is accomplished. Yet, they are originally conjoined, because the regard that moves in ek-stasis and ek-stasis itself are auto-affected, such that nothing enters into the light of the visible that has not already come into oneself in the invisible embrace of its own pathos.

Because these two modes are heterogeneous, the impossible leap from the former into the latter should never be attempted. The becoming conscious of the unconscious is a process that unfolds exclusively within the field of representation; it is the very movement of this representation; it is the passage to actuality of what would otherwise remain virtual; that is to say that it has not yet been formed by the act of consciousness that will let it be seen and will represent it. Because these two modes are originally conjoined, the actualization of representation as well as the contrary prohibition of it both presuppose the auto-affection of the process of this coming into the light of the ek-stasis, *the affect that either produces or represses representation*. That is why the fate of representation is subjected to the fate of affects, and that is why in the cure the abreaction and the repetition that take place in transference are the conditions for awareness [*prise de conscience*]. Contrary to the illusion of classical philosophy and hermeneutics, awareness is never the end for which the modification of affects and drives would only be a means, as if the goal were not life itself, well-being, or happiness but, once again, awareness, the intentional knowledge of a meaning that is objective and "true."

That is also why it is fallacious to place unconscious representations and affects on the same foundational level of the Psyche, under the title of the mental "representatives" of the drives. Affectivity and representation are precisely not situated on the same plane, because the former *is natura naturans* [*naturant*] and the latter is *natura naturata* [*naturé*]. Because the very designation of the affect as a "representative" falsifies its own being, this already illustrates the attempt of a metaphysics of representation to recapture into itself and reduce to its structure something that escapes it in principle. The affect, moreover, is not an equivalent of the drive, as if it were its psychic double. The task of a radical phenomenology, which alone can give psychoanalysis a philosophy,[30] is instead to think their identity. The internal connection of Force and Affectivity is not only due to the fact that, as the auto-affection of force, Affectivity forms the proper essence of every force. Because, in its auto-affection, the affect is radically passive with regard to itself and thus is laden with its own being even up to the unbearability of this weight, it seeks to discharge itself. It is thus the movement itself of the drive, which Freud rightly designates as the endogenous excitation that never ceases. In other words, it is auto-affection as constitutive of the essence of absolute subjectivity and of life.

The hermeneutic reading of psychoanalysis does not only have the immense merit of systematically elucidating the domain of meaning, understood as intentional meaning. By first giving rise to a confrontation between phenomenology and psychoanalysis and then to a collaboration between them, it has brought up many decisive problems and requires us to be more keenly aware of the presuppositions that have guided up to now the developments of the great thoughts of our times in a domain that determines what makes the humanity of the human. By inviting us to reflect on these presuppositions that are often the same and by calling them into question, it has opened up the investigation of new horizons.

Translated by Scott Davidson

Notes

1. Paul Ricoeur, *Freud and Philosophy: An Essay on Interpretation*, trans. Denis Savage (New Haven, Conn.: Yale University Press, 1970).
2. Ricoeur, *Freud and Philosophy*, 432.
3. Ricoeur, *Freud and Philosophy*, 347.
4. Ricoeur, *Freud and Philosophy*, 375.
5. See Husserl, *Cartesian Meditations*, §9.

6. See Husserl, *Crisis*, §55.
7. Ricoeur, *Freud and Philosophy*, 378.
8. Ricoeur, *Freud and Philosophy*, 378.
9. Specifically, Alphonse De Waelhens and Antoine Vergote, who are cited by Ricoeur in *Freud and Philosophy*, 379ff.
10. Ricoeur, *Freud and Philosophy*, 379.
11. Ricoeur, *Freud and Philosophy*, 381.
12. Ricoeur, *Freud and Philosophy*, 386.
13. Ricoeur, *Freud and Philosophy*, 385.
14. Cited by Ricoeur, *Freud and Philosophy*, 410.
15. Cited by Ricoeur, *Freud and Philosophy*, 413.
16. Ricoeur, *Freud and Philosophy*, 412, 414.
17. Ricoeur, *Freud and Philosophy*, 429.
18. See Ricoeur, *Freud and Philosophy*, 134–51, 455–58.
19. Ricoeur, *Freud and Philosophy*, 430.
20. Ricoeur, *Freud and Philosophy*, 424.
21. Ricoeur, *Freud and Philosophy*, 431.
22. Ricoeur, *Freud and Philosophy*, 436.
23. Sigmund Freud, "An Outline of Psychoanalysis," in *The Standard Edition*, vol. 23, 159.
24. Sigmund Freud, "A Note on the Unconscious in Psychoanalysis" (1912), in *The Standard Edition*, vol. 12, 260.
25. Ricoeur, *Freud and Philosophy*, 386.
26. Sigmund Freud, "A Difficulty of Psychoanalysis" (1917), in *The Standard Edition*, vol. 17, 143–44.
27. Freud, "A Note on the Unconscious in Psychoanalysis," in *The Standard Edition*, vol. 12, 261.
28. Sigmund Freud, "Papers on Metapsychology" (1915), in *The Standard Edition*, vol. 14, 177.
29. Ricoeur agrees with this, stating that "this function of *Repräsentanz* is certainly a postulate. Freud gives no proof for it" (*Freud and Philosophy*, 136).
30. See François Roustang, "Une philosophie pour la psychanalyse?" *Critique* 163 (1985): 1172–80.

Part 3

Politics, Art, and Language

9

The Concept of Being as Production

1

Ever since human beings have inhabited the earth, they have been producing their livelihood, namely the means of subsistence necessary to their sustenance. Ever since human beings have produced their livelihood, they have represented this production to themselves through representations which occupy their minds almost exclusively, precisely because these representations refer to their quotidian activity, to the condition of their life and their survival. If by ideology we understand these representations as a whole, then we must say: ideology is the thought of the essential. There are two reasons for this. On the one hand, what ideology represents, what it takes up in its gaze, is precisely the essential production of life, which cannot suffer interruption, for even a day. The essential is the object of this thinking. On the other hand, it is also its subject. The essential thinks in this thinking: the essential determines this thinking, not only by assigning it its object, but also by prescribing to it the very modalities exhibited by this thinking. Consequently, the production of life, the essential, determines the categories and forms of thinking. Ideology, as Marx so profoundly said, is the "language of life,"[1] that is to say of the production of life by itself, of its activity.

However, representations of production, important as they may be, from the start and for the most part with the primitives, for example, have been only imaginary, sensory representations, and not yet thinking in the proper sense, namely conceptual thinking. It is only with the advent of philosophy in Greece that the thought of production has become a concept. This emerged with the Aristotelian theory of the four causes. First of all, it is obvious that this theory, which was to play a very important role in the history of Western thought, only makes sense with reference to production as it was practiced in Greece, with reference to craft production. Take the example of the making of a silver vessel destined to be offered to the gods. There are four causes or four principles of the existence of this chalice. Firstly, the matter—silver—of which the vessel is made, and which is responsible for its existence in the sense that, without this silver, the chalice would not be. Secondly, the form, the exterior appearance which makes the chalice precisely what it is—a chalice and not something else. Thirdly, the sacrifice to which the chalice is destined and for which it was made, namely the *telos* which, in conjunction with the matter and the form, is co-responsible for the existence of the vessel. Lastly, the silversmith who formed, worked, the silver, who made the chalice. We thus have four causes: material, formal, final, and efficient.

At this point, however, we must take heed of Heidegger's commentary, which holds that what has just been said about the fourth cause is fundamentally inaccurate. The fourth cause is indeed the silversmith, but not his concrete activity, which is material in some way, not his manipulating the silver, not his hammering it, not his giving it shape. I quote Heidegger from "The Question Concerning Technology": "the silversmith—but not at all because he, in working, brings about the finished sacrificial chalice as if it were the effect of a making; the silversmith is not a *causa efficiens*."[2] Heidegger adds that Aristotle does not know the cause which bears this name, nor does he have a name with which to designate it. The production of the chalice thus has nothing to do with what we mean today by production—namely, a determinate activity. In that case, it would be a bodily activity having as its result, as its effect, the object produced, or at least the shape which defines it. If we take our bearings by Heidegger's text, the production of ancient Greece is not work.

How, then, is the silversmith co-responsible for the existence of the chalice, if it is not by fabricating it? What does "to produce" mean for him? Instead of providing us with an understanding of what production is, the silversmith's activity can on the contrary be understood only through production and its essence. There is an essence of production, which is the very essence of being and which is fulfilled in accordance with the four conjoined modalities, the four causes, the four principles of Aristotle. To produce the chalice is to respond to the chalice's being there before us, ready to be offered in a sacrifice. To produce means to promote entry into presence, to lead something to its appearing, to let it come forth in its presencing. To give us an understanding of what the essence of technology is, Heidegger quotes Plato's *Symposium*: "Every occasion for whatever passes over and goes forward into presencing from that which is not presencing is *poiesis*, is bringing-forth (*Her-vor-bringen*)."[3] To bring-forth, to pro-duce, therefore means to effectuate the transition from non-presence to presence. The text on *The Principle of Reason* furnishes the ultimate characterization of production: "To pro-duce the world before oneself."[4]

Granted, what is at stake is the production of the chalice, but if the production of the chalice designates its coming into presence, it is in the world precisely and as coming into the world, as the advent of the world, that this production takes place. Aristotle has more or less confused the ontic determinations with the ontological determinations, but what he aims at, in the end, is the being of the chalice and its coming into being. That is why, if we are to be able to characterize what being a cause means to him, we must take the *In-der-Welt-sein* as our point of departure.

If this is so, if the essence of production is coming into presence, then this production, *poesis*, not only designates the production of the chalice by the silversmith, namely, the poetic and artistic act which renders manifest insofar as it couches something in a form or endows it with the aspect of thinghood; production, *poesis*, also designates nature itself, *phusis*, within which the thing discloses itself to presence. For example, *poesis* designates the blossoming of a flower. Heidegger says that through production "the growing things of nature as well as whatever is completed through the crafts and the arts come at any given time to their appearance."[5] This is so because, in the end, production is unconcealment itself, *aletheia*.

We can already discern that when, at the dawn of Western philosophy, production becomes the theme of thinking, it is purely and simply reduced to truth, it is the production of truth. From the very start, the thinking of production reduces production to thought, to the ontological milieu where thought unfolds itself, and to the foundation of this milieu.

This becomes even clearer when Heidegger thinks the essence of technology. Technology is not the set of means laid out with a view to productive fabrication. Neither machines nor their cogs nor pistons nor hammers constitute its essence. The essence of technology is to be understood on the basis of unconcealment and as one of the modes according to which this unconcealment occurs and calls upon us. In the past, *techne* was this unconcealment as such; *techne* was the unconcealment which produces the truth in its radiance, and the beautiful was this radiance of the truth. Heidegger says: "the production of the true in the beautiful."

Today technology is no longer like that. However, and in spite of what it has become, its essence still resides in unconcealment, of which it is only a differentiated mode. Which mode? The one wherein man lays bare nature, but as that which must be utilized by a manufacturing activity and as a means to this activity. Nature is disclosed, freed so as to release the energy it harbors. It is in this way that the earth's crust discloses itself as a coal basin, the river as that which must deliver its power to the electrical plant, etc. This unconcealment which delivers nature as a standing-reserve, as a stock of raw materials and energy, as a resource to be exploited in such a way that this exploitation is maximized, Heidegger calls provocation. Provocation summons nature to deliver us all that can be made into something. This provocation of nature is the way in which being calls upon us today. That is why such a provocation, which rules the essence of technology, characterizes nothing less than the last age of Western metaphysics. The latter can be described and understood as follows.

It is a metaphysics of the will—of the will to will; it is a radical objectification of all things; it makes objects of all beings—objects for a subject, objects offered for the domination and action of a subject, which represents these things and ascertains them in its very representation. We are then in the epoch of epistemologies that immediately interpret Being as a being that is the object of a subject. The project inherent in these theories, the project of reaching an unconditional domination of beings, is equally a project of reaching absolute certainty—as can be seen in Descartes and Hegel. The supremacy of reason arising in the West is the supremacy of a dominating and calculative reason. This reason orders beings, and through it the will masters things. Wanting to exert mastery over things, the will wants nothing else but the reign of its own willing and that is why it is indeed a will to will.

Now, what will concern us in this world of technology, as Heidegger understands it, is what it presupposes—namely, the erasure of any distinction between theory and praxis.

Theory, in its original sense, means to behold the aspect through which a thing appears, to see this thing in its appearing, to see this appearing itself. Original theory is the sight of truth. Doubtless, in the theory of knowledge, and even more so in scientific theories, this original sense becomes altered. Theory no longer gazes at truth. It aims at dominating the real and, to that end, at grasping the real in accordance with characteristics that render this subjection possible. In the words of Max Planck, theory now says: "The real is what is measurable." What is at stake everywhere is achieving mastery over the real through measurement, through morphology, through the exhibiting of causal series that render the phenomena predictable, etc. Theory delimits its objects; it structures them in accordance with categories that permit their subsumption under theory, their subjection to the grasp of theory. Nature is no longer *phusis*; it is, for example, a complex of computable forces.

If we now turn our attention toward praxis, we see that it is generally understood as the application of theory, as the operationalization of theory to useful ends. But if practice is a realization of certain goals, a disposition of things in accordance with an order that suits us and offers them to our grasp, that allows our transforming the world to our convenience, then one must say that theory has already accomplished all that.

As soon as the rational organization and the computing of things come into play, as soon as the reign of the will begins, as well as the project to enframe beings in their totality, then theory and praxis are conjointly at work.

However, theory and praxis are not only identical because they exhibit a common project, but by virtue of a weightier reason: because they draw their possibility from the same essence, which dwells in each of them. We have seen that theory—even scientific theory—is only one way of grasping beings and thus of disclosing them. Heidegger writes: "within 'theory,' understood in the modern way, there yet steals the shadow of the early *theoria*."[6] But practice, *techne*, equally presupposes the work of unconcealment, not only because original *techne* is only the production of truth, but because the essence of modern technology as well proceeds from truth and as its destiny.

To sum up the Heideggerian interpretation of technology, we can say that it compels us to link production and unconcealment, to say that production is much more the doing of unconcealment than of technology; and that technology itself, in reality, qualifies as production only insofar as it too belongs to unconcealment and is a form of it.

As a consequence of these analyses, practice is reduced to theory and both are reduced to truth. In all this, to understand being as production means to understand being as coming into the truth of the world.

It is this reduction of praxis to *theoria*, this definition of production as production and manifestation of a world, that I would like to question in this paper. First of all, if we go back to the Aristotelian theory of the four causes of the existence of the sacrificial vessel, we see that its great weakness is to enumerate these causes in such a way that this enumeration is based on nothing but an external description of crafts production in ancient Greece. Of course, the apparently philosophical character of the intepretation offered by Heidegger of Aristotle's theory consists in seeking the unity of the four causes, namely, in understanding the reason behind this fourfold stratification of the essence of the foundation. I say "apparently philosophical character," for the attempt to think the four causes from a fundamental ontological unity, and as four modes of activity of this single essence, is a mystification if one of the causes turns out to be ontologically heterogeneous to the other three. To hold the four causes in the unity of a thought and of a single foundation is to forget, to disguise, the specific mode of being of that cause which is different from the others; it is to forget and to disguise the fundamental mode of being of being itself.

When considering the silversmith's making of the chalice, is it licit to put his deed, the concrete activity that he accomplishes, on a par with the silver of which the chalice is made, or with the chalice's form or purpose? Since what is at stake here is an ontological quest for ultimate foundations, our question is given the following formulation: is the being of action homogenous with that of, for example, silver? In other words, is the mode of revelation of action itself the same as the mode of revelation of what is there before us?

To cut the matter short, I would like to make the following observations about Heidegger:

1. The production of nature, the blossoming of the flower, is identical to the production accomplished by the artist or the craftsman, the worker in general.

2. In the production genuine to the craftsman, Heidegger considers the doing itself, the activity, as something negligible, which he labels pejoratively with the word "fabrication." I quote from "The Question Concerning Technology": "Thus what is decisive in *techne* does not lie at all in making and manipulating nor in the using of means, but rather in the aforementioned revealing."[7] However, by reducing the act of making and of manipulating to unconcealment, Heidegger reduces it to unconcealment as he understands it and as it accomplishes itself in nature, namely, to the unconcealment of the world.

3. It is true that there is a sense in which Heidegger distinguishes the unconcealment of technology from the unconcealment of things in nature. The natural thing produces itself before us, whereas what technology discloses is not produced without the intervention of the craftsman. But nothing more is said about the matter, and it probably is a mere empirical curiosity. On the other hand, modern technology unconceals in a manner specific to it, namely, in the mode of manipulating and enframing. The specificity of this mode of unconcealment resides in that the mode takes hold of beings, that it is therefore not the original *theoria* which lets things appear in their presence, and that, in this way, it obscures unconcealment as such—Heidegger says that it "blocks the shining-forth and holding-sway of truth."[8] But the specific unconcealment of technology which masks the essence of unconcealment is only possible through and within this essence: it is in the world and against the background of the truth of the world that being is enframed and manipulated by modern technology.

4. Lastly, if we consider the unconcealment proper to modern technology as it is described by Heidegger, we notice that it is one and accomplishes itself globally: within this unconcealment, the fate of the activity of the one who works is identical to that of the raw materials, of form and of its end. The essence of technology is like a structure: the elements co-constituting it receive their intelligibility and their definition

from that structure. Just as the Greek silversmith was co-responsible for the chalice within one single production, similarly, within modern technology, the fallenness of unconcealment maintains the homogeneity of the four causes and here again dodges the specificity of action and of work as such.

The fourth Aristotelian cause—the silversmith and his deed—has later been interpreted—and as early as the Romans—as *causa efficiens*, as what is really in deed, as what produces an effect or the produced object. If what we have just said is correct, the interpretation of the fourth cause as efficient cause refers to the essential and does not, as Heidegger would have it, signify a loss of what is essential. Consequently, could not the guiding thread of the thought of what production is in its being consist in an analysis of the concept of cause as efficient cause, an analysis of the history of this concept in Western thought? If we were to follow such a course, we would unfortunately witness the decay and the dissolution of this concept of cause. For Malebranche, cause in the sense of a real action really followed by an effect is the privilege of God only—it is thus absent from our experience. With Hume, it suffices to bracket God for causality to vanish altogether. This inability, on the part of Western thought, to think causality as real activity finds its last and purest expression in the positivism that gradually comes to dominate philosophy until our time, and that holds sway over it today more than ever: causality is a metaphysico-religious illusion that we must get rid of: there exist only successions or structures of phenomena whose regularities are extricated by science. In these times of the distress of metaphysics, Kant of course attempted to salvage causality. But what did he make of it? He turned it into a category of thought, namely of the representation of the world and of its truth.

It is true that salvation often appears at the bottom of the abyss. One could note here that precisely at the moment of positivism's imminent establishment and extension of its reign, if not over philosophy, then at least over European culture, a thinker of genius showed himself able to apprehend a true causality in the sense of real action, of bodily action, such as, for example, the action of the Greek silversmith or of workers in general. In this case, two things are noteworthy: (1) this thinking of concrete production was only possible through a conscious overthrow of the entire traditional philosophical horizon; (2) this philosophy, which constitutes the only philosophy of our world—I mean of the world of work—was to remain shut in the silence and solitude of its depth. I shall not, however, speak of Maine de Biran here. I only mention his name to say that without him our reflections on production might not have been possible.

If we look back to the epoch under consideration, to the end of the eighteenth and the beginning of the nineteenth centuries, we witness a decisive event. This event is not a cultural, philosophical, or ideological event. It is not relative to the thought of production but concerns production itself; it is the extension and formidable development of production in the form of large-scale modern industry. It is thus production itself which calls upon thinking and compels it to thematize production. That epoch sees the blossoming of the science of political economy, or at least an extraordinary development of this science which appears as the echo of the development of production. The most remarkable results of this new science are concentrated in Adam Smith's famous book *An Inquiry into the Nature and Causes of the Wealth of Nations* of 1776. In this work, Smith rigorously circumscribes the real essence of production and of the new world to which it gives rise: this essence is work. An entire problematic—that of political economy—organizes itself around the issue of work. Political economy does not, however, radically elucidate the concept it uses: that is to say, the elucidation that it does perform fails to go back to being. Smith places work at the foundation of political economy, but he does not raise the question of the being of work, of the ultimate essence of production.

At the end of the eighteenth century, Smith's book is translated into German and read by a philosopher, by the philosopher Hegel. As Aristotle had thought the Greek craftsman's production, similarly Hegel thinks the production beheld by the newly constituted political economy. It is a crucial cultural event that dominates modern thought to a large extent. Focalized in Hegel's thought, how does Western philosophy think the production that unfolds its essence in modern industry? The answer to this question is to be found in the notes written by Hegel in Jena during the years 1803–04, shortly after his reading of Adam Smith. In these lecture notes, Hegel does not directly focus on the topic of work, but he seeks the conditions of possibility of the existence of consciousness. Language manifests itself as the first of these conditions, because immediate consciousness is sensory consciousness, because sensibility is a ceaseless vanishing, and because consciousness only escapes this vanishing insofar as it speaks, insofar as, for the vanishing sensation, language substitutes the name, the word, wherein consciousness finds a stable and durable existence, the permanent existence of being. This stable being of language is like a bridge thrown over the abyss of sensory vanishing: the stable being of language confers being upon consciousness. In the Jena manuscripts, we can read: "Language is the existing concept of consciousness . . ."[9] But the existence bestowed upon consciousness by language is yet only an ideal and theoretical existence, that of the word. To be sure, the empirical intuition ideally [*idéellement*] posited in the word acquires the transparency of universality in the word. The transparency of universality lifts the empirical intuition from its intrinsic obscurity, but empirical intuition achieves only a manner of ideal reduplication in the word. This reduplication leaves the intuition unchanged and perhaps fails to capture its ineffableness.

That is why Hegel abruptly opposes the necessity of action to this theoretical and ideal existence of consciousness. By "action" he means the concept of work he has just discovered in Adam Smith. We must therefore raise the following question: what is the being of work as Hegel understands it, what is the being of production? One could as well say: what about being itself—if it is true that being resides in production? As early as the Jena manuscript, from the moment Hegel thinks about production, he interprets work as what allows consciousness to transform itself into something objective, and this objective something is the instrument—what Hegel calls a middle term. The instrument appears then as the very existence of consciousness, as its real, durable, effective being, as opposed to the objective but yet ideal being of the word within language. I quote: "Consciousness acquires a real existence opposed to the preceding ideal existence insofar as, in work, consciousness changes itself into this middle term, which is the instrument."[10] The instrument bestows the permanence of real being upon work by locating it within objective universality. There we find the reason for Hegel's paradoxical statement that the instrument, which is only a means, has more value than the end. Because the instrument is the objectification of action, it is not merely the object of action; it is rather action as object, action entering the effective condition of objectivity.

This connection between action and objectivity which requires that action produce itself as objective, is discernable in yet a second feature of work: the necessity for work to accomplish itself in accordance with a rule, a method. Individual activity, indeed, is only work to the extent that it fits into a way of proceeding consisting in a concatenation of defined processes, a concatenation which is there before us, the same for all, and to which one conforms oneself insofar as one performs a certain action. It is such and such work, which must be executed in such and such a manner, by going through a sequence of operations, which I see and can show. This manner of proceeding, this universal method, constitutes the essence of work as objective essence. Hegel writes: "there is a universal method, a rule for all work . . . But this universal rule is, for work, the true essence."[11] Doubtless, to the individual about to submit to the rule, the rule gives itself as something external to him, as "something existing for itself . . . as inorganic nature."[12] But this external being is precisely what the individual must learn, what he must assimilate, what he must become and into which his activity must blend in order to be effective and, by the same token, recognized. Skill, that is to say in the end, work itself, is nothing else but the process through which the individual transcends himself so as to give his activity, and thus his very being, the form and reality of the universal. In the same passage, Hegel writes: "Work is not an instinct, but a rational activity that, in the people, makes itself into a universal and, consequently, stands in opposition to the singularity of the individual, a singularity that must be overcome."[13]

The connection between work and objectivity is also exhibited by the fact that work does not aim at satisfying the needs of the individual performing it but the needs of all, that it is universal work in the service of universal need. "The work of the entire people inserts itself between the set of needs of a singular individual and his activity."[14] This means that, in its content, the work of each individual has as its goal the satisfaction of the needs of all other individuals, that this work is therefore not in itself what it is for this individual, but what it is for all, and that it thereby becomes, in itself and in its own reality, a universal reality.

The dialectic of the product fully brings to light the presupposition undergirding the analysis of work. In the product, the reality of individuals has become entrusted to the power of objectivity, and the product is precisely their very being, henceforth posited outside themselves. "But," says Hegel, "this being-exterior is their action; it is only what they have made of it: they, as acting and suppressed, are this being-exterior."[15] It follows that this being-exterior of individuals is their real being; that, posited outside themselves, it is what they can perceive, what shows itself to them, their "spirit"; and that this spirit, as reality and objectivity, in the end exists in itself and for itself, independently of them, who thereby find themselves—and this proposition should be taken literally—entirely suppressed. The quoted text continues with the following essential assertions: "And in this exteriority of themselves, in their being grasped as suppressed-being, as middle term, they behold themselves as a people. And this product which is theirs is thereby their own spirit itself. They produce their spirit, but revere it as being for itself. This spirit is for itself, for their activity, through which they produce it, is the suppression of themselves."

The radical origin of the connection between work and objectivity thus reveals itself. This origin resides neither in the instrument nor in the method to be followed by any activity claiming to be work, nor in the product. Instrument, method, and product only bind action and objectivity against the background of their common essence, which is the essence of action. This essence of action is objectification as such. Being, for Hegel, is what is there, what offers itself in the light of objectivity. To understand being as production is to understand it as the production of this objectivity. Action intervenes everywhere in Hegel's philosophy as the instauration of the horizon of the visibility where the Being of any possible being resides. Action has therefore an ultimate ontological meaning. What comes to be through it, what becomes actualized in it, is not this or that, the making of such and such an object, the production of such and such a content of experience; it is rather the production of this content in experience, in the light itself. This is why action occurs—so that light is, so that being is. This is why action occurs as objectification, because light is, for Hegel, the light of the world.

It may sometimes seem that Hegel speaks of action abstractly, that he ignores the particular character of the multiple actions that compose the course of the world and their specific laws, so as to reduce them to the monotonous scheme of alienation and of the overcoming of alienation. The reason for this is that Hegel considers the action of action, namely, what it truly does. In a flash of metaphysical seeing, he understands that what action does is not a determinate thing but that action makes it possible for this thing to be, for it to come into the light of reality. He understands that action, that production, is this coming into the light of the world, or, to appeal to a language already used, that it is the *In-der-Welt-Sein*.

What I propose to show is that in interpreting production as production of being and as production of the being of the world, Western philosophy exhibits its inability to think the real being of action, the being of real action. In order to establish this point, I shall have recourse to a thinker both well and little known, namely Marx. I shall attempt to understand the meaning of the radical overturning that takes place in his thought when production is no longer thought on the basis of truth, and when, on the contrary, truth is grasped in its originary being as production.

Through a philosophical recapitulation, we shall attempt to relive the stupendous overthrow that shook up the very foundations of Western thought in 1845 or, at least, one of its most steadfast presuppositions. Before undertaking this task, we must make another remark. Of all philosophers, Marx seemed the least prepared to carry out such an overturning because his philosophical education took place within the horizon that was to be overturned.

Marx thought about the essence of work in the *Economic and Philosophic Manuscripts* of 1844 for the first time. He had just read the English economists, in particular Adam Smith. He thought like the neoHegelian philosopher that he was then. Marx's situation is comparable to that of

Hegel in Jena, a situation in which Western thought, with its own presuppositions, finds itself face to face with the concrete problem of production. What is so noteworthy is that in 1844 Marx says about work exactly what Hegel said about it in the manuscripts of 1803: in both cases, we find the ontological interpretation of work and production as objectification. I should also mention that in 1844 Marx is Feuerbachian, materialist. It is striking, therefore, to see Feuerbach's materialism and Hegel's idealism say exactly the same thing about work: thanks to this example, it is clear that philosophy must always go beyond doctrines, their explicit content, and their conceptual systems to the hidden presuppositions really guiding them.

To end this first part of my paper, I want to recall briefly what Marx says in 1844 about work, namely that its essence is constituted by the process of objectification as such—and this is said in such a way that Marx himself acquires an awareness of the identity between his thesis and Hegel's. The third manuscript of 1844 states: "The greatness of Hegel's *Phenomenology* and of its final result is . . . that he thus grasps the essence of work and conceives objective man—true, because real man—as the result of his own work."[16]

It is true that in the *1844 Manuscripts* man and no longer consciousness objectifies itself. Feuerbach taught Marx to replace consciousness with the human species. However, the human species is in many respects only an unconscious reduplication of Hegelian consciousness. What is the human species, for Feuerbach? What characteristic sets it in opposition to the other species, to the other animals? The animal is, as it were, buried in its individual life, it is identical to its need, its activity is nothing but its need instinctively striving after satisfaction. The object of this activity is a particular object, which the animal consumes and which becomes a part of the animal, vanishing in it.

What characterizes the human species is precisely its relation to the species. This means that, far from being directly and exclusively turned toward sensory singularities, man is capable of opening up to the universal, that is, to the genus of things, to their laws, to their concepts. As such, human activity does not, as does animal activity, obey simple individual drives. It is able to model itself after the genus of things, and, through this, it becomes work. Work takes the universal laws of nature as its laws for building. It creates objects in conformity with these laws, having an internal finality, a finality of their own, capable of subsisting in their conformity with the structures of being. In short, work creates universal objects. "Man," says Marx, "gives shape in accordance with the laws of beauty."[17] Doing this, creating in accordance with the aesthetic laws of nature, the laws of things and their genus, man renders these laws manifest in the objects he creates. Better yet, he renders manifest and objective in the objects his ability to create in accordance with the laws of the genus: he manifests his relation to the genus. But the relation to the genus is the relation to the universal; it is Hegelian consciousness. One therefore understands how in the *1844 Manuscripts* human work really takes place as self-consciousness: because its object—the object created by work in the objectification of work which constitutes it—is nothing but the objectification of the relation to the universal, thus the objectification of consciousness itself.

Next, we shall try to show how Marx, burdened as he was by the unconscious Hegelianism of Feuerbach's thought, abruptly broke away from it, how he came to understand that the process of coming into the objectivity of a world is not real action, and moreover, lets the originary essence of being escape.

2

How the production of objectivity—the letting-come-before into this foreground of light that the world itself is—does not constitute a real action, that is what Marx attempts to establish from the third manuscript of 1844 onward, in his radical critique against Hegel. This critique still relies on Feuerbach: it asserts that in objectifying itself in the world, consciousness is unable to create any real being. Indeed, what characterizes real being is that it is a sensory being and, as such, a singular and individual being. Singularity and individuality belong to the phenomenological effectiveness of being, to its concrete givenness, and that is why Hegel could not ignore these ontological features. But he immediately falsifies them, interpreting them as moments of the process of the universal's unfolding itself, that is to say, of thought's unfolding itself. This attempt to explain the singularity and individuality of effective being on the basis of universality is a constant in Hegel. For example, it is from the universal essence of will that *The Principles of the Philosophy of Right* proceed in order to give an account of the system of right and of the political system as a whole, of the state and of its concrete determinations. How so? Pure and universal will in itself is still undetermined, unreal. If it is to realize itself, an effective act of the will must be accomplished, namely a singular act; and this singular act of will, in turn, is only something real if accomplished by an individual, if an individual carries it out. In this way, one deduces the existence of the individual from the universal essence of the will—which is also thought. For the will to realize itself, someone must make the decision, a ruler is needed: the existence of monarchy and the existence of the king of Prussia receive their legitimacy from the essence of pure thought.

The mystification by virtue of which being is recognized in its singularity and individuality only to be reduced to a moment of the Idea, to a phase of its realization, is visible in Hegel's *Logic*. In order to reach its truth, its reality, the Idea must objectify itself, give itself to itself in the form of otherness—and this being-other of the Idea, which is its reflection, its phenomenon, which here again takes on the form of particularity, of objective determination, is nature.

Nature is thus the objectification of thought. In nature, thought becomes alien to itself, posits itself as other, but this alienation, consequently, is not different from thought's own action: it is its objectification. Alienation and objectification are identical for two reasons: (1) what thought posits in the form of otherness, before itself, is itself; it is therefore thought that assumes the appearance of exteriority, of nature; and (2) thought itself carries out this positing of itself before itself, this positing of itself in the other.

From this, it follows that what is posited by the objectification of thought in the form of otherness not only proceeds from thought but is nothing but thought itself. It is thought in the form of otherness and exteriority. In relation to thought, this otherness and exteriority are therefore merely a pseudo-otherness, a pseudo-exteriority, a pseudo-reality, by no means a reality really different from thought.

That is why this alienation, being but a pseudo-alienation, is so easily overcome. Indeed, what is needed to abolish it? It suffices to know all that we just described; it suffices to know that the object posited by thought in its objectification as other than itself, as nature, does not differ in reality from thought itself. As soon as thought knows that, as soon as knowing knows that what stands before it, its object, is only other than it in appearance, differs from it only in appearance, it knows that its object is in reality only itself: it knows that before its object, alongside its object, it is in reality alongside itself, that it dwells close to itself in the other.

Alienation is therefore overcome, sublated, but this sublation is identical to its being maintained: it lets the opposite term, the other, the object, nature, subsist. What is at stake is not the real suppression of the object, the action upon it, but only the knowledge that what appears as other than thought is in effect not different from it. That is why this other term need not be suppressed, but, on the contrary, it needs to be maintained and preserved, for it is the manifestation of thought itself, its objectification identical to its reality. That is why thought confirms this other term, reaffirming it as the reaffirmation of itself. In this way, Marx retrieves from the depths the meaning of the Hegelian *Aufhebung*, that of a negation preserving what it negates. The negation of the being-other, of the object, of nature, is nothing but *the negation of the meaning of being-other that it had*, not the suppression of its real being. The negation of the meaning of being-other that the object had goes hand in hand with the affirmation of a new meaning, that according to which this being other is in effect the same as thought, its objectification, its realization.

As such, the action at stake here is only an action bearing upon ideal meanings, upon propositions; it is an action that is itself ideal, abstract, that does not change reality and is not a real action. In *The German Ideology*, the entire polemic against the neo-Hegelians only carries this evidence to its extreme: the neo-Hegelians assert that they are fighting only sentences, but they forgot to add, says Marx, that to these sentences they themselves oppose only sentences. With the action of thought, what is at stake is not to change real being but only to interpret it otherwise. That is why real being remains unchanged under these ideal modifications which slide over it without reaching it. Thus, for Hegel, the real world, the alienated world of politics, of the state, of religion, etc., is not abolished, but rather preserved once it is endowed with the meaning of being not the other of spirit, but its objectification, its realization.

Now, however important this critique of Hegel by Marx may be, we must step back from it and discern its ambiguity. This critique is founded upon Feuerbach's materialism. This materialism opposes sensible, singular, and individual being to Hegel's ideal being and—with respect to the faculty that gives us beings—opposes intuition to Hegel's thought. Now, I want to say that Feuerbach's materialism—and materialism in general—is burdened by a deep-seated ambiguity. One says: real being is sensible being, the being of nature; and man himself, according to Marx in the *1844 Manuscripts*, is a "being of nature." But to be sensible, to be a being of nature, means two things: on the one hand, sensible being is what is sensed, a stone, a wall, a machine, any being belonging to nature, what Feuerbach calls material being, matter; sensible being, on the other hand, means to be susceptible of sensing, to bear within oneself the capacity to open up to exterior being, and, within this opening, to receive it, to sense it. What is at issue in the second case is a sensibility in the sense of the transcendental aesthetic, an ontological sensibility. Intuition is such a faculty, and it is this intuition that Feuerbach and Marx oppose to Hegelian thought. This opposition means that whereas Hegelian thought pretends to create its content—beings, nature—intuition is, on the contrary, a receptive faculty and does not create beings. Marx's critique of Hegel has thus the clearest signification: it is a refusal to grant the power of creating beings to the action of thought, a refusal to grant ontic creativity to thought. Thought cannot reduce beings to itself. Beings are not a moment of the unfolding of thought, not something ideal.

If Marx's critique of Hegel has a very clear ontic meaning and designates the impossible creation of beings by thought, it is important to point out now that, in 1844, this critique still has no ontological import. For what is the intuition set in opposition to thought? Intuition does not create beings, it receives them, discloses them. It is the power that wrests beings from the night wherein they dwell in principle, so as to offer beings to the light and to turn them into phenomena. Intuition grants Being to beings by turning them into sensible things. But how does intuition render beings sensible? How does it promote them to the rank of phenomena? By turning them into objects. Feuerbach and, after him, Marx in the *1844 Manuscripts*, only speak of sensible being as a sensible object. What therefore becomes evident is that the structure of Feuerbachian intuition is identical to the structure of Hegelian thought: in both cases, the structure is the process of objectification wherein objectivity "objects" itself. If one wishes to call this process wherein the world accedes to the light a production, one must repeat that this is not a real production, not a real action. In what does real action consist? Wherein does its originary being reside? Neither in thought, nor in intuition! The explanation of Marx's rejection, in 1845, of Feuerbach's materialism is thus to be located in the fact that materialism rests upon intuition, that, according to Marx's own phrase, it is an "intuitive materialism," in the fact that materialism and idealism are identical.

What is neither thought nor intuition, what does not unfold itself in the light of a world, Marx calls praxis. Why is praxis neither thought nor intuition, why, more deeply, is praxis not the coming into the light of a world? Praxis designates a real action, that of the craftsman or the worker. It designates the concrete activity of the one who manipulates, strikes, lifts, carries, carves, etc. But the substantiality of this concrete action, the deed, the acting of action is not contained in the event of the world, in the ek-stasis of its horizon. If we place ourselves within fundamental *theoria* and if we live in it, we intuit, we see, we do not act. Intuition sees the object, it discovers it and contemplates it. Action does not do anything of the sort. Doubtless, we may very well act and at the same time intuit or contemplate the world. We may also have an intuition of the action that we are performing. In that case, we gaze at what we are doing. But action as such has nothing to do with this gaze of intuition, with the discovery of a spectacle, with the appearance of an object.

One must thus posit the structural ontological heterogeneity of intuition and action and recognize that in intuition we do not act and that, conversely, in action we do not intuit. One must not only say that we may very well act without having an intuition of our action, that is to say, without beholding it, without giving it to ourselves as an object. It is true that this is the manner in which we act most often, that this is the way in which the majority of the movements in our daily life are carried out. When we drive a car, for example, we do not look at what we do. It is under that condition that we know how to drive, under the condition that there be neither sensory nor intellectual representation of this action of driving. This is so with all the things that we know how to do, with the professional or private practices which mark out our daily existence.

One must go even further. One must not only say that we may act without intuiting our deeds, but also that our action is necessarily foreign to all intuiting, *that it is possible only insofar as it is not intuition*, that it is neither intuition itself, nor intuition of some object. If action were intuition, it would be gaze, sight, contemplation, and no longer action. Thus, we are led to the reciprocal exclusion of the essences of intuition and action, to the reciprocal exclusion of the essence of *theoria* and the essence of praxis.

I repeat what this means: through an analysis of the essence of intuition, of the appearance of the object, one cannot find action in intuition, but only its contrary, seeing. Similarly, through an analysis of the essence of action, one cannot find intuition in action, since, if intuition were present in it, it would not act. That is why when intuition takes place at the same time as action, this "at the same time" signifies a radical exteriority: it means that an intuition occurs somewhere else, outside action, and that it is to the extent that this intuition takes place outside action and not within it that action can carry itself out, that action is possible and real.

The radical exclusion of intuition from action must be thought to its limit. That action is bereft of all intuiting, of all seeing, means that nothing is or can be seen in it. What, then, is the praxis which, while expelling all seeing out of itself, excludes all objects from itself? The first sentence of the first thesis on Feuerbach describes it: it is subjective. Materialism was faulted for grasping reality "only in the form of the object or of intuition, but not as activity . . . not as practice, not subjectively." The subjectivity of praxis must be thought as Marx thinks it, namely in its radical opposition to *theoria*, in its opposition to Feuerbach's objective intuition and Marx's objective intuition as it can be found in the *1844 Manuscripts*. Objective intuition is understood here in the sense that man is an objective being to the extent that he has an object outside himself to which he relates himself, this relation occurring precisely in intuition in the sense that "intuition" designates the relation to the object. It is therefore this relation to the object, the coming into the world and the production of a world, which are excluded from subjectivity when it constitutes the essence of praxis. What is foreshadowed by the concept of praxis is an absolutely new meaning of the concept of subjectivity: it is originary subjectivity in its radical immanence.

It is not in keeping with our philosophical habits to think that thought hands us over to the world and to the reign of exteriority, whereas action is foreign to this world and hands us over to what is most interior to us. And yet when action abruptly calls upon us, we plunge into our depths, into the abyssal night of absolute subjectivity, into this place where our body's powers slumber and where, joining ourselves to these powers, we set them into motion—where the potentialities of organic subjectivity suddenly actualize themselves, where the fundamental "I can" that constitutes our existence unfolds itself, where we are one with ourselves in the originary unity which is bereft of transcendence and of world.

In contradistinction to this, we shall consider, one last time, *theoria* and the essence inherent in it. All seeing accomplishes within itself the negation of its particularity; seeing is this overcoming which, from a point of view, allows it to be a gaze, to raise itself above the gazer to the level of what is seen. It is in this manner that what is seen, as it is in itself and for all, is reached. All theory rests upon the transcendence operative within it and constituting it as a faculty of universal objectivity. As for praxis, however, it does not raise itself above itself, and at no time does it dismiss the particularity and individuality that are consubstantial with it. That praxis is subjective means that it remains within the internal experience of itself, that it is this lived tension of an existence shut up within the experience of its own act and coinciding with its deed. It is precisely nothing but its deed, but it is all that it does, and it undergoes its doing without the least respite, incapable of any distance on itself, of escaping from itself. In this principal impossibility of escaping from itself and of unfolding the stepping back of a distance on itself, selfness [*ipseitas*] takes shape and experiences itself: in this way, the monad of originary being as production is radically opposed to the universality of thought.

Such is the implicit content of the theses on Feuerbach, such is the scope of the overturning performed by the theses, overturning which may well be the overthrow of Western thought. That is indeed what Marx means. But how does he say it? In other words, what conceptual means does Marx have at his disposal in the spring of 1845 in order to formulate his explosive intuition? The conceptual means available to Marx are provided to him by the systems of Hegel and Feuerbach: they are the set of categories pertaining to intuition and thought. This means that in order to think the absolutely new essence which he has in view, Marx has no appropriate concept, no appropriate philosophical material at his disposal.

This predicament explains his manner of proceeding: to set Feuerbach's intuition aside, this intuition decomposing being by turning it over to the condition of object, Marx has recourse to action, but to action as he finds it in the philosophical horizon of 1845, to Hegel's action, namely the action of thought, the action of idealism. But the action of thought is not real action, and to get rid of it Marx appeals to Feuerbach: to indicate that the activity aimed at is a real and not an ideal one, that it is not the activity of thought, he clumsily calls it "sensible." Marx thus dismisses materialism through the action of thought, action whose structure is that of objectification, alienation, and sublation of alienation—whose structure is that of dialectic—only to dismiss this dialectic through materialism. Materialism and dialectic represent the two terms, the two philosophies which Marx radically rejects. This twofold rejection is carried out in such a way, however, that Marx could jettison materialism only by means of dialectic, and jettison dialectic only by using materialism. What Marx aims at remains hidden under this purely conceptual circle. To express what Marx has in view, dialectical materialism represents the quintessence of nonsense.

We shall return now to the concept of being as production insofar as it designates the radical subjectivity of praxis. Does not such a statement provoke objections? One will object that praxis takes place in the world, that, from the world, it borrows its raw materials, its instruments, its laws, the forms it creates and thereby its ends. But the discourse emitting these objections is precisely the discourse of theory, the one receiving its formulation in Aristotle's theory of the four causes, the one pretending to reduce praxis to *theoria* and to a mode of realization belonging to *theoria*. We shall, on the contrary, accomplish the overturning announced by the theses on Feuerbach: at issue, then, is no longer the beholding of praxis in the gaze of theory, but the founding of theory in praxis.

To found theory in praxis is to recognize firstly that theory itself, gazing, is not autonomous and that the very modalities of its realization, its categories, are prescribed to it by praxis. In other words, the ideal content of the categories cannot receive its legitimacy from itself, that is, from analysis. In this, resides the general sense of the concept of ideology. Ideology means that theory does not constitute the foundation of being, or the site of any independence whatsoever. If one appeals to Marx, it is truly absurd to oppose ideology to theory, to science. If the concept of being as production is understood in the way just outlined, ideology designates the status of theory in general.

To found theory in praxis is to affirm, secondly, that the content of seeing, the object of theory, is no more explained by theory than its forms. Intuition does not explain sensible reality. I quote Marx: "Even when the sensuous world is reduced to a minimum, to a stick, as with Saint Bruno, it presupposes the action of producing this stick."[18] This constitutes the theme of the critique directed against Feuerbach, who does not see that the object given to intuition is only the product of the activity of a series of generations.

The object of intuition is not only the product of praxis; it becomes a truly concrete object only when it is constituted by praxis itself: it is social activity in all its forms that constitutes the content and the substance of our world.

One will object: is it not precisely intuition which yields this activity and the entirety of social phenomena? At this point, we must reaffirm our thesis: intuition is incapable of giving us the real being of action, it can only represent it, reproduce it in the way a photograph represents a real event. Let us consider the silversmith engraving the chalice, hammering and molding the silver. As object of intuition, as empirical, objective, sensible phenomenon, his activity is there for each and every one. But the beholders look and do not act. It is thus not the empirical intuition of this activity, its objective appearance, which can define it, for it is only its appearance. The reality of this activity, that of work, resides in, and only in, subjectivity. Against Hegel, we must say: there is nothing objective about work: it is neither instrument, nor method, nor product. With Marx, we must say: machines do not work. They do not work, for they have their site within objectivity, where there are only third-person processes; the movement of a piston no more qualifies as work than the water falling in a cascade.

Because the essence of work is subjective, its laws are also subjective. On the one hand, work is originarily only the activity of need; it finds its first determination in the potentialities of subjectivity which delineate the bundle of these needs. On the other hand, the mode of accomplishment of this activity itself finds its determination within the structures of organic subjectivity, and work is only the actualization of these structures. We always follow paths that are already laid out. These are not only the paths laid out by human beings before us. The paths which we tread are outlined within us. They are the paths of our body, and those paths do not lead astray. They delineate the field of our possibilities and assign its destiny to our life. The whole of social activity, which seems to take place outside us, in reality finds in us and in our subjectivity both its rootedness, its reality, its predetermination, and its laws.

To say that praxis is subjective is thus not to formulate one philosophical interpretation among others. It is to offer a means to understand the world wherein we live. The world of our lives is an economic world, which is to say that its principle resides in work. In its own way and no matter what its paradoxes may be, the economic universe, in its very existence, bears witness to the originary truth of being and refers us to the concept of being as production. The economic world, however, is constituted by objective determinations, each of which is given to intuition—for example, the price of a piece of clothing or of a pound of sugar. Moreover, these objective determinations are ideal, quantitative determinations, of which one can form a theory, a science. What relation is there between such determinations and the silent effectuation of organic subjectivity within us? There is no relation. We immediately understand, then, what the economic world is, we understand that the whole economy is nothing but a vast system of substitution, that it is the entirety of the ideal equivalents that we attempt to have correspond to what is most intimate in our personal lives. One speaks of a day's work, of skilled and unskilled labor, where, between sunrise and sunset, there is only the unqualifiable unfolding of a singular life. This explains the immense malaise that affects any economic universe, as well as the dissatisfaction that shoots through it. It is not only a matter of determinate injustices, but, more importantly, of the principial inadequacy existing between subjectivity and any objective equivalent that is supposed to correspond to it. This principial inadequation furnishes the foundation of the radical critique that Marx directed against right, equal right, against any possible right, a critique propounded in the "Critique of the Gotha Program." This sheds light on what must have been Marx's ultimate project—what he called socialism: to construct not a just world, which is a meaningless project, but to construct a world that will do away with the problem of this equivalence between subjectivity and money. Such a society, which would render useless an impossible justice, is a society of overabundance, not one defined by the overabundance of products, but one whose wealth would allow each to realize the potentialities of his or her own subjectivity. It would be a world of the realization of praxis, a world of life, where the activity of life would be defined, wanted, and prescribed by life.

Meanwhile we live in an economic world, that is to say, in a world of value and money. These economic determinations are foreign to praxis and yet founded upon it: they represent it. The value of a product represents the labor necessary to its production. It follows that economic determinations, economic phenomena in their entirety are nothing but a translation of what takes place on the real level of praxis. These phenomena never find their explanation in themselves but only in this real praxis. Strictly speaking, there are thus no economic laws, no economic system, no science of economy. There is only room for a philosophy of economy, which accounts for what takes place on the economic level through a foundation that is heterogeneous to it. I shall choose only one example, the great law of the capitalist system, the law of the tendency of the rate of profit to fall. Understanding this law leads us back to real production, to the history of productive forces in the modern world.

According to Marx—with this, all of the teachings of Aristotle and Heidegger are overturned—the productive forces comprise two kinds of elements, which are heterogeneous to each other: objective elements, that is, raw materials and instruments, and subjective elements, praxis itself, the actualization of bodily subjectivity. The history of these productive forces, which is going to determine the history of the world, shows not that they are becoming ever more powerful, but that their internal structure is undergoing a modification; it shows that the objective element in these forces is ceaselessly increasing—the formidable development of the instrumental framework, of machines and factories—while the subjective element, living subjectivity, is ever diminishing. This fundamental phenomenon has two effects: an economic one and a real one.

On the economic level, it signifies the decline and ruin of capitalism, for capital is value and surplus-value, both of which are produced exclusively by subjective labor. If this living power progressively disappears from a production becoming more and more objective, it is the production of value, therefore of capital, which also disappears. Imagine a limiting case: an entirely automatized system of production. It would produce a considerable quantity of use-values, which would be valueless. Such is the absolute limit of capitalism, in which one sees that its fate rests upon the destiny of subjectivity in production.

However, if we consider this history of productive forces in itself and not in its economic effect, then we see that it implies a profound shakeup in the very structures of being, or rather of our existence. Two things that have been linked over the entire course of history—subjectivity and production—are diverging gradually. That they have been tied to each other in the age-old past of humanity means that the life of human beings was their work, that their life consisted in what they were doing so as to live and to survive. Production coincided with their life, defined their existence. In *The German Ideology*, Marx states: "What they are . . . coincides with their production . . ."[19] What will happen when the productive forces become entirely objective, when they coincide with the instrumental network set into place by a more and more elaborate technology, and when consequently, the subjectivity of individuals is left to itself? How will they be able to live, when life no longer receives its rhythm and its protection from material tasks, from work? We can say of future life: it will be a spiritual life or it will not be. The great malaise that is already spreading over the world, the doubt that is taking hold of life as it escapes from the hard necessity of maintaining itself alive each day, shows that the destiny of being works itself out in its originary site, at the heart of subjectivity.

In conclusion, it must be said that the interpretation of praxis implies an overturning of the traditional concept of truth. According to the philosophical tradition, truth finds its essence in *theoria*. But *theoria* is never more than and can only be the gaze cast upon exterior and, as such, always enigmatic being. For the thought performing the overturning of theory into praxis, truth, the power of revelation, belongs from now on and exclusively to deed. Only the one who does, who acts, knows, although through and within this deed, what being, which is this very deed, is about.

If a theoretical proposition subsists in its pretension to express truth, it does so in a very peculiar manner, insofar as it no longer contains this truth and no longer offers it to "gazing" within itself, but indicates outside itself, as the absolute other of itself, the site where truth is accomplished. In an ontology of praxis, theory can only take on, in the last analysis, the form of a prescription.

This is the predicament of religions, which are only reduced to theology, that is, to the theory of being, at the price of an absolute misinterpretation—for example, Feuerbach's. What characterizes religious discourse is the extenuation of theoretical content and the abrupt rise of an imperative. Its abruptness stems from the absence of any theoretical context. Religious discourse offers itself as naked speech, as an isolated proposition beginning with a certain word and ending with another one, a proposition to be taken as it is. Religious speech resounds in the midst of the clouds, in the obliteration of the objective universe, in doubtful and unsure circumstances. In this bracketing of the world, who speaks? Is it a man, a prophet, or an angel? Is it Moses or Christ? At any rate, the word that was heard, the law that was promulgated, gives itself as absolute. An absolute utterance is tied to nothing, has no extrinsic justification. Does this justification reside in it? How could an isolated proposition receive theoretical justification by being so isolated, in view of the fact that theoretical legitimation always consists in a series of analytical implications traceable to first principles or axioms?

Might not legitimation reside outside theory—in praxis? Because it constitutes the originary dimension of being, praxis, and praxis only, can reveal within itself and in the effectiveness of its doing what being is about. That is why one must not be too hasty in rejecting the ethical imperative, morals, the prescriptions with which life once surrounded itself, if prescription is the movement by which theory moves beyond itself toward the most originary site of being. "One must" means "one must do." In the second thesis on Feuerbach, Marx says: "Man must prove the truth, i.e., the reality and power of the this-worldliness of his thinking in practice."

One last remark: the thinking that thinks of being as praxis must not be mistaken about itself. It naturally inclines toward the idea that being produces itself, that it is self-production. To be sure, of being envisaged in itself we must say, along with traditional philosophy, that it is *causa sui*. This amounts to speculating about being, but speculative thinking has its rights. On the level where we situate ourselves, on the level where we grasp praxis as it grasps itself, we do not say that, however. On the contrary, we say: the power that unfolds itself in us and that we ourselves are in this radical unity which allows us to be one with it and to act, that power is powerless with respect to itself, it did not produce itself. That the power residing in us suffers a fundamental powerlessness with respect to itself is what makes life of it. For life undergoes itself as it undergoes what is given to it. Life is the passion of being arising in it and ceaselessly arising in it. Life is an invisible and silent life. The thought of praxis necessarily moves beyond itself to the site of existence, and that is why of course one must act and why truth resides in praxis, for it dwells in life.

Translated by Pierre Adler

Notes

This chapter was originally published as "The Concept of Being as Production," *Graduate Faculty Philosophy Journal* 10, no. 2 (1985). The editors thank the *Graduate Faculty Philosophy Journal* for granting permission to reprint the English translation here.

   1. Translator's note: Karl Marx and Friedrich Engels, *The German Ideology* (Moscow: Progress Publishers, 1976), 42.

   2. Martin Heidegger, *The Question Concerning Technology and Other Essays*, trans. William Lovitt (New York: Harper and Row, 1977), 8.

   3. Heidegger, *The Question Concerning Technology*, 10. Translator's remark: in this sentence, the phrase "every occasion" renders "*aitia pasa*," usually translated as "all causes." In the translation of Heidegger's text, the verb "to occasion" designates "the essence of causality thought as the Greeks thought it" (*The Question Concerning Technology*, 10).

   4. Martin Heidegger, *Vom Wesen des Grundes* (Frankfurt: Vittorio Klostermann, 1955), 39: "Dieses Vor-sich-selbst-bringen van Welt..."

   5. Heidegger, *The Question Concerning Technology*, 11.

   6. Heidegger, *The Question Concerning Technology*, 165.

   7. Heidegger, *The Question Concerning Technology*, 13.

   8. Heidegger, *The Question Concerning Technology*, 28.

9. Translator's remark: since the text of Hegel's from which Henry quotes has not been translated into English, I shall quote the German text. G. W. F. Hegel, *Jenaer Systementwurfe I*, ed. K. Dusing and H. Kimmerle (Hamburg: Felix Meiner Verlag, 1975), 288: "Sie ist der existirende Begriff des Bewusstseyns..."

10. Hegel, *Jenaer Systementwurfe I*, 280–81: "der theoretische Process geht in den praktischen Process uber, in welchem sich das Bewusstseyn ebenso zur Totalitat macht, so hier eine der vorigen idealen entgegengesetzte reale Existenz erhii.lt; indem es in der Arbeit zur Mitte des Werkzeugs wird..."

11. Hegel, *Jenaer Systementwurfe I*, 320: "es ist eine allgemeine Weise, eine Regel aller Arbeit... aber diss allgemeine ist fur die Arbeit das wahere Wesen..."

12. Hegel, *Jenaer Systementwurfe I*, 320: "eine Regel aller Arbeit, die etwas for sich seyendes ist... als unorganische Natur..."

13. Hegel, *Jenaer Systementwurfe I*, 320: "die Arbeit ist nicht ein Instinct, sondern eine Vernllnftigkeit, die sich im Volke zu einem allgemeinen macht, und darum der Einzelheit des Individuums entgegensetzt ist, die sich uberwinden muss..."

14. Hegel, *Jenaer Systementwurfe I*, 322: "Es tritt zwischen den Umfang der Bedurfnisse des einzelnen und seine Thatigkeit dafur, die Arbeit des ganzen Volkes ein..."

15. Hegel, *Jenaer Systementwurfe I*, 316: "aber diss aussere ist ihre That, es ist nur zu was sie es gemacht haben, es sind sie selbst, als thatige aufgehobene..."

16. Karl Marx, *The Economic and Philosophic Manuscripts of 1844*, trans. Martin Milligan (New York: International Publishers, 1972), 177. Translation modified: compare *Marx Engels Werke*, Erganzungsband, Erster Teil [Supplemental volume, First Part] (Berlin: Dietz Verlag, 1981), 574.

17. Marx, *The Economic and Philosophic Manuscripts of 1844*, 114. Translation modified: compare *Marx Engels Werke*, 517.

18. Translator's note: Marx and Engels, *The German Ideology*, 47–48.

19. Translator's note: Marx and Engels, *The German Ideology*, 37.

10

Difficult Democracy

The democratic principle, as it is shown to us in modern societies, can be understood as the transposition of a more "ancient" Idea onto the political plane. The substance of this Idea is derived from its roots in the spontaneous course of human experience. This takes the form, first of all, of working together. When a difficulty arises in carrying out this work, the concerned parties gather together and consult one another. From the confrontation of their points of view, there results a decision that seems best to them. *In being held in common, this decision has a sort of legitimacy*, and that is why everyone will submit to it. It is in this situation that the democratic Idea is formed, the idea of a community that itself decides its organization and its ends.

Inasmuch as the democratic Idea is born on the level of social activity, a decisive split occurs: this activity is duplicated; it is not only social but also political. Instead of being accomplished spontaneously, it is interrupted to become the object of a reflection. This is motivated by the need to integrate a particular action into a much wider set and ultimately into the totality of a group's actions. This consideration of the global system of actions marks the opening of a new and absolutely original field—the political—which refers to knowledge and no longer to action. This shift is decisive because it concerns *the very phenomenality of the phenomena that are in play*. In place of a real action immersed in life and revealing itself in its pathos, the unfolding of a properly political dimension substitutes representations, ideas, and an ideology—but first of all, the milieu of light where these representations and ideas show themselves. It is not by chance that the democratic principle came to light in Greece, where the opening of a world is experienced for itself. It is also in Greece—how could one forget?—that the surprising definition of the human as a "political animal" appeared.

Before going into the study of modern democracy, it is necessary to make a remark about its provenance. If we take a look back at more archaic societies, we have reasons to believe that they were all religious societies. The specific trait of primitive religion is not animism or polytheism. We are only able to understand this specificity if, paradoxically, we pose the most general question: Why is there a religion in human societies? What does the religious fact signify as such? It signifies that the human is not its own foundation. This truth is not something that primitive people apprehended in a conceptual system; they experienced it in their everyday life. They experienced this life in a radical passivity. It was not only passive with regard to natural phenomena and in being exposed to their fluctuations. It was passive with regard to life itself, its continually renewed needs, and the efforts it was forced to make in order to satisfy them. In addition to the external dangers that one can avoid by moving, by taking flight, etc., there is the much more menacing internal danger from which it is no longer possible to withdraw oneself. It is from itself that the greatest anguish [*angoisse*] arises in life: from its condition of being delivered over to itself and to everything that it lives through independently from its power. It is this condition of being thrown into life without having wanted it that for all living beings constitutes the original experience of the sacred and turns it into a religious being. Religion does not belong to the human as a singular experience but as its essence. It designates the inner connection of the living to the life from which it derives its condition as alive, in which it experiences [*éprouve*] all that it experiences.

Because the archaic experience of the sacred is inscribed in the very condition of the living being [*le vivant*], it is within itself before every conceivable form of experience. Although this antecedence of the life within itself can indeed project itself in front of the regard of the primitive in multiple forms and forces, these all refer to its condition as a living being who is immersed in life and subjected to it. This is the reason why, regardless of whether it is an animism or polytheism, these forms and forces are sacred.

The pathos-filled experience of the power of the life that throws the living into itself does not only manifest itself in the form of representations and beliefs; it "acts" out in oneself the rituals and practices that mark out one's daily life. Among these rituals, sacrifices have an exemplary significance. They attest that primitive man knows the generation from which he proceeds and that, in knowing this, attempts through these sacrifices to repay that which, in his fear and in the various experiences [*expérience*] of contingency, he experiences [*éprouve*] that he owes it.

The radical immanence of the archaic experience of the sacred can be understood better if one compares it to what we today call art or "aesthetics." Concerning the beautiful, the primitive has no more idea than that of the sacred: the primitive lives it in the immediacy of his pathos. That is why, in all civilizations and even in Greece, the archaic works prevail over all the others: *the power from which they proceed is the same as the one that generates the living being.* It is this hyper-power of life surpassing in oneself the living being that it generates that turns someone into an artist, and more generally, a cultural being. For culture never expresses anything other than this transcendence in immanence that casts each living being into itself at the same time as it pushes it to go beyond every given being, thus giving rise in oneself to an infinite desire. Art is only one form of the sacred. In a general manner, when the living is nothing more than a living traversed by life, the pathos-filled intersubjectivity in which it is inscribed among other living beings is a religious society.

When and how this decomposes is something of which our most recent history, the one which leads to modern democracy, provides a frightening example. The last religious society in the West is the Christian society. It is religious in an eminent sense because it explicitly interprets the absolute as Life and it gives Life a radical phenomenological meaning: a pathos-filled self-revelation that is foreign to the world and thus invisible. It is this absoluteness of life that it places in a no less explicit manner at the head of the social organization as well as of each individual's existence. Today we know almost nothing about this Christian world built on the Christian principle. On the one hand, the key that unlocks its intelligibility has been lost. On the other hand, in its visible manifestations, it has been almost entirely destroyed. For example, in Russia, out of the tens of thousands of sacred buildings that covered the country, there only remain today a few repainted copies for the use of tourists.

The elimination of Christianity is tied to the emergence of a new principle, the Galilean principle that puts life out of play to the benefit of the material world. The objective knowledge of the world—modern science—provides the exclusive prototype of knowledge. On the practical level, it is modern technology stemming from the new science that becomes the organizing principle of society and of the whole world. At the same time as life is struck to the heart, the formidable edifice of culture, which is based on it, collapses.

Here we are not proposing to describe the decomposition of the last religious society in the West, but rather the way in which it will appear afterwards to the society that succeeds it. Rituals, sacrifices, and the entire set of religious practices were experienced [*vécu*] by living beings as the ways for it to experience its relation to the absolute, to actualize it and thus to conform to it. Religion was an ethics. Because it was an ethics, it entered into social practice entirely. This social practice with the sacred flowing through topples over into a monstrous exteriority, when life is excluded from the new knowledge as well as the world that it will govern. Emptied of their substance, religious behaviors appear as extravagant actions. To what are gestures of adoration aligned if there is no longer anything to adore? Religious institutions and ceremonies are uncovered as objective phenomena. And when the edifices connected to these institutions and ceremonies have themselves lost their religious meaning, then an "aesthetic" approach emerges—an aesthetics separated from its content, which is itself empty. But if the religious world founded the totality of values regulating social activity, then where will the latter find the principle of its organization?

Within itself. It is then that the democratic Idea is put forward, not as being able to institute a political regime preferable to the others, but as the new principle of social life. This new principle is the social community itself, choosing its own norms and ends. The relation of this new principle to the old one is discovered as a relation not of succession but of opposition. Democracy defines itself against religion, and it does so with a violence that is not only manifested at the beginning of the new era by a revolution. When the first excesses have calmed down, democracy seeks to have its new "spirit" prevail: concord and tolerance. But even if it proclaims itself "neutral," recognizes the freedom of opinion, of belief, of religion, an opposition in principle remains. The more that democracy seeks to locate the presupposition of social practice in the community of humans considered as such, the more it will run up against the authority that, for centuries, has fulfilled this function. According to the democratic principle, the law that governs the social body proceeds from itself alone. If there can still be a religiously inspired moral law, its application is limited to the sphere of private life, just like religion. If a contradiction should appear between civil law and the ethical-religious law, it is the former that would prevail. In the case of a crisis, but in reality permanently, the transcendent origin of the ethico-religious law appears to all humans as an unacceptable exteriority. Religion has become the religious State, a sum of prescriptions coming from the outside and thus in direct conflict with what, in the eyes of democratic authority, could only come from itself. That is why the freedom in which the community of assembled human beings formulates its autonomy accomplishes itself as a liberation that is pursued along the whole history of modern democracies in the form of multiple successive liberations, for example, sexual liberation, in direct conflict with the Mosaic law.

Provisionally, let's set aside this conflictual relation between democracy and Christianity in order to consider the democratic principle in itself. There are thus all those who are concerned about an affair who have the capacity to debate about it. Regardless of whether it is debated by some or by many, such an affair is called general. But the more general is the affair, the more numerous are the individuals involved in it, and the fewer (in proportion) are those who can participate in the deliberations concerning it. They will thus not do it themselves but through the intermediary of delegates, and representatives who will from then on legislate in their place in organizations that have been established for this aim and that are the various political powers. In order to be realized, the democratic principle has invented political representation, but political representation is the negation of the democratic principle: instead of people assembled in an actual community, it has substituted a few individuals who are charged to deliberate in their place. Devoted to the service of public affairs, to the study of the issues, to participation on multiple committees and their specific tasks, their activity differs from that of their constituents. They think quite differently and henceforth form a separate class: the political caste.

Another difficulty arises which is much more serious because it is no longer tied to the question of political representation, but touches on the democratic Idea itself. Let's place ourselves in the hypothetical situation of a political power accomplishing the profound will of an entire community, and let's suppose that this will felt by everyone is to annihilate the population of a neighboring ethnicity or that of a group situated within itself. If the democratic Idea requires everyone to rally around the decision of the majority and to carry it out, then the actions that are the object of our hypothesis and that constitute nothing other than a genocide are no less democratically founded. One will say that this presupposition is arbitrary. But that is definitely not the case. If a democratic election had been organized in the Hitler regime before Stalingrad, there can be no doubt that a majority would have voted for this regime And the same remark could be made if the consultation had taken place in the U.S.S.R. in the era of Stalin, at the same time period, for example.

This difficulty is not only theoretical but also tragic; it requires democracy to provide another foundation for itself. What could limit the application of the majority principle and force it to respect instead of destroy individuals and persons, if not the affirmation of their absolute value? Absolute, that is to say, situated outside of the field of action of every political principle whatsoever and no longer depending on it. This is how we discover the serious failure of political theory which is now placed before a requirement that it is unable to face. This requirement is the requirement for an ethics.

We will translate this difficulty onto the political level by saying that formal democracy must give way to a material democracy. By a formal democracy, we mean the democratic idea such as it has been presented up to now. Recognizing that the unilateral use of the majority principle can lead to crime, we are contrasting it with the idea of a material democracy which has a content. This content is a set of values that all express, in various ways, the same fundamental value, namely, that of the individual. This content is so essential to the concept of democracy that it was affirmed forcefully by democracy at the time of its modern foundation. Whether in America or in France, this foundation is accompanied everywhere by a solemn Declaration, that of "Human Rights."

But "human rights" can only found true democracy on the condition that they themselves are founded. This is why a Declaration, however solemn it may be, does not suffice. There must exist somewhere, as an undeniable reality, the ultimate principle that will establish human rights in such a way to make them imprescriptible, inalienable, and inviolable. What radical principles does democracy use to found the rights without which it becomes unable to distinguish itself from regimes of terror and death?

Here it is necessary to dispel the illusion whereby democratic regimes claim to justify the principle on which they are based by a hidden recourse to this same principle. Human rights, one will say, are not only the object of a formal Declaration; they determine the system of laws, and to the extent that they are applied as they are in a state of law, they permeate society completely. This is the concrete situation that results from civil law in its actual application. It is, for example, the law that prohibits or authorizes the voluntary termination of pregnancy. But the problem that we are discussing presently is one concerning the foundation of civil law. The answer, which is self-evident in democratic regimes, is that this law was voted on by political representatives. It is the recourse to the majoritarian principle that we have shown is precisely unable to found the material content of democracy. The formal principle of the majority that defines civil law only avoided crime by referring to a prior system of values independent from it: "human rights." But when the time comes to found them, it is the majoritarian principle of formal democracy that is called upon. The attempt of democracy to constitute itself in an autonomous reality and thus to found the autonomy of individuals and persons politically comes to die in this circle.

This is the reason why human rights, even if they are proclaimed by a democratic assembly, can never cease to claim another foundation. They could not depend on a contingent vote that could abolish them as well as affirm them. What is required is a true foundation tied to these Rights by some type of internal necessity which is co-substantial with them—an ultimate, absolute foundation that is able to found itself at the same time as the human rights implicated by it and, in a certain way, as identical to it.

The first article of the "Declaration of the Rights of Man and of the Citizen" which was placed at the beginning of the 1791 Constitution declares that "men are born and remain free and equal in rights." This famous text is remarkable in more than one way. The first is that it concerns material democracy. Freedom and equality are values; they belong to the axiological content of democracy, not to the formal majority principle. It appears, moreover, that these values are totally independent from it. By vote, an assembly can indeed proclaim them, but they do not result from this vote; they do not derive their nature or validity from it. They exist and they exist as "values" before every vote of this kind, before every gathering of a democratic assembly, before the political invention of a "democracy." Democracies, assemblies, and votes can only recognize them after the fact, without undermining them and without changing them. Human beings are *born* free . . . and they remain so. The same goes for the equality of rights. Freedom and equality are thus not derived from democracy, but from human nature. Whether one wants it or not, democracy points us outside of itself, to the metaphysical question of knowing what the human being is. Democracy presents itself everywhere and today more than ever as the foundation of freedom and equality, but that is one of its primary mystifications. Neither freedom nor equality have their source in it—nor does the fact that they are both "values" bringing into it something like the radical demand of a realization. But this requirement—which tears the content of democracy from political theory in order to confer it on an ethics—seems itself to be rooted in a deeper truth, founding ethics itself, situated at the heart of the human, or rather engendering it and making it what it is. Democracy refers to this ultimate reality from which the human being proceeds *as "free" and "equal."*

Before asking ourselves about this ultimate reality, let us glance briefly at the new values to which modern democracy appealed. Ultimately, what truth does a political regime need when it seeks to promote a profound agreement between human beings, if not a truth whose nature is precisely to fulfill such an agreement: a truth whose essence is universality? For such a truth exists; it is the Galilean principle that has provided it. By drawing a sharp contrast between the sensible experience which is individual, variable, and contingent, and the geometric knowledge of the world, Galileo proposed a new truth made out of rational propositions and as such universally valid. For the universality of the new science is not only formal; it has content. Whereas sensible knowledge only provides things as an appearance, geometrical knowledge is rigorously adapted to the forms of extended material objects; it represents them as they are—it is true. How could democracy, which does not only seek to ensure the artificial unity of a community, but also the proper values that provide an uncontestable support for this unity, not turn toward this science that is so capable of fulfilling its secret expectation? This is how the alliance is knotted *between the Galilean principle and the democratic principle on which modernity will be constructed.*

The affinity between science and democracy can be seen in the way in which the latter will privilege the former to the point of turning it into the sole model of knowing. The "sciences" that supposedly hold true knowledge are invading the university curriculum and are monopolizing its credits, to the detriment of literary disciplines whose dismantling coincides with that of the traditional culture that has been stripped of any significance for truth. To the extent that the human can be totally excluded from knowledge that is essentially oriented toward the objective knowledge of the material processes of nature, the new "human sciences" themselves seek to be objective, whether it concerns their methodology or their "object": the human is reduced to homogenous phenomena, ultimately to those that are studied by the hard sciences. Morality does not escape from these presuppositions; it is a naturalistic morality that will be taught in the schools.

The attempt of democracy and of science to found together the new moral unity of humanity runs up against an insurmountable difficulty: *in the field opened by Galilean science, there are none of the values that democracy needs*—none of those that compose what we have called its material or axiological content.

The first article of the 1791 Constitution thus declares that "men are born free and equal in rights." But, if it is a question of biological birth, which is the only birth that science knows, it follows that no "freedom" can result from birth, but only biological processes that are foreign to anything that can be understood under the title of "freedom." Something like the birth of a freedom is thus totally inconceivable in the horizon of science. If democracy seeks to know what it is talking about and to give meaning to what it says, it must first situate itself outside of the scientific field instead of seeing it as the location of every possible truth.

The question of equality is even more troublesome. The first article says "equality in rights," but equality in rights results from a prior equality in relation to which it can only be the consequence. In the horizon of science, the prior equality would have to exist between various biological organisms, but this is not the case. How can one deny the differences of all kinds that are operative between them, such that these differences are generative of inequalities that are themselves multiple? This *de facto* inequality becomes precisely the principle of an eventual action exercised over living organisms and seeking to make them better, even to select them. This task is offered to the new science as Francois Jacob says: "Perhaps one will also be able to produce at will, in as many copies as desired, the exact copy of an individual, a politician, an artist, a beauty queen, or an athlete, for example. Nothing prevents us from applying from now on to human beings the processes of selection used for race horses, laboratory mice, or dairy cows."[1]

The inability of Galilean science to give a meaning to the concepts of freedom and equality, however, refers to a much more fundamental, but hidden, inability. When democratic constitutions speak about "human rights," it is clearly the rights of each person in particular, of each individual. It is only in this way, because they are the rights of each one, that these rights are the rights of all. It is in belonging to each one and thus to all, that human rights draw the revolutionary power by which they exploded societies in which these rights were still the privilege of only a few. And even in these societies ruled by privilege, it was always for individuals—the privileged—that freedom and equality meant something. The concept at the center of human rights is thus the concept of the individual. It is because the new science does not have the least idea of what an "individual" is that freedom and equality are empty concepts in its field of knowledge.

The important thing is to observe that, no less than in contemporary biology, traditional thought has never experienced as an enigma what constitutes the internal possibility of the individual. It has been too quickly contented by what it saw: individual things like this rock, this tree, this human being. Is all that not evident? Evident, that is to say, showing itself in the world as what it is: this rock, this human. What makes a thing be what it is and unlike every other thing—which is called the principle of individuation—depends on the way in which this thing is shown in the world, that is to say, in space and time. It is the place that it occupies in space and in time that individualizes it. Thus, according to Husserl, two identical audible tones of the same note are different because the one succeeds the other. The trouble is that in this conception, the individuality of a human being is of the same order as that of a pebble. Thus it is necessary to recognize that the traditional principle of individuation is unable to explain something like an individual having rights, who is free, etc. And the ultimate reason for this failure is the type of phenomenality from which thought seeks individuation, namely, the phenomenality of the world and its ecstatic categories where *all that is given to us, is the identity of a thing with itself but never the Ipseity of a Self.*

As for individuality and thus the individual, they only exist in reality in life, in the only life that exists: the absolute phenomenological life that comes into itself by experiencing itself [*s'éprouvant*], in such a way that this in this experience [*épreuve*] of itself an original Ipseity is built whose phenomenological actuality is a singular transcendental Self, which resides in every me [*moi*] and every ego conceivable; every individual as a living individual; every possible human, as a human is only possible as this one or that one, as an individual.

From the transcendental birth of every living individual, there follow two essential phenomenological determinations of one's own life: one's "freedom" and one's "equality."

As for freedom, it should be understood in its ambivalent meanings. On the one hand, experiencing itself in the self-experience of life, every living individual enters into possession of its own being and of everything that it carries within itself, for example, all of the powers of its own living body: taking, moving, etc. The hyper-power of life in which each of its powers is given to itself founds the power that an individual is able to exercise whenever and as often as it wants to. The transcendental Self has become an "I Can." Actual concrete freedom is the power of this "I can" to do all that it can.

The fact that the "I can" is only placed in possession of itself through the self-givenness of life is what refers its power to a non-power that is much older, to its transcendental birth in which it is for nothing and which it has neither chosen nor willed. Yet, it is in this birth that the human being is free: in the internal and imprescriptible relation of the living to life, a relation in which it is given to itself *as this "I can" and henceforth free.* If *religio* is this internal connection of the living to life, it must be said that all freedom is religious and thus, like this connection, imprescriptible, inalienable, and irremissible—or "sacred." If one can speak about freedom as a right—a human right, a right of the individual—this is only to the extent that Roman law happened to be invested with the formidable values of Judaism and Christianity, values taken from the definition of man as a "Son of God," that is to say, as living in life.

Here there appears an undeniable tension between the democratic conception of freedom and its Judeo-Christian foundation. Beyond its "Declarations," democracy naturally tends to attach freedom to the Idea that it has of itself, namely, the Idea that it is a concrete community that chooses its own organization, which is only valid when it is chosen by itself. In other words, an actual organization is only legitimate in the form of a self-organization. Freedom means autonomy, self-organization, self-foundation of laws and rules. Each individual's right to freedom can be understood on the basis of this autonomy of the community and has the same nature as it. Choice and freedom rule all throughout democracy and turn it into a sort of system of freedom. But autonomy, the self-organization of the community as its self-foundation, refers to a secret foundation—to speak like Marx—to "the existence of living individuals." But in this foundation, the law of democracy sees the end of its reign.

In §44 of *Being and Time*, Heidegger asks, "Has Dasein as itself ever freely decided and will it ever be able to decide whether it wants to come into 'Dasein' or not?" The negative response does not only exclude all decision and thus all conceivable freedom from the domain taken into consideration here. Because the question put in play refers to the ultimate possibility of what it is to be human (and determines in the end its "rights"), it only has a sense in a radical phenomenology. That *Dasein*'s entrance into itself is not the deed of *Dasein*, that is to say an ecstatic truth, means phenomenologically that the arrival of the human into itself is never accomplished in *Dasein*, the "outside of itself" of a world, but in life and according to the mode of phenomenalization belonging to it: in the pathos of its original Ipseity. It is only for this reason that, given to itself in the Ipseity of Life, every human being is a "living individual." It is only for this reason that it is born and can be free. Free through a freedom prior to any decision, to any freedom. A freedom that the individual derives from its birth and that is one with it, with the process of the self-givenness of life in which it is given to itself. This is why one cannot touch the freedom of the individual without touching it, or touch it without touching Life. If the face of the Other sometimes rises up in front of us with its threatening majesty, and especially when we undermine the other's freedom, this is because the power in which the other looks at us suddenly comes to be felt within ourselves as the Before that has always preceded us and in relation to which we are nothing.

For such a situation also makes equality possible. We have seen that the existence of multiple objective dissimilarities cannot signify in itself any sort of inequality between biological organisms that have been deprived in principle of individuality. After they have been experienced [*vécues*], however, the "objective" differences are modalities of life that are as indubitable as life. At the same time, they affect individuals. Isn't what characterizes individuals, after all, an inequality in principle since, as Marx observes in his critique of law, which "tacitly recognizes as a natural privilege the unequal talents of workers" such that "it is a law of inequality, like all law"?[2] But all the capacities of individuals are diverse: force, intelligence, imagination, sensibility. Are there not, for example, irreducible differences between feminine sensibilities and masculine sensibilities? Does not Paul's striking declaration that places humans beyond every objective or subjective particularity—"Neither Jew, nor Greek, neither slave, nor free man, neither man nor woman"[3]—thus remain paradoxical? And beyond these differences of kind, if one might say, does not the fact of belonging to one individual rather than another separate forever, precisely by radically individualizing them, all the modalities of all the lives of all the living?

If we consider a specific modality of the feminine sensibility as it takes place in the life of this woman or the force or weakness of this man, as he lives through them, then we will discover what we are seeking: for each impressional tonality whatsoever, it is the given to oneself in the self-givenness of life, it is this self-givenness of life itself that is Identical and that transforms even the most radical difference into an absolute equality, unequivocally designating the original place of it, its only possibility.

Let's summarize. If democracy cannot borrow its values from science, and if it cannot make them emerge from itself, this is because the concept of autonomy does not allow us to think the human. Before the human, there is the power that throws it into its own condition and that, in this way, always precedes it. This is indeed the aporia of democracy: *How could what is before every decision result from it, and be founded by it?* What is before every decision—the values of democracy—refers to what is prior to the individual, which refers to the most original Before. In life, the most original Before is the process of self-generation that generates within itself the Ipseity of every conceivable individual and in this way, the "values" that are only the various formulations of its true condition. Thus equality, for example, is not the product of an evaluation, or consequently of an actual counter-evaluation or a possible resentment. Humans who continually struggle to prevail over their fellow men, to seduce them or to put them down, are born free and equal, such that freedom and equality can only be actualized by the reactivation of the inner connection that rejoins every living being to life. But this reactivation of the religious connection is ethics. At the time of its establishment—but also constantly in order to maintain its supposed autonomy, that of the human and its rights—democracy struggles against religion which is perceived as an external constraint, an outmoded transcendence. *But by struggling against religion, democracy struggles against its own foundations.* It is this unperceived contradiction that leads to its ruin right before our eyes.

To conclude, let's ask what our reproach here to democracy means, namely, that it eliminates the foundation of the values on which it depends. For it is all too true that the values of democracy are the by-products of the values of Christianity on which the West was built. The essence of the West and what makes it an exceptional culture is the place recognized for the Individual—a place that is unintelligible without the Judeo-Christian prerequisite. The freedom of the Individual does not primarily mean that everyone ought to be free and that society should be organized in such a way that the individual is free. Much more importantly, it means that in the ontological or rather meta-ontological order, in the order that is not that of Being but of Life, life always engenders the Individual as its own self-generation. It is this inscription of the Individual at the heart of the internal process of the absolute as a process of the self-revelation of Life that makes the individual this infinite value that is announced by nothing in the world.

One final look at democracies' forgetting of their own foundation explains why they were condemned to remain "formal." This is because the site of their foundation circumscribes the site of their realization: this arch-dimension of life in which "living individuals" live. Because these individuals are the real content of society, history, the economy, and because Galilean technology is defined by its exclusion of them, then what occurs to them in their work, or in its elimination, can alone define their fate and can say what is and what will be for each of them the possibility of accomplishing themselves in the power of Life.

Translated by Scott Davidson

Notes

This article was originally published in French in *Michel Henry: L'Épreuve de la vie* (Actes du Colloque de Cerisy 1996), ed. Alain David and Jean Greisch (Paris: Cerf, 2000), 39–54.

1. François Jacob, *La Logique du vivant* (Paris: Gallimard, 1970), 344.
2. See Karl Marx, "Critique of the Program of the German Workers' Party."
3. Galatians 3:28.

11

Kandinsky and the Meaning of the Work of Art

The question of the meaning of the work of art can only be tackled if one first resolves the question of its nature or, as we say, its site. So it is a question of knowing in which dimension of being the aesthetic object arises and what status it should be recognized to have for the entire content of this specific experience known as "art." Otherwise, this unavoidable problem leads to an aporia.

On the one hand, the work of art is an imaginary reality. Here we adopt the brilliant guidelines provided by Husserl in §111 of *Ideas I*.[1] In the aesthetic contemplation of Dürer's engraving *Knight, Death, and Devil*, we are not directed towards the engraved plate any more than towards the figures that appear in black lines upon it, but rather towards other realities that are portrayed or depicted in "represented realities" [*les realités figurées*], and which comprise not the engraving as an object of the world, but the engraving-object as a work of art, its aesthetic reality. Thus we can make an essential distinction between the material elements that serve to support a work of art, which belong to the real world of perception, similar to all other real things, and, on the other hand, the work of art as such, which no longer has its place in the world but is actually outside of it, as we say, in that it is purely imaginary.

The tiles of a mosaic, the wood or copper of an engraving, the canvas of a painting, the colors that cover it, are part of the world that surrounds us. But in the aesthetic experience (whether it is the creator's or the spectator's), these material elements are only used to give shape to a reality of another order, the reality represented by the painting, engraving, or mosaic. One can perceive a painting's canvas, examine its grain, its cracks, which is what you do if you want to date it precisely. In the case of a painting on wood, you would assume it is Flemish if it is oak, French if it is walnut, and Italian if fir. When the aesthetic vision begins, however, when the "canvas" or "wood" becomes a painting and penetrates the actual dimension of the painting, these material elements are neutralized. They are no longer perceived or posited as objects of the world, but as entities that have no other function than to produce the reality represented in the painting—which is also neutralized and belongs no more to the real world than the elements that represent it, forming with them a single, new dimension of being inside of which they are unified by relations of resemblance and which is the ontological dimension of art.

As to the difference between this and the real world of perception, I will offer only a single proof: a very small real space on the canvas can represent an immense space, like that of the landscapes seen through the windows of some Flemish primitives. Generally, the entire painting can be viewed as a "window," as a hole in the real world, a hole or window through which the gaze is carried away into a radical elsewhere. In traditional painting the difference that we are talking about between the real and the imaginary, this "elsewhere" in which it has effectively thrown us, is first expressed in the fact that the painting is constructed in such a way that it causes an illusion, that of a three-dimensional space or, if you will, of depth where, however, there is, in the real world of perception, only the flat surface of a wall, a piece of wood, or a canvas.

In addition, every aesthetic work appears, one must remember, as a totality and is intelligible only as such. In a painting each color has value only according to all the others, whether they are contiguous or tied to it, in respect to a distance from or opposed to the canvas, by some subtler relation. It is the same for every form and every volume: each element in what, for this reason, we call a composition is necessary to its appearance and so is granted a precise meaning. Now, here is the important point that should be stressed: *this composition is an aesthetic composition*, and the relations out of which it is made, the elements between which these relations arise, are themselves aesthetic in nature; they are situated within this principal dimension of irreality which is that of the painting. When the painter puts a color on the canvas, he does not examine it, he looks at the composition, he looks at what in it corresponds to this feature or that spot, in short its aesthetic effect, which is integrated into the ensemble of effects, in other words, into this Whole that is the painting. Thus in facing a painting by Frans Hals one must take a few steps back to the place where his broad brushstrokes suddenly transform into the blush of a cheek or, on the face of the officer of Hadrian's army who slowly turns toward us, into the Eye of Life that gazes at us across time.

The aesthetic composition is thus not a kind of palette that the canvas has become due to the effect of the strokes of the brush or of the palette knife, but is only possible starting from there. Since each of the composition's plastic elements is shaped from a material element, they presuppose the existence of a material element. To the plastic totality of the composition that is the painting itself an organic unity of the substrate necessarily corresponds; to the particular resemblance that is established each time between a part of the canvas and its aesthetic equivalent corresponds the overall resemblance of the painting and its support. This is offered as a continuum, it has a kind of unity. This is not an internal unity, which is only that of the painting, since the material use of the colors is determined by the aesthetic effect that it produces. For this reason, however, this use is necessary in its own state. It is the continuum presented by the material substrate of the painting that causes its analogue to emerge and is the basis from which it will be able to emerge and to unfold in its own dimension of existence.

That is why this continuum must at all costs be preserved, restored, and re-created when it has been damaged or destroyed. The restoration of an artwork must be done according to the aesthetic unity of the work and not at all by taking into account the support itself, for example, by removing everything that had been redone in the past in order to conserve only the elements that belong to the original work. The "scientific" restoration of artworks as practiced today, for example, by removing the reconstituted parts from previous restorations of frescoes and replacing them with empty spaces, that is, with trails of white plaster, basically results in their criminal destruction, as can be seen in many places like Daphne, Serbian monasteries, Arezzo, Florence, etc. This scientific restoration (employing processes such as carbon-14 dating) proceeds from a crude materialism that does not recognize the true status of a work of art as unreal, as a pure imaginary creation.

In opposition to this concept of the work of art that strives to recognize, through a precise phenomenological analysis, a specific domain of existence, there is another whose authority comes from one of the greatest artists of our time as well as the strength of its own evidence, namely, the thesis that the ontological dimension in which art moves is that of sensibility. Let's consider these crucial statements by Kandinsky: "what is right artistically can only be attained through feeling," and "since art affects the emotions, it can only exert its effect by means of the emotions."[2] Thus the famous laws of the beautiful, being laws of sensibility, only have the appearance of ideal, objective, mathematical laws. Even though one might succeed in giving forms, and the relationships that arise between the plastic elements of a composition, a rigorous mathematical formulation, this would never be more than an ideal approximation of proportions and equilibriums that occur within sensibility and which find in it, and in its own laws, their possibility, the demands to which they respond, their ultimate reason. That is why, as Kandinsky said, "proportion and scale are not to be found outside, but within the artist."[3]

But if art arises from sensibility, if art draws from sensibility its own laws and the demands to which they strive to find a response, does the work of art not at the same time have its place in the real world, which is precisely the sensible world, a world given to sensibility and defined by it, by its forms and content? Thus we find ourselves caught in the aporia that desires the work of art to both belong and not belong to the real world. Before trying to overcome this difficulty, whose solution will allow us to understand the true nature of the work of art as well as its meaning, we should consider several implications of the definition of art, such as finding its essence in sensibility and in the dimension of being that it circumscribes.

In this regard, a bit more should be said about sensibility itself and about the world that it is the condition of. Sensibility is the Opening of this world, the transcendence in and by which the first Outside is born, this foreground of light that is the entire world such as it is. Sensibility is the ek-stasis of Being. Since this transcendence resides in each of our senses, they are able to constantly go beyond themselves towards what constitutes their proper object (the seen, heard, touched . . .) and reach it, in and through this process of transcendence, and thus in the ek-static Dimension where everything that appears to us offers us its face, a facet or an aspect of its being, everything that is given as object.

For sensibility by no means exhausts its being in this pure relation to a world considered as such and as self-sufficient—a relation whose phenomenality would be reduced to that of this world and its emergence. In any relation of this kind, actually, in any affection by any being whatsoever—an affection turning it into an object—the trait of affectivity reigns. It is neither something extra nor contingent, but on the contrary, affectivity determines sensibility as its own Ground [*Fond*] and as what makes it ultimately possible. Thus our attitude toward things is never reducible to a pure gaze or to its insensible or indifferent displacement. This gaze is never a simple seeing, but precisely a sensing, a feeling of things, because the seeing that opens us to things is above all and necessarily a seeing that feels itself seeing—"*sentimus nos videre*," as René Descartes said—that experiences itself and affects itself before being affected by the world, in such a way that the actual phenomenality of this original auto-affection is affectivity itself as such.

That is why the world is essentially a sensible world, because the relation to the object, which is ultimately the ek-stasis of Being in which every world and even the relation itself are founded, is auto-affected in its very transcendence, such that within it, on the basis of this auto-affection that originally reveals it to itself, such a relation is by necessity an affective relation: a sensibility. That is why Kant, in seeking the conditions of every possible experience, which is to say of every possible world, began his investigation with a transcendental Aesthetic, specifically by an analysis of sensibility. No doubt this analysis unfolds on a plane that is still that of factuality; it encounters sensibility with the birth of the world without truly understanding the reason for the sensible character of this birth. But this reason is there for us: the world is a sensible world because the relation to the world is affective according to the innermost possibility of its ek-static deployment.

Consequently, if we assume that the proper site of art is in sensibility, that it consists of putting sensibility's powers to work, then we must say: art in no way constitutes a separate domain, reserved to artists, aesthetes, or specialists; on the contrary, it overlaps with the world itself, every possible world in general, insofar as it is a sensible world whose source is in sensibility and borne by it. Thus the concrete world where humans dwell falls entirely under the categories of aesthetics and is only comprehensible through those categories. It is necessarily a beautiful or ugly world; if it is neither one nor the other, it exists in a kind of neutrality that is only one aesthetic determination among others, a certain state of the sensibility with which this world is endowed in principle.

Moreover, it is a fact well known by historians, anthropologists, ethnologists, etc., that one of the principal activities in all forms of civilization known up to now, except perhaps our own, is art, and the productions of art are often all that remain to us of this amazing past. Why then is it like this, why does every culture include art as one of its essential dimensions? Because every possible world, and consequently ours, is by necessity an aesthetic world, because every human as an inhabitant of this world is potentially an artist, one in any case whose sensibility functions as the transcendental condition of this world and its emergence. A world that is aesthetic by its very nature and an art inherent to every culture: these are the first two implications of the thesis that the work of art arises from sensibility and belongs to it.

We can see that we are in an aporia due to the fact that the definition of the aesthetic object as a pure imaginary leads on the contrary to the consequence—drawn by Sartre from his reading of Husserl—that, being foreign to the real world of perception, the field of art is as such neither beautiful nor ugly. This is a difficult thesis to support, particularly today. We basically live in the era of technology, which ravages the world of our daily existence, disfiguring its landscapes, its sites, cities, and monuments bequeathed by the past, causing the horrible and hideous to appear everywhere. How would this devastation of the universe, which we are the powerless witnesses of, be possible if, as sensible, this universe was not suffused, at least in a virtual way, with aesthetic categories?

Similar evidence leaps before our eyes when we probe deeper into the reasons why technology plunges our world into this abyss of ugliness: because it proceeds from an entirely new knowledge, which appeared during Galileo's time and whose assumptions and decisions came to overthrow the humanity of humankind, making it what it is today, European man, whose model, however, is imposed on the entire world. In order to attain an objective knowledge of the world, Galilean science decided to abstract its sensible qualities, sensibility itself, and to retain, as constituents of its true reality, only the geometrical forms of things, their ideal properties which are able to lend themselves to a mathematical and as such rigorous determination—the same for all, the universally valid, the "objective," the scientific, instead of its sensible, subjective, individual, and changing appearances. By thus defining a world of science as the only "true" and real world, it hypostasized not only an abstraction—insofar as this world of science necessarily refers to the real sensible world of which it is only an idealization and which grants it its only possible meaning—it again eliminated everything which causes this world to be an aesthetic world. Organizing social activity in light of the infinite possibilities in which the sensible world is rooted is, however, not part of that world. We say that a tree is green, that the street is noisy, that ugliness causes us to suffer—but in the things themselves there is neither color, nor sound, nor suffering. Color, sound, and suffering can only be "felt," "experienced," or "lived," where something feels and experiences itself so as to be able to feel and experience anything else whatsoever: in the previously deployed essence of auto-affection as absolute subjectivity, as Life.

In order to definitively clarify the site of the artwork, we should distinguish in a rigorous manner between what we will call the original-being and the constituted-being of the sensation or impression. The original being of the impression is its experiencing itself, the auto-impression in which it feels itself without any distance, in a primal feeling that is its actual affectivity. And so it is always through pain that we know pain, through color that we know color, etc. The impression originally given to itself by its affectivity is, however, capable of being given to us a second time by a regard, by an intentionality—which occurs when it slides into the past and the first division [*écart*] of time separates us from it, that a "retention" proposes to us as "having just passed," when it then appears in the world as one of its sensible qualities: the green of the tree, the sound of the street.

Here it should be repeated, however, that the sensible quality of the real, "objective" thing is only possible as the projection in "resonance" or "tone," this invisible subjectivity of life where the impression, whether of a color or form, draws its original being.

The musical character of these metaphors should not mislead us. They refer purely and simply to the absolute subjectivity of which every impression is originally a modality, which serves each time as the basis for its objective constitution—for its noematic appearance. The proof of this is the fact that these terms are habitually associated with that of interiority, which for Kandinsky always qualifies the original and abstract content of art, namely and specifically life. And basically it is always a question of "its interior," of "inner sound," of "inner resonance," or even of "intrinsic living tension"—all of these are radically subjective elements that comprise together, outside of the world, in the invisible of our Night, both the principle of our being and that of art. In music Kandinsky discovered this intention and capacity to immediately reproduce the hidden determinations of the Soul, thus recognizing in it, in its indifference to all objective reality "the most immaterial art"; he then assigned painting the same task: to no longer express the world but, like music, the ground of Being and of Life. It is by conceiving its task in the image of what music had already realized, and not as the task of expressing music (this would, on the contrary, be the goal of an artist like Auguste von Briesen),[4] that painting will capture its metaphysical and precisely salvific signification for modern culture and, in order to do so, it will become, in turn, consciously and deliberately "abstract."

If what is said above is true, then we will have grasped the crucial distinction Kandinsky established between two essentially different meanings of the concept of the pictorial element—and by this, he means the colors and forms out of which all paintings are made. On the one hand, each of these elements, grasped in its apparent immediacy, is presented as an objective content: this point that we see, this line with its many possible variations—straight, curved, zigzag, etc.—these colors with their infinite shades and nuances. On the other hand, however, the analysis of these elements brings to light the decisive fact that each of them, every kind of point or line, every color, is related to a subjective impression that is characteristic to it and that Kandinsky correctly calls its "inner sound," its "inner value," its "deep sound," in short, its inner or abstract content. This principal reference of each objective element to a specific subjective determination puts us in the presence both of the means and aims of art. It clarifies, in a startling manner, what we call the site of the work of art as well as its ultimate meaning.

Art, in short, has no other goal and no other meaning than to express those subjective determinations that constitute the ground of our being and perhaps of being itself, the soul of things and of the universe—if it is true that all entities and all objective appearances have their own inner resonance and initially rest within it. It is because this subjective dimension of Being is equally the essence of the universe and the abstract content, in other words absolutely real, that art wants to express it, that Kandinsky was able to call it "cosmic depth" and say that "the birth of a work of art is of cosmic character."[5]

Thus, to paint is not to naively represent an external object which guides one like a prior visible given, with properties that would actually belong to it and that would be legible in it: its noematic form and color. Instead, to paint is to return to this invisible reality that is indissolubly that of the world and of humankind itself: this is truly what art has been assigned to represent. Consequently, to paint is no longer to be guided by any external model whose imitation would remain moreover senseless (since the model is always superior to any copy); it is to choose and most often to invent "objective" elements for which only the subjective equivalent matters, for which the "inner resonance" is actually the same as what one wants to express; it is to construct, using those representative minima such as points, lines, surfaces, and other elements falsely called geometric, and using colors too, a composition whose inner vibration is the feeling that constitutes its prototype as well as its exclusive purpose. But if the content of art, its "abstract," "cosmic" content, becomes intelligible to us, it is the way to express this content and the nature of this expression that is yet to be clarified. "One knows much more often *what* one wants," as Kandinsky says in "The Cologne Lecture," "than *how* to attain it."[6]

As to the question of art's means—in this case of painting—we are, however, in a position to give a confident answer. If each objective element—form and color considered under their external appearance—is accompanied by a specific subjective determination that acts as its support, is it not advisable to demonstrate those specific tonalities that mark the reverberation within us of each type of "object," the inevitable and precise way that we have of experiencing it? And this task itself is twofold. First, it is a question of revealing or rather experiencing this inner tonality of which our daily activities, caught in their exclusively practical ends, have caused us to become unaware. In addition, it is a question of these inner tonalities that have been made "sensible" anew, of somehow taking inventory of them and of releasing the laws of their possible combinations. Kandinsky's theoretical writings consist specifically of the systematic study of the subjective tonalities in which colors and forms are presented to us, in the recognition of their relationships, which are similarly subjective and which constitute the foundation of every conceivable work of art—Kandinsky significantly calls such a work a "composition."

The description of the subjective tonality that accompanies each objective element has given rise to wonderful analyses in Kandinsky's writings. If, for example, one considers a letter, one sees that it appears as a "total form" which has, as such, a characteristic happy or sad tone.

In addition, it is comprised of variously oriented lines that produce, in turn, such and such a subjective impression. The overall tenor of these impressions or sounds defines the "inner life" of the letter. It follows that every letter produces a dual effect: it acts on the one hand as a sign having a definite purpose and serves in this regard to form words which also bear specific meanings. That is the practical, utilitarian purpose of the letter, which Kandinsky calls its "external effect." And yet, it is also possible to consider the letter while forgetting its external effect, its function as a sign. One then realizes that the letter is tied by its pure form to an "inner effect" that constitutes its proper pictorial meaning and can function completely independently of its utilitarian function. What is more, it is when this utilitarian function is out of sight that the inner effect that results from the letter's form alone is felt with all its force.[7]

Now, what we have said about a simple letter is also true for any external element whatsoever. A line, for example, serves in ordinary life to delineate an object and thus to designate it. But if in a painting one frees oneself from this obligation to draw a particular object, if it no longer represents any recognizable thing, then its "purely inner resonance" becomes perceptible; it acquires, says Kandinsky, "its full inner force." "Full" because this resonance is no longer weakened or masked by the utilitarian meaning that effaces it as long as it functions as the sign or representation of an object. "Force" because, seen in and for itself, a line manifests in each of its angles, its inflections and curves, by each of its changes in direction, the effect of a force that, no longer being that of any objective process (which has vanished), basically only exists within us, in our subjective body where all real force has its effective seat—a force that, for this reason, Kandinsky qualifies as "inner."

Kandinsky has given an impressive account of the subjective reality of all objective elements in regard to movement. The mysterious and magical power of the unfathomable subjectivity of Being is able to be felt within us as soon as it is no longer concealed and camouflaged by the tangle of objective, practical relationships that comprise the world of daily banality.

> A very simple movement, whose purpose is unknown, produces of its own accord a significant, mysterious, and solemn effect. This action lasts as long as one remains unaware of the external, practical purpose of the movement. Then it has the effect of a pure sound. A simple, concerted action (e.g., preparing to lift a heavy weight) produces, if its purpose is unknown, an effect so significant, so mysterious and dramatic and striking, that one involuntarily freezes as if in the presence of a vision of life upon another plane.[8]

This magical vision of another world—that always remains on the hidden side of the spectacle and never appears within it—is precisely the vision which art lays claim to. Art leaves us to contemplate or rather, as we have mentioned, to feel this vision within ourselves, as this original reality that is both that of the cosmos and our own.

The long and painstaking analysis of colors, which occupies a good portion of Kandinsky's theoretical writings, has the same goal as his analysis of form (to which moreover color itself belongs), namely to show that any objective element and especially noematic color has its original reality and place of vibration (its auto-affection makes it into an impression) in subjectivity. It is according to this, to its particular resonance, that each color should be chosen; its "inner necessity" constitutes the only possible motivation for its inclusion within a painting. In "The Cologne Lecture," Kandinsky recounts an important memory from the years of his apprenticeship: "I was often," he said, "so strongly possessed by a strongly sounding, perfumed patch of blue in the shadow of a bush that I would paint a whole landscape merely in order to fix this patch."[9] It is the intensity with which he experienced the subjective reverberation of each color, but also of each form, that led Kandinsky to gradually abandon the "objective support" and hence the very idea of a figurative painting, so as to leave the field free to the power of color and of "pure abstract form," in other words, to the subjectivity of life.

If the goal of art is to snatch the inner abstract content of subjective tonalities from their dissolution in objectivist perception, and instead to isolate them, abstract them in order to restore the power of their original resounding, then the problem is that these inner resonances are actually never isolated any more than their objective elements—forms and noematic colors—that correspond to them in the painting. Thus it is only on a theoretical level that one can consider each element separately in either the exteriority of its graphic or pictorial form, or in the interiority of its subjective force. In the concrete context of the artwork, on the contrary, this isolating of the element no longer exists; its particular tonality is thus no longer directly graspable. In order to experience it in itself, it is appropriate, then, to modify its position and to bring into play its surroundings. Thus, still following Kandinsky, when one considers a point located in the center of the pictorial plane (i.e., the sheet of paper or blank canvas), it is simply in moving this point towards one side of the plane that one comes to perceive its particular resonance, as well as the mysterious latent resonance of the pictorial plane itself, each of which had been until then confused and unrecognized, especially that of the plane.

The difficulties related to the grasping of the subjective tonality of isolated elements constitute nothing other, however, than the actual principles of the Kandinskian composition. It suffices to multiply the elements and their possible relations to open the infinite field of abstract plastic invention. These elements are three in number: form, color, and object (to which could be added plane). Since each of these elements exerts, due to its subjective value, an action upon us, it is important that the artist, in substituting himself precisely for Nature, consciously implement these three factors and combine their effects, that is to say, the set of affective tonalities that they arouse within us, in order to construct the painting in conformity to inner Necessity, to what could be called the original composition within us of these various tonalities, a composition which is both the cause and the result of the plastic composition: a state of the Force and pathos of the Life within us. By starting from this state, that is, from the subjective tonalities of the objective elements, the abstract artist arranges them according to principles, criteria, and directions that are, in the final analysis, nothing other than the most profound urges of his or her Soul and Desire.

The meaning of the work of art is to express this Soul which is thus both that of each of us as well as the soul of the universe, if it is true that to each element of the universe, to each objective determination, there corresponds a determinate pathos, such that the world is the totality of these subjective tonalities by which the world really exists within us. As Kandinsky says, "The world sounds. It is a cosmos of spiritually affective beings. Thus, dead matter is living spirit."[10]

If this is the universal meaning of the work of art, and not only of abstract painting, it follows that abstract painting has only been taken as an example, and that the theory of abstract painting that we have sketched with Kandinsky's help is in reality a theory of all possible painting. If one contemplates a classical painting representing a religious scene such as an adoration of the magi, a deposition, etc., then one will see that the forms (for example, the angle at which the figures are presented) and the colors (for example, of the clothing) have no objective model and are chosen solely for their expressive power, that is, for the subjective tonality to which each of these forms or colors is linked in principle. Thus traditional painting is only figurative in appearance. A truly figurative painting, that is to say one whose principle of construction would be the pure and simple reproduction of external elements, with their ordinary, that is to say extremely weak, inner resonance—like that which developed at certain times or in certain schools—would collapse into insignificance.

One last remark to highlight the dynamism and beneficent character of art—and remind us, unfortunately, how societies, like ours, that cut themselves off from art and culture in general, find themselves threatened by destruction, by the degeneracy known as barbarism. The aim of art is indeed not to express a subjective state understood as a state of fact, a state of affairs, and it is in this sense that Kandinsky could say, "I do not want to paint states of mind."[11] Art paints life, in other words a capacity for growth. Life as subjectivity, that is, as experiencing itself, is the power of attaining oneself and thus of expanding oneself at each moment. That is why each eye wants to see more and each force wants to swell, to become more efficient and stronger. Art is the endlessly repeated attempt to carry each of life's powers to its highest degree of intensity and thus of pleasure; it is the response given by life to its most intimate essence and to the will which inhabits it—to its desire to surpass.

Translated by Michael Tweed

Notes

1. Edmund Husserl, *Ideas Pertaining to a Pure Phenomenology and to a Phenomenological Philosophy: First Book*, 261–62.
2. Wassily Kandinsky, "On the Spiritual in Art," in *Kandinsky: Complete Writings on Art*, trans. Kenneth C. Lindsay and Peter Vergo (New York: Da Capo, 1994), 176. All subsequent Kandinsky references are also to this edition.
3. Kandinsky, "On the Spiritual in Art," 176.
4. See Michel Henry, "Dessiner la musique: Théorie de l'art de Briesen," in *Phénoménologie de la vie*, vol. 3 (Paris: Presses Universitaires de France, 2004), 241–82.
5. Kandinsky, "The Cologne Lecture," 394.
6. Kandinsky, "The Cologne Lecture," 394.
7. See Kandinsky, "On the Question of Form," 245–46.
8. Kandinsky, "Concerning the Spiritual in Art," 204–5.
9. Kandinsky, "The Cologne Lecture," 394.
10. Kandinsky, "On the Question of Form," 250.
11. Kandinsky, "The Cologne Lecture," 400.

12

Material Phenomenology and Language (or, Pathos and Language)

The brief comments that I am proposing here on language are given in the name of phenomenology. The phrase "the phenomenology of language" can be understood in two senses. On the one hand, phenomenology can be understood as a method of investigation, in which case the phenomenology of language consists in the application of this method to a specific problem. In this "application," phenomenology has the opportunity to demonstrate its fecundity as an original discipline by displaying the means which define it. Husserl had followed this path after the turning point of 1900. The intervention of a method which was not yet elucidated but which was already the method of intentional analysis, gives rise to one of the greatest analyses of language that contemporary thought has at its disposal. Whether they acknowledge it or not, philosophy and other disciplines such as linguistics will come to borrow a variety of insights from this analysis.

The implementation of a defining method requires phenomenology, however, to thematize itself, and, more generally, to become radically self-conscious. The presuppositions upon which phenomenology is based then progressively come to light for it. Today, we can recognize them in the famous section seven of *Being and Time*, and formulate them as follows.

1. Phenomenology is not defined first in fact as a method, but by means of its object. This object does not designate the set of phenomena, but what makes each phenomenon what it is, that is, the phenomenon's phenomenality considered as such—its appearance, its manifestation, its revelation, or yet the truth understood in an originary sense.

2. One of the first consequences of this definition of phenomenology is paradoxical; the definition eliminates the question of the method; the question of the method is at any rate absorbed back into the question of the object. The genuine object of phenomenology is phenomenality, because phenomenality constitutes our access to the phenomenon; in its very phenomenalization, phenomenality opens the path which leads

right up to the phenomenon. Now, in its ultimate possibility, the method is nothing other than this openness of a path leading to the phenomenon; it allows us to apprehend the phenomenon and to know it.

Moreover, we see the phenomenological reduction which constitutes the essential core of Husserl's method disappear from Heidegger's analysis of truth. The substitutes that some attempt to discover for it, the Difference between Being and the being (as Heidegger himself says), anxiety according to Jean-François Courtine, are only diverse formulations of the originary event of the pure phenomenality which constitutes the unique donation of Being. With Husserl, of course, the method remains at the center of the problematic, but we will see that the method constantly confronts the prior question of phenomenality; in fact, the method remains so dependent on phenomenality that its possibility as well as its many difficulties are based on it.

3. At the same time as it is taking the place of the method, and basically for the same reason, phenomenality is given in section seven of *Being and Time* a still more decisive importance. Insofar as it founds the possibility of an access to the phenomena, phenomenality also constitutes the possibility of language. Indeed, solely because phenomenality blazes the path by which things and phenomena advent to an encounter with us in order to offer themselves to our apprehension, because they show themselves to us, we can speak of them, name them, refer ourselves to them in this nomination, describe them, produce on their subject the many predications out of which our knowledge and our discourse are simultaneously composed.

If, therefore, appearing constitutes the incontrovertible condition of every conceivable language (which it does by discovering, first of all, everything that this language speaks about at the same time as what it is saying about it and will be able to say about it), then the sense of a "phenomenology of language" has been totally reversed. Far from being proposed as one theme or object among others for the work of phenomenological elucidation (a phenomenology of language just as there can be a phenomenology of social forms, of the work of art, etc.), language belongs, on the contrary, to the internal conditions of this process of elucidation; it is this internal condition if it is true that it bears within itself the capacity for making us see what it designates by naming it before pursuing the analysis of it either in the spontaneous assertions of common sense or in the advanced propositions of scientific knowledge. But, not only must the things be able to show themselves to us (the things to which these propositions refer), but also these propositions themselves must be able to show themselves, and they can do this only in a monstration proper to language, a monstration which constitutes its originary essence, its *Logos*. The primitive Saying is never therefore on the side of what is said, that is, on the side of what is shown; it is what shows.

4. The discovery of the original connection between phenomenality and language—the second finding its possibility in the first—brings before us an urgent question. Insofar as all systems of language (beyond their diversity, beyond the diversity of their structures and their own rules) refer to a prior possibility of speaking and hearing which is no longer a phenomenon but precisely the phenomenon's possibility—since only by adventing in the phenomenal condition is anything, regardless of what it is, susceptible of being said—then one has to explain what this advent is, this *phenomenalization of the pure phenomenality* which defines conjointly the object of phenomenology and the ultimate foundation of every possible language.

Now, if one questions the way phenomenology historically developed from Husserl, one has to see that phenomenology has left this question which is crucial for it in the dark, the question of pure phenomenality. Let us consider as a sort of example the principles that this phenomenology has explicitly recognized as its own. The first, "so much appearance, so much being," does not specify what is here understood as "appearance"—it would be better to say "appearing"—on which however being itself depends. The subordination of ontology to phenomenology thus leaves the principle of this subordination totally undetermined. Likewise, another principle, no less decisive since it founds the methodological postulation of phenomenology so much so that it serves as its slogan: *"Zu den Sachen Selbst!"* ("To the things themselves!"), also leaves undetermined what defines this immediate access to the things, an access which is nothing other than their own appearing.

Nevertheless, if we look closely here, we see that, behind the phenomenological indetermination of the principle of phenomenology, and due to this indetermination, a certain conception of phenomenality slips in surreptitiously. This is the very conception which presents itself first to ordinary thought and also constitutes the oldest and the least critical presupposition of traditional philosophy. It is the conception of phenomenality which is borrowed from the immediate perception of mundane objects; at the end of the account, it is borrowed from the appearing of the world itself. This disastrous confusion of the appearing of the world with the essence of all conceivable appearing overtakes phenomenology as a whole and notably its theory of language, since the latter is based on appearing.

In Husserl's phenomenology, it is the "principle of all principles" which exposes the full scope of this confusion. This principle posits intuition, "every originary donative intuition [as] an in principle source of knowledge" (*Ideas I*, section 24). What gives in intuition and what makes it be a donative intuition is the structure of consciousness, such as Husserl understands it, insofar as it is intentional. Certainly, fulfilled intentionality qualifies *stricto sensu* the concept of intuition, but intuition owes its phenomenological power (the power to institute in the condition of being a phenomenon by making phenomenality emerge) to intentionality. This emergence consists in the movement by which intentionality is thrown outside of itself by overcoming itself toward its intentional correlate insofar as it is a transcendent object. This distancing into the primitive "outside" where intentionality unfolds itself constitutes phenomenality in its purity.

When appearing is accomplished as the making-see of intentionality, the subordination of language to phenomenality (phenomenality understood as distancing) opens the way to the intentional conception of language which will always be Husserl's great discovery. Although it is the original making things be seen in perception, intentionality is still the making-see which is limited to signifying them in language. This ability to economize on perception is what distinguishes the human from the animal at the same time as it constitutes the principal foundation of humanity's immense power. Dissociated from perception, composed of meanings, intentional language is still however subordinated to, entirely dependent on, one sole conception of phenomenality.

If we return to section 7 of *Being and Time*, we see the phenomenological situation we are describing being taken to its most extreme point. The connection established between the monstration in which the phenomenon and language (which everywhere presupposes this donation) are given entails the decisive consequence that the nature of originary language is defined by the nature of the monstration to the point of being identified with it. Now, the nature of monstration does not remain more indeterminate than in the case of intentionality; it is explicitly understood on the basis of the Greek concept of *phainomenon* and its root, *pha, phos*: the light. To show itself, to advent in the condition of being a phenomenon means then to come to light, to enter into the light of a world. More profoundly, the appearing of the phenomenon designates the advent of the world itself, the emergence of the "outside," in such a way that this advent of the outside from the Outside constitutes the phenomenalization of phenomenality. When phenomenality is analyzed for itself and understood as ecstatic temporality in division two of *Being and Time* (the ontic considerations of *Dasein* having been finally eliminated), the definition of ecstatic temporality as pure exteriority appears decisive. "*Zeitlichkeit ist das ursprungliche 'Ausser- sich' an und fur sich selbst*" ("Temporality is the 'outside of itself' in and for itself"). And the phenomenality which is clarified in this way in the temporalization of temporality is precisely that of the world. "*Die Welt . . . zeitigt sich in der Zeitlichkeit. Sie 'ist' mit dem Ausser-sich der Ekstasen 'da'*" ("The world . . . temporalizes itself in temporality. It 'is' with the outside of itself of the ecstases, 'there'") (*Being and Time*, sections 65 and 69c).[1]

The reference of the originary nature of language to the ecstatic truth of Being constitutes the explicit content of the essays collected in *On the Way to Language*. The saying of speech is revealed there to be nothing other than the Greek appearing, this advent of the outside in which all of what we see and all about which we speak is given to us: "*Sagen, sagan, heisst zeigen: erscheinen lassen, lichtend-verbergend frei-geben*" ("To say," *sagan*, means to show: to give to be seen, to make appear, to set free in a clearing"). This assimilation of saying to the appearing of the world is constant: "*Aus dem Sagen, worin sich das Erscheinenlassen von Welt begibt*" ("On the basis of the saying, in which the letting-appear of the world is set forth"). The assimilation is authorized by a pedantic etymology which aims to make the German "*zeigen*" (to show) and the Old German "*sagan*," from which the Modern German "*sagen*" (to say) is derived, say the same thing: this "showing" which means "saying" and this "saying" which means "showing" (*Unterwegs zur Sprache* [Pfullingen: Neske, 1959], pp. 200, 208).[2]

This reciprocity of appearing and speech is the object of a precise analysis. What speech gives to see and of which it speaks is the being. To give the being to be seen, nevertheless, is to give something else and something higher to be seen, namely, the advent into presence in which the being comes to us. "*Das Wort . . . ist nicht mehr nur benennender Griff nach dem schon vorgestellten Anwesenden, nicht nur Mittel der Darstellung des Vorliegenden. Dem entgegen verleiht das Wort erst Anwesen, d.h. Sein, worin etwas als Seiendes erscheint*" ("The word . . . is no longer an instrument for giving a name to something which is there, already represented, a means for exhibiting what lies before us. On the contrary, the word first bestows the advent of presence, that is, Being, in which something appears as a being") (*Unterwegs zur Sprache*, p. 227).[3]

We have to ask then if there is a specific word for saying this "other rule" of the word in which the word renounces the saying of the being in order to say Being. "*Das alteste Wort für das so gedachte Walten des Wortes, für das Sagen, heisst Logos: die Sage, die zeigend Seiendes in sein es ist erscheinen lasst. Das selbe Wort Logos ist aber als Wort für das Sagens zugleich das Wort für das Sein, d.h. für das Anwesen des Anwesenden*" ("The oldest word for the rule of the word thus thought for saying is logos: saying which in showing lets beings appear in their it is. The same word logos, however, is insofar as it is the word for saying also the word for Being, that is, for the advent into presence of what is present" (*Unterwegs zur Sprache*, p. 237).[4]

If *Logos* is the word for the advent into presence of all of what shows itself, it depends, obviously, on the nature of this advent. Such a dependence is rigorous and must be analyzed in its own right.

Three characteristics define the advent into presence which consists in the appearing of the world. First, the unconcealing appearing is different from what is unconcealed in it to the point that the unconcealment consists in this difference. In section 44 of *Being and Time*, Heidegger distinguishes the originary truth (the unconcealment) and what is true (the unconcealed). Nevertheless, it seems to us that such a difference is posited only when the originary truth is understood as the "outside of itself" of the world.

Second, because the unconcealing appearing in the "outside of itself" of the world differs from what is unveiled in it, it is totally indifferent to it, the ek-stasis of the world dispensing its light indifferently upon every being—"over the just as well as over the unjust."

Third, the indifference of the appearing of the world to all of what shows itself in it refers to a still more decisive situation, to the incapacity of this appearing to posit the reality uncovered in it. This appearing, according to Heidegger's explicit assertion, does not create this reality; it is limited to unconcealing it ("*macht nicht, offnet*"). It is impossible not to see here a paradox which strikes at the heart of phenomenology's very principle. According to this principle, it is phenomenality which provides being. By appearing and only inasmuch as it appears is anything whatsoever susceptible of being. And yet, here it has been conceded that what appears owes its existence precisely not to the power of the appearing, since the power of appearing is limited to uncovering a being which preexists it and which would not be able, therefore, to depend on it in a genuine ontological sense.

Now, *these three characteristics of the appearing of the world*—here briefly sketched but obviously decisive—*are precisely those of the language which is founded upon such an appearing* and that, for this reason, we will call from now on *the language of the world*.

First, each word constitutive of this language is different from the particular reality—different from the "being"—which it intends each time it is used. Therefore, just as the ecstatic appearing reveals itself as being indifferent to all of that to which it gives appearance precisely because it differs from it, this difference which separates it from all that it designates is the reason why each word of the language of the world turns out to be indifferent to this referent. In an extraordinary epistle (3:6),

Saint James denounces this indifference when he says that "the tongue is . . . evil in its universality."

In fact, by means of its indifference to the thing designated, the word could just as well name something else, one word being applied in this way to two different realities in a disastrous confusion that nothing (besides a pure convention) is able to dispel. Conversely, and always by virtue of the indifference which is established between word and thing, two different words are able to qualify one reality. This is the situation that Saint James denounces as the universal perversion of the tongue when "with it we bless the Lord and the Father and with it we curse men who are made in the image of God. From the same mouth come blessings and curses" (3:9–10).

Solely because language blesses and curses in turn that which is the Same—the Lord and his image, God and his sons—solely because it fails to penetrate into what it claims to say and about which—in praise or in blame—it can only slander, language does not contain within itself the reality of which it speaks. Difference and indifference are here only the consequence of this primary ontological insufficiency. But then, does not this third characteristic of the language of the world obviously carry within itself the characteristic of the appearing of the world, that is, the original and definitive incapacity of such an appearing to posit the reality that it "unconceals" but never "creates"? The most decisive characteristic of the language of the world which human speak and which, since always, defines in their eyes the prototype of every conceivable language is contained in this impotence, which is immediately copied off the impotence of appearing (on which language depends).

Let us consider the first stanza of Trakl's poem entitled "A Winter Evening":

> Wenn der Schnee ans Fenster fällt,
> Lang die Abendglocke läutet,
> Vielen ist der Tisch bereitet
> Und das Haus ist wohlbestellt.
>
> Window with falling snow is arrayed,
> Long tolls the vesper bell,
> The house is provided well,
> The table is for many laid.[5]

We are following Heidegger's commentary by observing that the things named by the poet—snow, the bell, the evening—as called by their name, come to presence. They show themselves to us while we read the poem.

And yet, they do not take their place among the objects which surround us, in the room where we are sitting. They are present, but in a sort of absence. Present in this way: evoked by the poet's word, they appear; absent in this way: *although appearing, they are not there.* This is the enigma of the poet's word: to make the thing appear and thus seem to give being to it in such a way, however, that, although said by this word, the thing does not exist. The word gives being by withdrawing being from the thing; it provides the thing, but as not being.

Now, the poet's word is not the only kind of language which gives in such a way as to withdraw being as it gives it. Every human word does the same; it offers what it names only in a pseudo-presence so that the thing named, as long as it exists only in this nomination and by means of it, does not really exist. The one who says, "I have a thaler in my pocket," does not possess one by saying that. However, this incapacity of human language to produce through its word the reality of all of that about which it speaks is not based exactly on speech as such, but on the appearing to which it asks for its ultimate phenomenological possibility. The impotence that speech manifests everywhere flows from the mode of this appearing and from it alone.

Thus are we referred to our introductory remarks: (1) to the original connection of speech and the appearing on which it rests; (2) to the disastrous reduction, in Husserl's as well as Heidegger's phenomenology, of this appearing to the one of primordial "outside" of the world; (3) to the genuine origin of the impotence of human language which is based on the fact that, throwing all reality outside of itself in order to render it manifest in this self-exteriority, it also strips it of its substance, reducing it to these sorts of efflorescences on death that the poem provides. Evanescent apparitions about the world's foundation in nothingness or noematic meanings of intentional language, both are struck with the same irreality in principle. The world, this vast world where everything comes to presence only in a primary absence, an absence Augustine called memory—the memory in which everything is there, but in which nothing is ever present. And, likewise, when Kant fixed the *a priori* conditions of what he calls "all possible experience" and which was in fact only the experience of the world, he too could not—on the basis of these phenomenological, ecstatic forms of both pure intuition and the concept (both of which he called representations)—posit the least bit of existence; he had to ask sensation, that is, he had to ask life.

Life is the original appearing that from now on we are going to designate with the word "revelation." In this way, the reduction, in which classical phenomenology engages, of all conceivable appearing to the appearing of the world, will be dispelled. In a rigorous way, we must dissociate the characteristics which define the appearing of the world from those which define the revelation of life. These characteristics are exactly opposed to one another.

The first feature of the revelation of life is that it is accomplished as a self-revelation. Life revealing itself means that it experiences itself. This self-revelation could not be assimilated to a tautology. In self-revelation, the Same would not, so to speak, be named twice, the first time as what reveals or affects, the second time as what is revealed, with the result that the affecting and the affected would be presented as two different realities, each finding itself defined by its function. Only in the world's "being outside of itself" does the self-revelation of life divide itself by destroying itself. The dialectical process which illustrates this situation is only the advanced expression of a conception of phenomenality which has placed phenomenality in the oppositional structure of Difference: in the world's "outside of itself."

Irreducible to tautology, the self-revelation of life marks the place of an original and absolute generation. Experiencing itself, life takes hold of itself; it increases itself, enriching itself with its own substance by being submerged into it. Experiencing oneself has therefore nothing to do with the formal and empty equality of "A = A," an equality which can be seen only in the difference of these terms. In contrast, life is an immanent process, the eternal process in which life comes to itself; life pulls itself in against itself and plays with itself, producing its own essence insofar as this essence consists in and is complete in this self-enjoyment. Thus, the process in which life reveals itself to itself is identical with the process of its generation insofar as this is understood as self-generation. Life is a self-movement which experiences itself and never stops experiencing itself in this very movement, and this happens in such a way that nothing ever detaches itself from this self-experiencing movement, in such a way that nothing slips out of this moving self-experience.

But in this self-experiencing movement something advents which is still more admirable. In the endless advent of life in its self-experience, an Ipseity is born without which no experience of this type would be possible. Inasmuch as this self-experience is a self-experience which is phenomenologically actual and thus singular, the Ipseity in which this experience is accomplished is also singular; it is a singular Self generated in Life as the Self of the First Living Being in which life experiences itself and thus is revealed to itself—as its Verb.

Here, the guiding thread of our investigation again demands our attention at the same time as what we have called phenomenology is specified in its ultimate motivation. On the basis of the "First Logical Investigation" in an implicit way and in *Being and Time*'s section seven in an explicit way, the essential connection between language and appearing would be uncovered as a decisive theme if it is true that the nature of language depends on that of the appearing that it always presupposes. If this is true, then this other incontestable fact asserts itself: if, as we have just established, *phenomenality phenomenalizes itself originally according to a mode of phenomenalization radically different from that of the world, namely, life itself grasped in its pure, phenomenological essence as self-revelation, then there must also be another language than the language of the world* (a language different from the language constructed out of noematic meanings foreign to the reality of their referent; in other words, different from the language to which we generally limit the concept of language); *this other language would be dependent on the mode of phenomenalization proper to life inasmuch as the appearing of life is opposed feature for feature to the appearing of the world.*

On the basis of the phenomenological properties of life, we can grasp *a priori* the essence of this other language (which is based on life's self-revelation and which is usually obscured) as the very way through which life reveals in its self-revelation. For *the way in which life reveals is the way in which it speaks.* And, inasmuch as it reveals in its self-revelation, without starting outside of itself in the difference of the world, then as opposed to every other language, which is always related to a referent exterior to itself, the speech that life speaks presents the extraordinary characteristic that it never speaks but of itself.

It does not speak like a bore who, throughout his conversations, never has any other intention than to refer to himself. Life's speech intends precisely nothing—and itself less than everything. It contains in itself no intentionality. Someone might object that life, in its self-revelation, must be related to itself if it itself constitutes the content of this revelation. Does not this self-relation also make the essence of the Self that it generates by generating itself? What would life say, what would remain for it to say if, while having no external referent at all, it were deprived at any rate of saying itself?

But what is important in a radical phenomenology is the phenomenological essence of this self-relation. *Every relation which does not stand out against the horizon of the world and which does not render the world manifest in its way draws its possibility from pathos.* Pathos designates the mode of phenomenalization according to which life phenomenalizes in its originary self-revelation; it designates the phenomenological material out of which this self-donation is made, its flesh: a transcendental and pure affectivity in which everything experiencing itself finds its concrete, phenomenological actualization. In this pathos, the "how" of revelation becomes its content; its *Wie* is a *Was*. If life originally reveals nothing but its own reality, this is solely because its mode of revelation is pathos, which is this essence entirely concerned with itself, this plenitude of a flesh immersed in the self-affection of its suffering and joy. In the immanence of its own pathos, this reality of life is then not any life whatsoever. It is everything except what contemporary thought will turn it into, that is, some impersonal, anonymous, blind, mute essence. In itself, the reality of life bears necessarily this Self generated in its pathetic self-generation, this Self which reveals itself only in Life as the proper self-revelation of this Life—that is, as its *Logos*.

We see then in complete rigor what the *Logos*, what the *Speech of life* is. To the impotence of the speech of the world, which is incapable of positing the reality of which it speaks, obliged therefore to find it as a mysterious existence which precedes it and which owes nothing to it, the Speech of life opposes its hyper-potency, that of generating the reality of which it speaks. This does not mean that it "creates," since every creation is that of a world in the appearing by means of which all of what it shows is irrealized. The speech of life generates reality inasmuch as it reveals as life does: life generates its own reality by experiencing itself in the Self in which it self-reveals itself. Thus, the Speech of life reveals simultaneously the reality of life and the Self without which no life is living. The unthought of our ultimate, phenomenological condition, that of being living beings in life, consists of this double revelation.

Certain responses have taken shape for the constellation of problems connected to the phenomenological definition of Speech. How does this speech speak? What does it say? It speaks insofar as it is life. What does it say? It says itself. But to whom does it speak? This is an inevitable question, since every language is addressed to someone and makes sense only as being addressed. Heidegger's merit lies in having seen in its radicality a state of things which passes for being obvious. As one can see in *On the Way to Language*, a speech everywhere already present—which gives itself and which says itself—addresses speech to us, allowing us to speak in our turn. This privileging of speech over human speech determines their relation and defines what it is to be human: "*Das so Ereignete, das Menschenwesen, ist durch die Sprache in sein Eigenes gebracht*" ("What has thus taken place, human being, has been brought into its own by language") (*Unterwegs zur Sprache*, 34).[6]

To put this phenomenologically, if the appearing speaks insofar as it shows, the one who can hear its speech is the one who is open to the monstration of this appearing, is the one who is defined by this openness, being nothing other than it. But who is this, the one who can hear the speech of appearing? *How and why is he a Self*—irreducibly singular, always mine? By conceiving Speech on the basis of the anonymous Event of a pure exteriority, one can indeed define some sort of agency abstractly through its openness to such an Event. How can one not see that something like an actual Self is found here purely and presupposed like common sense, if it is true that the possibility of such a Self and thus of every conceivable "I"—if the essence of Ipseity, which is immediately annihilated in every form of exteriority—is born nowhere else than in the place where life engenders itself by experiencing itself in the pathos of its self-revelation? Only in this way does the original Speech, which precedes everything, not speak in the desert; only in this way is there in fact someone who hears it, the one to whom it has given a Self to be, a Self given to itself in its self-donation to speech—a Self living in Life.

What the original Speech of life says to every living being is therefore its own life. Thus is it possible to recognize this speech in each living being or in each of the modalities of its life. Let us consider the suffering that I experience. The suffering does not say, for example, that "I suffer, someone is guilty," which lets one think that one ought to add ultimately some cause or something like that to the suffering one feels. In its nudity, in its naïveté, in its total exposure, *in its pure self-experience*, what suffering says is itself and nothing else. But it does not say that either—it does not say itself—by saying at any rate "I suffer," by forming the "suffering" meaning whose connection with the "I" meaning would constitute the substance of its speech. It says itself in such a way that, in order to know what it is talking about, it would not be necessary for the intentional language to have already produced these meanings; it also says itself in such a way that it would not be necessary for the saying of the suffering to be composed of these meanings and to be itself something ideal. But in itself suffering is nothing ideal. If suffering says to us what it says to us without recourse to any moment in the language of humans, then we must ask, "how does it say it?" In its suffering and by it. We see therefore why suffering is a speech, why it is suffering who speaks and suffering who says: the revelation of what, in this way, it tells us is done in and by the flesh of its suffering so that what it tells us is itself, this suffering flesh and nothing else. At the same time as this speech of suffering, which is only an example, we find before us an infinite number of speeches which draw their saying from the infinite number of the modalities of the lives of numerous living beings; we find ourselves before this "language of real life," as Marx says, without which there would no other language—these other languages only ever signify emptily, *après coup*, the first epiphanies of our flesh. Without this language of real life, no speech of any kind would ever be able to speak.

As soon as we ask, "how does suffering speak?" inevitably we sense that it says to us something in addition to its own suffering flesh. It says itself to us; this is what is added to its own suffering flesh and, in fact, this is what makes it possible. For no suffering ever advents as the suffering of no one. Since it bears in itself the Self who suffers it, we are obliged to reconsider the question "How" according to which this suffering speaks. It does not speak by itself, if it is true that its own revelation is not precisely its own doing. Only in the self-donation of life and inasmuch as the latter is accomplished does each suffering experience itself, in its own Self, but first in the originary Self that absolute life generates in itself in its self-revelation to itself. In this way, within the very heart of suffering, life has already spoken otherwise, in an older suffering, this older suffering in which life embraces itself in the process of its self-advent, in the love and enjoyment of itself—this older suffering which lives in every modality of life, suffering or joy, because in either suffering or joy, it is this older suffering which gives suffering or joy to itself inasmuch as in this older suffering, in this original pathos which belongs to it, absolute Life gives itself to itself.

Insofar as absolute Life reveals itself in the older suffering by giving it to itself, the speech of Life speaks in every living being. It is addressed to every living being not as a being that it happens upon, who would have no means of hearing it, but as the being that the speech of life has engendered in its own generation. What each living being hears by experiencing itself—and no matter what the vicissitudes of this experience may be is this Speech of life. Each living being has heard this Speech of life in the first shudder of his own life, when he experiences himself for the first time, this Speech of life whose embrace with itself, whose Speech, has joined him—and forever—to himself in the very emergence of his Self. Thus, the possibility of hearing the Speech of life is for each living Self consubstantial with its birth, on the condition of being a Son. Forever do I hear the noise of my birth. The noise of my birth is the noise of life, the infrangible silence in which the Speech of Life constantly tells me about my own life, in which my own life—if I understand the Speech which speaks in it—constantly tells me the Speech of Life.

Let us summarize. The renewal of the question of language which results from its connection to the question of phenomenality presents two successive phases. In the first, we find that, when language is no longer understood as an autonomous power, all of its characteristics turn out to be established on the basis of those of the appearing in which it must first of all make that of which it speaks be seen, its speech consisting in this making to be seen as such. As long, nevertheless, as this appearing is that of the world, the phenomenological determination of language will be imprisoned within the unbreachable limits assigned to the concept of phenomenality since Greece. Within these limits, the renewal of the question of language can only be an apparent renewal. We really see this in Kojève's work, which leaves its mark in the French—philosophical, psychoanalytical, literary, linguistical, and anthropological—thought of the second half of this century. From the young Hegel to Heidegger, as the synthesis that Kojève attempts shows, it is the same presupposition, language as negation, negativity, abandonment, and loss of reality, a presupposition which extends the reign of its mortuary fascination everywhere.

If the ultimate possibility of the *Logos* resides in pure phenomenality, only the apprehension of pure phenomenality in its originary mode of phenomenalization can indicate the overthrowing of our understanding of language. Another speech comes then into question, a speech which speaks otherwise, which says something else, which says it to the one that it generates in its very speech, who draws from it his condition of living, who has never been separated from it and cannot be it. The speech of life and not of death. Truthful speech where reality says itself, unaware of the difference, the indifference, the lie and annihilation. All the characteristics traditionally attributed to language by the thought of the world are now flotsam and jetsam. A set of problems which are entirely new emerges.

We are going to limit ourselves to some programmatic remarks.

1. The radical opposition which separates the language of life from the language of the world does not exclude their relation; in fact, it's the opposite. This relation consists in that the first founds the second, but this founding would not be possible without there being a relation. We can form for ourselves *a priori* an idea of the relation, if we do not lose sight of the presupposition of a phenomenology of language. Inasmuch as the language of the world is based on the appearing of the world in which it shows to us all of what it says, while, in the same way, the Speech of Life is the Verb, the originary Self in which life reveals itself to itself, it becomes obvious that the relation of the two languages conceals the relation of the two modes of phenomenalization of phenomenality and can be understood only on the basis of this relation. In order to limit ourselves to one particular formulation of this immense problem, we can say that every linguistic intentionality, which intends a transcendent meaning, can relate itself to that meaning only on the condition of having already entered into the possession of itself in the self-donation of the pathos which turns it into a life. Thus, at the same time as it presupposes the making-see which defines this linguistic intentionality, it presupposes this originary revelation in which there is neither intentionality nor seeing, in which nothing is ever seen.

2. An "example" will be able to emphasize the importance of this founding relation between the two languages. When Marx declares that "ideology is the language of real life," in no way does he want to reduce

this life—hunger, cold, striving, suffering—to the discourse of ideology. Instead, he asserts that, while this discourse is of another order and is irreal like the meanings with which it is composed, it is unintelligible in its own order, and therefore is explained only in its reference to the multiple modalities of the life of "living individuals."

3. The immanent relation of life to what we call in an equivocal way its "expressions" must be carefully distinguished from the intentional relation of life to the noematic meanings in which life is always allowed to signify itself. The cry of suffering is an expression of life entirely different from a linguistic proposition such as "I'm in pain." The proposition is a noematic irreality foreign to the reality of the suffering which it signifies. In contrast, the cry belongs to the immanence of life as one of its modalities in the same way as the suffering which the cry bears within itself is one of life's modalities. It is true that its belonging to life can be recognized only if the cry is grasped in its subjective utterance, as a phonic act of the living body possessing the phenomenological status of life, and not as a behavior of the objective body uncovering itself to us in the world.

Would we not, however, hear this cry resounding in the world like another noise, like finally a proposition thrown in anger by a schoolteacher at a recalcitrant student? *But the cry of suffering does not speak in this way; it speaks in and through its own pathos; its speech is the speech of life.* We also hear it as a sound which resonates in the proximity or distance of an "outside," solely because of the duality of the appearing; we hear it this way because, in the exteriority of the world, the noise to which our corporeality is open in hearing is added over and above to the original revelation of the suffering which is pulled in tight against itself in its pathetic flesh and which is striving always in this pathos to free itself through its cry. The two speeches speak in one same and most simple cry, because the philosophy of language refers to and is possible only on the basis of a phenomenology whose radical presupposition is the duplicity of appearing.

4. The analysis of the speech of life which speaks in its pathos raises still other problems. We are saying that this speech is the original speech, but what "origin" means must be specified. In a sense, the speech of suffering is the origin of the cry which proceeds from it, the cry being second in relation to the suffering; this secondary status is the case even if its utterance belongs to the same phenomenological milieu as the suffering, in this case the milieu of the living body. But, as we have suggested, suffering itself has nothing original about it; it does not bring itself forward in its flesh. Because of this, it characterizes our human life; our human life is a finite life which is given to itself only in the self-donation of absolute life, just as every human Self is joined to itself only in the original Ipseity of the First Self—of the Verb of this life.

This is why the Verb of life and human speech speak in two different ways. While human speech is incapable of engendering suffering, in fact, presupposing it so that our life is always told to us as what we undergo in a passion stronger than this speech (even if this speech composes the web of the stronger passion)—the Verb of Life constantly engenders itself in the self-donation process of this Life inasmuch as it is in the Verb that Life is revealed to itself. Thus it constantly says, in itself, life before it says life to all living beings.

If, following the famous Prologue of Saint John's Gospel, we take into consideration the abyssal assertion according to which "in the beginning was the Word, the Logos, the Verb, and the Word was made flesh," that is, made man, that is, one sole person in the figure of Christ, then the singular fact that Christ speaks in two ways becomes intelligible. He speaks the speech of a finite life which speaks of its tiredness, a speech in which He asks the Samaritan, "give me something to drink"; he also speaks the speech of the Verb in which absolute Life says itself to itself, with its radical phenomenological determinations: "before Abraham was, I am"; "I am . . . the Truth, the Life."

5. By pursuing the examination of these two ways of speaking— that of the man Jesus who asks for a pillow on which to lay his head, who weeps over the death of a friend or over Jerusalem whose destruction he sees across the centuries, and that of the Verb which says its condition of being the Verb—we encounter new difficulties. In Christ, the two ways of speaking are speeches about life. They tell us (the one) about the suffering, the complaints, the despair finally of the man who is making his way towards the torment of an infamous death and (the other) about the eternal generation of Life in the Verb, the relation of phenomenologically reciprocal interiority which unites them. They tell us about Life and the Living, about the Father and the Son: "Do you not believe that I am in the Father and the Father in me?" (John 14:10).

In the Scriptures, however, these two ways of speaking—as essential as they are and especially the second—can claim no other status than that of being "speeches of the world" in the sense that we have analyzed; they are propositions, structures of meaning intending each time determinate realities, meanings, and "realities" uncovering themselves to us in the appearing of the world. In the New Testament, several types of speakers formulate these propositions. First, there are the Evangelists who recount the story of Jesus, the principal events and characters connected to this story. Nevertheless, the narratives which compose the New Testament are punctuated with quotation marks. These are then the very speeches of Christ that we hear and, if Christ is the Verb, we hear the speeches of God. Even when Christ speaks of himself and of his own condition of being the Verb, the speeches of God are addressed to humans in the language they use to communicate among themselves—this language of the world whose ontological insufficiency is, as we have emphasized, what is most decisive. Therefore, how would the text of the Evangelist, although it is given as though it were written by those who directly witnessed or by their disciples, be equal to proving the truth of what it relates, that these characters, lost for us in the haze of centuries, have really existed, that these miracles have really taken place, that Christ has truly pronounced these extraordinary words? But the problem is more serious if we suppose that these words had been formulated and belong still, let us say, to a language which is incapable of positing through itself the reality of which it speaks. How would the most decisive words—"I am the truth"—prove their own truth, namely, that the one who has pronounced them is himself, in his person, the self-revelation of the absolute life of God, his Verb?

There is no answer to these questions as long as we remain enclosed in the proposition according to which we believe that it is language that gives us access to reality. Language such as we have heard it since always: the Greek *Logos*, the appearing of the world in which all that this language tells us shows itself, in which no life is ever shown. Therefore, where and how to reach life? Where this life in itself reaches, and in the way in which it reaches it, in its Speech. In the ageless process in which life has joined us to ourselves in our Self, by being given to itself in its Verb. The speech which does all of that, which says all of that, is the speech which speaks in us by generating us, by revealing us to ourselves in speech's self-revelation to itself: it is the Speech of Life.

But what about the Scriptures? Where do they come from, these foreign meanings which do not bear in themselves the reality that they signify any more than they are capable of "creating" this reality from themselves? What speech has dictated them? But first what do they say? They say that we are the Sons, that we have been given to ourselves, in this Self that we are forever, in the process through which absolute life is given to itself in its Verb. They say the truth of what the meanings foreign to reality would not be able to establish. *But there in what they say is what we are.* The speech which has constituted these meanings in a human speech and which has dictated these texts is the Speech of the Life which speaks in us, which has generated us in our condition of being Alive. Thus, we hear it, so to speak, twice and we can understand it. We hear the speech of the Scriptures inasmuch as what the speech which institutes us in Life self-hears itself in us.

The material phenomenology which offers an entirely new phenomenological bedrock to our conception of language does not only concern the metaphysical destiny of humanity. Or, if you prefer, nothing escapes from this destiny. Because it consists of its self-revelation, the Speech of life speaks everywhere where there is life, in its most elementary modalities. It speaks in the most simple sadness in which Descartes saw the prototype of the *cogitatio*, which prohibits us from relating it to the world, from inserting it into an extended body. The exclusive consideration of an extended body by contemporary thought and especially by scientific thought developed after Galileo bars our access to the genuine body and keeps us from conceiving it as having speech, as having the speech of the life that speaks in every living body. With this language of the body, that of the spontaneous gestures which accompany everyday life, that of dance, of mime, of sports, etc., an immense domain uncovers itself for us. It would be a mistake here to think that the term "language" is merely a metaphor: a hand given and open arms have an immediate meaning just as words do. We really see this in the language by which we communicate with animals, which excludes all intellectual meaning. Like the intelligence of ordinary language, the intelligence of this complex language refers to a phenomenological bedrock, its complexity being based precisely on the fact that it implies, like the language of the body, for example, not only the appearing of the world—where the body is an object—but also the pathetic flesh of our living corporeality. Because it makes the duality of appearing intervene, the analysis of this language would lead back to the problems to which we have alluded. In the end, what is at issue is to reduce the illusion of ordinary language in which the meanings delivered by ordinary language (whether they are conceptual or practical) seem to come exclusively from the world and seem to find a sufficient explanation in the world.

We will get an idea of how far the domain of the pathos of language extends by noting that the economy, for example, can be considered in a non-metaphoric way as a language. Are not the "objects" that the economy deals with—the "work" about which economists speak and which they reduce to a calculable object, consumer goods, use-value, money, prices, capital, the various taxes on profits, interest, etc.—precisely parameters whose definition and analysis arise from a science, which is itself objective and whose "evidence" is carved out unilaterally against the horizon of the world? But if, as Marx established, such objects are only ever the products or the substitutes of an action of life, and are subjective like life, substitutes for the suffering striving of humans, of "their subjective work force," of "living work," as Marx's last writings repeat impatiently, then we must address our questions concerning the meaning of this language called economy, concerning its capacity to say reality or be its denaturation, whether or not it is a delusional ideology, to a primitive Speech, the Speech of Life.

We should make not only economy but every form of culture be the object of an interrogation as to whether it can be considered as a language. Let us consider painting. Does not painting show us the world and all of what peoples it? If painting shows us the world, does it not say the world in its own way? But what exactly does it show us? Beings or their monstration (for example, space, spatialization, perspective, etc.)? Rather than singular objects, their way of appearing? Light rather than what is illuminated? Every great painting sets up this question anew. What do Turner's last paintings represent? These landscapes at sunrise reduced to blinding patches of whiteness; properly speaking, these are not things but their emergence, their abolition in this emergence itself. Is not the language of painting the same as the language that Heidegger entrusts to the poet, the language which leaves the being destitute in order to say its advent in presence?

However, if a material phenomenology interrogates the painting concerning its phenomenological bedrock, which has evolved into painting's own theme, into what it tries to make be seen or said, then the question divides in two. Because every speech is also and first that of Life, painting must paint the invisible. Such was Kandinsky's astonishing intuition. Even if today we still take this intuition as circumscribed within the sphere of abstract painting whose eruption it marks, this does not forbid it from actually concerning every possible type of painting, the most archaic as well as the most classical. And this is the case for essential reasons: the fundamental elements out of which every painting is composed—that is, color and form—both draw their original, phenomenological material from life. Color draws its phenomenological material from life by way of pure impression (the color spread across the object, the "noematic color," being only the pure impression's projection). Form therefore has a site in life like color, inasmuch as a form is nothing but the outline of a force; it draws from life the pathetic dynamism without which there is neither force nor form.

And what can we say about music? Is it not the immediate expression of pathos in the sense that a cry can be the immediate expression of suffering? But not only higher forms of culture provide us with all the illustrations of its profound nature. Is it not the case that, already in its elementary strata, by means of the diverse modes of existence—by means of cooking, work, leisure, eroticism, the relation with others, with the living and the dead in general—what is said each time is a way in which life says itself in each living being, a modality of its speech?

In regard to the world itself, would it be paradoxical at this point to see in it as well a speech of life? Is its ecstatic appearing, however, not the phenomenological basis of an entirely different language? Have we not shown that, since it is different from and indifferent to all of what it says, it turns out to be in principle incapable of positing its reality? But then, it is this reality which becomes a problem, since the unconcealing of world never takes into account what is unconcealed in it—its content. We have asked: what if this content has no other provenance than Life? On the one hand, life, action, the set of human, subjective activities, the living body which is the seat of action shows itself in the world under the appearance of external behaviors. In these behaviors, life is constantly hidden, however, from constituting its unique reality. On the other hand, this very appearance still owes to life what it appears to be; these colors, these sounds, these odors, these flavors that we can uproot from nature, as Galileo wanted, only on the condition of returning them to their original reality, to their impressional self-revelation in the pathos of life. World-of-life, *Lebenswelt* in a radical sense; it is still life which speaks in the world, in the world which secretly speaks the language of life to us. *Coeli enarrant gloriam Dei.* The world is the speech of God.

Let us dispel one last illusion, which could come about from material phenomenology itself. In overthrowing the traditional conception of language, material phenomenology discovers, let us say, a Speech which is older, silent, and ignorant of humans, which was covered over by the noise of their voices. This is the speech of Life, which says itself in its pathetic self-revelation, which is in itself its own speech, its Verb. When classical phenomenology practices the transcendental reflection of the phenomenological reduction by opposing life to itself in this reflection, by putting life outside of itself, by giving it to be seen, by making itself the "Spectator" of it, classical phenomenology is devoted to the task of rediscovering this life, but as if life were not saying itself, as if life were not its own Verb. This counter-direction is carried as far as possible, when Fink writes: "In the performance of the phenomenological reduction, transcendental life, in producing 'the Spectator,' puts itself outside of itself, splits itself and divides itself. *This division is the condition of the possibility of adventing to itself for transcendental subjectivity.*"[7]

Material phenomenology neither uncovers nor reveals life. The task of making life advent to itself is really beyond its powers; in order to accomplish this, philosophy truly comes too late. We are always already in life; always already life is given to us by giving us to ourselves in the pathos of its Speech.

What is phenomenology good for? Material phenomenology exercises in complete lucidity the power to think *après coup*, to meditate on life (this power that we have also received). Then it is *capable of founding the phenomenological method by proceeding to its radical critique.* Husserl wanted to see and grasp—*Sehen und Fassen*—life in an apodictic evidence. Unfortunately, there is no possible evidence of transcendental subjectivity because in the divergence of an Outside, in the language of the world, all life vanishes. Faced with this observation which knocks it off course, the Husserlian method instinctually substitutes the transcendent essence of life offered to the sight of intentionality for this singular life which eludes it, a noematic essence which is at once irreal and given as irreal. This phenomenology is in mourning for reality. But there is more. How can one construct an essence of life, even if the essence is irreal, if one is unaware of life, if one is in the absence of its reality? On the basis of its images, by varying them? But, from where do we get the archetype which will tell us that these images themselves are its replicas?

The material phenomenology which gives speech to Life resolves not only the problems upon which classical phenomenology came to founder. If our world pursues everywhere, in a sort of daze, the edification of a universe of idealities more and more monstrous, the listening to this voice in the place where it speaks and in the way that it does speak will perhaps appear to a humanity out of joint with itself and devoted to nihilism as the unique means of its salvation.

Translated by Leonard Lawlor

Notes

This English translation was originally published in *Continental Philosophy Review* 32, no. 3 (1999): 343–65. It is reprinted here with permission from Springer.

    1. Martin Heidegger, *Being and Time*, trans. John Macquarrie and Edward Robinson (New York: Harper and Row, 1962).

    2. Martin Heidegger, *On the Way to Language*, trans. Peter D. Hertz (New York: Harper and Row, 1971), 93 and 101.

    3. Heidegger, *On the Way to Language*, 146.

    4. Heidegger, *On the Way to Language*, 155.

    5. Martin Heidegger, *Poetry, Language, Thought*, trans. Albert Hofstadter (New York: Harper and Row, 1975), 194.

    6. Heidegger, *Poetry, Language, Thought*, 208.

    7. Eugen Fink, *Sixth Cartesian Meditation*, trans. Ronald Bruzina (Bloomington: Indiana University Press, 1995), 23 (trans. modified).

Part 4

Ethics and Religion

13

Ethics and Religion within a Phenomenology of Life

I would like to present a few remarks on ethics and religion. However brief they may be, they are within the scope of an investigation that implies certain presuppositions—namely those of a phenomenology of life. The phenomenology of life is not a phenomenology that devotes itself to one particular object among other possible objects, but rather an ideal phenomenology that strives to recognize that by which the subject of phenomenology should be defined, namely appearing, or phenomenality as such. Now, the systematic elucidation of appearing (not of things but of the way in which things offer themselves to us) presents us with what I would call the duplicity of appearing. This means that the mode of appearing, considered in itself, is twofold. On the one hand, there is the appearing that consists of a coming outside [*venue au-dehors*], of such a kind that here phenomenality is that of this "Outside"—which is also called the "world." On the other hand, there is a more original revelation that does not project outside of itself what it reveals, that does not divert toward anything external, anything other, anything different, whose phenomenality is not the visibility of any sort of "Outside," of an ek-stasis. This original revelation reveals itself to itself, in other words, it is a self-revelation. There is only one self-revelation of this kind: life. Life reveals itself to itself, it experiences [*s'éprouve*] itself in such a way that in that experience there is neither an "Outside" nor a "world"—nothing visible. The phenomenality of this experience is a pure pathos.

The question regarding the relationship of ethics and religion unfolds within life and only encounters the appearing of the world in a subordinate manner.

If it is a question of problematizing the relationship of ethics and religion within life, we cannot avoid noticing that such a "program" has already been carried out, namely by Christianity. That is why we will borrow our references from it.

Basically, Christianity conceives the essence of things—God—as Life. Furthermore, this life is phenomenological; it is a revelation, specifically a self-revelation. *God reveals himself.* Christianity is not a monotheism in the usual sense. It is not limited to affirming the existence of a unique God, an always problematic affirmation. Christianity states what God is, namely, Life. From then on for each living being, this "affirmation" is nothing other than itself—if it is true not only that all the living presuppose life within them, but that their own life is in itself nothing other than this presupposition. How to understand this, how to understand the inner bond [*lien*] that unites every living being to life, this is religion's theme. *Religio* refers to a bond—the sole bond uniting us to the absolute. Because such a bond is situated in life, it is lived in various ways, though all of them are prescribed by the originary essence of life and the process by which it generates within itself the living.

The way in which this bond should be lived is ethics. As the foundation of ethics is in religion, let us examine what should be thought under the headings of religion and ethics and their relation, doing so according to the presuppositions of a phenomenology of life or, if one prefers, of Christianity.

Christianity is monotheistic only because it asserts that the absolute has but one constituent Life—a single, unique life in all possible living beings. Life is absolute in this fundamental sense, in that it is not a facticity but the process of its own self-generation, which is accomplished as a self-revelation, and thus as *Logos*. Therefore life always comes into itself by experiencing itself in such a way that in this experience of itself is implied an Ipseity, the phenomenological actuality of which is a Self without which no living would be possible. Thus there is no Life without a living being, without the Self of this Original living being [*Premier Vivant*] which is as old as Life itself. In this way, the generation of the Original living being in the process of the self-generation of absolute life belongs to this process as that without which it could not occur. To the extent that the generation of the Original living being belongs to the self-generation of Life as its condition, it is consubstantial with it. To the extent that the phenomenality of this process is exclusive of all difference, what is engendered remains within the power that engenders it, not only as its own condition but phenomenologically. The pathos of life, the place where it experiences itself, is the pathos of the Original living being, just as the pathos of the Original living being, the place where it experiences itself, is the pathos of Life. Such is the reciprocal relation between the phenomenological interiority of Life and the Original living being, as formulated in the following: "Believe me that I am in the Father and the Father is in me" (John 14:11).[1]

Now in a paradoxical, yet fully intelligible manner, the reciprocal phenomenological interiority of Life and of the Original living being also concerns every possible generation of any living being whatsoever, for example, the generation of this living being that I myself am. To be clear, here we are employing the language of classical phenomenology. In its eyes, the living being that I am is the transcendental ego or, as found in §55 of the *Krisis*: "the absolutely unique ego functioning as ultimate authority."[2] Now, such an ego is a final authority only in its function of constituting the world. And in order to fulfill such a function, this ego is presupposed. It must already be conveyed in the condition which is its own, be given to itself as this absolutely unique ego. Such is, in effect, the condition of the ego: to be given to itself, to experience itself in such a way that it never brings itself into this condition of experiencing itself, that this self-givenness is never its own work but rather that of life. Instead of being an ultimate authority, the ego is the product of a generation, it has a birth.

We are able to expose this transcendental birth of the ego: every ego must be stated in the accusative; as Jean-Luc Marion has recognized in Descartes, there is only a transcendental *me* (*moi transcendantal*) as long as the experience that it has of itself is not its own doing. To experience itself, to relate to itself without having given rise to this relationship itself, to be united to itself in the passive immediacy of a non-ekstatic pathos, such is the condition of the transcendental Self presupposed by every conceivable me [*moi*] and ego. However, this transcendental Self is itself only possible if it is joined to itself within the Ipseity of the Original Self co-generated within the self-generation of life.

Leaving aside the extraordinary originality and profundity of this definition of humankind no longer starting from the world—as being of/from the world—but from life, we will stick to its consequences for ethics. The inner religious bond between man and God in life defines in fact his condition as the "Son of God." The Son of God and not of another human, since only the life capable of engendering itself is capable of engendering any living being whatsoever: "And call no one your father" (Matthew 23:9). If religion is organized around this human condition as the Son of God, ethics consists, according to us, in different ways of living. Now, these ways are neither multiple nor equivalent. For humans, there are two: to lose this condition, or at least to forget it—this condition that is his transcendental birth, his entry into life. For that is what it is to be born—not to come into the world, as is naively said, but to come into life. One can either thereby lose one's condition of living or at least forget it or, on the contrary, if it is lost, rediscover it, and thus be born a second time, in a second birth, be reborn.

As to the loss of the condition as Son, I will limit myself to one remark. This loss must be possible and its possibility lies in the status of the ego, in its transcendental birth. Unlike natural birth, which sees the child separate from its mother and then leave to follow its own path in the world, the transcendental birth is neither a point in time nor an event [*ni ponctuelle ni événementielle*]; the transcendental ego is given to itself only in the self-givenness of life and for as long as this self-givenness takes place. Son of God, this is one condition that nothing can interrupt. But this condition as Son is paradoxical.

On the one hand, the ego is given to itself as a Self only in the self-givenness of absolute life and in the Ipseity that belongs originally to that life. In other words: in each ego, its Ipseity does not proceed from it, but rather the ego proceeds from Ipseity, from this original Ipseity co-generated within the self-generation of life. Hence the ego is nothing. Everything is given to it, beginning with this Self without which no ego is possible.

On the other hand, however, it is advisable to grasp the positivity of this condition and follow the process of the transcendental birth of the Son up to the moment when, through a mutation as decisive as it is unexpected, this generation that was again only that of a me in the accusative, becomes that of an ego, strictly speaking. Given to itself in the self-givenness of absolute life and in its Ipseity, the me passively experiences itself as such, and yet it suddenly discovers itself to be much more than this passive me that is expressed in the accusative. Given to itself, experiencing itself in the Ipseity of life, it takes possession of itself at the same time as it takes possession of each of the powers traversing it. By taking possession of those powers, it is able to exercise them. A new capacity is conferred upon it, no less extraordinary than that of being a me, even when that is but a simple consequence. It is the capacity of the me to be in possession of itself, to become one with it and with everything that it bears within itself and which belong to it as the multiple components of its real being. Among these are the body's powers: the ability to take, to move, to touch, to extend one's limbs from within, to shift one's eyes, etc. There are also the powers of the mind: those of forming ideas and images, of willing, etc. It is by being a me that the me possesses all its abilities. It is in the pathos-filled[3] experience of those powers that it takes possession of each of them and coincides with them so as to be able to implement them and to act. Taking possession of each of them inasmuch as it has taken possession of itself in the original Ipseity of absolute life. So here, at the term of its transcendental birth, the me is put in possession of itself and of all its capacities. As long as it advances armed with all its powers and keeps them available, this me is an I. "I" means "I can."

Thus, the transcendental birth of the Son occurs as a transition from the me to the ego, a transition that is a reversal [*retournement*]. The me, which given to itself in the Ipseity of Life, has become the point of origin for a multiplicity of powers and acts that it accomplishes whenever it wants. From passive it has become active. Whereas nothing depended on it because its own condition of a living transcendental me does not depend on it, now everything depends on it because it is a bundle of powers that it freely uses whenever it wants.

The ego that is free to exercise any of its powers at will, experiences itself as such. Experiencing its freedom in the exercise of each of its powers, the ego now takes itself as their source, their origin. It imagines that it possesses these powers, that they are its own in a radical sense, as what it itself has produced. As the source and origin of the powers that comprise its being, it considers itself as the source and origin of its very being. Thus is born the transcendental illusion of the ego, an illusion in which the ego takes itself for the ground of its own being.

It is this transcendental illusion of the ego that Paul strikes at the heart of: "What do you have that you did not receive? And if you received it, why do you boast as if it were not a gift?" (1 Corinthians 4:7). The question of whether this is truly an illusion is answered in the Epistle to the Galatians: "For if those who are nothing think they are something, they deceive themselves" (Galatians 6:3). The denunciation of the transcendental illusion of the ego takes on an unheard-of violence when coming from the mouth of Christ. It is a question—in the parable of the shepherd and his flock—of all those who want to enter the pasture where the sheep graze—where the living live—without passing through the gate to the pasture, which Christ says is himself. "I am the gate" (John 10:9). Consequently, to be a living Self without passing under the triumphal Archway of the Arch-Ipseity in which every Self is thrown into itself in order to be this living being that it is forever more, such is the scandal that nonetheless coincides with the most ordinary experience. Such, in effect, is the one who, lifting a weight, believes that he is the one who lifts it. "Liar!" for how could one exert this power if life hadn't given it to him together with all of his other powers? Liar and "Thief" too! For to lay claim to what does not belong to you is, by all accounts, theft. And when the theft concerns not the object taken but the power that takes it, the theft is one in principle, so to speak. This then explains the strange, yet fully intelligible words of Christ: "All who came before me are thieves and bandits" (John 10:8).

The transcendental illusion of the ego establishes the system of transcendental egoism, a system that is itself paradoxical. The ego that experiences itself in each of the powers of its body or mind is thrown with them into the world; it cares about things, but only in regard to itself. Such is its relation to itself now: the being that is concerned with itself in the world. And this is the paradox: the ego concerned with itself, which thinks only of itself and acts only in light of itself, lives in the complete concealment of its true Self that is never ekstatically related to itself but only related to itself within the immanence of life: an invisible Self, with neither a face nor a regard, that no image separates or protects from itself. The more the ego thinks of itself, and that's all it does, the more its true condition escapes it. One must attempt to grasp the abyssal character of this Forgetting. Given to itself in the non-ekstatic pathos of life, the Self arises only in the coming into itself of this absolute life, a coming that has always already been accomplished, which is for every conceivable Self the absolute Before to which it could never return, of which it will never have any recollection, which it could never reunite with in thought: the forever lost Immemorial.

It is, however, this lost condition of the Son of absolute life that ethics claims to recover. But how? If the access to life cannot be made in a thought, in a knowledge, through any memorial—because life never appears where thought thinks or where memory looks—then the first prescription of ethics becomes completely clear; it is formulated by Christ himself: "Not everyone who says to me, 'Lord, Lord,' will enter the kingdom of heaven, but only the one who does the will of my Father" (Matthew 7:21). The presupposition of Christian ethics is therefore that the possibility of the second birth does not consist in knowledge or cognition but in doing, in action. Now this presupposition takes on a decisive significance only because, in a phenomenology of life, the status of action is itself overturned. Instead of displaying itself in the world and finding its reality within the world, within its objective result, action unfolds its essence in life and in life alone. That's not all: it is not only action that unfolds in life, but the action of life itself, a self-transformation of life desired by it and destined to lead back to its absolute essence: "the one who does the will of my Father." To do the will of the Father refers to the mode of life in which the life of the Self is accomplished in such a way that what is accomplished in it henceforth is the absolute life according to its essence and its own necessity. Such is the goal of ethics, the second birth, the restoration of the religious bond. But we shall proceed step by step.

In the world, action appears in terms of an objective behavior that cannot be distinguished from a natural process. Or else, to try to recover the act in itself, it consists of a process of objectification, for example in a pro-duction [*pro-ducere*] that is identified with this coming into the outside. The possibility of this coming outside is not thought, and in any case, no life is possible in this because life has no Outside. In a phenomenology of life that presupposes the duplicity of appearing, everything is dual, for example, our body as well as the actions rooted within it. On the one hand, it is true that an objective movement does develop, but this is only the external aspect of an action whose possibility and thus reality reside solely in the self-givenness of the power that acts. It is due to this, due to being put in possession of itself, that this power is a power, that it is the I Can of which we have spoken. Because reality remains in the invisible embrace of life, the world is no longer the place where the thing offers itself to be seen in its nudity; this is only an appearance, the contrary perhaps of how things fundamentally are. "Woe to you, scribes and Pharisees, hypocrites! For you are like whitewashed tombs, which on the outside look beautiful, but inside they are full of the bones of the dead and of all kinds of filth" (Matthew 23:27).

The duplicity of appearing doesn't only introduce a world of hypocrisy, where the latter reigns if not *de facto* then at least as a principal possibility, but also a world of the incognito. "But when you fast, put oil on your head and wash your face, so that your fasting may be seen not by others but by your Father who is in secret; and your Father who sees in secret will reward you openly" (Matthew 6:17, 18). Now the significance of this incognito reveals itself to be twofold. The phenomenology of life spontaneously practiced by Christianity does not only oppose the behavior perceived externally to the truth of the world and the invisible reality of action. It is within action itself that it introduces a mysterious division. In addition to the pathos of the revelation of action to itself in the effort of the one who accomplishes it, there is its revelation to God and the revelation of God himself. This is not an inexplicable addition or a mere postulation—rather, it is the reaffirmation of the transcendental birth of the ego and of its condition as Son. Meaning that the power that acts is given to itself only in the self-givenness of Life. This is the all-seeing Eye that observes all of the me's actions and never turns away from them as long as they are occurring and in order for them to occur—"your Father who sees in secret," the ineluctable "before God" in which there is neither before nor outside, the Parousia without memory to which every ego owes its being as an ego and as a living being [*un vivant*]. Before attempting a final elucidation of this inner relation to life, which is also that of ethics and of religion, first a brief remark.

For it is not only action that Christianity, turning its back on tradition as well as modern thought, uproots from the world—the law by which ethical action is regulated undergoes an analogous displacement. Here the critique of the Law is introduced, the motivation having been set forth in a brilliant manner by Paul. It refers to the central thesis of Christianity that places reality within life. It is because the law is transcendent, external to life and perceived by life to be outside of it, as a content that is intelligible in and through this exteriority, that it is found to lack reality. And by the same token, it is lacking that which finds its effectuation in the reality of life: action. Unreal and impotent, such is the Law. On the one hand, it prescribes under the form of an injunction perceived in total clarity: "Thou shalt not commit adultery." On the other hand, the clearly stated commandment is incapable of producing the act that would conform to it: "Did not Moses give you the law? Yet none of you keeps the law" (John 7:19).

To see what must be done without having the power to do it, such is the hopeless situation in which the Law has placed humankind. Such a law—which defines the infraction and the crime and opens their gaping possibility before humanity without granting the power to avoid either of them—is a cursed Law. It would be better to be in a state of innocence in which the possibility of the fault would not appear before the gaze. The Law damns all those who do not put it into practice; it damns them all since it does not give anyone the power to uphold it. The Law multiplies the crime, as the Apostle said in a striking comment: "Moreover the law entered, that the offence might abound" (Romans 5:20).[4]

Unlike Paul, it is not through the establishment of a complex, and in many regards splendid problematic, that the critique of the Law in the Gospels is made. In the Gospels, to the contrary, an act occurs that does not take the Law into account, but simply ignores it. Christ heals the paralyzed invalid on the day of the Sabbath. Doing so on the Sabbath goes against the Law of the Old Covenant. Whence the scandal for all those who still live under the Law and want to define their actions according to it—even though, in practice, this is precisely what they do not do. "Therefore the Jews started persecuting Jesus, because he was doing such things on the sabbath" (John 5:16). This annulment of the old Law and thus of an ethics, and perhaps of a religion, must have a powerful motive. This motive, which concentrates the central tenets of Christianity, is delivered in one blow. "But Jesus answered them, 'My Father is still working, and I also am working'" (John 5:17).

With this abrupt reply, unsuitable as it is by not taking the Law into account, Christ essentially shifts the object of the debate, transposing it from the domain of the Law, which is not reality, to that of life. Again, it is not to a factical life that he appeals but to its absolute essence: the process of the self-generation of life that continuously engenders itself [*autoengendrer*] or, as it is said in John, the "Father" who "never stops working." Thus the Law no longer constitutes the principle of ethics, but life; it is life that commands, that constitutes the new Law. And so new questions arise such as: how does the new Commandment command, where and how does it exercise its power, what does it command, and whom does it command? But all this can only be asked of life, if it is life that commands.

In a phenomenology of life, the relationship of the Commandment to that which is commanded is revealed with an extraordinary clarity: it is the relationship of Life to the living, the relationship of filiality, the transcendental birth of the ego—not the human as it has always understood itself on the basis of the world, but the transcendental Christian human defined by its condition as Son—as the living Self generated in the Ipseity of absolute life. This carves out the abyss separating the Old Law from the new Law: while the former is incapable of positing what it commands, the action that it prescribes, the latter has already fulfilled the prescription, it has already plunged into Life those to whom the injunction to be living beings [*vivants*] is made.

What does the task of living mean for one who is already alive? To live and to act in such a way that in him is accomplished the predestination inscribed in his condition as Son—the predestination according to which man is destined to be this living being generated in the self-generation of absolute life, living only from that, being able to accomplish his own essence only within the essence of absolute life. It is this predestination that Paul has in mind when he writes to the Romans: "We know that all things work together for good . . . who are called according to his purpose. For those whom he foreknew he also predestined to be conformed to the image of his Son, in order that he might be the firstborn within a large family" (Romans 8:28, 29).

Those called are those called by life, called by life to be its Sons. Hence life has known them in advance because it is by uniting with itself in the Ipseity of the First Living that it has united each of them to himself; it is by revealing itself to itself in its *Logos* that each of them has been revealed to himself. The predestination was therefore that, in its birth, each transcendental living Self repeats in it the conditions of the Arch-generation of the Arch-Son so "that he might be the firstborn among many brethren."

The predestination implied in the condition of the Son to be in absolute life was also perceived by John as the commandment of Love. Love is not what is commanded, as Kant believed. Love is what commands, it is the commandment of Life. The commandment of Life is a commandment of love only because Life is love—because, constantly experiencing itself in the self-enjoyment [*la jouissance de soi*] of its Ipseity, it loves itself in the life of an eternal love. Consequently, life commands all the living to love by giving them life, by begetting them as its Sons—those who, experiencing themselves in the experience of themselves and in the love of Life, are predestined to no longer be anything other than this experience and its love.

The predestination implied in the condition of the Son can only be fulfilled if the system of transcendental egoism is destroyed, namely, the ek-static relation to oneself in Care [*Souci*], and with it every ego and every Self pertaining to the phenomenality of the world. Theoretical ethics is the examination of concrete situations in which this abolition is effective, as in the parable of the good Samaritan or in the "works of mercy" which were defined later.

The study of ethics was not our topic. All that interested us here was the relation between ethics and religion, a relation located in life and thus actualized only in action. For this reason, the limits of a theoretical approach are easily perceived.

Translated by Michael Tweed

Notes

The French text of this essay was originally presented in 1996 in Rome at the symposium entitled "Philosophy of Religion between Ethics and Ontology," and was published in *Archivio di Filosofia* 64 (1996): 89–97.

1. Except where noted, all biblical references are from the New Revised Standard Version.

2. Translator's note: In order to maintain consistency with what follows, I have directly translated Henry's French. In Edmund Husserl, *The Crisis of European Sciences*, trans. David Carr (Evanston, Ill.: Northwestern University Press, 1970), 186, this phrase is rendered as "the absolute ego as the ultimately unique center of function."

3. Translator's note: For one explanation of Henry's use of the terms *pathos* and *pathétique*, see *I Am the Truth*, ix. Again, the important point is to avoid any misreading that might occur due to the meaning of "pathetic" as now commonly understood.

4. Here I have used the King James version because it better reflects Henry's intention.

14

Theodicy from the Perspective of a Radical Phenomenology

What does it mean to speak of theodicy from the perspective of a radical phenomenology? The question of the justice of God raises such great difficulties, is shrouded in such mystery, even scandal, that all those who have reflected upon it are placed in a paradoxical situation: that of having to justify God—of cleansing him of the suspicion of being the cause of the evil that is in the world. Indeed, precisely this evil had been the gravest objection one could raise against the existence of a supposedly good and omnipotent creator. Those preoccupied by these problems, most notably philosophers, have thus been moved to formulate a series of considerations, arguments, interpretations, and hypotheses meant to render evil comprehensible—more precisely to render it compatible with the idea of a supreme Good, that is to say with God himself. Leibniz's *Theodicy* is the most famous example of this discursive problematic, meant ultimately to reconcile good and evil while maintaining that the former is everything and all-powerful and the latter is nothing and powerless.

Phenomenology begins with the bracketing of all interpretations and all hypotheses, in order to return to the things themselves and encounter phenomena in their nudity—in this case evil itself; suffering and pain in their immediacy, in their incontestable presence. Therefore, if evil can and must be recognized as inevitable or necessary, it is in evil itself, in its very substance and phenomenological flesh, that this recognition must somehow occur. Phenomenology always already deprives itself of all the principles and all the conceptual mediations, of all the clever arguments by which we might be tempted to induce something as evil in order to reinstate it into an order of things good in themselves. And we can well see why: it is because any reason given to explain the irruption among us and within us of suffering in any form leaves that suffering intact in its suffering, only to render it all the more apparent and unbearable. One will perhaps even come to regard these efforts toward a rational validation of evil as something of a scandal; as when Leibniz declares that, in the eyes of supreme Providence, and for its ultimate decision regarding their salvation or damnation, "men are selected and sorted not so much according to their own excellence as according to their convenience for the plan of God."[1]

Here it must be noted, however, that the most inventive speculations of the most ingenious minds are never as free as they seem—by which I mean detached from the phenomena whose rational explanation is ultimately their only purpose. Leibniz's *Theodicy* does not escape this rule. It relates to "phenomena" in two ways: insofar as it undertakes to justify evil and suffering, it is thus obliged to take into consideration these characteristics of the given experience. But a subtler aspect of the phenomenological reference of the *Theodicy*, as without a doubt most theological constructions preceding or following it, should now be considered. This consideration will provide the justification for my entire approach, that of treating the justice of God not only from a phenomenological point of view, but from the point of view of what I call, against historical or classical phenomenology, a radical phenomenology.

Leibniz's point of departure in his attempted justification is precisely not evil; his point of departure is evil in the world. A mere tautology, one will say. Far from it! Evil, which we henceforth will understand exclusively in the sense of suffering—suffering, therefore—is precisely *not* in the world, so that speaking of suffering *in the world*—as though this were its place of origin or its natural site—is to change completely, without even noticing it, that which we want to consider, by falsifying and distorting it. To "explain" a phenomenon disguised in its very givenness, in its phenomenality, a phenomenon always already estranged from its true essence, is to embark on a path which, instead of leading us to where we want to go, leads us astray. Insofar as the "explanation" offered rests in turn and precisely on the world where suffering is believed to exist, it is in fact nothing other than an explanation of the world itself—a statement of its characteristics; its ontological structures; its phenomenality.

This world is the world of representation. The phenomenality that makes of it the world is precisely that of representation—an engendered phenomenality, produced by being-placed-before, by the fact of being placed before as such, which is to say exteriority itself, which is to say the world. The fact that in the modern metaphysics of representation the world is a fallen world, the correlate, the ob-ject of an ob-jectifying Subject, does not change its original status as a world—by which we mean its pure phenomenality, which is the Greek phenomenality—the light where everything shines; that light in which suffering never shows itself and with which, never being seen and seeing nothing, it has precisely nothing to see.

What must be promptly established is how the world determines the whole of Leibniz's problematic—the world and not suffering or evil;

how, believing to speak of the latter, he in fact speaks only of the former. "I call the world," says Leibniz, "the entire series and the entire collection of every existing thing" (ibid., 112). Yet this totality of existing things refers us to another totality, to the milieu of their manifestation, to the world understood this time as this pure milieu, as the horizon of exteriority in which all these things give themselves to us as existing in a world and thus as a whole. This referral from an ontic totality to a phenomenological Whole is indicated to us by the contingency of each one of these existing things. For this Whole, this pure milieu of manifestation, could be occupied by other things than those which currently fill it, as Leibniz observes starting from space, time, and mater which function then as the pure milieus which are able to receive all things as not determined by them, as contingent. These things, "all that which we see and experience, are contingencies and have nothing in them which renders their existence necessary—it being manifest that time, space, and matter, unified and uniform in themselves and indifferent to all, could receive any other movements and figures and in a different order" (ibid., 111).

In this empty phenomenological totality that is the world and which in itself is indifferent to everything which can form its content—just as light is indifferent to that which it illuminates—these existing things form a totality in a second sense, in the sense that they constitute a series where they are linked by causality. Each existing thing in itself, contingent, is however necessary as considered in this series, in a world in the sense of a coherent ontic group. But this world in turn, as a collection of things internally linked by necessity, is itself contingent to the extent that, in the empty space of the pure world and within the empty horizon of pure time, an other ontic totality, an other system of cause and effect, could have taken place. Each world, though internally necessary, is still only a possible world. Or, to speak like Leibniz, "the universe, whatever it be, is all of one piece," "nothing can be changed in it (any more than in a number) except its essence . . ." (ibid., 113). That is to say: it can only be changed as a whole, into an other world, into an other series of cause and effect.

Why is each world nothing but a possible world, contingent? For the same reason that, within this world, each particular existing thing is contingent: because beyond that particular existing thing and beyond the ontic totality where it is held, a horizon arises which surpasses them on all sides and releases them into it as something dead, indifferent, and opaque—something which never carries its principle in itself and thus is found to be without principle, and thus contingent, and thus merely possible; it can be replaced in the empty and undifferentiated space of this horizon by something else. Because in this space of light which expands ceaselessly before us as the world, there is in fact always room for something other than what actually appears there. In the world each thing is without reason, not as a result of what it is in its particularity and specificity, but because it is in the world. The principle of reason is the word of the world. It demands an answer to the why-question, a question which is without an answer as soon as it is formulated. And this is because it arises at the same time as the world; it is the horizon developed beyond all that is, and it is what lets be all that appears within that horizon, with no other principle than its pure and simple being-there—as this ob-ject, as this external thing which exteriority never justifies.

The contradiction of every rationalism which is only ever a cardboard rationalism, inasmuch as each reason invoked by it is an unconscious formulation of the contingency in which it moves in principle—this contradiction entails a movement from Leibniz's problematic of the contingent world to a cause of this world, which would not itself be in the world, because this cause would carry *in itself* the reason [*raison*] for its own existence. "It must therefore look for the reason for the existence of the world, which is the entire group of contingent causes, and it must look for it in the substance which carries with itself the principle for the world's existence . . ." (ibid., 112). But this displacement from the question of the world to God—from that which in the world, that is to say in its own exteriority in relation to itself, turns out at the same time to be without principle, to the substance which carries the principle for its existence with itself, in itself—this displacement is emptied of its sense by Leibniz, for whom it appears strictly illusory. The authentic sense of such a displacement would be to substitute for the phenomenological and ontological milieu of exteriority another domain of being and of appearing where that which exists—in this case evil or suffering—would no longer be discarded as a contingent phenomenon in the horizon of the unanswerable question of why, but would be revealed to itself in this interiority where there is nothing other than itself, where existence and reason are made one—there where all love is experienced in the abundance and enjoyment of its own being without the ability to pose on its own to the subject the question of why it is the case, because the horizon where such questions arise never arises within it; there where "the rose has no why, flowering because it flowers" because it does not relate to itself in a world, because, as the second obscured verse that we are quoting from the famous text by Angelus Silesius says, the rose "does not care about itself, does not want to be seen."

It is true that this radical immediacy—which is originary Being, which is Life, which is Force—is also God, is also the substance which carries the principle for its existence within itself. Yet in Leibniz's problematic, this decisive situation is cited only to be immediately obscured. The recourse to God precisely does not imply any displacement of the problematic from exteriority—where beings only exist in the void of nothingness—to the phenomenological interiority where life experiences itself in the Night of its own abundance—where it is Being pure and simple, without mediation of any sort, without discourse or external justification. Quite the contrary; the God of Leibniz is thought only in its relation to the world and ultimately on the basis of it. Rather than the condition of substance (i.e., the fact of having the principle of its existence in itself) being explored and described *per se*—phenomenologically and thus ontologically—as the interior essence of life, this condition is understood through the notion of a cause and, moreover, as a cause of the world. The ultimate principle of life, which is only and can only be life itself—the joy and happiness of living—is interpreted on the basis of the being which is in itself devoid of this happiness, which does not feel itself and is thus nothing.

The worldly origin of substance taken as a cause of the world (and thus having lost its interior principle) becomes blinding in that this cause is immediately designated as an intelligent cause. "It is also that this cause must be intelligent, because this world which exists is contingent, and an infinity of other worlds are equally possible and equally worthy of existence, it must be that the world-cause had respect for or relation to all these possible worlds in determining one. And this respect or correlation of an existing substance to mere possibilities could be nothing other than understanding which has (the) ideas of such possibilities" (ibid., 112). The correlation of understanding to ideas or to the possibilities that it represents to itself and thus to the structure of representation, the relation of the cause of the world to all possible worlds, the "relation to" as constitutive of the world as such in its ek-static structure: that is the unthought phenomenological foundation of Leibniz's entire analysis of evil and suffering. This analysis consists ultimately in asking why there is evil or suffering in the world and in responding that each possible world is a series or totality of co-necessary things, and the best of these series is the one which has been chosen by God, who in his goodness has chosen the best. If none of them had been the best, God would not have chosen any.

What I have briefly recalled and have attempted to establish at greater length elsewhere is that the phenomenological presupposition of Leibniz's theodicy is the presupposition of classical thought in general and of contemporary phenomenology in particular, that it is the repetition, fallen and blind, in a metaphysics of representation, of the Greek presupposition that the phenomenon is that which shows itself in the light. What I would like to clarify here is why such presuppositions are totally inadequate for thinking the problem of a theodicy, which is to say, in short, the legitimation of suffering.

The inadequacy of the presupposition of the world to the question of suffering is precisely on the order of phenomenology. It implies, therefore, a redefinition of the concept of phenomenon and thus a reassessment of historical phenomenology itself, in view of the elaboration of a radical phenomenology. The inadequacy is this: in the world, which is to say in the transcendental process of the externalization of exteriority, nothing like suffering ever occurs, because in exteriority everything is external to itself, never touches itself, does not feel itself and thus feels nothing. This is the reason why, for example, as Descartes profoundly understood, there is nothing sensible in the world—no color, no pain, no sensation—because all sensation finds its ultimate possibility in the fact of internally experiencing oneself. Here, "internally" means that there is no exteriority, no world, in the being with itself and in itself of sensation, such that sensation does not relate to itself in a world; it is never an external sensation. What we refer to as this patch of color spread over things, this pain in our arms, is nothing but the noematic projection of what is always already constructed internally as sensation. Radical phenomenology thematizes this prior interior construction which it considers to be phenomenality itself.

How does sensation phenomenalize itself outside of the phenomenality of the world? How does it experience itself in its primal self-embrace? In and through its affectivity. Affectivity is therefore not something, some phenomenon in the sense of a being. Rather, it relates to Being pure and simple, to pure phenomenality; it defines this phenomenality in its original form, and defines it in itself: it is in and through the flesh of its affectivity that everything affective reveals itself. Thus a pain—a suffering—does not reveal itself in the world or in the ek-stasis of Being, in the becoming visible of some horizon of visibility, but only in itself, in its affectivity. Hence suffering, and it alone, teaches us what suffering is.

As the original essence of phenomenality, affectivity is also the original essence of all phenomena—not only affective phenomena such as those which occupy us now (i.e., pain, suffering), but of all phenomena in general—for example, of the objects which show themselves to us in the world. These objects, we shall say, feel nothing; they do not feel themselves. This is true. So they would be nothing if they did not give themselves to be felt by and in a subjectivity, there where it gives itself to feeling in its affectivity.

Modern, and notably scientific, thought, as it has developed in the West since Galileo, has expelled the sensible qualities and thus sensibility and as their ground affectivity from the world—in order to promote an absolute objectivity, rationality, and universality—and has left us blind to the true reality of every possible world. This reality is precisely the pathos of affection in which everything which can be felt and, in this way, everything which is, is given to be felt. If there is nothing which is not a pathos in its possibility of being, then the world never subsists in its pure objectivity, but only as a living cosmos, having its ultimate reality in pathos. Suffering is not in the world, but the world is in suffering. "The world," said Kandinsky, "is full of resonances. It constitutes a cosmos of beings exerting a spiritual action. Dead matter is a living spirit."[2]

To the extent that everything is referred in its possibility of being to pathos as the essence of life, it will be asked: why does this life carry suffering within itself, instead of being pure bliss, simple happiness? Returned to its proper place, to its pure interiority to itself, is suffering able to account for itself? Is the question of why definitively set aside because, in this radical interiority of life, there is neither horizon nor world? But who is posing this question, who wants to cast this horizon beyond what is? It is suffering itself. Why? This is not because, situated in a world, it could only show itself as a pure and simple being-there without reason, but because it suffers. It is from the ground of the interiority of suffering that the cry of this question emerges to the subject. By casting the horizon of the question beyond itself, suffering instinctually invokes the work of exteriority which, putting everything outside of itself, would unburden suffering of itself. But this distancing of suffering from its internal and living reality, this way of alienating itself from itself and casting off the weight of its own being, does not and cannot ever occur. This is because suffering is affective—and it belongs to the essence of that which is affective to experience itself at each moment of its being, internally correlated to itself, such that what is experienced and what experiences are insurmountably and forever the Same. But this way of being insurmountably and forever itself is Being's original way of being; it is Being as Living and finding its ownmost possibility in Life.

If suffering carries in it this primordial essence of Being which throws it into itself in order to be what it is, do we not still have to ask what relation it maintains with this primordial essence—with life? Is it a contingent relation, or do they rather belong together in a more subtle way, as a quasi-necessary property? We have observed in suffering the birth of a will, the will to get rid of itself, and at the same time the impotence of this will. The same impotence is inscribed in the very being of suffering insofar as, in its radical immanence to itself, it adheres to itself without ever being able to recoil vis-à-vis itself. Suffering's will to get rid of itself leads us back to this inability to get rid of oneself; it is the result of it, but first of all the ordeal [*épreuve*] of it. In this impotence at the very heart of the will and made manifest by it, suffering tells us something more about itself. It tells us that it is not pure and simple suffering, but first that which leads to it; not a phenomenon but the way of access to the phenomenon. This road consists in the phenomenality of the phenomenon, in the Suffering [*Souffrir*] of suffering [*souffrance*]. Just as, in suffering, we regard the primal Suffering which gives it to itself, so also do we thereby regard Life. We are therefore able to understand why suffering does not happen in Life as the consequence of an unfortunate accident, as the result of an unpredictable catastrophe, but rather insofar as Life is Life. It is not because Life and suffering are identical and absolutely coextensive, but because suffering is a principal possibility of Life. It is this point that must be further developed.

Note first that the two characteristics that we have recognized as those of suffering—the will to get rid of itself and the inability to accomplish it—are precisely two characteristics of Life. Life is absolute subjectivity, the experiencing of itself immediately and without distance, in and through pathos. Subjectivity must therefore be understood in a new sense—that of a subjectivity which is no longer reduced to a relation to the world. Life finds its essence in the radical immanence of absolute subjectivity, in the new sense that we are giving to it. It is feeling itself as suffering itself—it is this primal suffering that is precisely Life. Life is not something which exists, but rather its tireless arrival into itself. In this is constantly drawn a dichotomy which psychology finds everywhere yet explains nowhere. In the unbreakable experience of this arrival and in its primal Suffering, life is able to suffer and, in a certain way, makes suffering necessary by its very essence—that which is free, not required essentially, being the ways by which it does so. To be alive *qua* suffering and not to know suffering is a fiction which can only be maintained so long as, in treating suffering as a being or as a fact, we fail to see its transcendental rootedness in the Event [*Événement*] by which Being arrives or its ultimate identity with that Arrival [*Avènement*].

This Event is thus the auto-experience of Being *qua* Life—its auto-affection. In auto-affection there is firstly a being-affected, the possibility of being affected. In the possibility of being affected, there is suffering. Not as the result of that which affects us, of some unfavorable event, but as its condition, as the condition of any possible affection in general. Suffering is not in the content of the phenomenon, but in its very phenomenality, in the How of its coming into us. For this arrival is accomplished as our subjectivity, as this Suffering which is the obligatory place where we feel all that we can feel.

Suffering in the last analysis is the phenomenological mode of actualization of the Suffering which constitutes the essence of all life, the way in which it experiences itself, such that the more this experience intensifies, the more suffering (whereby this experience effects itself) intensifies also. If Affectivity is in its Suffering the original essence of revelation, if it is the primal knowledge included in all possible knowledge and therefore in genuine science, then indeed it must be said: *qui auget scientiam auget et dolorem.*[3]

What science? What knowledge? The knowledge that life has of itself. In and through its Suffering life comes into itself; it is the experience of itself adhering to itself at each moment of its being; it comes into possession of its own being, it enjoys itself, it is enjoyment, it is joy. And the more intense the suffering will be in which Suffering actualizes itself and pursues its own limit, crushing life against itself and letting it feel all that it is, the more lively will be the enjoyment that this life has of itself, the inebriation of the pathos where it surrenders and entrusts itself to its being. Thus suffering is both a way and a road: the way for the arrival of life into itself; the road which leads to Being as the proper destination of Being in itself, in the plenitude of itself. In Nietzsche's words, suffering is the Mother of Being.

In life there is a movement, a temporality that is not the ek-static temporality of the world—not that temporality which flows from the future to the past by way of a present that is never present, but an ideal limit where the represented being slips at each moment from a dead presence into the non-present. The immanent temporality of Life in which life enters into itself and never ceases to be wholly present to itself, where there is neither dehiscence nor nothingness, is the passage from Suffering to joy, as the simple fulfillment of the experience of life and thus of life itself. We think always in terms of representation, here one thing and there another. Here suffering and there joy. We do not conceive of suffering as the substance out of which joy is made, as the experience of the ontological event in which Being embraces itself in its own pathos, in which Life is the happiness of living and thus the highest Good.

This brilliant yet unconvincing essay that is Leibniz's *Theodicy* at times offers remarks which resonate in a strange way. They are the ones which establish a connection between evil and good itself, when the first is no longer given as the antithesis of the second, but binds itself secretly to it as its condition. We learn then that sickness allows us to savor health better, that "a little evil makes good more noticeable, which is to say, better," and indeed that "God derives courtesy of sin far greater good than that which arrived before sin" (ibid., 115–14). The fact that the connection between the fundamental affective tonalities of good and evil, of happiness [*bonheur*] and woe, are still only designated externally and not taken as constitutive of the internal phenomenality of Being and thus as its very substance, does not prevent it from being named at the very least and points toward the Essential.

Two other themes of the *Theodicy* are worth noting, as long as we are able to recognize their radical phenomenological meaning. The first is that there is more good than evil [*maux*], but that unfortunately we only pay attention to the latter. And why is this attention accorded uniquely to evil and not to good, notably to physical goods such as health, the normal exercise of our forces, the harmonious functioning of our bodies? Because, according to Leibniz, we do not reflect upon that activity which takes place spontaneously within us and do not take it into account; we can only see it as a good when we are deprived of it. What if life, we ask, the simple deployment of our bodily forces, for example, had no need of self-reflection for its well-being? Even if it were on the condition of this non-reflection, of its immediacy, that it could first be and act, in its sleepwalking pathos—there where life is simply life, and the life of God himself.

The last decisive theme of the *Theodicy* is that of the justice of God, strictly speaking. This concerns the penalty inflicted upon whoever has committed an offense and particularly the eternal punishment, that of damnation. It is then no longer a general law, a general will—that which ties reward to good and punishment to evil—which is invoked, but ultimately the internal essence of Being as Life. "God," writes Leibniz, "could not change his nature, his justice is essential" (ibid., 288). But this supreme justice is no longer a distributive justice which punishes and rewards according to laws that it would have itself established. The law is here the phenomenological structure of absolute subjectivity inasmuch as, in its auto-affection, it adheres moment by moment to what it is, in such a way that it is what it is, unconditionally, absolutely. "The damned remain wicked, they cannot therefore be drawn from their misery." And again: "Where sin does not cease, neither can the penalty," so that "the damned are themselves the cause of the continuation of their torments" (ibid., 288, 289).

Throughout this essay we have assumed the equivalence of evil and suffering. There is, however, in mere suffering a kind of innocence, of naïveté, which differentiates it in every case from the evil that one calls moral. We have indicated the point of their divergence. It intervenes in suffering itself when the latter, instead of surrendering itself to the work of life within it and to its slow conversion into joy, is no longer able to support itself, begins to turn against itself, and to get rid of itself. This is when Evil begins, the terrible process of *ressentiment*, of bad conscience, of flight from self and of self-destruction. The modern world, which carries nihilism to its extreme point, demonstrates vividly that, in spite of appearances and the worldly and allegedly scientific explanations that proliferate today, what is happening in the world can never be explained starting from the world, but only starting from that life of which we are speaking. The interest of a theodicy today is to return us to this ever-present and ever-active source of all that is, and in inviting us to renew the effort to understand, beginning from that source, our own destiny.

Translated by Justin Boyd

Notes

1. G. W. Leibniz, *Essais de théodicée* (Paris: Aubier, 1962), 170.
2. Kandinsky, "On the Question of Form," 250.
3. Translator's note: This is a reference to Ecclesiastes 1:18, rendered in the King James Bible as follows: "For in much wisdom is much grief: and *he that increaseth knowledge increaseth sorrow.*" I have italicized the quoted portion.

15

The Experience of the Other: Phenomenology and Theology

When philosophical reflection comes across an essential question, its first topic of investigation must be to confront the phenomenological presupposition that serves as the support and ultimate possibility for the reality at stake in it. This phenomenological presupposition is phenomenality itself, or even, as one might also say, pure appearing, pure manifestation, pure revelation. We will see that these terms belong just as much to the language of theology as to that of phenomenology. Prior research, to which I cannot return here, has taught us that there are two ways of appearing, two modes according to which pure phenomenality and hence every conceivable "phenomenon" are phenomenalized. On the one hand, there is the appearing of the world, which consists of the Outside coming into the outside, in an ek-static horizon of visibility. This horizon is the "world" itself, and everything that belongs to the world shows itself within it. On the other hand, there is the revelation of life, which is no longer the revelation of some other thing but only of itself. It is thus a self-revelation that excludes all forms of distancing and any possible seeing. It is an invisible revelation of an invisible. Its mode of phenomenalization is the Arch-passibility of a primordial and pure pathos.

    The conception of any reality obviously becomes completely modified depending on whether the phenomenological support assigned to this reality is the ek-static appearing of the world or the pathos-filled self-revelation of life. Accordingly, the comprehension of the body is turned upside down depending on whether it is understood as a body in the world or as our living flesh. The phenomenological underpinnings of the appearing of the world, which the Greeks assigned to it and which is explicated in exemplary fashion in Heidegger's *On the Way to Language*, assumes that one must see or be able to see anything one discusses or everything one says about it. This question of language arises anew when it becomes replaced by the Logos of Life mentioned in John's first letter. For example, there suffering is said by suffering, and this is a suffering one cannot see. Yet in its invisibility it speaks with a force greater than any language that speaks about things—with a force that is invisible and cannot be overlooked. The same is true of the experience of the other [*d'autrui*].

A coherent and systematic problematizing of the experience of the other, which refers its final possibility to the revelation of life, would first have to show why such an experience fails in the appearing of the world (i.e., just as much in the "outside of itself" of intentionality or of classic consciousness, which is always understood as a relationship to something, subject/object, *cogito/cogitatum*). This sort of critique goes beyond the framework of this discussion. Let me restrict myself here to affirming that the experience of the other implies the relationship between a plurality of "me's" [*moi*], none of which is possible in the appearing of the world. A self [*un moi*] can certainly continually operate within the appearing of the world and just as much in a phenomenology of intentionality, but it is always presupposed without ever being founded.

In contrast, the distinctive feature of a phenomenology of life is to establish, or rather to recognize, a primordial phenomenological reciprocity between Life itself and an Ipseity that belongs to it in principle. Another connection, itself also primordial, is discovered here: a connection between a phenomenology of Life and theology in the sense of a specifically Christian theology. For the absolute in Christianity or what it calls "God," when it comes down to it, is Life. Contrary to what one usually thinks, the concept of Life escapes any equivocity. There is no "biological" life, no natural life. ("Today's laboratory research is no longer concerned with life," says François Jacob.)[1] There is only a single Life, the Life of God, that is to say the Life of the absolute. This should be understood as absolute Life, which is itself brought forth in Life, that is, in the pure fact of experiencing itself [*s'éprouver soi-même*]. An Ipseity without which no experience [*épreuve*][2] of self is possible is constructed in this coming of Life into its "experiencing itself." To the extent to which we do not speak of a concept of Life, but of phenomenologically actual and real Life, the Ipseity, within which this Life comes to itself, must be understood as phenomenologically effective and concrete. At stake is a singular Self, the First living Self in which absolute Life experiences itself and reveals itself in this First Self that is its Word. A relation of reciprocal phenomenological interiority is accordingly accomplished as the very structure of the process of absolute Life, a relation between this absolute Life and the First living Self as far as it experiences itself in Him who experiences himself in it. Speaking from the phenomenological point of view, one should not forget that such a relation must be grasped where it is accomplished, outside the world, before it, in the Arch-passibility of its primordial pathos. To experience oneself, enjoy oneself, love oneself in such a way that this self-enjoyment [*jouissance de soi*] occurs *within absolute Life* as Life's generation of the First Self in which it hence experiences itself and loves itself—the First Self experiencing itself within this absolute Life that loves itself in Him—bears the result that everyone loves himself in something "other" [*autre*] than him (any exteriority being here out of play). This other is never exterior to it, but is interior and consubstantial. The unheard-of relation just mentioned, "You have loved me before the foundation of the world" (John 17:24), is accomplished in this way.

Even within its formal structure, the Johannine context never stops affirming that this relation of phenomenological interiority between absolute Life and the First living Self is reciprocal. The phenomenological interiority of the Father to the Son is constantly posited in it as the Son's interiority to the Father: "As you, Father, are in me and I am in you" (John 17:21), "The Father is in me and I am in the Father" (John 10:38), "Do you not believe that I am in the Father and the Father is in me?" (John 14:10).

What is surprising in both Christianity and a phenomenology of life is that this internal structure of the process of absolute Life as relation of phenomenological interiority between Life and its Word recurs in the relationship between this absolute Life and the human being as it happens, between the Word of Life and any conceivable transcendental Self. I am a living transcendental Self, but I have neither brought myself into this Self that I am, nor have I brought myself into this life that is mine. Yet this life only lives by coming about as a Self, this Self only comes about in the Ipseity of the Word, in the process of the self-generation of absolute Life as generation of the First living Self. This is why Meister Eckhart says: "God self-engenders as myself" (Sermon no. 6).[3]

The experience of the other is possible if one starts from these radical presuppositions, and one must understand it starting from them. Inasmuch as it is situated within life, it must be understood as foreign to the world. No self [*moi*] is possible within the world. Yet this experience also does not occur starting from me [*moi*] as an ego conceived as a point of departure or, even worse, as the starting point and source-point of an intentionality. Not only is intentionality, as the openness to the world, out of play here, but the me [*moi*] or the transcendental Self is no longer the source, the origin, the *natura naturans* of its relation to the other. One must precisely not start from this Self. If every transcendental Self—the other's as much as mine—is generated in the process of absolute Life's self-generation in its Word, then one must start from this very process. In it alone resides the ultimate possibility, not only of each transcendental living Self, but also of their relations [to each other]. The relationship of transcendental Selves thus is held within them before them. It occurs at the place of their birth, within the process of absolute Life in which they come into themselves and in which they remain as long as they are living. Inasmuch as they are living in one single identical Life, as they are Selves in the Ipseity of a single identical Self, they can be together in a being-with that always precedes them, namely absolute Life in its primordial Ipseity.

Any conceivable community takes birth and is formed in its primordial phenomenological possibility in this way. Consequently it has certain essential traits. The first concerns what is shared in this community, if you wish, its content: this is transcendental life. Such a content is not originally (and consequently not necessarily) a "rational" content. In the sense in which it is commonly understood, reason is not what originally gathers together; it isolates just as much. One quite rightly calls the fool someone who has lost everything except reason. Besides, reason can reveal itself as destructive not only on the individual plane. One must simply consider what happens under our very eyes today for a measure of the extent to which reason, when left to itself, to a pure objectivism, to the calculating abstraction of modern technology, can strike at the very core of the human. It strikes at what is most distinctive about the human and threatens his "humanity." At the same time, it constitutes a threat to humanity as a whole to the point of leading it to ruin. The content of any community is in reality everything that belongs to life and finds its possibility in it. Suffering, joy, desire, or love, even resentment or hatred bear in themselves a gathering power infinitely greater than that attributed to "reason." Properly speaking, reason has no power to gather together, inasmuch as one cannot deduce the existence of a single individual from it. It has nothing to do with what must be gathered into a "community."

Life is what any community has in common. Accordingly, the community actually offers the second essential trait, namely, that of being a community of the living in the sense of living transcendental Selves. Such Selves are possible only within it and, in turn, it is not possible without them. It cannot do without the primordial Self in which life comes in itself, and which contains the potential and indefinite multiplicity of all possible selves [*les moi possibles*].

But it is the third trait of life that must be stressed here: before defining the shared content, Life in its primordial Ipseity constitutes the transcendental possibility of being-in-common of what is in common, that is, relationship as such, "being-with" in its priority. However, it can no longer be a question of life in general, of a finite life like ours, but of absolute Life.

These remarks have three consequences. (1) First, any community is essentially religious. The relationship between the transcendental Selves presupposes in any respect and in any manner the relationship of each transcendental Self to absolute life, the *religious bond* (*religio*). This is not because, inasmuch as it bears this bond, each self generates its relation to another [*autre*] but, quite to the contrary, it is because from this bond he receives his own Self and, at the same time, the possibility to relate to the other. (2) Second, any community is essentially invisible. To be sure, it "appears in the world" for the same reasons as our own life, our Self, and our flesh do, but this appearing is here still only a mere appearing cut off from reality. Even more than our life, our Self, or our visible flesh, this visible community thus bears in it the possibility of pretense and deceit. Is this not the place where indifference and all other shameful feelings are constantly masked by social ritual? (3) Third, the reality of community as invisible, as foreign to the world and to its phenomenological categories, such as space and time, opens a domain of paradoxical relations, which form the core of Christianity. Kierkegaard brilliantly intuited this. In this way, a real relationship can be established between transcendental Selves that never see one another and belong to different eras. One's life can be turned upside down by reading a book from a different century or by an unknown author. One can become contemporary to an event that happened two thousand years ago. The presuppositions of a phenomenology of life are here discovered to function as an introduction to Christianity's decisive intuitions and, especially, to its extraordinary conception of intersubjectivity.

If the Word really is the condition within which each living Self comes and can come into itself, then is it not the condition for each living Self different from mine, the path one must necessarily take in order to enter into relationship with the other? In this way, absolute Life reveals itself in its Word as the phenomenological access to the other Self just as it is for me access to mine: the Ipseity in which I am given to myself and come into myself, in which the other is given to and comes into him- or herself. In this Ipseity I can come to the other and the other can come to me. In this sense Life is being-with as such, the essence of any community, being-in-common as well as what is in common.

Therefore, it should not escape us that the phenomenological presuppositions I am developing are identical to the doctrine of the mystical body of Christ. Each living transcendental Self, being given to itself and being given to itself only in the self-givenness of absolute Life in its Word, is found to be in this Word, with Him. Henceforth I am myself given to myself in Him together with these others who are similarly only given to themselves in this Word. Accordingly, each living transcendental Self is in the Word before being with itself. And the Self is with the other [*l'autre*] in this Word before the other is given to himself. The other is in the same situation of being in the Word before being with himself or with me—in the Word in which he is with himself as with me—just as I am myself with him or her and with myself in this Word. Each transcendental Self therefore, as it is with the other there where it is given to itself, is precisely with the other before any ulterior determination—before being man or woman.

And these, in fact, are the immediate phenomenological presuppositions of the doctrine of the mystical body of Christ. Indeed, this body presupposes all of them, the first by reason of founding relations, the second by reason of relations founded on the first, at the same time discovering their origin and the principle of their development in them. This is an immanent development drawing its insurmountable consistency from the force of this origin remaining in it. In this way, one can at least in abstract fashion make out successive phases in this construction or this growth of the body of Christ because within it there is always an element that builds up and another that is built up.

Christ, as the "head" of the body, is the element that builds up. The members are all those who, sanctified and deified in him and by him, henceforth belong to him by becoming parts of this very body, precisely its members. To the extent to which there is a *real* Incarnation of the Word, Christ first builds up each living transcendental Self in its primordial Ipseity, which is that of absolute Life; he joins it to himself. By giving each Self to itself, he allows it to grow from itself in a process of continual self-growth [*auto-accroissement*] that turns it into a "becoming" (the opposite of a "substance" or of a "thing"). At its depth [*fond*], this process is no other than the process of absolute Life. A critique of the Husserlian problematic of Impression would show that if "there is always a new impression" in the internal flux of time-consciousness, this is never by virtue of the Impression itself. The pathos-filled process of absolute Life's self-givenness is always already at work so that this flux, in itself foreign to any intentionality, is neither linear nor indeterminate: it is impressional, at first fleshly, according to the Arch-passibility of this Life, and then it obeys an obvious affective dichotomy inasmuch as this Arch-passibility phenomenalizes itself in the primordial phenomenological tonalities of pure Suffering and the pure Rejoicing issuing forth from this Suffering. In this way finally this flux, this apparently absurd parade of modest pleasures and oppressive thoughts, is secretly oriented toward deathly agony, toward the ultimate move from the ultimate suffering of despair to the irruption of a joy without limit—as Kierkegaard recognized and as the hidden Parousia on the wood of the Cross attests.

The givenness to itself of each transcendental Self is a givenness in which one is built up on the inside as if growing from oneself and hence from one's own becoming. The Word repeats this operation of the Word in each conceivable transcendental Self, past, present, and future. Accordingly, the mystical body of Christ grows indefinitely from all those who are sanctified in the flesh of Christ. In this potentially indefinite extension, the mystical body of Christ is constructed as "the shared human person" and "that is why he is called the New Adam."[4] This building-up does not proceed by accumulation of additional elements, like "stones," properly speaking, in an edifice constructed by human hands. Quite the opposite, building-up occurs in Christ, in the Word. Therefore it continues as a building-up of transcendental Selves, each of which, given to itself in the Word and one with him, at the same time discovers itself given to itself in the same unique Life of the same unique Self in which all the other Selves are given to themselves. Accordingly, the Self is one with all of them in Christ, and because Christ is not divisible—being the unique Life in which the power of living is held—they are not separated either. Instead they are one in Him, with Him, and within Him they are just as much one with all the others who are also in Him. In this way the "universal person" of humanity, as the Fathers also say, turns out to be precisely this "shared person" that Cyril mentions: *the reciprocal phenomenological interiority of all the living in the unique Self of absolute Life, in the reciprocal phenomenological interiority of this Self and of this Life, of the Father and of the Son.*

Within this shared person one cannot fail to distinguish between what builds up and what is built up, between the head and its body. Therefore, one must say with Augustine that "the head saves and the body is saved." Yet because the one who builds up enters into everything that is built up, because the head and the body are one, because this body made up of all the living who live and are united in him thus becomes "the whole body" of Christ—therefore it is up to this body to accomplish and to achieve what had not yet been achieved in Christ. This explains Paul's extraordinary declaration, citing his own sufferings experienced over manifold tribulations and persecutions undergone in the service of Christ as sufferings still missing in Christ's own body: "In my flesh I am completing what is missing in Christ's sufferings" (Col. 1:24). In this way Paul completes this body, achieves it—namely, in the radical sense that Paul's sufferings are the sufferings of Christ himself and belong to Christ's body. This is possible because Christ remains in his enlarged body, in his "whole" body. This is what the Fathers also call his Church. He remains in this "whole" body that is his mystical body as what gives each of his members to him- or herself. What he gives to each of his members is hence himself.

It is true that not all of them live what gives them to themselves as their God. Most live idolatrously: they have no concern at all for the power that gives them their life, living in it only for themselves, in all and sundry things only concerned with themselves. But to those who are members of his body, to all those who, given to themselves in the self-givenness of the Word, now live only by the infinite Life that is experienced in this Word—*to those who love each other in Him in such a way that He is the one they love in each other, Him and all those who are in Him*, eternal Life will be given, in such a way that in this Life that has become theirs, they may be deified and saved.[5]

Translated by Christina M. Gschwandtner

Notes

1. Henry's reference is to François Jacob's *La Logique du vivant* (Paris: Gallimard, 1970).

2. Translator's note: The French *épreuve*, of course, suggests more than the English word "experience" to the extent that it refers also to a test or an ordeal that is undergone.

3. Translator's note: The full context from the German Sermon no. 6 (ed. Quint) or 65 (ed. Pfeiffer) is as follows: "The Father bears his Son in eternity like himself. 'The Word was with God and God was the Word': the same in the same nature. I say more: he has borne him in my soul. Not only is she with him and he equally with her, but he is in her: the Father gives birth to his Son in the soul in the very same way as he gives birth to him in eternity and no differently. He must do it whether he likes it or not. The Father begets his Son unceasingly, and furthermore, I say, he begets me as his Son and the same Son. I say even more: not only does he beget me as his Son but he begets me as himself and himself as me, and me as his being and his nature. In the inmost spring, I well up in the Holy Ghost, where there is one life, one being, and one work." *The Complete Mystical Works of Meister Eckhart*, trans. Maurice O'C. Walshe, rev. Bernard McGinn (New York: Crossroad, 2009), 331.

4. Cyril of Alexandria, *Commentary on John*, trans. David R. Maxwell, ed. Joel C. Elowsky (Downers Grove, Ill.: Intervarsity, 2015), 105.

5. One finds an admirable synthesis of these converging interpretations of the doctrine of the mystical body in the Fathers in the work of Louis Laneau, *De la déification des justes* (Geneva: Ad solem, 1993). A seventeenth-century Jesuit missionary, sent to Siam [Thailand], he wrote this synthesis in prison. It establishes an explicit relationship between the doctrine of the mystical body and that of salvation as *identification* with God, precisely as *deification*. I thank the poet Franck Viellart for having told me about this book, which is of an exceptional depth and clarity.

16

Speech and Religion: The Word of God

By "Word of God," we mean first of all the Scriptures. Thus it concerns a text, like all the others, written in a language that can be comprehended according to principles that are relevant to language in general. This language can be called a "word" because it can take the form of a sonorous utterance and also because, according to what is evident in the significations that it conveys, it is addressed to someone.

All the same, the word of the Scriptures bears a distinctive characteristic: it is not merely addressed to someone, to us men, but it is addressed to us by God. Understanding the word of the Scriptures is possible only if the divine provenance of this word is perceived at the same time as it is.

This is why the text of the Gospels (to which, lacking time, we will limit ourselves) displays a constant attempt at legitimization, making reference to other sacred texts, to the Prophets whose confirmation, or something like it, they give themselves out to be.

The most categorical affirmation of the divine provenance of the evangelic word resides in the quotation marks that punctuate the story. In these instances, it is Christ himself who speaks; it is the very word of God that we hear—and that is so because Christ is defined as the Word of God. Organized around this divine Word, the evangelical text as a whole is transformed, dismissed from its linguistic station, banished from its properly textual place toward its divine referent: not only the words spoken by Christ, but his acts—washing feet, remitting sins, resurrecting the dead.

It is still the case that these acts are said, like the words of Christ. Both are significations borne by linguistic terms, moments, and parts of a language, of a speech, incapable of doing anything but adding meaning to meaning, without crossing the abyss that separates all signifying truth from reality itself, not to mention this Archi-reality to which one gives the name "God." The words of Christ stand out from between the quotation marks with an impressive force, but these words are words, a language whose referential reality is never posited by it. After all, this collection of texts is perhaps only making up a clever tale whose central character is invented or, if Christ really existed, perhaps, as Rilke suggests, "he was played the fool by his love as was Mohammed by his pride." And in such a case, the words of the Gospel, in spite of their loftiness and their profundity, are still human words, not bearing in them the mark of their divinity. For, as Sartre said, "It is always I who decide that this voice is the voice of an angel."

The question is therefore this: composed of linguistic terms and of significations, language, a word homogeneous with every other—can the evangelic word attest in some way to its divine provenance, thereby establishing its truth, the divinity of Christ, that is, the truth of what he says and what he does? In other words, how is one to know that the Scriptures are the word of God? Who, what word will tell us this?

And here is our answer: there exists another Word besides that which, composed of linguistic terms, forms the substance of the Scriptures. This other Word differs by nature from all human words; it includes neither linguistic terms nor significations, neither signifier nor signified; it does not have a referent; it does not come from a speaker properly speaking; and it is not addressed to some interlocutor, to anyone, whoever he might be, who would exist before it—before it has spoken. It is this other word that tells us that the word delivered in the Scriptures is of divine provenance. And it is this other Word, telling us that the evangelic word is of divine origin, that alone is the Word of God.

Let us therefore examine the nature of these two words, each in turn—the one set forth in the Scriptures, like unto the word that men use among themselves; and this other word, more ancient, which is the sole one to let us understand that the word delivered by the Scriptures is of divine provenance—this other word that is the Word of God.

The human word is based on language, which is composed of signs relating to objects. In this regard, the linguistic term is an instrument, a means, which by conferring a name on something that is already there allows one to have power over it, to manipulate it symbolically. But however one might conceptualize it, this instrumental function refers to a phenomenological essence that is the essence of the Word. For the linguistic term can say the thing only if it gives it to be seen, if "it delivers the thing as thing into the bursting forth of the appearing [*das Ding als Ding zum Scheinen bringt*]."[1] To speak truly, in the term that names the thing, the Word does not just render visible the being about which it is spoken or what is said about it; it does this only because previously it let appear, because, according to Heidegger, it grants the arrival in presence itself—because it gives Being.

The term to designate the phenomenological essence of the word inasmuch as it lets appear and thus gives Being, is *Logos*. There is therefore a co-belonging of *Logos* to Being and Being to *Logos*, but this does not indicate any reciprocity between these two terms. It is only because the Word grants the appearing that, at the same time, it grants Being. In other words, Being does not have any word that would be proper to it; it does not have a name. It does not have a name not because it would be beyond all names, but in contrast because there is always a name before it. A Word has always already spoken before it, one that delivers the appearing to which Being owes Being and beings with it.

Only if the Word that frees the appearing comes before Being is it necessary to say not what it "is," but what sort of appearing it frees, what sort of appearing appears as the very essence of the Word as *Logos*. It no longer suffices to assert that the Word is phenomenological through and through, that its essence is phenomenality as such; it is incumbent upon us to recognize how it is phenomenalized, that is to say, what is the pure phenomenological material of which it is made. The final question relative to the word, no longer the question of the essence of the word [*das Wesen der Sprache*] but of the word of the essence [*die Sprache des Wesens*], is the question of knowing how the Word speaks, in what tongue, and, in this fashion, what it says.

Now explicitly in Heidegger, and implicitly in most theories of language, the phenomenality that serves as support for the saying of the word is interpreted as that of the world. According to Heidegger, "To say means to show, to make appear, *to present a world in a clearing.*" Or: "*The Said gives the 'is' in the clearing.*"[2] Already in *Sein und Zeit*, the word, as an existential of *Dasein* (discourse), found its explicit phenomenological possibility in the opening of Being-in-the-world. In other forms of thought, across different systems of conceptualization, the phenomenality that supports the word, which, for example, grounds the relation of the sign and the thing, is always the light of an "Outside." It is accordingly the coming outside of this Outside—a sort of original exteriorization of exteriority, finding its origin there and consisting in its very deployment—that constitutes the clearing power of this light, its Lighting. Thus, to say, to express, is to exteriorize and to make seen in this way, while the expressed is what is outside [*Das Ausgesprochene ist gerade des Draussensein*].[3] Let us call this Word that finds its phenomenological possibility in the coming outside of an Outside the Word of the World.

What is said in the Word of the World displays several characteristics.

1. It is given by showing itself outside, like an "Image."
2. It is automatically given as a non-reality. Consider, for example, the snow, the bell, the evening about which Trakl speaks in the poem "Winter Evening."[4] The poet having called them by their names, these things come into presence and yet they do not take a place among the objects that surround us in the room where we are standing. They are

present, but in a sort of absence: present in that they appear, absent in that, though appearing, they are not there. What sort of appearing gives, lets beings appear such that, thus giving them Being, it withdraws Being by the same move, gives it as not being? What *Logos* is carried out like a murder? It is the *Logos* that reigns in the Word that the poet speaks, in the Word of the World, *Logos* whose appearing is the World as such.

3. It is therefore not only the things said by the poet that come to presence in a sort of absence, that show themselves as not being. This is the case for all beings. For "all can be said." The Saying of the World on which the poet himself relies, as well as every man who speaks in this Saying, is such that, showing what it is made of, it withdraws Being from all that it shows. And this is because *giving in Exteriority and thus placing each thing in its own exteriority, it empties them of their own reality*. If a difference must be made between the things about which the poet speaks and those that surround me in the room where I am, it is precisely not the word of the poet, *it is not the appearing of the World that can make it*. But what will I say about myself, seated in this room, making an effort to read and to understand? What does the Word of the World say about the ego?

This word wants to make the ego visible by positing it before, by installing it in the light of a clearing, that is, in the language of modern metaphysics, by representing it. But if the ego in its ipseity expels all conceivable exteriority from itself and therefore its light, the ego's appearing before itself can signify only its own disappearance. Thus Lacan reduces the subject to the fact of saying itself to the intention of an other and the *cogito* to its utterance. Holding, in the wake of Kojève and Hegel, that by virtue of its constitutive negativity, the subject can be posited only by denying itself, Lacan finds the saying of the Word of the World to be an exemplary illustration of his theses, or perhaps even their ground. The subject who is said in language by abolishing all real referent is itself abolished therein. Saying "I" is to say "I am not"; "it is in sum always to say 'I am dead,' or 'I am nothing.'" The self-utterance of the subject is the utterance of this nothing. Or "the subject of the utterance disappears by appearing in the subject of what is uttered."[5] It appears only in this disappearing, snatched up by it, such that its act of birth is also its obituary.

Descartes did not share the romantic theories of language to which we just alluded, but every analysis of the *cogito* that means to stick to its utterance, to the texts in which it is formulated, runs up against the same aporia—namely, in itself *cogito* is the contrary of what the word of men says about it. Thus this word that makes visible and that wants to see says that *cogito* is what is seen clearly, evidently—while in itself, having issued from hyperbolic doubt, *cogito* happens when all evidence has been annihilated—when the Word of the World has fallen silent.

We arrive now at our question: what do the Gospels say about the ego, what do they say about us? They say that we are the Sons. Now Sons and filiation are found only in Life. In the world, by contrast, no such thing as birth is possible. Things are not born, and, for this reason, they do not die, except metaphorically. In the world, things appear and disappear without anything living ever being able to arrive in their appearance or being able to disappear in their disappearance.

Only Sons have a birth; they are born in Life, begotten by it, being one of the living only as such, as Sons. Life is the Word of God. To understand Life as the very Word of God is possible, however, only if by this term "word" we refrain from understanding something that might resemble the words that men speak. The Word of God no doubt has one characteristic in common with the Word of the World: it is phenomenological through and through. This is why the saying of the divine word is a revelation. But how does the divine word reveal, what sort of appearing does it deliver, and what does it say to us? This is the crucial question; it is that of phenomenology—of a phenomenology that grasps itself—and perhaps also that of theology, a theology that grasps itself—not as discourse on God but as the Word of God himself. The Word of God reveals, speaks, as Life. Life, that is to say, the original word, is the Archi-Revelation as self-revelation, as auto-affection. This is to say that life reveals in such a way that what it reveals is itself and nothing other. It affects in such a way that the content of its affection is itself and nothing other. In distinction from the Word of the World, which points away from itself and always speaks of something else, of something else that in this Word is carried outside itself, thrown out of line, deprived of its own reality, reduced to an image, to a content without content, at once opaque and nonetheless empty—the Word of Life gives life. It is called the Word of Life because its *Logos* is Life, namely, self-givenness, self-enjoyment.

Giving in this way, speaking this *Logos*, Life begets its Sons in it. The transcendental birth of Sons, of those who, in the Word of the World, will be called ego, self, men, individuals, persons, and so on, is a birth intelligible in life and in it alone. And this is because there is no other way to come into life except through life itself. In the process of its incessant coming into itself, which is that of its eternal auto-affection, life undergoes itself in such a way that a Self results each time from this ordeal as identical to its pure "undergoing itself." Such an ordeal is singular on principle, undergoing what it undergoes, phenomenologically defined by the content of this ordeal. Life is the essence of ipseity; it is carried out by giving birth to the latter, by giving birth to it in it and without ever departing from itself. But all ipseity, as living, is a singular Self.

Thus life is begotten, carried out, undergone as a singular Self, as this Self that I myself am. Life auto-affects itself as myself. If with Eckhart, one calls life "God," then one will say with him: "God is begotten as myself." But this Self begotten in Life, holding the singularity of its Self only from ipseity and holding its ipseity only from the eternal auto-affection of life, bears the latter in it, inasmuch as it is borne by it and arrives in each instant in life only through it. Thus life communicates itself to each of the Sons by penetrating him as a whole, such that there is nothing in him that would not be living, and moreover nothing—inasmuch as its Self arrives only in the auto-affection of life itself—that would not contain in itself this eternal essence of life. "God gives birth to me as himself."[6]

The mystery of the transcendental birth of Sons in Life stems from the fact that in this birth two passivities collapse into each other: the radical passivity of life vis-à-vis the Self in its eternal auto-affection (in theological language, the eternal *jouissance* of God) and, on the other hand, the passivity of the singular Self begotten in this auto-begetting of absolute life. For this Self is passive with regard to itself only within the auto-affection of Life that begets it and the passivity proper to this life. Life throws the Self into itself inasmuch as it is thrown into itself, in its eternal auto-affection and thus through it. The phenomenality of these two passivities—that of Life, that of the Self—is the same. It is a nonecstatic pathos, which is why neither of them can be said to be even the least bit passive in relation to something exterior in the phenomenological sense and thus visible.

The fact that the Self can subsist only in the eternal auto-affection of Life in it invites us to make a more precise distinction between two concepts of this auto-affection. The auto-affection that expresses the essence of absolute life signifies that the latter affects itself in the twofold sense that it is carried out as productive of its own affection and at the same time as the content of this affection. Life is what affects and what is affected. This life can be called absolute because it needs nothing other than itself to exist. Phenomenologically, there is after all nothing else to it. That is why this life can still be called infinite, because the finitude of the ecstatic horizon of a world is totally foreign to it. It can be called eternal because the temporality that deploys this ecstatic horizon has no place in it either. The phenomenological passivity that characterizes all life inasmuch as it is pure self-enjoyment—even in sorrow—can just as well be thought as a pure Act since in the case of this absolute life, it is it itself that produces the affection constitutive of its essence, which is self-begotten.

In the case of the auto-affection of the singular Self that I am, autoaffection has changed its meaning. The Self auto-affects itself; it is the identity of the affector and the affected, but in such a way that it has not itself posited this identity. The Self auto-affects itself only insofar as absolute life auto-affects itself in it. Passive, it is so not just in regard to itself and each of the determinations of its life, in the way that each suffering is passive vis-à-vis itself and is possible only as such, getting its affective tenor only from this passivity whose pure phenomenological tenor is affectivity as such. The Self is passive first in regard to the eternal process of the auto-affection of the life that begets it and is forever begetting it. This passivity of the Self in life is not a metaphysical determination posited by thought; it is a phenomenological determination constitutive of the Self's life and which, as such, is forever being lived by it. This determination is so essential, the ordeal that is undergone so unrelenting, that our life is nothing other than this feeling of being lived. If one sticks to the experience proper to it, the Self therefore should not be called what auto-affects itself, but what is found unrelentingly auto-affected. How is it that the specific mode of the singular Self's passivity as auto-affected in the eternal auto-affection of Life does not define simply a general characteristic of its own life? How is it that this particular mode of passivity begets in this life all its essential modalities, which are as such filled with pathos—for example, the anxiety or the drive that originates directly in the phenomenological structure of the Self and is identical to it? Here is not the place to show this. For us, the problem is rather to understand the relation between these two passivities collapsed each into the other in the transcendental birth of the Self as the birth of a Son in Life. In sum, the issue is this: by pushing phenomenology to its limit, as radical phenomenology, as material phenomenology, to understand man's relation to God, to at least circumscribe what, as phenomenology, it can say about this relation.

What this phenomenology has established, at the point we have arrived at in our analysis, is the quasi-identity of the essence of man and that of God, namely, Life. Such an essence is not merely phenomenological; it is that of an Archi-phenomenality. It is this Archi-phenomenality of life which makes it a Word, an Archiword that speaks of nothing else but itself, at once the how and the content of what it says, of what it says *to us*, inasmuch as in its saying a singular self is built up. If we are in the word and speak only in its wake, if this word is addressed to us[7] and enjoins us in such a way that no one can evade it, this is simply because, as the Word of Life finding its essence in Life, it is first in itself, in an absolute immanence that nothing can break. Next, it is because in the immanence of its auto-affection, a singular Self is begotten each time, to which it is addressed henceforth and to which it can address itself and address itself inevitably—in this auto-affection that has become no longer the auto-affection of Life but that of the Self.

This phenomenological essence common to man and God grounds their phenomenological relation, begets man as a man who knows God—"*ein Gott wissender Mensch*";[8] "we worship what we know"[9]—while, begetting man in the auto-affection of his own auto-begetting, God knows man, reads the depths of his heart in the very act by which he begets him. This commonality of a phenomenological essence could be expressed metaphorically by saying: the Eye with which I see God and the Eye with which God sees me is but one and the same Eye—it being understood that phenomenologically speaking, here there is neither Eye nor vision nor world, nor anything like that.

That man knows God is an outrageous proposition, one barely heard today. What is it other than the inevitable response to the most simple question: Is it conceivable that the living know nothing of life? Where and how, why, what formidable hatred for life has gathered in the world where we live that the innermost certainty that life has of living has been hidden, not simply hidden, but to speak truly, denied, thus committing in this long series of murders that is the history whose horror Voltaire saw, a quite particular murder, a theoretical murder in some ways, general, putting to death no one in particular, but stripping each living thing of its living quality and doing so by stripping life of what makes it life. But let us leave aside these questions that pertain to modernity and return to our own question, which belongs to no time and now stands out in its simplicity: What do the living know about life?

In a certain sense, nothing, if it is a matter of that knowing which guides the modern world and modern thought. And this is because such a knowing is excluded from the internal structure of life. In another sense, inasmuch as the essence of the living stems from the Archi-revelation of life, doesn't it know all there is to know about it? Let us try to glimpse this extraordinary knowing, without anything held back or left over, where in the absolute immanence of a pathos-filled auto-affection, the living has already laid hold of all that which, in this taking possession, is henceforth under its power, one of its powers. For it is but the most humble drive, the most elementary act that presupposes—in order to be carried out without thought, without representation, without imagination, without perception, without conception, without being preceded in any way, and without wanting, without showing itself in any world—nothing but the auto-affection of the living contemporaneous with its transcendental birth and identical to it.

Isn't it significant that Heidegger, when he wanted to think life, taking his inspiration from the biologists of his time, was compelled to turn to the immanence of an original being-inpossession-of-itself belonging to the drive and its specific phenomenality, thought negatively as fascination [*Benommenheit*], or else in categories totally foreign to the analytic of *Dasein*, as Didier Franck has shown?[10] And if in other texts Heidegger believed he could radically separate philosophy and theology and affirm that "faith does not arise from *Dasein*,"[11] isn't this simply because the analytic of *Dasein*, like the later thought of Being, was entirely ignorant of life? For Faith is not some sort of lesser knowledge deprived of its own position and thus of all possible justification. It is simply a name for the unshakeable certainty that life has of living and for its hyperknowing. Faith does not come from the fact that we believe, it comes from the fact that we are the living in life. It is our condition as Sons that makes us believe what we believe, namely, that we are Sons; and it is for this reason alone that Faith can befall us.

Do the living know everything about life? Haven't we said that the auto-affection of the living differs from the auto-affection of life insofar as only the second produces itself in the sense of an absolute auto-affection? If the singular Self is auto-affected in its transcendental birth—that is to say, begotten as a Self—only in the auto-affection of life, doesn't the latter precede it as an already to which it will never be able to return, as a past that it will never be able to rejoin and that will remain forever closed to it—an absolute past? In his magnificent work *L'Inoubliable et l'inespéré*,[12] Jean-Louis Chretien reintroduced the concept of the Immemorial. I will take it up here to designate the antecedence of life to all of the living.

That there is no memory of the Immemorial means first that we cannot represent it, form a memory of it, relate to it by any thought whatsoever. The Archi-ancient never turns toward thought. In this sense, the Immemorial is struck by an insurmountable Oblivion. This Oblivion is not something like the correlate or flip side of a possible memory; it is not the forgetting into which memory changes when we no longer think of it. In their mutual correlation, forgetting and memory each proceed from a single place, from that place which is freed by the Word of the World, from "that clearing that every appearance must seek out and every disappearance must leave behind."[13] In the Immemorial of the antecedence of Life no clearing of this sort is ever given out, and this is so simply because there is no possible memory or forgetting of it, no conversion of the one into the other. Now, the absolute Oblivion that banishes all memory and all forgetting, that never goes out to meet thought—does this forgetting bar all access to the Immemorial or does it constitute this access as such?

That thought does not have to remember, that the clearing where all appears appears and all that disappears disappears, does not open the path to the Immemorial but forbids access to it—this is what renders untenable the claim to submit God to the priority of Being, and this is what justifies the problematic of Jean-Luc Marion.[14] For one can well say "God is," but since Being itself is subordinated to the priority of the givenness of appearing, the meaning of Being is decided only in the latter. From now on, submitting God to the priority of Being implies at least two absurdities. The first is the presupposition that God is in himself foreign to Revelation and consequently obliged to ask an exterior revelation for the right to show himself in it, in the place that it assigns to him and in the way that it prescribes. But the second presupposition is even more mistaken because it has already identified the light to which God would owe his shining for us with that which is deployed in the Difference of the world and things—thus reserving, it is true, a small corner for God in the Fourfold. One must therefore reverse Heidegger's propositions, according to which "the experience of God and of his manifestedness, to the extent that the latter can indeed meet man, flashes in the dimension of Being";[15] "the sacred . . . comes into the light of appearing only when Being has been clarified beforehand."[16] For it is only when this light of appearing is extinguished, outside the clearing of Being, that access to the Immemorial is possible—in Oblivion.

The Oblivion that passes beyond all memory belonging to thought, and thus all conceivable Memory, gives us access to the Immemorial. We can mitigate the paradoxical character of this thesis by validating it in the case of our Self itself. For it must be observed that in the ego's relation to itself, that is to say, in the ipseity of its Self, there is no memory. The project that seeks the essence of my self in its unity and sameness and wants to ground the latter on memory as the sole faculty capable of unifying its fragmented states is one of the most superficial in philosophical thought. For if it is a matter of the *living ego* and thus of its life, any intrusion of a memory separating from the Self what it would present to it as itself would have already destroyed the very possibility of the Self, namely, the auto-affection of life and the ipseity in it. Far from gathering life into a possible unity and thus into unity with itself, memory deploys a place where no life is possible, only what no longer is and as such, as remembered object, never was. Husserl saw clearly that a life given in retention would be a life in the past. But a life in the past is a phenomenological nonsense, something that excludes the very fact of living.

This is why the idea of a subjectivity self-constituting itself in retention and protention would mean only self-suppression for the living defined transcendentally by such a subjectivity. There is life as there is affect: only in the present. Not in this present that itself comes into time and in it slips into the past, which is only a temporal form, but in what stands outside time and thus outside all memory—in the Oblivion of the Immemorial. This is why if it is said of the Immemorial of the antecedence of life to the living that it is an absolute past, it must be seen that in this absolute past there is nothing of the past. For this antecedence is that of life, while in the past there is only death. What is more, it is from the self that the Immemorial designates the antecedence of life and thus its absolute essence.

To better understand the Self's relation to the life that precedes it in Oblivion, it is necessary to grasp more clearly what this Oblivion signifies in the Self's relation to itself. Far from separating my self from itself, from dispossessing it of a quality or a power, Oblivion integrates this power into my self as what is so inward that, being able neither to represent it nor to think it, it can no longer lose it and bears it in itself as an innate capacity belonging to it and which has been put in it since forever. Of this belonging to my self in Oblivion, of all its powers, the Body offers the most striking example. It is only in the Oblivion of its Body that the self is found in possession of all its powers, one with them, in such a way that in this Oblivion they precede and inhabit it as the very forces that life confided to it in the act by which it begets it eternally. In contrast, all movement of the living body is interrupted at once if it is placed or forced outside itself in the Exteriority of a "world." All thought of the Body destroys it, renders action impossible, as the modern dualism imputed to Descartes demonstrates. This is because, standing in Oblivion, the Body could be glimpsed by thought only if the latter does not attain it and leaves its power to act intact.

It is not just particular experiences that establish this. It is a universal law of the Self that wherever it seeks to show itself—either as apprehended object or if it casts itself ahead of itself in a project—a limitless nostalgia penetrates it along with an irrepressible feeling of impotence. This nostalgia is only too evident in the case of memory, which never proposes to life anything but its own absence. It can also be spotted in the indefinite progress of knowing, in the speech of men that itself never stops, in every form of being-in-the-world insofar as the ipseity of the Self is identified with it or with a mode in which it is enacted, with the resoluteness or abiding character of a decision. Finally, this same nostalgia or despair can be found in all action that intends an objective referent or believes itself able to be defined thus.

The Oblivion constitutive of the ipseity of the Self is its absolute immanence. An immanent Self is a non-constituted Self, non-constituted as a Self—Self without Self, without image of itself, without anything being proposed to it in this form, as Self or even as this Self that it is. Self without face and that will never admit being seen. Self in the absence of all Self. In such a way this absence of Self in the Self is constitutive of its ipseity as well as of all that will be possible on the basis of it. For it is only because no image of itself is interposed like a screen between it and itself that the

Self is thrown into itself without protection and with such violence that nothing will ever defend it from this, no more than from itself. It is only because this violence is perpetrated against it on account of its being one of the living in life and thus in self-Oblivion that the Self is possible as this Self to which no memory will ever refer its image, that nothing will ever separate or deliver it from itself so that it is this Self that is forever.

Doesn't the Oblivion that constitutes the ipseity of the Self bear within it something like the shadow of a more ancient forgetting—a more obscure zone in the obscurity of the Night of absolute subjectivity? Actually, the Immemorial does not merely circumscribe the domain of a specific phenomenology: this nonecstatic pathos where, in the immanence of its ipseity, without memory and without Self, the Self accomplishes itself as a "living" [*vivre*]. Immemorial means that when the Self arrives in and through this ipseity, the auto-affection of absolute life is already accomplished. Immemorial thus does not first designate the Self's memoryless relation to itself but, more essentially, its relation to life. As this relation no longer to self but to life is itself forgotten, this phenomenological homogeneity does not yet exhaust a difference that must be explained in full, does not say if this difference is itself phenomenological.

There are therefore two auto-affections: that of life which auto-affects itself absolutely and thus auto-begets itself, and that of the Self auto-affected and thus begotten as Self in Life. Nevertheless, there is but one life, the living live nowhere else but in this single and unique life that begets itself absolutely. Thus, the auto-affection in which the auto-affected Self arrives at its condition as Self is not other than the auto-affection of absolute life. That the power of self-begetting itself would never be the Self's own deed but only that of the anto-affection of life, and that thus the Self would live only begotten in it, means precisely that the auto-affection that throws it in itself is that of life, that there is none other besides the former, and that there is thus nothing else in it but this absolute auto-affection. This, then, is why God begets me "as himself," why the Self is passive vis-à-vis itself only inasmuch as it is passive vis-à-vis absolute life, why, finally, to the forgetting of self in which the Self is given to itself as a Self without Self, the Oblivion of Life is added—which is the greatest forgetting of all, the Immemorial in which alone we are the living, where our transcendental birth is carried out.

The transcendental birth of the ego thus has nothing to do with our birth as a man—not only because the latter appears as an arrival in the world and is understood as such, while our transcendental birth as the Self's coming into its Self stands entirely outside the world. In addition to this radical phenomenological difference and as its consequence, our transcendental birth is opposed to our birth as a man because in distinction from the latter—which designates only a moment in the time and history of this man, a moment at the end of which, having cut the umbilical cord, he will set out as an almost autonomous being following, nay creating, his own destiny—our transcendental birth never ends if it is true that the arrival of the Self in its Self as auto-affected in the auto-affection of absolute life happens only inasmuch as this auto-affection happens. Being a Son does not designate the result of some event that happened at another moment and is now past. Being a Son designates a condition, the Condition from which no one can cut himself off and for which he can make no other arrangements, a "gift that must be received each day without being able to make any other arrangements for it."[17] Our transcendental birth is never past because there is no past in the Self, because there is no past in the absolute past of the Immemorial of the antecedence of Life. This is why if we say that we are born in this transcendental birth, we have to say also, more profoundly, that we are "unborn,"[18] never separated from the auto-begetting of life, being begotten only in it. There is thus all the more reason for us to say that we are uncreated, since by creation one means that of the world.

We have described the Self's self-forgetting before describing its forgetting of Life. The second forgetting nonetheless precedes the first, since the Self is related to itself only on the Basis of Life, of its absolute auto-affection. If the Self is related to itself only in life, it can be said that there is no self anywhere but in God. More precisely: "In him we have life."[19] It is necessary to pass through God, through life, in order to come fully into life, just as the Self must pass through this life in order to come fully to itself and each of its "states." That God—or, if one prefers, Life—is more intimately within me than myself is not a mystical pronouncement, but a phenomenological one. It is included in the affirmation that we are Sons. The affirmation that we are Sons—the living in life—is not a simple tautology, it overturns just about everything that has ever been said about man since man has been spoken about, since the Word of the World has spoken of man.

That the Oblivion of Life gives access to Life and the forgetting of the self to the Self, are notions that might seem strange. Forgetting Life, that is what we do every day and all day; but for all that we do not cease to be the living. That the Oblivion of Life, far from separating us from Life or from our Self, gives us access to both makes sense only in a phenomenology—a phenomenology of life that does not demand the unveiling of its object from a process of intentional elucidation or from the clearing of Being, but from this object itself, precisely from Life and the original world of its Archi-revelation. It is because Life is revealed in the radical immanence of its pathos-filled auto-affection that it does not care for itself or desire to be seen, that it does not think and especially does not think about itself or remember itself, that it lives in Oblivion. In this Oblivion, life never stops embracing itself and never quits itself. If there is something "that one can forget without losing," as Jean-Louis Chrétien says of the Plotinian Good,[20] this is only because this "something," this "Good," is only a name for Life. It is only to the extent that the Non-ecstatic to which no thought ever fully arrives is not a phenomenological Nothing but precisely the phenomenological essence of the pathos in which Life arrives and arrives incessantly in itself in its eternal Archi-revelation—only to this extent is the Oblivion of this Non-ecstatic, the Oblivion of the Immemorial, changed into what cannot be lost. What can never be remembered is precisely what can never be forgotten. The phenomenology of the Immemorial is the same thing as a phenomenology of the Unforgettable: it leads irresistibly from the first to the second. This phenomenology must be named at least once: "'Unforgettable' is a suffering of what we lack the power to detach ourselves." The unforgettable is "the misfortunes themselves to the extent that they cannot be put behind us."[21]

Because Life in its Oblivion archi-reveals itself, it is a Word, we have said. Every Word must be heard and understood. In what does this Understanding consist? Of the Word, Heidegger says: "We hear it only because we belong within it [*Wir hören Sie nur weil in sie gehören*]."[22] How do we belong to the Word? This is what must be made clear if the mode of this belonging is the only thing that tells the nature of the Understanding. And it is here that the phenomenological presupposition that commands the worldly interpretation of the Word, at the same time that it hides its original essence, denatures the relation that it must maintain with those to whom "understanding" falls. As soon as the Understanding is taken as being-open-to-the-world, and when this existential determination counts as much for the speaking as for the hearing that are grounded on the Understanding structured like it,[23] it follows that there is hearing only with regard to what is outside itself; it also follows that in this Gap constitutive of the Understanding as well as the hearing that rests on it, a fundamental uncertainty slips in: differing in principle from what is said and understood, I am reduced to its subject, to conjectures and interpretations. This is what stands out clearly and distinctly in the privileged case where it is supposed that it is the same one who speaks and hears, who consequently listens to his own word. Isn't it remarkable that in this situation—namely, that of the moral conscience and its call, a call explicitly defined as that which *Dasein* addresses to itself—this call, issued from *Dasein* but coming to it in the opening of the world, comes to it "from afar" even if it is cast "unto afar."[24] The object of many mistaken interpretations, this distant and mysterious call demands, if it is to be comprehended, that one take on a bold problematic whose ultimate result repeats the initial phenomenological presupposition, claiming that *Entschlossenheit* is nothing other than *Erschlossenheit* itself grasped in its truth. What remains simply presupposed in this presupposition is the thesis claiming that *Dasein* is "mine," so that the exterior identity of the caller and the called in the moral conscience can pass for an ontological theory of the essence of ipseity, which exists nowhere else but in life.

At the same time, it is, in the lectures of the 1950s, the affirmation of a "we" belonging to the Word, taking a place in it, steeped in it, that seems groundless. And nonetheless, for every word it must be known who hears it and how. This connection of the Word and the Understanding which is appropriate to it in its essential ipseity and singularity inasmuch as it is that of a "we," that is to say, of an "I" or of a "me," escapes from the contingency of a factual correlation only if it is phenomenologically grounded. Being phenomenologically grounded does not mean simply: showing itself, appearing. No more than to a speculative affirmation, the belonging of a "we" to the word could not belong to a simple observation, in the sense of what can be seen. Being grounded phenomenologically means—for this "we," for this "self," for this "ego," for the "listeners" whoever they might be, as well as for the link that has already inscribed and buried them in the word—that the latter precedes them radically, but in such a way that, exhausting its essence in life and confiding to them this essence which is its own, it at the same time confides to them their ipseity, an ipseity that belongs to them and by which they find themselves determined in themselves as Selves and egos.

What the Word of Life confides to those who hear it is their own "existence." Between it and each of them there is an absolute relation. If this existence is each time that of a self, that of an "each individual," this is so only to the extent that the Word which gives it bears the ipseity in itself and, giving its own essence, giving this ipseity, it gives each to itself as this self that it is insurmountably and forever.

But because the Word of Life consists in life and the latter never goes outside itself, something remains to this Word of Life confided to each of the living: standing only in itself, it stands in itself only insofar as it holds it in itself, in its own life, in this unique life that is literally that of all the living, that which gives them life as a life that is each time their own and that is theirs only inasmuch as it remains in itself, as it is its own—it in them, and them in it.

How do we belong to the Word of Life, how do we understand it, if this Understanding is other than the mode of this belonging? We belong to the Word of Life in the auto-affection where we are begotten: our understanding is our birth—our Son-ly condition. I am forever hearing the sound of my birth. Because understanding the Word of Life (the hearing in which I hear this Word) is equivalent to my own life begotten in the auto-begetting of absolute life, this Understanding affords no freedom to him who understands. It is not the Understanding of a call to which the living would have license to respond or not. To respond to the call, to understand it appropriately, but also to be able to avoid it, it is always too late. Always already, life throwing itself into itself has thrown us into ourselves, into this Self that is like unto no other and that marks our irreplaceable place in life. Here, as the advertisement for the Great Circus of Oklahoma says, "Here there is a place for everyone."[25]

This place is given in life by Life, a place that intrudes upon that of no one else, never taken from another nor occupied by him, because in the auto-affection of life which gives the Self to itself, life is given in its entirety, without division or any part being kept in reserve. Who has ever been free of birth, and who, receiving life, has never received it in its entirety, crushed beneath its profuseness and bearing it inside as what, making it a Self, grants to it in each instant, in its auto-affection which is that of life, the capacity to grow by itself and thus to "live"? For to live is nothing other than that: to grow by oneself, to be exceeded by oneself, inasmuch as the Self itself is exceeded by life, exceeded by what makes it a Self.

In this way, the Understanding in which we understand the Word of Life can be grasped by a model different from that of life itself. Because this Understanding is our birth, our primal belonging to life, its phenomenological substance is exhausted in the passivity of the living auto-affected in the auto-affection of absolute life and in the pathos proper to this passivity and constituting it: it is Suffering and Joy. Suffering and Joy are the fruits of life, its unique Word—in the final analysis, the sole thing that anguished men amid the troubles of the world desire to understand. But what does this Word say to them? Nothing other than itself, namely, their own "existence"—the ineffable happiness of the ordeal and of living.

It is thus that an abyss separates the Word of Life from that of the world. The Word of the World is not merely different from all that it says, the appearing in which it is deployed stemming only from the Difference as such. Such Difference manifests an absolute indifference, the indifference of this word to all that it says, since it can say anything and everything, as the light cares not for what it illuminates, letting it slip out of the clearing that it opens, like an object that is lost without ever taking precautions against it. The most obvious, most simple, most terrible characteristic of this indifference found in all Difference and implied by it is surely the following: *never does the classification of what is said in the Word of the World result from the classification of this word, namely, from the mode of appearing that it conveys.* Whether it be a stone, a tree, a broken tool, an equation, a goat, or a hydroplane, it matters little as long as the nature of what is disclosed owes nothing to its disclosure, as long as the latter, its saying—not penetrating the inner essence of what it says and, in that way, grasping nothing—is limited to a simple observation, to saying and to repeating: "that is," "there is."

Life is so little a stranger to what it reveals that it resides in it as its very own essence—it contains and retains it in itself with an unbreakable grip and as was described above: as this eternal auto-affection in the auto-affection of which it became one of the living. This is the reason why, in distinction from the Word of the World, *the Word of Life confers its classification on what it reveals*, never disclosing it outside itself as what would have no relation with it, as anything whatsoever, but in it as that whose flesh it is. And this is why, in distinction from the beings about which the Word of the World speaks—entering or exiting from the clearing at the whim of this Word or owing to the gratuitousness of the discourse that speaks, remembers, or forgets them and that can hearken back to what it speaks about just as well as to what it says about this—he who is born of the Word of Life does not have the leisure to remove himself from the Parousia of its Revelation. Whether it be remembered or forgotten depends only on thought, not on its condition as living. Life has only one word, this word never hearkens back to what it said and no one can evade it. This Parousia without memory and without project, this Parousia of the Word of Life, it is our birth.

At the end of this short journey a question arises: Since immemorial Life has begotten us as its Sons and showered us with good, and since this birth is incessantly being accomplished in us, what need is there for a Memorial? We speak nonetheless of the Scriptures, and these Scriptures in their entirety—what are they if not a Memorial? What is more, what they say to us in the farthest reaches of what they want to convey, isn't this done to preserve in memory, to celebrate this Memorial together? In the Gospels in any case, isn't this extreme point the institution of the Eucharist: "Do this in memory of me"?[26]

One could contemplate establishing the necessity of this Memorial on the very nature of the Immemorial. Because the latter consists of an unfathomable Oblivion, we could gain some knowledge of it only through what is said to us about it in the Scriptures, and thus by a sort of favor granted to he who is gifted with reading them. This, it seems, is Chrétien's thesis: "The necessity for Scripture comes precisely from the fact that it is the sole memorial of what is inaccessible to our memory."[27] But what would happen if the knowledge of the Scriptures, that is to say, the assurance of their divine provenance, could be established only in the place held by the Immemorial itself and thus by means of it? Truthfully, it is not the memorial that grounds our access to the Immemorial, but the latter alone that, giving us to understand who it is, at the same time gives us the possibility of understanding, by recognizing it, every conceivable authentic memorial as the memorial of the Immemorial.

How can we not notice that, in the words that report the institution of the Eucharist, a strange displacement occurs. That which must be preserved in memory is not exactly words, not even those that relate the institution of the Eucharist: "Do this." From the beginning, with unexpected force, the text designated another place besides its own, the one where something like "Doing" happens. But doing, we have tried to show, is possible only in the Oblivion of the body, which is possible only in the most abysmal Oblivion, there where I am Son, in the place of my birth.

The Scriptures say that we are the Sons. Relative to their worldly word, this referent—the condition Son—is external to them. But this referent that is external is what we are as one of the living; this is the essence of the divine Word that begets us in each instant. By saying: "You are the Sons," the Word of the Scriptures points away from itself and indicates the place where another word speaks. To speak truly, everything affirmed by this word of the Scriptures carries out the displacement that leads out of it to this other place where the Word of Life speaks. For example, all Christian "morality" has this radical phenomenological signification of *referring from the word that makes visible by absenting to the one that begets in Life.* "It is not those who say to me: Master! Master! who will enter into the Kingdom of Heaven, but he who does the will of my Father."[28] Here alone reigns the word whose saying is a doing, the Word of Life that makes us the living. And it is not the word of the Scriptures that gives us to understand the Word of Life. It is the latter, by begetting us at each instant, making Sons of us, which reveals in its own truth, the truth that the word of the Scriptures acknowledges and witnesses. He who hears this word of the Scriptures knows that it speaks truly, for the Word that institutes it in life hears itself in it.

What need have we of the Scriptures? Are they there only to be acknowledged after the fact, on the basis of a truth that we already bear in us and which in its prior accomplishment, in the already accomplished accomplishment of life in us, could easily do away with them? By virtue of the Oblivion that defines its ownmost phenomenological essence, life is ambiguous. Life is what knows itself without knowing itself. That it knows all at once is neither extra nor added on. The knowing by which one day life knows what it knew ever since forever without knowing it is not of another order than that of life itself. It is life itself that knows at one fell swoop what it knew ever since forever. The knowing by which life knows what it knew ever since forever without knowing it is an upheaval in life itself. In such an upheaval, life undergoes its auto-affection as the auto-affection of absolute Life; it suffers the depths of its own Basis and is suffered as identical to it. To the extent that life is susceptible of this upheaval, it is Becoming.

When we ask if life already knows all that it knows, and if in this case something more can still befall it, we are speaking of it in the manner that one speaks of things which, in their releasement, already are all that they are. Life "is" not. Still less could it be "all that it 'is.'" That life is Becoming means: possibility remains open in it so that in it the auto-affection that strikes each of the living with the seal of its indelible ipseity—this auto-affection is undergone as that of absolute life. That this limitless emotion in which the auto-affection of each of the living is undergone as that of the absolute life in it and thus as its own essence—as this essence of life which is also its own—that such an emotion as the Revelation of its own essence befalls him who reads the Scriptures and inasmuch as these say to him nothing other than his condition as Son—there is nothing surprising here as soon as it is noted that this Son-ly condition is precisely his own and that thus *the condition of Faith is always posited.* Only the god can make us believe in him, but he inhabits our own flesh.

For this reason, the emotion that delivers the living to eternal life rises up in it each time that the truth of life is revealed to it, and all the more surely as it is revealed in its ownmost proper way—namely, as a revelation that is not first addressed to the Intellect but that consists in the very affectivity of life, as happens in the case of art that has no other end but to awaken in us the powers of life according to the impulsive, dynamic, and pathos-filled modalities that are its own.

But the upheaval of life that opens it emotionally onto its own essence does away with all condition in the sense of an encounter, of a circumstance or an occasion, of every cultural form of whatever order. It is and can be born from life itself as this rebirth that gives it to suddenly undergo its eternal birth. The Spirit blows whither it will.[29]

Translated by Jeffrey L. Kosky

Notes

This English translation was originally published in *Phenomenology and the Theological Turn: The French Debate* (New York: Fordham University Press, 2000), 217–41. It is reprinted here with permission from Fordham University Press.

Translator's note: What is being translated here as "Word" is the French term *Parole.* This French term can also be rendered as "Speech," as when rendering the distinction made, in French, between *langue* and *parole*, "language" and "speech." As such, it should be borne in mind that "Word" and "word" connote speech or a spoken word. Occasionally, the context will dictate that *parole* be translated as "speech"—in which case the reader should remember that this is the same term elsewhere translated as "word." In the title of this essay, both "Speech" and "Word" translate *parole*.

1. Heidegger, *On the Way to Language*, 125.
2. Heidegger, *On the Way to Language*, 107–8 (trans. modified).
3. Heidegger, *Being and Time*, 205 [162].
4. See Heidegger, *Unterwegs zur Sprache*, 17–22.
5. Mikkel Borch-Jacobsen, *Le Lien Affectif* (Paris: Aubier, 1991), 132. One finds, in this remarkable work, a radical requestioning of much of what contemporary thought has taken for granted.
6. Meister Eckhart, "Sermon 6," 187.
7. Above, see Heidegger, *On the Way to Language*, particularly 111–12, 75, 126, 76.
8. Eckhart, "Sermon 10."
9. John 4:23.
10. See Didier Franck, "Being and the Living," in *Who Comes after the Subject?* ed. Eduardo Cadava, Peter Connor, and Jean-Luc Nancy (New York: Routledge, 1991).
11. Heidegger, "Phenomenology and Theology," in *Pathmarks*, ed. William McNeil (Cambridge: Cambridge University Press, 1998), 43 (trans. modified) [*GA* 9:52].
12. Jean-Louis Chrétien, *L'Inoubliable et l'inespéré* (Paris: Desclée de Brouwer, 1991).
13. Heidegger, *On the Way to Language*, 126.
14. Jean-Luc Marion, *God without Being*, trans. Thomas A. Carlson (Chicago: University of Chicago Press, 1991).
15. Seminar at Zurich. Cited and commented on by Jean-Luc Marion, *God without Being*, 61 and 211, n. 16. See also Jean Greisch, *Heidegger et la question de Dieu* (Paris, 1980), 334.
16. Martin Heidegger, *Questions III* (Paris: Gallimard, 1966), 114.
17. Marion, *God without Being*, 175 (trans. modified).
18. "I am unborn," Eckhart, "Sermon 52"; English trans., p. 202.
19. Paul, Acts 17:28.
20. Chrétien, *L'Inoubliable et l'inespéré*, 41.
21. Chrétien, *L'Inoubliable et l'inespéré*, 106.
22. Heidegger, *On the Way to Language*, 124 (trans. modified). Translator's note: The English "Understanding" here translates the French *entendre*, since these are the respective English- and French-language renderings of Heidegger's *Verstehen* to which Henry refers in this passage. It should be borne in mind that the French *entendre* also carries the meaning "to hear" in the sense of hearing something spoken to one.
23. "Reden und Hören grunden im Verstehen . . . Nur wer schon versteht, kann zuhören—"Both talking and hearing are based upon understanding . . .

Only he who already understands can listen" (Heidegger, *On the Way to Language*, 208 [164]).

24. "Gerufen wird aus der Ferne in der Ferne"—"The call is from afar unto afar" (Heidegger, *Being and Time*, 316 [271]).

25. Franz Kafka, *Amerika*.

26. Luke 22:20.

27. Chrétien, *L'Inoubliable et l'inespéré*, 116.

28. Matthew 7:21.

29. The first part of this text was the object of a presentation made at the Colloque Castelli (Rome, January 1992). It was published in the acts of this colloquium, *Archivio di Filosofia* 1–3 (1992).

www.ingramcontent.com/pod-product-compliance
Lightning Source LLC
Chambersburg PA
CBHW032029290426
44110CB00012B/735